German

A Linguistic Introduction

Standard German is spoken by approximately 95 million people worldwide. This book provides an introduction to the linguistic structure of Standard German that is rich in descriptive detail and grounded in modern linguistic theory. It describes the main linguistic features: the sounds, structure, and formation of words, structure of sentences, and meaning of words and sentences. It surveys the history of the language, the major dialects, and German in Austria and Switzerland, as well as sociolinguistic issues such as style, language and gender, youth language, and English influence on German. Prior knowledge of German is not required, as glosses and translations of the German examples are provided. Each chapter includes exercises designed to give the reader practical experience in analyzing the language. The book is an essential learning tool for undergraduate and graduate students in German and linguistics.

SARAH M. B. FAGAN is Professor in the Department of German at the University of Iowa. Her recent publications include *Using German Vocabulary* (Cambridge, 2004).

Linguistic Introductions available from Cambridge University Press:

Romani: A Linguistic Introduction Yaron Matras
Yiddish: A Linguistic Introduction Neil G. Jacobs
Portuguese: A Linguistic Introduction Milton Azevedo
Ancient Egyptian: A Linguistic Introduction Antonio Loprieno
Chinese: A Linguistic Introduction Chao Fen Sun
Russian: A Linguistic Introduction Paul Cubberley
Introducción a la lingüística hispánica Jose Ignacio Hualde, Antxon Olarrea, and Anna
    María Escobar
French: A Linguistic Introduction Zsuzsanna Fagyal, Douglas Kibbee, and Fred Jenkins
Maori: A Linguistic Introduction Ray Harlow
German: A Linguistic Introduction Sarah M. B. Fagan

German

A Linguistic Introduction

Sarah M. B. Fagan

CAMBRIDGE
UNIVERSITY PRESS

CAMBRIDGE UNIVERSITY PRESS
Cambridge, New York, Melbourne, Madrid, Cape Town, Singapore, São Paulo, Delhi

Cambridge University Press
The Edinburgh Building, Cambridge CB2 8RU, UK

Published in the United States of America by Cambridge University Press, New York

www.cambridge.org
Information on this title: www.cambridge.org/9780521618038

First published 2009

Printed in the United Kingdom at the University Press, Cambridge

A catalogue record for this publication is available from the British Library

Library of Congress Cataloguing in Publication data
Fagan, Sarah M. B.
   German : a linguistic introduction / Sarah M. B. Fagan.
      p.   cm.
   Includes bibliographical references and index.
   ISBN 978-0-521-85285-2 (hardback) – ISBN 978-0-521-61803-8 (pbk.)
1. German language – Grammar.   2. German language – Textbooks for foreign
speakers – English.   I. Title.
   PF3112.F38   2009
   438.2′421 – dc22   2009006852

ISBN 978-0-521-85285-2 hardback
ISBN 978-0-521-61803-8 paperback

Contents

Contents vii

Figures

Tables

Acknowledgments

I am very grateful for the help and generosity of number of people who have contributed in various ways to this project. I owe very special thanks to colleagues who read and gave me valuable feedback on individual chapters and who discussed and helped clarify a number of issues: Michael Jessen, Catherine Ringen, David Fertig, Wolfgang Ertl, John te Velde, Orrin Robinson, Joseph Salmons, Robert Howell, Margaret Mills, Glenn Ehrstine, Mark Louden, and Barbara Fennell. Marc Pierce and Kirsten Kumpf provided valuable comments on the entire manuscript, for which I am very grateful. Several individuals helped with the figures in this book. I would like to thank Ingo Titze for permission to use modified versions of images from *Principles of Voice Production*, Julie Ostrem for her help in making these images available, and James Pusack for putting me in touch with Julie. Special thanks to Erin Chrissobolis, who helped modify and create the images used in the figures. I thank the editors at Cambridge University Press who have helped see this project through to completion: Andrew Winnard, Sarah Green, Karl Howe, and my copyeditor, Rosemary Williams.

Abbreviations

A	adjective
acc.	accusative
Adv	adverb
AdvP	adverb phrase
AP	adjective phrase
ASG	Austrian Standard German
Aux	auxiliary verb
C	complementizer
C	consonant
Con	conjunction
CP	complementizer phrase
dat.	dative
Det	determiner
DO	direct object
E	event time
Eng.	English
ENHG	Early New High German
F	foot
fem.	feminine
FWG	Foreign Worker German
gen.	genitive
Gk.	Greek
Gmc.	Germanic
Goth.	Gothic
GSG	German Standard German
IA	Item and Arrangement
IE	Indo-European
Infl	inflection
IO	indirect object
IP	inflection phrase
IP	intonational phrase
IP	Item and Process

IPA	International Phonetic Alphabet
Lat.	Latin
masc.	masculine
MHG	Middle High German
MLG	Middle Low German
N	noun
neut.	neuter
NHG	New High German
nom.	nominative
NP	noun phrase
OE	Old English
OHG	Old High German
OV	object–verb
OVS	object–verb–subject
P	preposition
PIE	Proto-Indo-European
PO	prepositional object
PP	prepositional phrase
Pro	pronoun
PRO	the understood subject of an infinitive
PS	phrase structure
R	reference time
REFL	reflexive
S	speech time
sg.	singular
Sk.	Sanskrit
SOV	subject–object–verb
Spec	specifier position of CP
SSG	Swiss Standard German
SUB	subject
SVO	subject–verb–object
t	trace
V	verb
V	vowel
VP	verb phrase
WP	Word and Paradigm
YP	phrase (e.g., NP, AP, etc.)
XP	phrase (e.g., NP, AP, etc.)

Introduction

1 German: speakers and geography

Standard German is spoken by approximately 95 million speakers worldwide (Gordon 2005). It is an official language in Germany, Austria, Switzerland, Luxembourg, and Liechtenstein. It is the national (sole official) language in Germany, Austria, and Liechtenstein; in Switzerland it is an official language along with French, Italian, and Rhaeto-Romansh; in Luxembourg it shares official status with French and Luxemburgish (Lëtzebuergesch), a Mosel Franconian dialect.[1] German is also an official regional language in Belgium, Italy, and Denmark, and is spoken in a number of other countries, including the Czech Republic, Kazakhstan, Poland, and Paraguay.[2]

Standard German is the variety of German that is described in grammars and dictionaries. It is the "official" form of the language; texts written in German typically follow the spelling and grammar norms of this variety of German. Standard German is the form that is typically used in school in German-speaking countries and the variety that is taught to non-native speakers studying German as a foreign language. Although non-standard varieties of German will also be treated here (German dialects, Foreign Worker German, etc.), Standard German is the variety that is the focus of this study. The chapters on the sounds of German, the structure of German words, the regularities of word order, and so on all deal with the standard language.

2 Objectives

This book aims to provide an introduction to the linguistic structure of Standard German that is rich in descriptive detail and grounded in modern linguistic theory. It includes a history of the language, a description of the major German dialects, and a discussion of sociolinguistic issues in addition to an analysis of the basic structural components of the language, namely, phonetics, phonology, morphology, syntax, and semantics. It is intended for a broad readership. It is written in such a way as to be accessible to university students in German and linguistics, teachers of German, and linguists with a variety of interests. Prior knowledge of German is not required, as all necessary glosses and/or translations are provided for the examples in German.[3] Professional competence in linguistics is also not essential; basic linguistic concepts are introduced briefly and specialist linguistic terminology is explained. A glossary of technical terms is also provided.

This book differs in its scope, depth, and focus from other linguistic introductions to German that are currently available in English.[4] It is not concerned simply with the purely structural aspects of German, but also presents a detailed view of the language in its historical, regional, and social settings. Where other texts introduce the reader to linguistics with German as the object of investigation, this book focuses on the linguistic features of the language and explains linguistic concepts only briefly. Emphasis is placed on linguistic detail and the elucidation of insights into the language afforded by current linguistic research.

The general theoretical framework employed here is that of generative linguistics, the view that a formal and explicit set of rules (a generative grammar) underlies the knowledge that native speakers have of their language. The components of this grammar, which are all interrelated, include phonetics, phonology, morphology, syntax, and semantics. In general, a more traditional approach to theoretical issues is taken instead of one that represents the most recent directions in the field. The expectation is that an approach that has the advantage of time and exposure will be accessible to a wide audience.

3   Organization

The first four chapters deal with the major structural components of the language. Chapter 1 treats the phonetics and phonology of German, including phonological processes, phonotactic constraints, stress, and intonation. Chapter 2, which presents the morphology of German, deals with inflection as well as the word-formation processes of derivation, compounding, and reduction. The discussion of the syntax of German in chapter 3 includes a description of the phrase structure of the language, from noun phrases to sentential phrases, and highlights the salient characteristics of German word order. Chapter 4, which deals briefly with lexical semantics, focuses on issues of sentence-level semantics: tense and aspect, modality, and voice.

The final three chapters of the book treat variation in the language, from diachronic and regional to social. Chapter 5 presents a history of German, beginning with a description of its Indo-European and Germanic ancestors and then presenting the important phonological, morphological, and syntactic characteristics of three of the major periods of the language. Chapter 6 deals with regional variation. It addresses regional variation in the colloquial language and presents the characteristics of the major German dialects. It also describes the varieties of German spoken in Switzerland and Austria and deals with the linguistic differences in Germany between the East and the West. Chapter 7 treats the sociolinguistic issues of style, forms of address, language and gender, youth language, the speech of foreigners, and the influence of English on German.

Each chapter includes exercises that are intended to give the reader practical experience in analyzing the language and an opportunity to put to use the information presented in that chapter. Solutions to the exercises can be found in the online answer key at www.cambridge.org/fagan.

NOTES

1 See chapter 6 for further discussion of German dialects and the relationship of these dialects to Standard German.
2 See Gordon 2005 for additional information on the countries in which German is spoken.
3 A number of the exercises do require a basic knowledge of German.
4 These include Russ 1994, Johnson 1998, Boase-Beier and Lodge 2003, and Fox 2005.

1 Phonetics and phonology

1.1 Phonetics of German

1.1.1 Introduction

The subfield of linguistics known as phonetics deals with the sounds of human speech. There are three branches of phonetics: articulatory phonetics, which is concerned with how the human vocal tract produces speech sounds; acoustic phonetics, which investigates the physical properties of the sound waves produced when we speak; and auditory phonetics, which deals with the way that speech sounds are perceived by listeners. This discussion of German phonetics focuses on the articulatory characteristics of the sounds of German.

Speech sounds are produced when an airstream is put into motion. In German, as in most languages, speech sounds are produced by pushing air from the lungs out of the body through the vocal tract. A diagram of the vocal tract is provided in Figure 1.1. To produce the different sounds of a language, the airstream is modified in various ways by manipulating the larynx (voice box), the velum (soft palate), the tongue, and the lips.

The larynx is made up of cartilages and muscle (see Figure 1.2). The vocal cords, two pairs of folds of muscle and ligament, are attached to the inner sides of the thyroid cartilage (the Adam's apple) at the front of the larynx and to the two arytenoid cartilages at the back of the larynx. The lower pair of folds can be spread apart or brought together by movement of the arytenoid cartilages. When the vocal cords are spread apart and the airstream passes freely through the space between them, the glottis, the sound produced is characterized as voiceless. The sound produced when pronouncing the *s* in *das* 'the', for example, is voiceless. When the vocal cords are brought close together, but not completely closed, and the air passing through them causes them to vibrate, the sound that is produced is voiced. An example of a voiced sound is the vowel *a* in *ja* 'yes'.

If the velum (the soft area at the back of the roof of the mouth) is raised against the back of the throat (pharynx), only allowing the airstream to pass

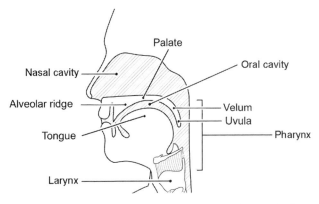

Figure 1.1 The vocal tract. Modified from I. R. Titze, "Principles of Voice Production: Second Printing." Copyright 2000 by the National Center for Voice and Speech, Iowa City IA 52242.

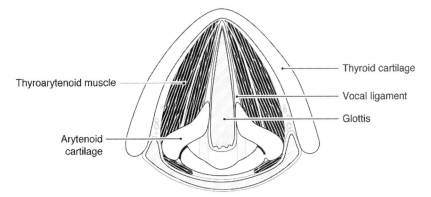

Figure 1.2 The larynx. Modified from I. R. Titze, "Principles of Voice Production: Second Printing." Copyright 2000 by the National Center for Voice and Speech, Iowa City IA 52242.

through the mouth, the sound produced is oral. All the sounds in the word *Lippe* 'lip' are oral. If the velum is lowered and air is allowed to pass through the nasal passages as well as through the mouth, the sound produced is nasal. The *m* in *Mutter* 'mother' is a nasal sound.

The tongue is a highly flexible organ of speech and plays an important role in the modification of the airstream. It can be lowered, raised, moved forward in the mouth, pulled back, and so on, so that it approaches or touches various surfaces in the mouth. Important parts of the upper surface of the vocal tract are the teeth, the alveolar ridge (the ridge behind the upper front teeth), the (hard) palate (the roof of the mouth), the velum, and the uvula (the small piece of soft tissue that hangs down from the rear portion of the velum); see Figure 1.1.

The lips, which like the tongue are very flexible, are the final articulators to modify the airstream as it leaves the body. The lips can be used together with the teeth, as in the production of *f* in *finden* 'to find'. They can also be used by themselves, in a rounded position, for example, as in the production of *u* in *Mutter* 'mother'.

Linguists use special phonetic alphabets to represent speech sounds in order to ensure a one-to-one correspondence between sound and symbol. The symbols of conventional spelling systems typically do not have this characteristic. The symbol *e* in the German spelling system, for example, can represent three different vowel sounds. Compare the conventional spelling of the following words with their phonetic transcriptions (phonetic symbols are placed between square brackets): *nett* [nɛtʰ] 'nice', *lebt* [leːptʰ] 'lives', *Sache* [zaxə] 'thing'. The symbols of the International Phonetic Alphabet (IPA) are used to represent speech sounds in this book.

1.1.2   The vowel sounds of German

Vowels are those speech sounds that are produced *without* a closure of the mouth or a narrowing of the speech organs to a degree that would produce audible friction when the airstream passes through the mouth. Five parameters are necessary to distinguish the different vowel sounds of German: tongue height, tongue position, lip position, length, and tenseness.

There is a direct correlation between the tongue height of a given vowel and the degree to which the mouth is open during the articulation of that vowel. The *i* sound in *Miete* [miːtʰə] 'rent' is a high vowel; the mouth is almost closed during the articulation of this vowel. The *e* sound in *Fee* [feː] 'fairy' is a mid vowel; the mouth is half open (the jaw is lowered somewhat) to pronounce this vowel. The *a* sound in *Saal* [zaːl] 'hall' is a low vowel; the mouth is open wide (the jaw is quite low) during the production of this vowel.

The parameter of tongue position refers to the location of the highest point of the tongue, from front to back in the mouth. The *i* sound in *Miete* [miːtʰə] is a front vowel; the highest part of the tongue during the articulation of this vowel is at the front of the mouth, under the palate. The *e* sound in *Mitte* [mɪtʰə] 'middle' is a central vowel; the highest part of the tongue is somewhat further back in the mouth than for *i*. The *u* sound in *Fuß* [fuːs] 'foot' is a back vowel; the highest point of the tongue is in the back of the mouth under the velum. The difference in tongue position between front and back vowels is especially apparent if you pronounce a front vowel like *i* [iː] and then a back vowel like *u*

Table 1.1 *Vowel sounds in German*

		front		central		back	
		unrounded	rounded	unrounded	rounded	unrounded	rounded
high	tense	iː	yː				uː
	lax	ɪ	ʏ				ʊ
mid	tense	eː	øː				oː
	lax	ɛ ɛː	œ	ə			ɔ
				ɐ			
low				a aː			

[uː]; you can feel the tongue being pulled back when it moves from the *i* to the *u* position.

During the articulation of a vowel, the lips can be rounded, as in the articulation of *o* in *so* [zoː] 'so'. The lips can also be spread apart (unrounded), as in the pronunciation of *e* in *See* [zeː] 'lake'. Lip position is thus a matter of lip rounding. We say that [oː] is a rounded vowel; [eː] is an unrounded vowel.

The length of a vowel is the duration of that vowel relative to the duration of other vowels. The *a* in *Staat* [ʃtaːtʰ] 'country' is a long vowel (length is represented using the length mark, ː). The *a* in *Stadt* [ʃtatʰ] 'city' is a short vowel.

The parameter of tenseness is commonly described as involving the degree of muscular tension necessary to produce a vowel. Tense vowels are said to be produced with greater muscular tension than lax vowels. Although this has not been verified experimentally, there are phonetic differences between tense and lax vowels. In German, tense vowels are produced further from the mid-central position of the vowel area (the natural, relaxed position for the tongue) and are higher than their lax counterparts. The *i* in *Miete* [miːtʰə] 'rent' is a tense vowel. It is somewhat higher and further forward than the *i* in *Mitte* [mɪtʰə] 'middle', which is a lax vowel. Tense vowels in German are long when they appear in a stressed syllable; they are short when unstressed. The *i* in *Musik* [muˈziːkʰ] 'music' is tense and long; in *musikalisch* [muziˈkʰaːlɪʃ] 'musical' it is tense but short because the syllable in which it occurs does not bear primary stress. (The raised vertical stroke, ˈ, indicates that the following syllable bears primary stress. Stress will be indicated in transcriptions only when relevant to the discussion. See section 1.2.6 for further discussion of stress.)

Table 1.1 lists the vowel sounds of German. Only the long variants of the tense vowels are included in this table. Examples of words that contain these vowels are provided in examples (1) through (3).

(1)   High vowels
       [iː] *lie*gen 'to lie'   [yː] *lü*gen 'to fib'
       [ɪ]   *Ki*ste 'box'   [ʏ]   *Kü*ste 'coast'
       [uː] *spu*ken 'to haunt'   [ʊ]   *spu*cken 'to spit'

(2)   Mid vowels
       [eː] *le*sen 'to read'   [øː] *lö*sen 'to solve'
       [ɛ]   *ke*nnen 'to know'   [œ]   *kö*nnen 'to be able to'
       [ɛː] *Kä*se 'cheese'
       [ə]   *bitte* 'please'   [ɐ]   *bitter* 'bitter'
       [oː] *O*fen 'oven'   [ɔ]   *offen* 'open'

(3)   Low vowels
       [a]   *Stadt* 'city'   [aː] *Staat* 'country'

Table 1.1 tells us that [iː] is a high, front, tense, long, unrounded vowel. It differs from [yː] only in lip position; [yː] is a high, front, tense, long, *rounded* vowel. If you say [iː] and then round your lips, the resulting sound will be [yː]. If you consider all the front vowels in Table 1.1, you will notice that there are three additional pairs of vowels that differ from each other in this way (lip rounding): [ɪ]/[ʏ], [eː]/[øː], and [ɛ]/[œ] in addition to [iː]/[yː]. The rounded vowels of these pairs ([yː], [ʏ], [øː], and [œ]; found in words like *süß* 'sweet', *fünf* 'five', *Öl* 'oil', and *Köln* 'Cologne', respectively) are particularly interesting because they have no counterparts in English: English has no front rounded vowels.

A sound that stands out in Table 1.1 is [ɛː]; it is the only vowel in German that is both lax and long. [ɛː] is typically represented by orthographic *ä* or *äh*: *Väter* 'fathers', *ähnlich* 'similar'. Although the [ɛː] pronunciation in such words is considered standard, speakers in northern and central Germany substitute [eː] instead: [feːtʰɐ], [eːnlɪç].

The low vowels, [a] and [aː], are not marked for tenseness, and both are considered central vowels. Although some studies treat the two different *a* sounds in German as qualitatively different (e.g., differing in tongue position), they are treated here (following Mangold 2005, among others) as differing only in duration.

It turns out that there is an interesting relationship between these two vowels. When long *a* is umlauted (in the formation of plurals, the derivation of *er*-nominals, etc.), the resulting vowel is [ɛː], as the pairs of words in (4) demonstrate:

(4)   *Zahn* [tsaːn] 'tooth'   *Zähne* [tsɛːnə] 'teeth'
       jagt [jaːktʰ] 'hunts'   *Jäger* [jɛːkɐ] 'hunter'
       Jahr [jaːɐ] 'year'   *jährlich* [jɛːɐlɪç] 'yearly'

As expected, when short *a* is umlauted, the resulting vowel is [ɛ], a sound that differs from [ɛː] only in length:[1]

(5) *Fall* [fal] 'case' *Fälle* [fɛlə] 'cases'
alt [altʰ] 'old' *älter* [ɛltʰɐ] 'older'
Kamm [kʰam] 'comb' *kämmt* [kʰɛmtʰ] 'combs (3rd person sg.)'

Two vowel sounds in German never occur in stressed syllables: [ə] (schwa) and [ɐ]. Both are mid central vowels that are lax, short, and unrounded. [ɐ] is somewhat lower than [ə]. In adjective and verb endings, <e> is pronounced as [ə]; [ɐ] is typically the pronunciation of <er> when this sequence occurs at the end of words (angle brackets, <>, indicate orthographic symbols):

(6) *alte* [altʰə] (*Leute*) 'old (people)' (*ich*) *lese* [leːzə] '(I) read'
alter [altʰɐ] (*Freund*) 'old (friend)' *Leser* [leːzɐ] 'reader'

The sounds we have discussed so far are monophthongs, vowels that do not show a change in quality (tongue height, tongue position) within a syllable. Vowels that do change in quality during a syllable (because of movement of the tongue during their articulation) are diphthongs. German has the three diphthongs illustrated in (7).

(7) [aɪ̯] *mein* 'my' *Mai* 'May' *Bayern* 'Bavaria'
[aʊ̯] *Haus* 'house' *Couch* 'couch' *Clown* 'clown'
[ɔɪ̯] *neu* 'new' *Mäuse* 'mice' *Boykott* 'boycott'

Diphthongs are represented phonetically by two vowel symbols, the beginning and end points of the vowel articulation.[2] One of the sounds in a diphthong is more prominent than the other. This is indicated by placing the diacritic ̯ under the less prominent of the two vowels. In the diphthongs in (7), the second vowel is less prominent.

In German, diphthongs also arise phonetically from two additional sources. A vocalic pronunciation of the *r*-sound, [ɐ], results in a number of different diphthongs. Some examples are [iːɐ̯] in *Tier* [tʰiːɐ̯] 'animal', [uːɐ̯] in *Uhr* [uːɐ̯] 'clock', and [eːɐ̯] in *Meer* [meːɐ̯] 'sea'.[3] A second source is non-native (but well-integrated) words that end in *-ion* or *-ation*, in which we find the diphthong [i̯oː]: *Emotion* [emotsi̯oːn] 'emotion'; *Operation* [opʰəʁatsi̯oːn] 'operation'. In this diphthong, unlike the others discussed here, the first vowel is less prominent.

German also has nasalized vowels (indicated with the diacritic ˜) in words that have been borrowed from French. Some of the nasalized vowels that occur in German are illustrated in (8).

Table 1.2 *Consonant sounds in German*

		B	LD	A	PA	P	V	U	G
Stop	voiced	b̆		t̬			k̬		
	voiceless	p		t			k		ʔ
	voiceless aspirated	pʰ		tʰ			kʰ		
Fricative	voiced		v	z	ʒ	j		ʁ	
	voiceless		f	s	ʃ	ç	x		h
Nasal		m		n			ŋ		
Lateral				l					
Trill				r				ʀ	

B = bilabial; LD = labiodental; A = alveolar; PA = postalveolar; P = palatal,
V = velar, U = uvular; G = glottal

(8)   [õ:] *Balkon* 'balcony'
        [œ̃:] *Parfum* 'perfume'
        [ɛ̃:] *Teint* 'complexion'
        [ã:] *Restaurant* 'restaurant'

A vowel is nasalized when the velum is lowered during its articulation and air is allowed to escape through the nasal cavity. Many of these words with nasalized vowels also have alternative pronunciations with an oral vowel followed by a nasal consonant in place of the nasalized vowel:[4]

(9)   [ɔŋ], [o:n] *Balkon* 'balcony'
        [y:m]   *Parfüm* 'perfume'

Because nasalized vowels do not play a major role in the sound system of German (they occur in a relatively small number of loanwords from French), they will not be treated further.

1.1.3   The consonant sounds of German

Consonants are those speech sounds that are produced by impeding the flow of air in some way. The consonant sounds of German can be described in terms of manner of articulation (how the airstream is impeded), place of articulation (where the airstream is impeded), and state of the vocal cords. Table 1.2 lists the consonant sounds of German.

   Stops are those consonants that are produced by a complete closure in the vocal tract. The articulation of a stop involves closure, a build-up of pressure during closure (because the airstream is trapped), and then release of the closure, resulting in an "explosion" of air (stops are also called plosives). The *p* sound in *Pass* 'passport', for example, is a stop. It is bilabial (both lips are used to form the closure) and voiceless (the vocal cords are apart during the closure). The *t* sound in *tief* 'deep' is an alveolar stop (the closure is formed by placing the tip and front part of the tongue against the alveolar ridge). The *k* sound in *Kuh* 'cow' is a velar stop (the closure is formed by placing the back of the tongue against the velum).

There are three kinds of stop sounds in German: voiced stops, voiceless stops, and voiceless aspirated stops. Stops are voiced when the vocal cords are together and vibrating during the period of closure; they are voiceless when they are apart and not vibrating during closure. A voiceless stop is aspirated if its release is followed by a period of voicelessness accompanied by a burst of air. The *p* in *Panne* for example, is aspirated (indicated by a superscript *h*); the *p* in *Spanne*, on the other hand, is not.

(10) [pʰ] *Panne* [pʰanə] 'breakdown'
      [p] *Spanne* [ʃpanə] 'span of time'

You can see the difference between these two *p* sounds if you dangle a sheet of paper in front of your mouth and say *Panne* and then *Spanne*. The burst of air that accompanies the aspirated *p* in *Panne* causes the paper to move. This movement of the paper is absent when you say *Spanne*, since the *p* in this word is not aspirated. This same contrast can be found in English and demonstrated with word pairs like *pin* (with aspirated *p*) and *spin* (with unaspirated *p*).

Examples of the three kinds of stop sounds in German are given in (11) through (13); see also Table 1.2. For each type of stop, there are three places of articulation: bilabial, alveolar, and velar.

(11) Voiced stops[5]
      [b̥] *Fieber* [fiːb̥ɐ] 'fever'
      [d̥] *wieder* [viːd̥ɐ] 'again'
      [ɡ̊] *logisch* [loːɡ̊ɪʃ] 'logical'

(12) Voiceless stops
      [p] *(ich) spare* [ʃpaːʁə] '(I) save'
      [t] *Stahl* [ʃtaːl] 'steel'
      [k] *Skalen* [skaːlən] 'scales'

(13) Voiceless aspirated stops
      [pʰ] ***P****aare* [pʰaːʁə] 'pairs'
      [tʰ] ***T****al* [tʰaːl] 'valley'
      [kʰ] *(die)* ***K****ahlen* [kʰaːlən] '(the) bald people'

There is an additional sound in German that is referred to as a "glottal stop" or "glottal plosive," [ʔ]. It is produced by closing the vocal cords, holding them tightly together along their entire length, and then releasing them suddenly into the articulation of a following vowel. The glottal stop is the sound that one typically hears before a stressed vowel at the beginning of a word:

(14)   [ʔ] *Öl* ['ʔøːl] 'oil', *offen* ['ʔɔfn̩] 'open'

In English, a glottal stop can be heard before the vowels in utterances like *uh-uh* (used to express disagreement or say "no") or *uh-oh* (used to express surprise). Although the glottal stop, [ʔ], is phonetically a state of the glottis rather than an articulatory stop like [p], [t], and [k], for example (Ladefoged 1971:16), it will be treated here as a stop.

Fricatives are those consonants that are produced by placing two articulators close together to create a narrow passage through which air is forced, producing a turbulent airflow. The *f* sound in *Fieber* 'fever', for example, is a labiodental fricative. The two articulators that create the narrow passage in the production of this fricative are the lower lip and the upper teeth. The *s* sound in *es* 'it' is an alveolar fricative. It is produced by raising the blade of the tongue (the area right behind the apex – the tip) close to the alveolar ridge. The *sch* sound in *schön* 'beautiful' is postalveolar, produced by placing the front part of the tongue behind the alveolar ridge, close to the front part of the hard palate. The lips are also strongly rounded, more so than in the pronunciation of English *sh*. The *ch* sound in *Licht* 'light' (known in German as the "*ich*-Laut") is palatal, produced by raising the front of the tongue towards the hard palate, with the tip of the tongue touching the lower front teeth. The *ch* sound in *lachen* 'to laugh', on the other hand (known in German as the "*ach*-Laut"), is a velar fricative, produced by raising the back of the tongue towards the velum (the soft palate). One of the pronunciations of the *r* sound in *Rede* 'speech' is the uvular fricative, produced by raising the back of the tongue towards the uvula. The *h* sound in *haben* 'to have', characterized here as a glottal fricative, is produced by slightly narrowing the glottis (Mangold 2005:52).[6]

There are two basic kinds of fricatives in German: voiced and voiceless. Examples of these two types of fricatives are provided in (15) and (16); see also Table 1.2. There are seven relevant places of articulation for fricatives in German: labiodental, alveolar, postalveolar, palatal, velar, uvular, and glottal.

(15)   Voiced fricatives
         [v] *Wein* [vaɪ̯n] 'wine'
         [z] *Reise* [ʁaɪ̯zə] 'trip'
         [ʒ] *Marge* [maʁʒə] 'margin'
         [j] *jener* [jeːnɐ] 'that'
         [ʁ] *Rede* [ʁeːtə] 'speech'

(16)   Voiceless fricatives
         [f] *fein* [faɪn] 'fine'
         [s] *(ich) reiße* [ʁaɪsə] '(I) rip'
         [ʃ] *Marsch* [maʁʃ] 'march'
         [ç] *Chemiker* [çeːmikʰɐ] 'chemist'
         [x] *Nacht* [naxtʰ] 'night'
         [h] *Hut* [huːtʰ] 'hat'

There are three nasal consonants in German. Nasals are produced by forming a complete closure in the vocal tract and lowering the velum so that air escapes through the nasal passage. Nasal consonants are similar to stops in that they involve a closure of the vocal tract. In German, nasals have the same places of articulation as stops: bilabial, alveolar, and velar. All German nasals are voiced.

(17)   Nasal consonants
         [m] *Mehl* [meːl] 'flour'
         [n] *Nase* [naːzə] 'nose'
         [ŋ] *lange* [laŋə] 'long'

The *l* sound in German can be classified as an approximant, a sound produced by bringing two articulators close together without producing a turbulent airflow. It is a lateral sound, articulated by placing the blade of the tongue against the alveolar ridge and allowing air to escape on either side of the tongue. Because the point of contact with the tongue is the alveolar ridge, *l* is classified as alveolar. It is a voiced sound. We will refer to it simply as a lateral.

(18)   [l] *Milch* [mɪlç] 'milk'

Many varieties of English have two different *l* sounds, in contrast to Standard German: a "clear" *l*, as in Standard German, and a "dark" or velarized *l*, [ɫ], which is produced by raising the back of the tongue towards the velum at the same time the blade of the tongue is making contact with the alveolar ridge.[7] In those variants of English that have both types of *l*, clear *l* is typically found in prevocalic position, whereas dark *l* is found postvocalically:[8]

(19)   English *l*
         [l] *lip, leave, late, lap, look*
         [ɫ] *hill, ball, fold, self, film*

Trills are the final type of consonant sound in German. A trill is produced by holding an articulator loosely close to another articulator, so that the airstream sets it in vibration. An alveolar trill, [r], a realization (pronunciation) of German *r* typically found in Bavaria and Austria, is produced by the tip of the tongue vibrating against the alveolar ridge. A uvular trill, [ʀ], another realization of German *r*, is produced by the uvula vibrating against the back of the tongue. Both types of trills are voiced.

(20)   [r] *Rede* [reːʈə] 'speech'
        [ʀ] *Rede* [ʀeːʈə] 'speech'

1.2   Phonology of German

1.2.1   Introduction

My goal here is to present a descriptive phonology of German, not a theoretical account that aims to compete with the most recent theoretical treatments. I do, however, take into account the recent literature and incorporate facts and ideas that are new and go beyond the traditional accounts of German phonology found in previous monographs and textbook descriptions. I express phonological generalizations in the form of rules and derivations rather than simply relying on prose formulations, since the formalization of rules helps to ensure accuracy and can reveal generalizations that might not be apparent in prose accounts. Because of length limitations I focus more on segmental than on prosodic phonology, and more on the word level than on the sentence level. I also focus more on "regular" than "irregular" phonology and do not treat those rules that are morphologically conditioned.[9]

Phonology is the subfield of linguistics that deals with the sound patterns of language, the regularities that underlie the sound systems of language. For example, if we consider the way in which *r* is pronounced in German, we see that there are two phonetically distinct pronunciations that are possible, a consonantal pronunciation, [ʁ], and a vocalic, [ɐ], and if we look at the distribution of these two pronunciations, we see a pattern. We find the consonantal pronunciation when *r* occurs at the beginning of words, the vocalic when it occurs at the end of words:[10]

(21)   Consonantal *r*
        Rat [ʁaːtʰ] 'advice', *Rippe* [ʁɪpʰə] 'rib', *rund* [ʁʊntʰ] 'round'

(22)   Vocalic *r*
        Bier [piːɐ] 'beer', *leer* [leːɐ] 'empty', *Uhr* [uːɐ] 'clock'

This pattern in the distribution of the *r* sounds in German is a characteristic of the language that is treated in the phonology. It is a characteristic of the sound system of German.

The minimal unit in the sound system of any language is the phoneme. Phonemes are more abstract units than the actual speech sounds (or phones) in a language. Although the two different pronunciations of German *r*, for example, are phonetically distinct, at some level both of these pronunciations are the same; they are both perceived as *r* by native speakers of German. They are two different phonetic realizations of the *r* sound, or *r* phoneme in German, /r/. Phonemes are written between slash brackets, //, to distinguish them from their various phonetic realizations, or allophones, which are placed between square brackets, []. At the phonemic level of representation, a word like *leer* 'empty', for example, is transcribed as /leːr/. At the phonetic level, it is transcribed as [leːɐ̯], since the *r* phoneme occurs at the end of this word and thus has a vocalic pronunciation.

Phonemes are the distinctive sounds of a language. They are the sounds that have the potential to bring about contrasts in meaning. If we substitute *r* for *l* in the word *Lippe* 'lip', for example, this yields a completely different word, *Rippe* 'rib'. A pair of words like *Lippe* and *Rippe* is called a minimal pair, two words that differ in meaning and that are identical in form except for one sound that occurs in the same place in each word. Given a minimal pair like *Lippe* and *Rippe*, we can say that /l/ and /r/ are phonemes of German. The discovery of minimal pairs is thus crucial in determining the phonemes of a language.

Sounds are considered to be allophones of the same phoneme if they are phonetically similar and in complementary distribution (they never occur in the same environment) or in free variation (the substitution of one sound for the other does not cause a change in meaning). The phoneme /iː/, for example, has two allophones, [iː] and [i], which are in complementary distribution: [iː] occurs only in stressed syllables; [i] occurs only in unstressed syllables.

(23) *Fabrik* [faˈpʁiːkʰ] 'factory' *Fabrikant* [fapʁiˈkʰantʰ] 'industrialist'
      Maschine [maˈʃiːnə] 'machine' *maschinell* [maʃiˈnɛl] 'mechanical'
      Musik [muˈziːkʰ] 'music' *musikalisch* [muziˈkʰaːlɪʃ] 'musical'

The two allophones of /r/, [ʁ] and [ɐ̯], are in complementary distribution in all environments except after short vowels, where they are in free variation. After short vowels, /r/ may be realized as [ʁ] or [ɐ̯], with no change in meaning.

(24) *hart* [haʁtʰ] or [haɐ̯tʰ] 'hard'
      Herr [hɛʁ] or [hɛɐ̯] 'sir'
      dort [tɔʁtʰ] or [tɔɐ̯tʰ] 'there'

The smallest unit in the analysis of phonological structure is the feature. Features are the characteristics of segments; they are the units that make up individual speech sounds. Features such as [round], [tense], and [high] play a role in the description of German vowels. The vowel [iː], for example, has the features [−round], [+tense], and [+high], among others ([+] means that a feature is present and [−] means that it is absent). Other features that are relevant in the description of speech sounds in German are those such as [voice], [continuant], [spread glottis], etc. These as well as other features will be presented and explained as needed in the discussion of phonological rules in section 1.2.4.

A feature that is capable of distinguishing one phoneme from another (or one set of phonemes from another set) is a distinctive feature. For example, the feature [round] is a distinctive feature of German because it distinguishes the phoneme /yː/ from /iː/. The single difference between these two phonemes is lip rounding: /yː/ is [+round]; /iː/ is [−round]. Features can be used to characterize not just individual sounds, but also classes of sounds. For example, the two features [−back] and [+round] describe the class of front rounded vowels in German. A class of sounds that share a feature or features is a natural class. Other examples of natural classes are voiced fricatives, nasal consonants, and back vowels. As we will see in section 1.2.4, many of the regularities that underlie the phonology of German can be expressed as rules that apply to natural classes.

The syllable plays an important role in the phonology of German. The distribution of the allophones of certain phonemes, for example, is best described in terms of where they occur in a syllable. A syllable is made up minimally of a nucleus, usually a vowel (a monophthong or a diphthong), which forms the core of the syllable. The onset of a syllable is made up of the segment or segments that precede the nucleus; the coda consists of the segment or segments that follow the nucleus. The word *schlank* [ʃlaŋkʰ] 'slim' is monosyllabic. The single vowel in this word, [a], is the nucleus; the first two segments [ʃl] form the onset; the last two segments [ŋkʰ] form the coda. The word *Physik* [fy.ziːkʰ] 'physics' is disyllabic (the period marks a syllable boundary). Its first syllable consists of the onset [f] and the nucleus [y]; its coda is empty. The second syllable consists of the onset [z], the nucleus [iː], and the coda [kʰ]. In a word like *kaufen* [kʰaʊ̯.fn̩] 'to buy', the diphthong [aʊ̯] forms the nucleus of the first syllable (its coda is empty).[11] The nasal [n] forms the nucleus of the second syllable (its coda is also empty). The diacritic ̩ is placed under the [n] to indicate that it is syllabic and thus forms the nucleus. The placement of syllable boundaries in the discussion of phonological rules in section 1.2.4 will simply be given. The principles that determine the placement of syllable boundaries will be discussed in section 1.2.5.

The foot also plays an important role in the phonology of German. A foot is a stressed syllable and any following unstressed syllables that intervene before the next stressed syllable. The phrase *widerlicher Geruch* 'disgusting smell' for example, with six syllables, two of which are stressed, consists of two feet: ₍F₎['widerlicher Ge]₍F₎['ruch]

1.2.2   The vowel phonemes of German

On the basis of the minimal pair test, we can assume the following vowel phonemes for German:

(25)   Vowel phonemes in German and their allophones
        /iː/   *Musik* [iː] 'music', *musikalisch* [i] 'musical'
        /ɪ/   *bitte* [ɪ] 'please'
        /yː/   *Physiker* [yː] 'physicist', *Physik* [y] 'physics'
        /ʏ/   *müssen* [ʏ] 'to have to'
        /uː/   *Jubel* [uː] 'jubilation', *jubilieren* [u] 'to jubilate'
        /ʊ/   *Mutter* [ʊ] 'mother'
        /eː/   *leben* [eː] 'to live', *lebendig* [e] 'lively'
        /ɛː/   *Prätor* [ɛː] 'praetor', *prätorisch* [ɛ] 'praetorial'
        /ɛ/   *Bett* [ɛ] 'bed'
        /øː/   *Goethe* [øː] 'Goethe', *Goetheana* [ø] 'works by and about Goethe'
        /œ/   *können* [œ] 'to be able to'
        /ə/   *bitte* [ə] 'please'
        /oː/   *Probe* [oː] 'test', *probieren* [o] 'to try'
        /ɔ/   *Gott* [ɔ] 'god'
        /aː/   *Drama* [aː] 'drama', *dramatisch* [a] 'dramatic'
        /a/   *Tanne* [a] 'fir'
        /aɪ̯/   *nein* [aɪ̯] 'no'
        /aʊ̯/   *Baum* [aʊ̯] 'tree'
        /ɔɪ̯/   *treu* [ɔɪ̯] 'loyal'

Given the minimal pair *bieten* [piːtn̩] 'to offer' and *bitten* [pɪtn̩] 'to ask', for example, we can posit the phonemes /iː/ and /ɪ/. With the minimal pair *spielen* [ʃpiːln̩] 'to play' and *spülen* [ʃpyːln̩] 'to rinse', we can add the phoneme /yː/ to the list. The minimal pair *Kiste* [kʰɪstʰə] 'box' and *Küste* [kʰʏstʰə] 'coast' yields the additional phoneme /ʏ/. Minimal pairs can be found for each of the phonemes listed in (25).

Although [ə] never occurs in stressed syllables, it contrasts with other unstressed vowels and can thus be considered a phoneme of German. Consider, for example, the minimal pair *Rebellen* [ʁeˈpɛlən] 'rebels' and *Rebellin* [ʁeˈpɛlɪn] 'female rebel' and the near-minimal pair *fehlend* 'missing' [feːləntʰ] and *elend* 'wretched' [eːlɛntʰ].

Minimal pairs can also be found showing that [ə] contrasts with [ɐ]: *Lehre* [leːʁə] 'teaching' and *Lehrer* [leːʁɐ] 'teacher'; *Reife* [ʁaɪ̯fə] 'ripeness' and *reifer* [ʁaɪ̯fɐ] 'riper'. However, notice that [ɐ] is always associated with the sequence <er>: the *-er* used to form nouns from verbs (*Fahrer* 'driver'); the comparative *-er* (*kleiner* 'smaller'); the *-er* adjective ending (*ein großer Tisch* 'a large table'), etc. In spite of the minimal pairs contrasting [ə] and [ɐ], we will not posit [ɐ] as a phoneme of German. We will instead represent it phonemically as the sequence /ər/ (see, for example, Benware 1986, Hall 1992, Kohler 1995, Mangold 2005). In section 1.2.4.10 we will discuss the rules that determine when this sequence will be realized phonetically as [ɐ] (as in *reifer* /raɪfər/ [ʁaɪfɐ]) and when it will be realized as [əʁ] (as in *reifere* /raɪfərə/ [ʁaɪfəʁə]).

Notice that all the tense/long vowel phonemes (not just /iː/, as mentioned in section 1.2.1) have long and short allophones. The long allophones occur in stressed syllables; the short allophones occur in unstressed syllables. This distribution of allophones can be expressed as a rule; it will be treated in section 1.2.4.

Although the diphthongs in German are represented phonetically as a sequence of vowels, they will be treated here, following common practice (Benware 1986, Kohler 1995, Mangold 2005), as single phonemes. As the following minimal pairs demonstrate, the diphthongs contrast with single vowels, both long and short.[12]

(26) *Mais* [maɪs] 'corn'   *mies* [miːs] 'lousy'   *muss* [mʊs] 'must'
      faul [faʊl] 'lazy'   *viel* [fiːl] 'much'   *voll* [fɔl] 'full'
      Meute [mɔɪtʰə] 'pack'   *Miete* [miːtʰə] 'rent'   *Mitte* [mɪtʰə] 'middle'

1.2.3   The consonant phonemes of German

The consonant phonemes that can be posited for German are listed in (27) through (31).

(27)   Stop phonemes in German and their allophones
         /p/ *Bass* [p] 'bass', *rauben* [p̆] 'to rob', *Raub* [pʰ] 'robbery'
         /t/ *Deich* [t] 'dike', *leiden* [t̆] 'to suffer', *Leid* [tʰ] 'sorrow'
         /k/ *Gabel* [k] 'fork', *lagen* [k̆] '(they) lay', *lag* [kʰ] '(I) lay',
              ruhig [ç] 'calm'
         /pʰ/ *Pass* [pʰ] 'passport', *Raupen* [p] 'caterpillars' ([ʁaʊpm̩])
         /tʰ/ *Teich* [tʰ] 'pond', *leiten* [t] 'to lead' ([laɪtn̩])
         /kʰ/ *Kabel* [kʰ] 'cable', *Laken* [k] 'sheet' ([laːkn̩])

(28)   Affricate phonemes in German and their allophones[13]
         /pf/ *Pfund* [pf] 'pound'
         /ts/ *Zunge* [ts] 'tongue'
         /tʃ/ *Cello* [tʃ] 'cello'
         /tʒ/ *Manager* [tʒ] 'manager', *das **Dschungelfieber*** [tʃ] 'the yellow
               fever'

(29)   Fricative phonemes in German and their allophones
       /f/   *falsch* [f] 'false'
       /s/   *Wasser* [s] 'water'
       /ʃ/   *Schule* [ʃ] 'school'
       /x/   *Nacht* [x] 'night', *nicht* [ç] 'not'
       /h/   *haben* [h] 'to have'
       /v/   *kurven* [v] 'to circle', *kurvt* [f] 'circles'
       /z/   *reisen* [z] 'to travel', *gereist* [s] 'traveled'
       /ʒ/   *Garage* [ʒ] 'garage'
       /j/   *ja* [j] 'yes'

(30)   Nasal phonemes in German and their allophones
       /m/   *machen* [m̩] 'to make'
       /n/   *neu* [n] 'new'
       /ŋ/   *singen* [ŋ] 'to sing'

(31)   Liquid phonemes in German and their allophones[14]
       /l/   *lachen* [l] 'to laugh'
       /r/   *leeren* [ʁ] 'to empty', *leer* [ɐ̯] 'empty', *bitter* [ɐ] 'bitter'[15]

Minimal pairs can be found in which the glottal stop contrasts with other consonants.

(32)   *neben* [neːb̥m̩] 'beside'   *eben* [ʔeːb̥m̩] 'even'
       mein [maɪ̯n] 'my'   *ein* [ʔaɪ̯n] 'one'
       dich [tɪç] 'you'   *ich* [ʔɪç] 'I'

However, the distribution of the glottal stop is predictable (see section 1.2.4.8). Furthermore, its presence is optional. The words *eben*, *ein*, and *ich*, for example, can be pronounced without a glottal stop with no change in meaning. Thus, the glottal stop is not given the status of a phoneme in German.

The phonemic status of the affricates in (28) is not uncontroversial. Some studies treat such stop–fricative sequences as sequences of two separate phonemes (Moulton 1962, Heike 1972, Benware 1986, Kohler 1995); others treat them as monophonemic (Hall 1992, Mangold 2005).

Another area of controversy involves the phonemic status of [ŋ]. Following studies such as Benware 1986, Kohler 1995, and Mangold 2005, /ŋ/ is treated here as a phoneme of German. Many studies, however (e.g., Seiler 1962, Vennemann 1970, Hall 1992, Wiese 1996), do not give [ŋ] phonemic status, but treat it instead as derived from the cluster /Ng/ or /Nk/, where /N/ is a nasal that is unspecified for place of articulation.

1.2.4   *Phonological rules*

The relationship between the phonemes of German and their phonetic manifestations can be expressed as rules, as statements that tell us how these phonemes are realized phonetically. For example, one of these rules tells us when the phoneme /iː/ is realized as [iː] and when it is realized as [i]. Phonological rules do not just apply to single phonemes; they also apply to classes of phonemes. The rule that describes when /iː/ is realized as [i] applies to all tense vowels, not just to /iː/.

Phonological rules relate the phonemic level of analysis to the phonetic. They derive the phonetic realization of words from their underlying or phonemic representation. Given the phonemic representation of a word like *Musik* 'music', for example, /muˈziːkʰ/, the phonological rules of German will yield the phonetic representation [muˈziːkʰ]. These rules will tell us that /uː/ is short in this word (because it is not stressed) and that /kʰ/ is aspirated (because it occurs before a pause).

Rules can generally be expressed using the following form of notation:

(33)   A → B / X _____ Y

A in this notation stands for an element in underlying (phonemic) representation (a phoneme or a class of phonemes) and *B* represents the change this element undergoes (how it is realized phonetically). The focus bar, _____, indicates the position of the segment undergoing a change, and *X* and *Y* describe the environment in which the segment must be located to undergo the change. The rule in (33) can thus be read as "*A* becomes *B* when it occurs between *X* and *Y*." *X* or *Y* may be absent. If *X*, for example, is absent, the rule is read as "*A* becomes *B* when it occurs before *Y*." Any additional symbols employed in the following discussion of the phonological rules of German will be explained as they occur. We capitalize the names of the rules formulated in this and other chapters (which apply to German) to distinguish them from terms used for general processes that may apply in other languages.

1.2.4.1 Vowel Shortening   The rule of Vowel Shortening in German states that vowels are shortened when they are unstressed (*V* stands for "vowel").

(34)   Vowel Shortening
        V → [−long]/ _____
                    [−stress]

Long vowels that are stressed are unaffected by the rule and thus retain their length. This rule yields the short allophones of the long vowel phonemes; the long allophones occur when the rule fails to apply. This rule allows us to represent the form meaning 'music' as /muːziːkʰ/ in both *Musik* 'music' and *musikalisch* 'musical' and account for the fact that the *i* in this form is pronounced as long and tense in *Musik*, but short and tense in *musikalisch*.

(35)   /muːˈziːkʰ/ → [muˈziːkʰ]
          /muːziːˈkʰaːlɪʃ/ → [muziˈkʰaːlɪʃ]

Notice that Vowel Shortening also accounts for the fact that the *u* in both words is short and tense (it is unstressed in both words).

> *1.2.4.2 Voicing Assimilation*   The contrast between the two sets of stop phonemes in German has traditionally been viewed as a one of voicing. Under the traditional view, the fortis stops (represented here as /pʰ tʰ kʰ/) are [−voice]; the lenis stops (represented here as /p t k/) are [+voice] (Wängler 1960, Moulton 1962, Wurzel 1970, Rubach 1990, Hall 1992, Wiese 1996). (I use the traditional terms "fortis" and "lenis" here simply as a means of distinguishing the two sets of stops.) An alternative position suggests that the relevant feature is [tense] or [spread glottis], not [voice] (Kloeke 1982, Meinhold and Stock 1982, Iverson and Salmons 1995, Jessen and Ringen 2002). Following Jessen and Ringen (2002), who provide experimental data in support of their position, we will assume that the contrast is one of [spread glottis]. Both sets of stop phonemes are [−voice].[16] The fortis phonemes, unlike the lenis, are [+spread glottis]. Sounds that are [+spread glottis] have an active glottal opening gesture; in stops, the feature [+spread glottis] is often signaled by aspiration, although aspiration may be absent due to the environment in which the stop occurs (Jessen and Ringen 2002:192). A [+spread glottis] stop that occurs before a syllabic nasal or lateral, for example, is not aspirated. Compare the careful pronunciation of *leiten* 'to lead', with schwa and a non-syllabic nasal following /tʰ/ (/laɪtʰən/ → [laɪtʰən]) and the pronunciation without schwa and a syllabic nasal (/laɪtʰən/ → [laɪtn̩]).

The lenis stops are underlyingly (phonemically) [−voice] and are often realized phonetically as voiceless stops:[17]

(36)   *Dach* 'roof'   /tax/ → [tax]
          das Dach 'the roof'   /tas tax/ → [tas tax]
          Hausdach 'house roof'   /haʊstax/ → [haʊstax]

When they occur between voiced sounds, however, they tend to be voiced. That is, lenis stops assimilate to their voiced surroundings.

(37)   *oder* 'or'   /oːtər/ → [oːtɐ]
          ein Dach 'a roof'   /aɪn tax/ → [aɪn tax]

Although voicing in this environment is typical, some speakers do not show voicing consistently, which suggests that voicing is phonetically conditioned, that is, that it has a phonetic explanation (Jessen and Ringen 2002:205).[18] Following Jessen and Ringen, we treat voicing assimilation as phonetic, not phonological (voicing assimilation is not expressed as a phonological rule). However, lenis stops that occur between two voiced sounds are transcribed phonetically as voiced, since they do tend to be voiced in this environment.

1.2.4.3 Fortition   There are some instances, however, where lenis stops occur between voiced segments yet are realized as [−voice]. At first glance, it appears that the lenis stops in the word pairs in (38) through (40) appear in roughly identical environments (all occur between [+voice] segments):

(38)   *neblig* 'foggy'   /neːplɪk/ → [neːp̊lɪç]
        erheblich 'considerable'   /ɛrheːplɪx/ → [ɛʁheːpʰlɪç]

(39)   *Handlung* 'action'   /hantlʊŋ/ → [hant̊lʊŋ]
        handlich 'handy'   /hantlɪx/ → [hantʰlɪç]

(40)   *nörglig* 'cranky'   /nœrklɪk/ → [nœʁɡ̊lɪç]
        kärglich 'sparse'   /kʰɛrklɪx/ → [kʰɛʁkʰlɪç]

However, if we consider the structure of these words, we see a difference between the two members of each pair:

(41)   *nebl-ig* 'foggy'   *erheb-lich* 'considerable'
        Handl-ung 'action'   *hand-lich* 'handy'
        nörgl-ig 'cranky'   *kärg-lich* 'sparse'

The lenis stop in the second member of each pair occurs immediately before a suffix (-*lich*); the lenis stop in the first member of each pair does not (the consonant /l/ occurs between the stop and the following suffix). This difference in structure can explain the difference in the realization of the lenis stop. Jessen and Ringen (2002:212) explain forms like *handlich* by assuming a constraint that requires stops at the end of a phonological word to be [+spread glottis]. Their account requires that one consider *handlich* (but not *Handlung*) to be two phonological words, an assumption that is independently motivated (Wiese 1996, Jessen and Ringen 2002).[19]

Beckman *et al.* (to appear) argue that this same constraint applies to fricatives as well as stops. It accounts for the fact that fricatives in word-final position are voiceless, as the following examples demonstrate.

(42)   *Gras* 'grass'   /kraːz/ → [kʁas]
        Gräser 'grasses'   /krɛːzər/ → [kʁɛːzɐ]
        grasreich 'full of grass' /kraːzraɪx/ → [kʁaːsʁaɪ̯ç]

We will express this constraint as the rule of Fortition (following Wiese 1996, curly brackets are used to indicate the boundaries of phonological words):

(43)   Fortition
         [−spread glottis]   →   [+spread glottis] / _____}

This rule states that sounds that are [−spread glottis] (lenis stops and voiced fricatives) become [+spread glottis] (fortis stops and voiceless fricatives) when they occur at the end of a phonological word. It accounts for the differences in pronunciation of the lenis stops in the word pairs in (41) and the voiced fricatives in the examples in (42).

1.2.4.4 Aspiration   As mentioned in section 1.2.4.2, not all [+spread glottis] stops are aspirated. There is much variation in the degree of aspiration, which is dependent on factors such as boundaries, stress, place of articulation, and so on (Jessen and Ringen 2002:192). For example, aspiration is stronger before stressed vowels than it is before schwa, an unstressed vowel, but it is present in this environment (Jessen 1998:93–94). The degree of aspiration is an issue of phonetics, however, and will not concern us here. The presence versus absence of aspiration, on the other hand, is an issue that we will address. The presence of aspiration is predictable, and can be accounted for by the following rule (*IP* stands for "intonational phrase"):[20]

(44)   Aspiration
$$\begin{bmatrix} -\text{continuant} \\ +\text{spread glottis} \end{bmatrix} \rightarrow [+\text{aspirated}] / \begin{cases} \underline{\hspace{1em}}[-\text{consonant}] \\ \underline{\hspace{1em}}[+\text{sonorant}, -\text{syllabic}] \\ \underline{\hspace{1em}}]_{\text{IP}} \end{cases}$$

The Aspiration rule states that stops that are [+spread glottis] are aspirated when they occur before a vowel, a non-syllabic liquid or nasal, or a pause (at the end of an intonational phrase).[21] The examples in (45) have aspirated stops in prevocalic position (before stressed and unstressed vowels); those in (46) show aspirated stops before non-syllabic liquids and nasals;[22] those in (47) have aspirated stops before a pause.

(45)   *Pass* 'passport' /pʰas/ → [ˈpʰas]
         Miete 'rent' /ˈmiːtʰə/ → [ˈmiːtʰə]
         Brücke 'bridge' /pʀʏkʰə/ → [pʀʏkʰə]

(46)   *Prüfung* 'test' /pʰryːfʊŋ/ → [pʰʀyːfʊŋ]
         weltlich 'wordly' /vɛltʰlɪx/ → [vɛltʰlɪç]
         Knie 'knee' /kʰniː/ → [kʰniː]

(47)   *schlapp* 'worn out' /ʃlapʰ/ → [ʃlapʰ]
        nett 'nice' /nɛtʰ/ → [nɛtʰ]
        Rock 'skirt' /rɔkʰ/ → [ʁɔkʰ]

Because the rule of Aspiration does not apply to [+spread glottis] stops that occur before syllabic liquids and nasals, it prevents aspiration in words like *leiten* 'to lead' when pronounced without schwa, since the absence of schwa requires a syllabic pronunciation of /n/: /laɪtʰən/ → [laɪtn̩] (see the discussion in sections 1.2.4.9 and 1.2.4.10).[23]

Notice that stops that are phonemically lenis ([−spread glottis]) are realized as [+aspirated] when they occur at the end of a phonological word and in an environment for aspiration.[24]

(48)   *handlich* 'handy' /hantlɪx/ → [hantʰlɪç]
        Neid 'envy' /naɪt/ → [naɪtʰ]

Because they occur at the end of a phonological word, they undergo Fortition, which causes them to become [+spread glottis]. They are then eligible for the rule of Aspiration – as long as they occur in one of the proper environments. In *handlich*, /t/ undergoes Fortition and is then eligible for Aspiration because it occurs before a non-syllabic liquid. The /t/ in *Neid* is eligible for Aspiration (after Fortition) because it occurs before a pause.

Stops that occur in an onset with a preceding fricative are not aspirated, as demonstrated by the word *Stahl* 'steel' [ʃtaːl]. Because the fortis/lenis distinction is neutralized in this position, it is not clear whether these stops are allophones of fortis or lenis stops. We will simply assume that they are lenis ([−spread glottis]), in which case the rule of Aspiration will not apply to them. A word like *Stahl*, for example, is represented phonemically as /ʃtaːl/.

1.2.4.5 Fricative Devoicing   Traditionally, fricatives in German are treated together with stops (they both belong to the natural class of obstruents),[25] and rules that affect stops (Fortition, for example) apply to fricatives as well. However, it turns out that German fricatives differ from stops. In particular, unlike their stop counterparts, they contrast in voicing. The fortis fricatives, /f s ʃ ç x h/, are [−voice]; the lenis fricatives, /v z ʒ j/, are [+voice]. Minimal pairs (or near-minimal pairs) demonstrate this contrast in onsets (word-initially as well as intervocalically):[26]

(49)   *vier* 'four' [fiːɐ̯]   *wir* 'we' [viːɐ̯]
        Grafen 'counts' [kʁaː.fn̩]   *braven* 'well-behaved' [pʁaː.vn̩]

(50)   *Seal* 'seal' [siːl]   *Siel* 'sluice' [ziːl]
        reißen 'to tear' [ʁaɪ̯.sn̩]   *reisen* 'to travel' [ʁaɪ̯.zn̩]

In word-final position, however, this contrast is neutralized by Fortition:

(51)   *reisen* 'to travel' /raɪ.zən/ → [ʁaɪ.zn̩]
        reis! 'travel!' /raɪz/ → [ʁaɪs]

(52)   *reißen* 'to tear' /raɪ.sən/ → [ʁaɪ.sn̩]
        (ich) reiß '(I) tear' /raɪs/ → [ʁaɪs]

The contrast in voicing is also neutralized when a fricative occurs before an obstruent:

(53)   *reist* 'travels' /raɪztʰ/ → [ʁaɪstʰ]
        reißt 'tears' /raɪstʰ/ → [ʁaɪstʰ]

The rule of Fricative Devoicing accounts for the [−voice] realization of lenis fricatives when they occur before an obstruent.

(54)   Fricative Devoicing
        [−sonorant]   →   [−voice] /_____ [−sonorant]

This rule states that all obstruents (stops as well as fricatives) are realized as [−voice] when they occur before an obstruent. The fricative /z/ in *reist* 'travels'(/raɪztʰ/), for example, is realized as [s] ([ʁaɪstʰ]) because it occurs before the obstruent /tʰ/. It is not necessary to add the feature [+continuant] and restrict the rule to fricatives, since all stops in German are phonemically [−voice] and therefore cannot be affected by the rule.[27]

1.2.4.6 Velar Fricative Assimilation   The phonemic status of German [ç] and [x] has long intrigued scholars and has resulted in extensive discussion in the literature (see Robinson 2001 for an overview of the research on this topic). The following examples, which show the two sounds to be in complementary distribution, with [x] after non-front vowels and [ç] elsewhere (after front vowels, after consonants, word-initially), would argue for a single phoneme:

(55)   *Buch* 'book' [puːx]
        doch 'but still' [tɔx]
        Bach 'brook' [pax]
        Brauch 'custom' [pʁaʊ̯x]

(56)   *ich* 'I' [ɪç]
        Bücher 'books' [pyːçɐ]
        brechen 'to break' [pʁɛçn̩]
        höchst 'highest' [høːçstʰ]
        Leiche 'corpse' [laɪçə]
        Bräuche 'customs' [pʁɔɪçə]

(57)   *Milch* 'milk' [mɪlç]
        durch 'through' [tʊɐ̯ç]
        manch 'many a' [manç]

(58)   *Chemie* 'chemistry' [çemiː]
        China 'China' [çiːna]

However, minimal pairs like those in (59) and word-initial [x], illustrated in (60), raise doubts about the validity of a single-phoneme analysis.

(59)   *Kuchen* 'cake' [kʰuːxn̩]   *Kuhchen* 'little cow' [kʰuːçn̩]
        tauchen 'to dive' [tʰaʊ̯xn̩]   *Tauchen* 'little rope' [tʰaʊ̯çn̩]

(60)   *Chanukka* 'Hanukkah' [xanʊkʰaɪ̯]
        Junta 'junta' [xʊntʰa][28]

Notice, though, that the differences in pronunciation of <ch> in the word pairs in (59) correlate with differences in word structure. *Kuhchen* 'little cow' and *Tauchen* 'little rope' contain the suffix -*chen*, where <ch> occurs at the beginning of a phonological word: *Kuchen*, *Kuh+chen*, *tauch+en*, *Tau+chen*. In addition, word-initial [ç] in the examples in (58) appears before front vowels, whereas word-initial [x] in (60) is found before non-front vowels.[29] The predictable differences in distribution between [ç] and [x] allow us to account for the data by assuming a single phoneme for German, /x/.[30] The palatal realization of this phoneme, [ç], is accounted for by the rule of Velar Fricative Assimilation.[31]

(61)   Velar Fricative Assimilation

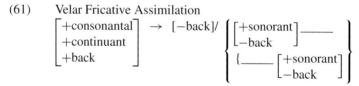

$$\begin{bmatrix} +\text{consonantal} \\ +\text{continuant} \\ +\text{back} \end{bmatrix} \rightarrow [-\text{back}]/ \begin{cases} \begin{bmatrix} +\text{sonorant} \\ -\text{back} \end{bmatrix}\underline{\quad\quad} \\ \{\underline{\quad\quad}\begin{bmatrix} +\text{sonorant} \\ -\text{back} \end{bmatrix} \end{cases}$$

This rule realizes the velar fricative, /x/, as [ç] when it follows [−back] vowels and /r/, /l/, and /n/ (the consonantal sonorants) and when it occurs at the beginning of a phonological word before these same segments.[32] It accounts for the [ç] pronunciation of /x/ in words like *ich*, *Milch*, *China*, and *Kuhchen*. This rule represents a process of assimilation whereby a [+back] fricative is realized as [−back] when it follows a [−back] sonorant (vowel or consonant) or when it precedes a [−back] sonorant at the beginning of a phonological word. When /x/ does not occur in these environments it will be realized as a [+back] fricative, that is, as [x] (/x/ in words such as *Buch*, *Chanukka*, and *Kuchen*). I assume that schwa is phonologically [−front, −back], which accounts for the [ç] pronunciation in the suffix -*chen* when schwa is pronounced: [çn̩]. I also assume that /a/ and /aː/, which are central vowels phonetically, are specified phonologically only for the feature [front]. Because they are [−front] (and not specified for the feature [back]), they will not cause /x/ to be pronounced as [ç] in words such as *Bach* and *Chanukka*.

1.2.4.7 Velar Spirantization As the following examples illustrate, [ḵ] can alternate with [ç] in related word forms.

(62) *ruhiger* 'calmer' [ʁuːɪḵɐ]   *ruhig* 'calm' [ʁuːɪç]
  beruhigen 'to calm' [pəʁuːɪḵən]   *beruhigt* 'relieved' [pəʁuːɪçtʰ]
  Könige 'kings' [kʰøːnɪḵə]   *König* 'king' [kʰøːnɪç]

If we assume that /k/ is the phoneme in all these forms, we can derive the forms with [ç] using the rule of Velar Spirantization (where $C_\emptyset$ stands for zero or more consonants and $ stands for a syllable boundary) and Velar Fricative Assimilation.

(63) Velar Spirantization

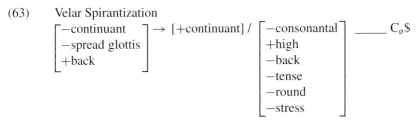

$$
\begin{bmatrix}
-\text{continuant} \\
-\text{spread glottis} \\
+\text{back}
\end{bmatrix}
\rightarrow [+\text{continuant}] /
\begin{bmatrix}
-\text{consonantal} \\
+\text{high} \\
-\text{back} \\
-\text{tense} \\
-\text{round} \\
-\text{stress}
\end{bmatrix}
\underline{\qquad} C_\emptyset\$
$$

  Condition: Does not apply to words in which /k/ is followed by a syllable containing /x/.

The rule of Velar Spirantization turns the velar stop /k/ into a voiceless velar fricative (spirant), [x], when it is in coda position following unstressed /ɪ/ (/k/ is phonemically voiceless), and Velar Fricative Assimilation realizes it as [ç], since it follows /ɪ/, a [−back] vowel.[33]

A condition on Velar Spirantization specifies that the rule does not apply to words that contain /x/ in the syllable following /k/. This condition prevents the rule from applying to words like *Königreich* 'kingdom', *königlich* 'royal', and *ewiglich* 'eternally', which have a /k/ that is realized as [kʰ] rather than [ç]:

(64) *Königreich* 'kingdom' [kʰøːnɪkʰʁaɪç]
  königlich 'royal' [kʰøːnɪkʰlɪç]
  ewiglich 'eternally' [eːvɪkʰlɪç] (cf. *ewig* 'eternal' [eːvɪç])

Words like those in (64) contain [kʰ] rather than [ç] because the standard language apparently does not favor two successive syllables ending in [ç] (Siebs 1969:100).

The rule of Velar Spirantization does not occur in southern German, where /k/ in words like *ruhig* 'calm' and *beruhigt* 'relieved' is realized as a stop:

(65)   Southern German
         ruhig 'calm' /ruːɪk/ → [ʁuːɪkʰ]
         beruhigt 'relieved' /pəruːɪktʰ/ → [pəʁuːɪktʰ]

In northern and central German, on the other hand, the rule of Velar Spiranti-zation is more general, applying to all instances of /k/ in coda position, not just those following unstressed /ɪ/:[34]

(66)   Northern and central German
         Sieg 'victory'/ziːk/ → [ziːç]
         gesagt 'said' /kəzaːktʰ/ → [kəzaːxtʰ]

Standard German is thus an interesting mix of southern and non southern pronunciation. In southern German (S), /k/ in coda position is realized as a stop; in northern and central German (N/C), /k/ in coda position is realized as a fricative. In Standard German, /k/ in coda position is realized as a stop in all positions except in the sequence /ɪk/, where it is realized as a fricative:[35]

(67)   /k/ in coda position   S   N/C   Standard
         After central/back vowel *Zug* 'train'   [kʰ]   [x]   [kʰ]
         After front vowel   *Sieg* 'victory'   [kʰ]   [ç]   [kʰ]
         In the sequence /ɪk/   *wichtig* 'important' [kʰ]   [ç]   [ç]

1.2.4.8 Glottal Stop Insertion   Although the glottal stop is not con-sidered a phoneme of German, its distribution is predictable. The glottal stop occurs before vowels and is most common at the beginning of a phonological word with initial stress and at the beginning of utterances (Kohler 1994). We can thus express the rule of Glottal Stop Insertion in terms of the phonological word ({), the foot (F), and the intonational phrase (IP). (Recall that a foot is a stressed syllable and any following unstressed syllables that intervene before the next stressed syllable.) According to Kohler (1994:42), the glottal stop is more commonly pronounced as glottalization (creaky voice) of the following vowel (with or without long glottal closure preceding the vowel) than as a sim-ple glottal stop (closure and release).[36] We will express Glottal Stop Insertion as the insertion of the feature [+constricted glottis] and leave the realization of this feature (creaky voice or glottal stop) to the phonetics.

(68)   Glottal Stop Insertion

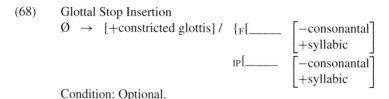

         Condition: Optional.

The rule of Glottal Stop Insertion inserts the feature [+constricted glottis] before a vowel at the beginning of a phonological word when that word bears initial stress or is utterance-initial. Because the glottal stop (glottalization) is not used universally, it is expressed as an optional rule. This rule accounts for the distribution of glottal stops in a phrase like the following (from C. Hall 2003:70):[37]

(69)   *Er hat die anderen beeindruckt.* 'He has impressed the others.'
       [ʔeɐ̯ hat ti ˈʔant̪aʁən p̌əˈʔaɪnt̪ʁʊktʰ]

The first glottal stop in this phrase is utterance-initial; the second two glottal stops occur at the beginning of phonological words and are also foot-initial. Words with stressed vowels that are morpheme-internal do not undergo Glottal Stop Insertion.[38]

(70)   *Theater* 'theater' [tʰeˈaːtʰɐ]
       Kloake 'sewer' [kʰloˈaːkʰə]

Although these vowels are foot-initial, they do not occur at the beginning of a phonological word.

1.2.4.9 Schwa Deletion   The status of schwa in German has received a good deal of attention in the literature, with some authors arguing that schwa is a phoneme of German that is deleted in some contexts (Kloeke 1982, Strauss 1982, Benware 1986), and others arguing that schwa is not a phoneme, but that it must be inserted in certain contexts (Wiese 1986, 1988; Giegerich 1987).[39] A third approach, expressed by Becker (1998), treats schwa as an allophone of /e/. I assume that schwa is a phoneme of German and that a deletion rule is necessary to account for schwa–zero alternations like the following:

(71)   *Cochemer* 'person from Cochem' [kʰɔxəmɐ], *Cochem* 'Cochem'
           [kʰɔxm̩]
       ebene 'smooth' [eːp̌ənə], *eben* 'smooth' [eːp̌m̩]
       Eselei 'stupidity' [eːzəlaɪ̯], *Esel* 'donkey' [eːzl̩]
       bittere 'bitter' [pɪtʰəʁə], *bitter* 'bitter' [pɪtʰɐ]

Assuming that both forms in each pair in (71) have a schwa phonemically, the rule of Schwa Deletion accounts for the forms in which schwa is not realized phonetically.[40]

(72)   Schwa Deletion

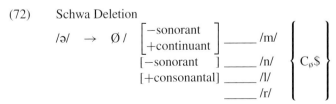

This rule deletes schwa before /m/, /n/, /l/, and /r/ when these occur in a coda, as long as certain conditions are met on the segments that precede schwa. Schwa is deleted before /m/ only if a fricative precedes schwa:

(73)   *tiefem* 'deep' /tʰiːfəm/ → [tʰiːfm̩]
         Cochems 'Cochem's' /kʰɔxəms/ → [kʰɔxm̩s]
         blödem 'stupid' /pløːtəm/ → [pløːtəm] (stop precedes schwa)

If schwa occurs before /n/, an obstruent (a fricative or a stop) must precede schwa. Thus the conditions on Schwa Deletion before /n/ are less restrictive than those before /m/.

(74)   *reisend* 'travelling' /raɪ̯zənt/ → [ʁaɪ̯zn̩tʰ]
         Faden 'thread' /faːtən/ → [faːtn̩]
         nehmen 'to take' /neːmən/ → [neːmən] (nasal precedes schwa)

The conditions on Schwa Deletion before /l/ are even less restrictive. The segment preceding schwa must be a consonant.[41]

(75)   *Löffel* 'spoon' /lœfəl/ → [lœfl̩]
         Mittel 'means' /mɪtʰəl/ → [mɪtl̩]
         angeln 'to fish' /aŋəln/ → [aŋl̩n]
         Greuel 'horror' /krɔɪ̯əl/ → [kʁɔɪ̯əl] (vowel precedes schwa)

There are no conditions on the segment that precedes schwa when it occurs before /r/; schwa is simply deleted before /r/ when it occurs in a coda (and /r/ is realized as [ɐ]).

(76)   *bitter* 'bitter' /pɪ.tʰər/ → [pɪ.tʰɐ]
         verbittert 'embittered' /fɛr.pɪ.tʰərtʰ/ → [fɛɐ̯.p̆ɪ.tʰɐtʰ]

Notice that /m/, /n/, /l/, and /r/ are all realized as [+syllabic] after a preceding schwa has been deleted. In addition, /r/ is realized as [−consonantal]. These details are addressed in the following section, which treats the realization of /r/.

1.2.4.10 r-Vocalization   The feature [−back] is one of the important features of /r/, since this is the feature that plays a role in Velar Fricative Assimilation, causing a [+back] fricative to become [−back]: *durch* 'through' /tʊrx/ → *dur*[ç]. Although the vocalic realizations of /r/ are [−back] ([ɐ] and [ɐ̯]), the consonantal realization ([ʁ]) is [+back]. The rules that state the distribution of the allophones of /r/ take this into account. The consonantal allophone of /r/ is produced by a rule that realizes /r/ as a voiced uvular fricative when it occurs in an onset:

(77)   Consonantal Realization of /r/

$$/r/ \rightarrow \begin{bmatrix} +\text{back} \\ -\text{sonorant} \end{bmatrix} / \$C_\emptyset \underline{\quad\quad}$$

This rule yields the consonantal pronunciation of /r/ in words like those in (78).

(78)   *Rede* 'speech' /reːtə/ → [ʁeːt̥ə]
         leeren 'to empty' /leː.rən/ → [leː.ʁən]
         Schrift 'writing' /ʃrɪftʰ/ → [ʃʁɪftʰ]

The vocalic allophones of /r/ are accounted for (in part) by the rule of r-Vocalization, which changes the [+consonantal] feature of /r/ to [−consonantal] when /r/ occurs in a coda:[42]

(79)   r-Vocalization

$$/r/ \quad \rightarrow \quad [-\text{consonantal}] / \underline{\quad\quad} C_\emptyset \$$$

The rule does not change the [−syllabic] feature of /r/; thus it realizes /r/ in coda position as [ʁ̥].

(80)   *leer* 'empty' /leːr/ → [leːʁ̥]
         leert 'empties' /leːrtʰ/ → [leːʁ̥tʰ]
         verkauft 'sold' /fɛr.kʰaʊftʰ/ → [fɛʁ̥.kʰaʊftʰ]

   The rule that accounts for the [−consonantal, +syllabic] realization of /r/ also accounts for the [+syllabic] realizations of the other consonantal sonorants, namely, /m/, /n/, and /l/.

(81)   Sonorant Syllabification

$$[+\text{sonorant}] \quad \rightarrow \quad [+\text{syllabic}] / \$C_\emptyset \underline{\quad\quad} C_\emptyset \$$$

This rule causes /m/, /n/, /l/, and /r/ to become syllabic and thus form the nucleus of a syllable when they find themselves in a syllable without a nucleus because of Schwa Deletion. This is exemplified for /l/ in (82).

(82)   /lœ.fəl/ *Löffel* 'spoon'
         →   [lœ.fl]   Schwa Deletion
         →   [lœ.fl̩]   Sonorant Syllabification

When Schwa Deletion occurs before /r/, the rule of r-Vocalization will yield a form with [ʁ̥]; Sonorant Syllabification will turn [ʁ̥], which is [−syllabic], into [ɐ], which is [+syllabic].[43]

(83)   /liː.fərn/ *liefern* 'to supply'
   →   [liː.frn̩]   Schwa Deletion
   →   [liː.fɐ̯n̩]   *r*-Vocalization
   →   [liː.fɐn̩]   Sonorant Syllabification

1.2.4.11 Nasal Assimilation   Schwa deletion has repercussions in addition to those that affect the syllabicity of a following consonant. In particular, when a stop precedes a schwa that is deleted before /n/, /n/ takes on the place of articulation of the preceding stop. It is realized as a bilabial nasal, [m], following a bilabial stop and as a velar nasal, [ŋ], following a velar stop:

(84)   *haben* 'to have' /haːpən/ → [haːp̚m̩]
        backen 'to bake' /pakʰən/ → [pakŋ̍]

The rule of Nasal Assimilation accounts for this change in place of articulation of /n/. This rule uses "alpha notation," where the Greek letter α serves as a variable and must have the same value each time it occurs.[44]

(85)   Nasal Assimilation
$$\begin{bmatrix} +\text{nasal} \\ +\text{syllabic} \end{bmatrix} \rightarrow [\alpha\ \text{artic}]/ \begin{bmatrix} -\text{continuant} \\ -\text{sonorant} \\ \alpha\ \text{artic} \end{bmatrix} \underline{\hspace{2cm}}$$

The rule of Nasal Assimilation states that a syllabic nasal preceded by a stop must have the same place of articulation as the preceding stop.[45] For example, if the stop is bilabial, /p/ or /pʰ/, the nasal has to be bilabial: the /n/ in *haben* 'to have' /haːpən/ is realized as the bilabial nasal [m] because it is preceded by the bilabial stop /p/ following Schwa Deletion.

1.2.5   Phonotactic constraints

Phonotactics deals with the permissible sequences of segments in a given language. What is permissible in one language may not be permissible in another. The sequence /kʰn/, for example, is perfectly acceptable in an onset in German, but not in English; compare German *Knie* 'knee' /kʰniː/ and English *knee* /niː/. The syllable plays an important role in phonotactics, since the constraints on permissible sequences of segments in a language can often be stated in terms of permissible onsets and codas.[46]

1.2.5.1 Syllable structure   Although some languages allow only very simple syllables (Hua, a Papuan language of New Guinea, allows only CV syllables; Blevins 1995:217), German allows a variety of syllable types ranging from syllables that consist solely of a nucleus to those that contain onsets and codas made up of multiple segments. In German, all combinations of onset, nucleus, and coda are possible (each syllable, by definition, must contain a nucleus):

(86)   nucleus   *Kakao* 'cocoa' [kʰa.kʰaː.o]
        onset + nucleus   *liefern* 'to supply' [liː.fɐn]
        nucleus + coda   *Chaos* 'chaos' [kʰaː.ɔs]
        onset + nucleus + coda   **kann** 'can' [kʰan]

Onsets can consist of up to three segments, and codas can have up to four segments.[47]

(87)   Onsets
        one segment   *lebt* 'lives' [leːptʰ]
        two segments   *klebt* 'sticks' [kʰleːptʰ]
        three segments *Sprache* 'language' [ʃpʁaː.xə]

(88)   Codas
        one segment   *mit* 'with' [mɪtʰ]
        two segments   *kalt* 'cold' [kʰaltʰ]
        three segments *filmt* 'films (3rd person sg.)' [fɪlmtʰ]
        four segments   *hilfst* 'help (2nd sg.)' [hɪlfstʰ]

Words in German can be syllabified using universal principles and language-specific constraints. Each vowel is assigned to a nucleus. The longest sequence of segments to the left of each nucleus that does not violate the phonotactic constraints of the language (see the discussion below) is assigned to the onset of the syllable with that nucleus. The remaining segments to the right of each nucleus are assigned to the coda. These principles yield syllabifications like those indicated in the following words.

(89)   *beschleunigen* 'to accelerate' /pə.ʃlɔɪ̯.nɪ.kən/
        gesprochen 'spoken' /kə.ʃprɔ.xən/
        Wagner 'Wagner' /vaː.knər/

The onsets of the second syllable in each of the words in (89) do not violate the phonotactic constraints of the language, since these are possible word-initial consonant clusters, as the examples in (90) demonstrate:

(90)   *schlimm* 'bad' /ʃlɪm/
        Sprung 'leap' /ʃprʊŋ/
        Gnade 'mercy' /knaː.tə/

An additional principle must be taken into account when syllabifying words like *Türöffner* 'doorman'. The above principles would yield the syllabification in (91), which would result in an unacceptable pronunciation.[48]

(91)   *Türöffner* 'doorman' /tʰyː.rœf.nər/ → *[tʰyː.ʁœf.nɐ]

In this syllabification, the /r/ in *Türöffner* is not in a coda – but it must be, because it must be vocalized (*Tü*[ɐ]*öffner*). The principle necessary for producing the correct syllabification, which has precedence over all other principles of syllabification, requires syllable boundaries to coincide with word boundaries. This principle locates a syllable boundary between the two words in the compound *Türöffner*. This yields the syllabification in (92), which results in an acceptable pronunciation.

(92)   *Türöffner* 'doorman' /tʰyːr.œf.nər/ → [tʰyːɐ̯.œf.nɐ]

    Many scholars assume that intervocalic consonants in German can be ambisyllabic, that is, that they can belong to the coda of one syllable and the onset of a following syllable (e.g., Sievers 1893, Jespersen 1904, Trubetzkoy 1939, Giegerich 1985, Benware 1986, Kohler 1995, Wiese 1996). In particular, an intervocalic consonant following a short vowel (the /tʰ/ in *bitte* 'please', for example) is assumed to be ambisyllabic. One argument in favor of such an analysis is based on the fact that word-final syllables in German do not end in a short (lax) vowel.[49] This leads to the conclusion that there must also be a constraint against word-internal syllables ending in a short (lax) vowel. Ambisyllabic consonants are thus required in order to satisfy this constraint. As Hall (1992:52) points out, however, a flaw in this line of reasoning is the assumption that generalizations that hold for word edges also hold for syllable edges. He notes that a number of studies show that this is not necessarily the case (Halle and Vergnaud 1980, Clements and Keyser 1983, Itô 1986). In addition, there does not appear to be clear-cut phonetic evidence in favor of ambisyllabicity.[50] The analysis of German syllable structure presented here thus does not recognize ambisyllabic consonants as being relevant for the phonology of German.

1.2.5.2 Onsets   The acceptability of word-internal onsets is typically determined by appealing to the acceptability of onsets in word-initial position. For example, because /tʰl/ does not occur word-initially in German, this sequence cannot function as an onset in a word like *Atlantik* 'Atlantic'. The onset of the second syllable in this word can consist maximally of one segment, /l/: /atʰ.lan.tʰɪkʰ/, not */a.tʰlan.tʰɪkʰ/. However, word-initial and word-internal onsets do not always behave identically when the onset consists of a single segment. For example, we do not find word-initial /s/ before vowels in native German words. Even initial /s/ in words of foreign origin is typically integrated into the phonology of German and pronounced as [z]: *Safe* 'safe' [zeːf], *Sex* 'sex' [zɛks] (Mangold 2005:691, 722). However, /s/ is a possible onset word-internally: *reißen* 'to tear' /raɪ.sən/. Similarly, /ŋ/ does not

occur in an onset word-initially, but does word-internally: *bringen* 'to bring'
/prɪ.ŋən/.

Except for /s/ and /ŋ/, which may occur in a one-member onset only word-
internally, all the consonant phonemes of German may occur in one-member
onsets word-initially and word-internally. This holds, for example, for /x/:

(93)   *Chemie* 'chemistry' /xeː.miː/   *Kuchen* 'cake' /kʰuː.xən/

The phonemes /h/ and /j/ also occur in both positions, but they never occur in
onsets that consist of more than one segment.

(94)   *Hand* 'hand' /hant/   *Ahorn* 'acorn' /aː.hɔrn/
        Jahr 'year' /jaːr/   *Boje* 'buoy' /poː.jə/

Only certain combinations of phonemes are possible in two-member onsets.
Obstruents (stops, fricatives, and affricates) are permissible as the initial segment in such onsets; sonorant consonants (liquids and nasals) are typically the
second segment.

(95)   stop + liquid   *Brauch* 'custom' /praʊ̯x/
        stop + nasal   *Knecht* 'servant' /kʰnɛxtʰ/
        fricative + liquid   *flach* 'flat' /flax/
        fricative + nasal   *Schnee* 'snow' /ʃneː/
        affricate + liquid   *Pflug* 'plow' /pfluːk/

In addition, a few obstruents (the fricative /v/ and the lenis stops) may occur as
the second segment in a limited number of two-member onsets.[51]

(96)   /ʃv/   *Schwein* 'pig' /ʃvaɪ̯n/
        /tsv/ *zwei* 'two' /tsvaɪ̯/

(97)   /ʃp/   *Spiel* 'game' /ʃpiːl/
        /ʃt/   *Stein* 'stone' /ʃtaɪ̯n/
        /sk/   *Skat* 'skat' /skaːtʰ/

Not all two-member onsets that are possible word-initially are also possible
word-internally in words made up of a single morpheme. For example, /fr/ can
form an onset word-initially and word-internally in a morphologically simple
word, but this is not the case with /ʃl/ (Hall 1992:68):

(98)   word-initial   *frei* 'free' /fraɪ̯/
        morpheme-internal   *Afrika* 'Africa' /aː.friː.kʰaː/

(99)   word-initial   *Schlaf* 'sleep' /ʃlaːf/
        word-internal   *be-schlaf-en* 'to sleep on' /pə.ʃlaː.fən/
        morpheme-internal   NA

These distribution facts would argue against positing morpheme-internal onset clusters that do not also occur word-initially. In particular, /tl/ would be questionable as an onset in words like *adlig* 'noble' and *Handlung* 'action' because it does not occur word-initially. These words would have to be syllabified with only /l/ in an onset and /t/ in the preceding coda:

(100)   *adl+ig* /aːt.lɪk/ → [aːt̬.lɪç]
         Handl+ung /hant.lʊŋ/ → [hant̬.lʊŋ]

This syllabification poses no problem for our analysis of German stops, however. The /t/ in both words is phonemically [−voice], but undergoes voicing assimilation (and is realized as a [+voice] sound, [t̬]) because it occurs between two [+voice] sounds (see the discussion of voicing assimilation in section 1.2.4.2).[52]

There are only five different three-member onsets that are possible. The first consonant in such a cluster is either /s/ or /ʃ/, the second is a stop, and the third is a liquid.

(101)   /skl/ *Sklave* 'slave' /sklaː.və/
         /skr/ *Skrupel* 'scruple' /skruː.pʰəl/
         /ʃpl/ *Splitter* 'splinter' /ʃplɪ.tʰər/
         /ʃpr/ *Spruch* 'saying' /ʃprʊx/
         /ʃtr/ *Strom* 'current' /ʃtroːm/

These clusters occur only word- or morpheme-initially. They do not occur as onsets in morpheme-internal position (Hall 1992:69).

1.2.5.3 Codas   With the exception of /h/, /j/, and /tʒ/, all consonant phonemes may occur in one-member codas in German. All single-member codas that are possible word-finally are also possible word-internally. However, some single-segment codas occur word-internally only in morpheme-final position, that is, not in morpheme-internal position (Hall 1992:111).

(102)   word-final   *mit* 'with' /mɪtʰ/
         morpheme-internal   *Atlas* 'atlas' /atʰ.las/

(103)   word-final   *Fisch* 'fish' /fɪʃ/
         word-internal   *misch-te* 'mixed' /mɪʃ.tʰə/
         morpheme-internal   NA

There are many combinations of consonants that can occur in two-member codas. Examples of those beginning with a sonorant consonant are listed in (104); those beginning with an obstruent are in (105):

(104)   liquid + liquid   *Kerl* 'guy' /kʰɛrl/
        liquid + nasal   *Helm* 'helmet' /hɛlm/
        liquid + obstruent   *halb* 'half' /halp/
        nasal + obstruent   *Hemd* 'shirt' /hɛmt/

(105)   stop + fricative   *Mops* 'pug (dog)' /mɔps/
        stop + stop   *nackt* 'naked' /nakʰtʰ/
        fricative + fricative   *Kochs* 'cook's' /kʰɔxs/
        fricative + stop   *Lust* 'pleasure' /lʊstʰ/
        affricate + fricative   *Kopfs* 'head's' /kʰɔpfs/
        affricate + stop   *rutscht* 'slides' /rʊtʃtʰ/

Codas made up of three segments that begin with a sonorant consonant are followed by another sonorant consonant and an obstruent or by two obstruents:

(106)   sonorant consonant + sonorant consonant + obstruent
        /rls/   *Kerls* 'guy's' /kʰɛrls/
        /lmtʰ/ *gefilmt* 'filmed' /kəfɪlmtʰ/

(107)   sonorant consonant + obstruent + obstruent
        /lps/   *Rülps* 'burp' /rʏlps/
        /nftʰ/ *sanft* 'gentle' /zanftʰ/

Codas made up of three segments that begin with an obstruent are followed by the obstruents /stʰ/ or /tʰs/:

(108)   obstruent + obstruent + obstruent
        /fstʰ/ *schaffst* 'create (2nd sg.)' /ʃafstʰ/
        /ftʰs/ *Stifts* 'pencil's' /ʃtɪftʰs/

Although there are three-member codas that can occur within a single morpheme, many occur only across morpheme boundaries:

(109)   /nstʰ/ *Kunst* 'art' /kʰʊnstʰ/
        /rxtʰ/ *Furcht* 'fear' /fʊrxtʰ/

(110)   /nx+s/ *Mönchs* 'monk's' /mœnxs/
        /x+stʰ/ *suchst* 'look for (2nd sg.)' /zuːxstʰ/

Codas that contain four segments always begin with a sonorant consonant and end with either /stʰ/ or /tʰs/:

(111)   sonorant consonant + sonorant consonant + /stʰ/
/lmstʰ/ *filmst* 'film (2nd sg.)' /fɪlmstʰ/

(112)   sonorant consonant + obstruent + /stʰ/ or /tʰs/
/lfstʰ/ *hilfst* 'help (2nd sg.)' /hɪlfstʰ/
/rktʰs/ *Markts* 'market's' /marktʰs/

Four-segment codas occur only rarely within a single morpheme. Two examples that Hall (1992:121) notes are /rpstʰ/ in *Herbst* 'autumn' /hɛrpstʰ/ and /rnstʰ/ in *ernst* 'serious' /ɛrnstʰ/.[53] The complexity (length) of German codas is thus due in large part to the inflectional morphology of the language. The second person singular ending -*st* on present tense verb forms in particular accounts for the majority of four-member codas.

1.2.6   Stress

1.2.6.1 Word stress   A stressed syllable is one that is perceived as more prominent than other syllables. Various factors that play a role in deter-mining prominence include length (duration), loudness, and pitch (the audi-tory property of a sound that allows listeners to place it on a scale ranging from low to high). In German, the strongest correlate of word stress is length; stressed syllables are longer than unstressed syllables.[54] Although there may be a number of different degrees of stress phonetically, at the phonological level we will recognize two: primary stress (represented by the raised verti-cal stroke, ', before the syllable receiving primary stress) and secondary stress (represented by the low vertical stroke, ˌ); all other syllables are unstressed (no diacritic).

It is necessary in German to recognize a level of secondary stress because of words like *Demut* 'humility', *biegsam* 'flexible', and *Bahnhof* 'train station'. All of these words have primary stress on the first syllable, but the vowels in the second syllable are all long, an indication that the second syllable in each word is stressed to some degree, since Vowel Shortening does not apply (Hall 1992:29–30):

(113)   *Demut* 'humility' ['teːˌmuːtʰ]
biegsam 'flexible' ['piːkˌzaːm]
Bahnhof 'train station' ['paːnˌhoːf]

In what follows, secondary stress will not be indicated unless it is relevant for the discussion.

A number of generalizations can be made regarding the placement of stress in German words. These generalizations are sensitive to the morphological structure of a word. The relevant categories are simplex words (those that have no affixes and are not part of a compound), complex words (formed with prefixes and/or suffixes), and compound words (formed from two or more lexical items).

1.2.6.1.1 Simplex words   Of the various generalizations that can be made about the assignment of stress in simplex words in German, three exhibit few exceptions and are thus highly reliable: the "three-syllable window restriction," the "closed-penult restriction," and the "final-schwa restriction" (Jessen 1999).

The three-syllable window restriction requires that stress fall on one of the last three syllables of a word (Jessen 1999:519). This accounts for the placement of stress in the following words:[55]

(114)   *Kle'o.pa.tra* 'Cleopatra'
         Har'mo.ni.ka 'harmonica'

The closed-penult restriction says that the main stress cannot occur farther to the left than on the penultimate (second-to-last) syllable if the penultimate syllable is closed (ends in a consonant) (Jessen 1999:520):

(115)   *Hi'bis.kus* 'hibiscus'
         Pla'cen.ta 'placenta'
         Rho.do'den.dron 'rhododendron'

As Jessen (1999:520) notes, syllables that end in diphthongs behave like closed syllables with respect to stress assignment:

(116)   *Ba.la'lai.ka* 'balalaika'
         Her.me'neu.tik 'hermeneutics'
         The'sau.rus 'thesaurus'

The third generalization (the final-schwa restriction) states that if the final syllable contains schwa and has an onset, stress falls on the penultimate syllable (Jessen 1999:521):

(117)   *Me'tho.de* 'method'
         Ta'pe.te 'wallpaper'
         Ka'nis.ter 'canister'

If the final syllable does not have an onset, the antepenultimate syllable is stressed (Jessen 1999:521):

(118)   *A'ka.zi.e* 'acacia'
         'Li.li.e 'lily'
         'Sta.tu.e 'statue'

Notice that both the closed-penult restriction and the final-schwa restriction result in penultimate stress assignment. Kohler (1995) in fact notes the tendency for stress to fall on the penultimate syllable in simplex words. Evidence that penultimate stress could be the default stress pattern in German comes from stress placement in foreign words and foreign names that have entered the language in written form (Kohler 1995:187). The word *Niagara*, for example, is pronounced by German speakers with penultimate stress (*Nia'gara*).[56] Wiese (1996:280–281) reports on an experiment involving words in Japanese that provides further evidence that penultimate stress is the dominant/unmarked pattern in German. For discussion of additional generalizations that can be made regarding stress assignment in simplex words, see Jessen 1999.

1.2.6.1.2 Complex words   *Suffixed words* Inflectional suffixes (e.g., plural endings on nouns, adjective endings, etc.) are unstressed and typically do not change the stress pattern of the words to which they are attached.

(119)   *'König* 'king'   *'Könige* 'kings'
        'mager 'meager'   *'magere 'Ernte* 'poor harvest'

Derivational suffixes fall into two basic classes with respect to stress: those that do not bear stress and those that do.[57]

The large majority of derivational suffixes that do not bear stress (or bear secondary stress) are Germanic in origin. These suffixes typically do not affect the stress pattern of the words to which they are attached.

(120)   *'düster* 'gloomy'   *'Düster-heit* 'gloominess'
        'Bruder 'brother'   *'Bruder-schaft* 'brotherhood'
        'Abend 'evening'   *'abend-lich* 'evening'
        'Spiegel 'mirror'   *'Spiegel-chen* 'little mirror'

(121)   *be-'greif-en* 'to understand'   *be-'greif-ˌbar* 'conceivable'
        'arbeit- 'work'   *'arbeit-ˌsam* 'industrious'

A small number of suffixes that do not bear stress can bring about a change in stress. Some of these suffixes are native (*-isch, -er*); others are not (*-ik, -or*).[58]

If *-isch*, for example, is added to a derived word (a word created using a derivational affix) or compound, it typically does not have an effect on stress:

(122)   *'Mörd-er* 'murderer'   *'mörd-er-isch* 'murderous'
        'Haus-hält-er 'houskeeper'   *'haus-hält-er-isch* 'economical'

However, when added to polysyllabic non-derived forms, it can bring about a change in the stress pattern:

(123)   *'Chaos* 'chaos'   *cha'ot-isch* 'chaotic'
         'Dämon 'demon'   *dä'mon-isch* 'demonic'
         Eu'ropa 'Europe'   *euro'pä-isch* 'European'
         'Japan 'Japan'   *ja'pan-isch* 'Japanese'

Notice that this change in stress results in and thus preserves a penultimate stress pattern (Kohler 1995:186).

The derivational suffixes that do bear stress are all of Romance origin (Latin, French). These suffixes are stressed on the last syllable that has a full (non-schwa) vowel as its nucleus (Kohler 1995:187):

(124)   *'Spion* 'spy'   *Spio'n-age* ([aːʒə]) 'espionage'
         'liefer-n 'to supply' *Liefe'r-ant* 'supplier'
         Haus 'house'   *hau's ier en* 'to paddle'
         Hu'mor 'humor'   *Humo'r-ist* 'humorist'
         so'lid 'solid'   *Solid-i'tät* 'solidness'
         ko'rrekt 'correct'   *Korrek't-ur* 'correction'

If a derived word contains several of these suffixes, only the last suffix is stressed:

(125)   *Nat-i'on* 'nation'   *nat-io'n-al* 'national'   *Nat-ion-al-i'tät* 'nationality'

Prefixed words. Stress assignment in prefixed words is sensitive to the lexical category of a word. In particular, verbal prefixes behave differently from non-verbal prefixes. Verbal prefixes are typically unstressed. The verbal prefixes *be-*, *ent-*, *er-*, *ge-*, *ver-*, and *zer-* (which are never separated from the verbal stem) are generally unstressed and do not have any effect on the stress of the words to which they are prefixed.

(126)   *'steig-en* 'to climb' *be-'steig-en* 'to ascend'
         'leb-en 'to live'   *er-'leb-en* 'to experience'
         'end-en 'to end'   *ver-'end-en* 'to perish'

The forms *durch-*, *hinter-*, *über-*, *um-*, *unter-*, and *wider-* can behave in the same way, that is, as unstressed, inseparable prefixes, and are analyzed here as such:[59]

(127)   *'blut-en* 'to bleed'   *durch-'blut-en* 'to supply with blood'
         'fahr-en 'to drive'   *über-'fahr-en* 'to run over'
         'nehm-en 'to take'   *unter-'nehm-en* 'to undertake'

These forms can also be stressed (e.g., *'durch-blut-en* 'to bleed through'), in which case they are treated not as prefixes but as part of a phrasal verb (like *Rad fahren* 'to pedal') and are stressed in their citation (dictionary) form according to the rules that apply to compounds (see section 1.2.6.1.3). Notice that the prefixed words in (126) and (127) preserve the penultimate stress pattern of their non-prefixed counterparts (Kohler 1995:187).

The verbal prefix *miss-*, as well as the set of prefixes that includes *über-* (when meaning 'too much') and *unter-* (when meaning 'too little'), are unstressed unless they are followed by an unstressed syllable, in which case they are stressed (Kiparsky 1966):[60]

(128)   *miss-'trau-en* 'to mistrust'   *'miss-ver-steh-en* 'misunderstand'
        über-'schätz-en 'to overestimate'   *'über-be-licht-en* 'to overexpose'
        unter-'schätz-en 'to underestimate' *'unter-be-licht-en* 'to underexpose'

Nominal and adjectival prefixes are typically stressed.[61] In particular, the nominal and adjectival prefixes *erz-*, *miss-*, *un-*, and *ur-* are generally stressed.[62]

(129)   *'Erz-bischof* 'archbishop'   *'erz-konservativ* 'ultraconservative'
        'Miss-brauch 'abuse'   *'miss-mut-ig* 'sullen'
        'Un-mensch 'monster'   *'un-reif* 'immature'
        'Ur-text 'original (text)'   *'ur-alt* 'ancient'

Interestingly, the stress pattern of these words is identical to the stress pattern of compounds. As Wiese (1996:294) points out, the stress pattern of a prefixed word like *'Miss-gunst* 'resentment' is identical to that of the compound *'Miss-wahl* 'beauty (Miss) contest'.[63]

1.2.6.1.3 Compound words   A compound is a word made up by adjoining two or more words. The compound *Haustier* 'pet', for example, is formed from the words *Haus* 'house' and *Tier* 'animal'. Although compounds can be made up of four words or more (*Kern+kraft+werk+unfall* 'atomic power plant accident', *Nudel+saucen+rezept+sammler+treffen* 'noodle sauce recipe collector meeting'), only two- and three-member compounds will be discussed here.

In a copulative compound, where all members of the compound are of equal status (and could be conjoined with *und* 'and'), each member is stressed.[64]

(130)   *'Schleswig-'Holstein* 'Schleswig-Holstein'
        'geistig-'seelisch 'spiritual-psychological'
        'schwarz-'rot-'gold 'black-red-and-gold'

In a subordinate compound, where one member of the compound further specifies or defines another (in the subordinate compound *Blutdruck* 'blood pressure', for example, the first member, *Blut* 'blood', specifies the kind of *Druck* 'pressure'), the unmarked pattern is stress on the initial member.[65] This holds for three-member as well as two-member compounds. In three-member compounds, the A constituent is stressed, regardless of the internal structure of the compound, A(BC), as in *Volkshochschule*, or (AB)C, as in *Autobahnkreuz* and *Übersichtskarte*.

(131)   'Haustür 'front door'
          'blaurot 'purple'
          'Überstunde 'hour of overtime'
          'Volkshochschule 'adult education center'
          'Autobahnkreuz 'expressway interchange'
          'Übersichtskarte 'general map'

In some compounds, however, the second (B) member is stressed, not the first. One set of compounds with this stress pattern, (AB)C compounds, is illustrated in (132).

(132)   Rot'kreuzschwester 'Red Cross nurse'
          Drei'zimmerwohnung 'three-room apartment'
          Zehn'fingersystem 'touch-typing method'

This type of compound differs in a number of ways from compounds with initial stress (Benware 1986:108): the A constituent is an adjective or a quantifier (number); the (AB) constituent shows the stress pattern of a corresponding noun phrase (*rotes'Kreuz* 'red cross'; *drei'Zimmer* 'three rooms'); the (AB) constituent does not occur independently as a compound (*Rotkreuz*, *Dreizimmer*).

Another set of compounds with stress on the B constituent, a set of A(BC) compounds, is illustrated in (133).

(133)   Beethoven-Kla'vierkonzert 'Beethoven piano concerto'
          Donau-'Dampfschiff 'Danube steamship'
          Weltge'sundheitsorganisation 'World Health Organization'

Benware (1987) argues that the A constituents in these compounds are semantically marked (less common), and thus exhibit a marked stress pattern by being unstressed. The A constituent in a compound with the structure A(BC) is usually indefinite. In 'Autowerkstatt 'car repair shop', for example, the A constituent refers to cars in general, not to a specific car. The same is true for compounds like 'Opernfestspiele 'opera festival' and 'Kunsthandwerk 'artistic handicrafts'. In compounds like those in (133), however, the first constituent is definite. There is only one *Beethoven*, one *Donau*, etc. The semantic markedness of these compounds is signaled by a marked stress pattern. See Benware 1987 for a discussion of other sets of A(BC) compounds that are stressed on the B constituent.[66]

1.2.6.2 Sentence stress   When words occur in stretches of speech rather than in isolation, not every word will contain a syllable with primary stress. Although the first syllable in *meine* 'my', for example, can in principle receive primary stress, it is unstressed in the following utterance (Fox 1984:7).

(134)   *Meine 'Schwester 'schreibt mir 'lange 'Briefe.*
         'My sister writes me long letters.'

In German, as in English, stressed syllables play an important role in the rhythm of speech. A stressed syllable, together with the unstressed syllables that follow it, forms a foot, and each foot takes up roughly the same amount of time.[67] German, like English, is thus a stress-timed language (stressed syllables recur at regular intervals of time), in contrast to languages like French, which are syllable-timed (each syllable takes up approximately the same amount of time).

In every utterance, which may contain a number of words with primary stress, at least one syllable stands out as being particularly prominent, the nucleus. In the sentence in (134), the syllables *Schwes-*, *schreibt*, *lang-*, and *Brief-* all bear primary stress, yet *Brief-* is particularly prominent and therefore forms the nucleus of the sentence. The nucleus plays an important role in intonation.

1.2.7   Intonation

The pitch of a speech sound depends on the rate of vibration of the vocal cords. Sounds with a high pitch are produced with a higher rate of vibration than sounds with a low pitch. The changes in pitch over the course of an utterance are known as intonation.

The nucleus in an utterance is associated with a noticeable change in pitch. In the sentence in (135), for example, there is a fall in pitch (indicated by the symbol `) between the first and second syllables of *Nachmittag*.

(135)   *Ich 'komme 'heute `Nachmittag.* (C. Hall 2003:120)
         'I'm coming this afternoon.'

In the example in (136), there is a rise in pitch on the word *müde* 'tired' (indicated with the symbol ´).

(136)   *'Sind Sie ´müde?*
         'Are you tired?'

Although the intonation patterns in (135) and (136) are associated with sentences, intonation patterns can be associated with other grammatical units. In (137), for example, there are two intonation patterns: falling, associated with a sentence, and rising, associated with a tag question.[68]

(137)   *Er `kommt ´nicht?* (Fox 1984:44)
         'He's coming right?'

Because intonation patterns can be associated with various kinds of grammatical structures, the term "intonational phrase" is used to refer to the stretch of speech associated with an intonation pattern.[69] Each intonational phrase has one nucleus. There is one intonational phrase and therefore one nucleus in the utterances in (135) and (136): *Nach-* in (135) and *mü-* in (136). The utterance in (137), on the other hand, has two intonational phrases and therefore two nuclei: *kommt* and *nicht.*[70]

The nucleus occurs normally on the last lexical word in an intonational phrase, unless that word is a verb (C. Hall 2003:133).[71]

(138)   *'Gerd 'schreibt ein 'Buch über `Mozart.*
        'Gerd is writing a book about Mozart.'
        'Gerd hat ein 'Buch über 'Mozart ge,schrieben.
        'Gerd has written a book about Mozart.'

If the nucleus occurs on any other word in an intonational phrase, stress is being used contrastively. That word is contrasted (implicitly or explicitly) with another.

(139)   *Gerd hat ein Buch über Mozart ge`schrieben (nicht gelesen).*
        'Gerd has written (not read) a book about Mozart.'

There are a number of different intonation patterns in German, three of which will be discussed here: the falling pattern, the rising pattern, and the level pattern.[72] The falling pattern is commonly used for statements (140a), commands (140b), and questions that begin with a question word (140c) (C. Hall 2003:124–125).

(140)   The falling pattern
        a. *Du 'hast jetzt ge`nug ge,arbeitet.*
            'You have worked enough now.'
        b. *'Gehen Sie 'bitte 'nicht `weg!*
            'Please don't go away.'
        c. *Wann 'kommst du nach `Hause?*
            'When are you coming home?'

The use of the falling pattern is very similar in German and English. In German, however, the fall is much steeper than in English.

The rising pattern is used in yes/no questions (141a), among other sentence types. In the example in (141b), the rising intonation turns the sentence into a question (C. Hall 2003:126).

(141) a. ˈKommst du ˈmit?
   'Are you coming along?'
  b. ˈDieter war in Iˈtalien?
   'Dieter was in Italy?'

The level pattern (indicated by the symbol ¯) is characterized by the absence of movement in pitch directly on or following the nucleus. The level pattern is used, among other things, for non-final intonational phrases (142a), in lists for all but the final element (142b), and for expressing a noncommittal attitude (142c) (C. Hall 2003:128):

(142) a. *Wenn wir nach ¯Hause ˈkommen, ˋessen wir was.*
   'When we come home, we'll eat something.'
  b. *Wir ˈkaufen ¯Butter, ¯Milch, ¯Eier und ˋBrot.*
   'We're buying butter, milk, eggs, and bread.'
  c. *¯Danke.*
   'Thanks.'

Fox 1984 discusses the general meaning conveyed by the two most important intonation patterns in German, the rising pattern and the falling pattern. According to Fox (1984:59), the rising pattern makes an "appeal to the listener, who is being invited, or challenged, to respond." The rising pattern is clearly appropriate for questions, as in (141a), but also for sentences that are statements on the surface but intended as questions and thus invite a response from the listener, as in (141b). The falling pattern, on the other hand, functions as an assertion. It makes the utterance self-sufficient, since it does not depend on the listener's reply. The falling pattern is thus appropriate for statements, as in (140a).[73]

Exercises

Solutions to the exercises can be found in the online answer key at www.cambridge.org/fagan.

1. Provide the phonetic symbols for the vowels in German that are phonetically (a) [+high, +round]; (b) [+front, −round]; (c) [−high, +back]; (d) [+low]; (e) [+high, −tense]; (f) [+long, −tense]; (g) [−high, +front, +round]; (h) [+high, +front, −round]
2. Describe the following consonants phonetically (for example, [pʰ] is a voiceless aspirated bilabial stop; [ʀ] is a uvular trill): (a) [p̆]; (b) [ŋ]; (c) [tʰ]; (d) [ç]; (e) [r]; (f) [ʃ]; (g) [l]; (h) [k]; (i) [s]; (j) [ʔ]; (k) [m]; (l) [ʁ]; (m) [v]; (n) [t̪]; (o) [ʒ]

3. Transcribe the following words phonetically, applying the rules discussed in section 1.2.4 (transcribe a glottal stop in the positions where glottalization can occur).

(a) *kommen* 'to come' /ˈkʰɔmən/; (b) *Gabe* 'gift' /ˈkaːpə/; (c) *lebt* 'lives' /ˈleːptʰ/; (d) *Teig* 'dough' /ˈtʰaɪk/; (e) *phonetisch* 'phonetic' /foːˈneːtʰɪʃ/; (f) *Tiere* 'animals' /ˈtʰiːrə/; (g) *Bier* 'beer' /ˈpiːr/; (h) *niest* 'sneezes' /ˈniːztʰ/; (i) *welcher* 'which' /ˈvɛlxər/; (j) *Buchhandlung* 'bookstore' /ˈpuːxˌhantlʊŋ/; (k) *lockige* 'curly' /ˈlɔkʰɪkə/; (l) *sonnig* 'sunny' /ˈzɔnɪk/; (m) *Theater* 'theater' /tʰeˈaːtʰər/; (n) *veralten* 'to become obsolete' /fɛrˈaltʰən/; (o) *flachem* 'flat' /ˈflaxəm/; (p) *grobem* 'coarse' /ˈkroːpəm/; (q) *knappen* 'scarce' /ˈkʰnapʰən/; (r) *Himmel* 'heaven' /ˈhɪməl/; (s) *Wasser* 'water' /ˈvasər/

4. Syllabify the following words (indicate syllable boundaries) using the principles and constraints discussed in section 1.2.5

(a) *halben* 'half' /halpən/; (b) *umschmeicheln* 'to flatter' /ʊmʃmaɪxəln/; (c) *bierernst* 'deadly serious' /piːrɛrnstʰ/; (d) *beknien* 'to beg' /pəkʰniːn/; (e) *besuchte* 'visited' /pəzuːxtʰə/; (f) *kopfüber* 'headfirst' /kʰɔpfyːpər/; (g) *Heizung* 'heating' /haɪtsʊŋ/; (h) *Königreich* 'kingdom' /kʰøːnɪkraɪx/; (i) *milchig* 'milky' /mɪlxɪk/; (j) *Milcheiweiß* 'lactoprotein' /mɪlxaɪvaɪs/

5. Indicate which syllable in each of the following words bears primary stress. (a) *Arbeit* 'work'; (b) *Zitrone* 'lemon'; (c) *Phantasma* 'phantasm'; (d) *Wette* 'bet'; (e) *Freundschaft* 'friendship'; (f) *Linguist* 'linguist'; (g) *transportieren* 'to transport'; (h) *verbringen* 'to spend (time)'; (i) *beschleunigen* 'to accelerate'; (j) *Spiegelbild* 'reflection'; (k) *Betäubungsmittel* 'anesthetic'; (l) *Lebensmittelgeschäft* 'grocery [store]'; (m) *Dreitagefieber* 'sandfly fever'; (n) *Taschenwörterbuch* 'pocket dictionary'; (o) *Beruhigungsmittel* 'sedative'

6. Locate the nucleus (nuclei) in each of the following sentences (assume that the sentences are uttered without contrastive stress).

(a) *Der Wirt kannte den Mann.* 'The proprietor knew the man.'

(b) *Er war gegen 3 Uhr in sein Lokal gekommen.* 'He had come into his bar around 3 o'clock.'

(c) *Inzwischen hat ein Projektentwickler das Gelände gekauft und will dort ein Hotel bauen.* 'In the meantime a project developer has bought the site and intends to build a hotel there.'

(d) *Die Skipässe werden jetzt elektronisch gelesen.* 'Ski passes are now read electronically.'

(e) *Ich habe Wasserfälle, Elche und eine Stabkirche gesehen.* 'I saw waterfalls, elk, and a stave church.'

NOTES

1 See Wiese 1996:21–22 for a discussion of the literature on the two *a* sounds in German and additional arguments for treating the two sounds as differing only in length.

2 German diphthongs are transcribed in a variety of ways in the literature. For example, the diphthong in *Häuser* 'houses' is transcribed as [ɔø] (Siebs 1969, Krech *et al.* 1982), [ɔɪ] (Kohler 1995), [ɔʏ] (Wiese 1996), etc. The transcription of German diphthongs employed here follows Kohler 1995, since the use of [ɪ] and [ʊ] as the second vowel in the diphthong is phonetically most accurate (Mangold 2005:36; Jessen 2007).

3 See section 1.2.4.10 for further discussion of the vocalic realization of *r*.

4 Nasal consonants are sounds like [m] in *Mutter*/*mother*, [n] in *Nacht*/*night*, and [ŋ] in *singen*/*sing*. See section 1.1.3 for further discussion.

5 I do not use the IPA symbols that are typically used to represent voiced stops ([b], [d], [g]). Instead, I use the diacritic for voicing (a wedge, ˇ) with the symbols for voiceless stops. I explain my reasons for this in section 1.2.4.2.

6 Because the turbulence during the articulation of [h] is produced primarily by the air passing through the entire oral cavity rather than through the glottis, [h] is probably more accurately characterized as a glottal approximant (see Ladefoged 1971:122, for example). However, following the general practice in the literature (e.g., Hall 1992, Wiese 1996, C. Hall 2003, Mangold 2005), [h] will be classified here as a fricative.

7 Dark *l* can be found in some German dialects, for example, in the Rhineland (Cologne) and in parts of Switzerland (C. Hall 2003:59).

8 There is a good deal of variation in the distribution of [l] and [ɫ] in the various dialects of English. Some speakers of American English, for example, have dark *l* in all positions. At the other end of the continuum are dialects like southern Irish English, where clear *l* may occur in all positions (see Cruttenden 2001:204).

9 The morphologically conditioned rules of *e*-Epenthesis and umlaut are treated only very briefly in chapter 2. See Wiese 1996 (and references therein) for further discussion of morphologically conditioned rules of German. For literature on sentence-level phonetics and phonology, see, for example, Kohler 1979, 1990, and 1995.

10 This is a simplified description of the distribution of [ʁ] and [ɣ]. See below (this section and section 1.2.4.10) for a more detailed description.

11 We follow Vater 1992 and assign the less prominent vowel in German diphthongs (e.g., [ʊ̯] in [aʊ̯]) to the nucleus. Hall (1992) takes a different approach, and assigns this vowel to the coda. See Vater 1992:109 and Hall 1992:142–153 for further discussion.

12 Only /aɪ/, /aʊ/, and /ɔɪ/ have the status of phonemes. Diphthongs like [iːɐ̯] arise from the sequence of a vowel followed by /r/ (see section 1.2.4.10 for details). The diphthong [i̯oː] in a word like *Emotion* 'emotion' arises from the sequence /ioː/ and a low-level phonetic process that results in a non-syllabic pronunciation of /i/ before vowels (Mangold 2005:42).

13 An affricate is a sequence of a stop followed by a homorganic fricative (a fricative with roughly the same place of articulation).

14 "Liquid" is a cover term for laterals and various types of *r* sounds.

15 Various pronunciations are used by speakers of German for consonantal *r*, for example, [ʀ], [r], and [ʁ]. The choice of these different *r*-sounds is dependent on factors such as dialect, style, content, etc. (see, e.g., Kohler 1995:165, Mangold 2005:53–54, and C. Hall 2003:65–66 for further details). I use [ʁ] as representative of consonantal *r*, since this pronunciation predominates (Kohler 1995:165).

16 The lenis stop phonemes in German are traditionally represented as /b d g/ and the fortis as /p t k/. However, since *b*, *d*, and *g* represent voiced stops in the IPA, and *p*, *t*, and *k* represent voiceless stops, this suggests that the distinction between lenis and fortis stops in German is one of voicing. Because both sets are voiceless, I use the symbols *p*, *t*, and *k* for both sets (lenis as well as fortis). I add the symbol for aspiration, [ʰ], to the symbols for the fortis stops to represent the [spread glottis] feature of these stops.

17 The space between words in phonemic and phonetic transcriptions is employed simply for ease of reading.

18 See Jessen and Ringen 2002:205–206 for a discussion of the phonetic/physical factors that account for the gradient nature of voicing assimilation.

19 Wiese (1996:67) argues that all consonant-initial suffixes are phonological words.

20 [continuant] is a feature that characterizes sounds made with free or nearly free airflow through the center of the oral cavity. Sounds that are [+continuant] are vowels and fricatives; stops, nasals, and laterals are [–continuant]. The feature [sonorant] characterizes sounds produced when air flows smoothly through the vocal tract. Vowels, nasals, and liquids are [+sonorant].

21 I follow Hall 1992:55 and use the notion of intonational phrase to indicate that fortis stops are aspirated syllable-finally before a pause.

22 Some authors argue that liquids following fortis stops are voiceless – that the stops in this environment are not aspirated (the diacritic ₀ indicates that a segment is voiceless): *Kreis* 'circle' [ˈkʀ̥aɪs], *Klasse* 'class' [ˈkl̥asə] (Kohler 1995:158, C. Hall 2003:31). However, it is difficult to distinguish experimentally between stop aspiration and (partial) sonorant devoicing when stops occur before sonorant consonants (Michael Jessen, personal communication, September 19, 2005). I follow Hall 1992:54, for example, and treat fortis stops before sonorant consonants as aspirated.

23 The application of Aspiration must follow the deletion of schwa, since the opposite order of application would yield the incorrect form *[laɪtʰn̩] (the asterisk indicates that this pronunciation is unacceptable).

24 We assume that the <d> in words like *handlich* and *Neid* is underlyingly (phonemically) lenis, /t/, since it behaves like a lenis stop in other related forms (it is voiced when it occurs between voiced segments): *Handes* 'hand (genitive)' [hant̮əs]; *Neides* 'envy (genitive)' [naɪt̮əs].

25 The class of obstruents includes stops, fricatives, and affricates.

26 Fully native minimal pairs for [s] versus [z] occur only intervocalically. The word *Seal*, for example, is non-native.

27 For more details on German fricatives, see Piroth and Janker 2004 and Beckman *et al.* to appear.

28 *Junta* can also be pronounced with an initial [j] (Mangold 2005:446).

29 There are some exceptions to this generalization. However, there is typically an alternative pronunciation for those words that exhibit [x] before front vowels and [ç] before non-front vowels: *Cholesterin* 'cholesterol' [k] or [ç] (listed in this order in Mangold 2005:241); *Xeres* 'sherry' [x] or [ç] (Wahrig 2000:1412; Muthmann 1996:457). This suggests that pronunciations with word-initial [x] before front vowels and [ç] before non-front vowels are non-native. As Robinson (2001:19) points out, "there is no native historical source for word-initial [x] or [ç]. *All* examples in Modern German are borrowings."

30 My analysis has benefited from the observation that [ç] and [x] are largely in complementary distribution in word-initial position (Michael Jessen, personal communication, September 4, 2007; Jessen 1988).

31 [back] is a feature that involves the placement of the body of the tongue and characterizes consonants as well as vowels; [+back] sounds are articulated behind the palatal region in the oral cavity. I assume that [ç] has the features [−back, +high, −coronal], which distinguishes it from [ʃ], which is [−back, +high, +coronal] ([+coronal] sounds are produced with the blade of the tongue raised from its neutral position). Sounds that are [+consonantal] are produced with major obstruction in the vocal tract. This feature is necessary in the formulation of this rule to prevent it from applying to /h/, which is [−consonantal].

32 This rule would also realize /x/ as [ç] when it follows /m/, which is [−back], but to my knowledge there are no sequences of /mx/ in German.

33 Notice that the rule of Velar Spirantization yields a fricative that is [−voice] and [−spread glottis] (when the rule changes the manner of articulation from stop to fricative, it does not change the [−voice] or [−spread glottis] feature of the stop). I assume that a low-level phonetic constraint realizes this and all other [−voice] fricatives as [+spread glottis]. (See Vaux 1998 for evidence that voiceless fricatives are [+spread glottis] in their unmarked state.)

34 According to Durrell (1992:13), this regional variation in pronunciation of -(i)g is followed "almost universally," whether used in colloquial or more formal speech.

35 The information in (67) is a modified version of information presented in C. Hall 2003:47. According to Hall (who makes a simple north/south distinction), "millions of German-speakers whose pronunciation is otherwise perfectly standard consistently use either the northern or the southern pronunciation" (2003:47–48). The standard language (reflected in the rule of Velar Spirantization) is actually the outcome of (arguably arbitrary) decisions made at a conference on theater pronunciation held in Berlin in 1898 (Robinson 2001:3). There is clearly something less than natural about Velar Spirantization, evident in the formulation of the rule itself – the complicated statement of the environment in which it applies and the condition on its application. Note that Velar Spirantization must apply before Fortition, since the opposite order would yield unacceptable forms: *saftig* 'juicy' /zaftʰɪk/ would be realized incorrectly as *[zaftʰɪkʰ] instead of [zaftʰɪç].

36 Creaky voice is produced with the arytenoids tightly together, but with a small length of the vocal cords vibrating (Ladefoged 1971:8).

37 We have modified Hall's transcription of stops to correspond to the convention we follow here.

38 Some authors claim that words such as *Theater* and *Kloake* contain glottal stops (e.g., Hall 1992:58, Wiese 1996:59). However, Kohler (1994) finds no evidence of glottal stops or glottalization in stem-internal vowel sequences (he mentions the word *Kloake* explicitly). Both *Theater* and *Kloake* are transcribed in Mangold 2005 without a glottal stop (words like *beanspruchen* 'to claim' are transcribed with a glottal stop: *be*[ʔ]*anspruchen*).

39 Hall (1992:22) argues that almost all instances of schwa are predictable and therefore epenthetic. He does consider schwa to be a phoneme of German, however, because its presence word-internally in many morphemes and certain prefixes cannot be accounted for by epenthesis.

40 The distribution of schwa is a complex matter. In the following pairs, which also exhibit a schwa–zero alternation, the "deleted" schwa is not represented in the orthography, unlike the deleted schwa in (71): *Atem* 'breath', *at∅men* 'to breathe'; *trocken* 'dry', *trock∅nen* 'to dry'. This schwa–zero alternation will not be treated here.

41 The condition that a consonant must precede schwa when schwa precedes /l/ is a bit of an oversimplification. The consonant may not be /r/, since schwa may not be deleted in a word such as *Minstrel* 'minstrel' [mɪnstʀəl]. However, since there are only two additional words that I am aware of that end in the sequence *-rel* (*Barrel* 'barrel', *Varel* 'Varel [city name]'), and all three are either borrowings or place names, I have chosen not to complicate the conditions on Schwa Deletion in order to accommodate these forms.

42 Recall that [ʁ] and [ɐ] are in free variation following a short vowel: *dort* 'there' /tɔrtʰ/ → [tɔʁtʰ] or [tɔɐtʰ]. Thus the rule of *r*-Vocalization is optional when /r/ follows a short vowel. For the sake of simplicity, however, I do not include this condition in the statement of the rule. I simply present the consonantal and vocalic allophones of /r/ as being in complementary distribution in all environments.

43 Note that the [−consonantal, +syllabic] realization of /r/ ([ɐ]) shares the features [−back, −high, −low] with /r/; it is not specified for the feature [front]. It will thus differ from the realization of /ə/ and /a/, both of which are specified for the feature [front] (/ə/ is [−front, −back]; /a/ is [−front]).

44 Alpha notation allows us to collapse several rules into one.

45 I adopt Giegerich's (1989:19) use of the feature [α artic] to express homorganicity (having the same point of articulation). This convention for expressing homorganicity goes back to Lass and Anderson 1975:262–263.

46 A number of studies have dealt with the phonotactics of German, for example, Moulton 1956, Seiler 1962, Tanaka 1964, Benware 1986, Hall 1992, Kohler 1995, and Wiese 1996. Benware 1986, Hall 1992, and Wiese 1996, in particular, emphasize the importance of the syllable in the treatment of phonotactics. See these studies for detailed tables and examples of possible onsets and codas in German.

47 Of the three words with five-member codas cited by Hall (1992:121), only *Herbsts* 'autumn (genitive)' is listed as a possible form in the *Duden* spelling dictionary (Dudenredaktion 2006:495). Wiese (1996:48), however, argues that such words "are probably not well formed and are clearly avoided." Hall does say that such five-member clusters are unpronounceable for many Germans and are made pronounceable by epenthesis of schwa, as in *Herbstes* (an alternative form also listed in the *Duden* dictionary).

48 An asterisk before a word (or a sentence) indicates that the form is unacceptable.

49 See Ramers 1992 for an overview of the various phonological arguments for ambisyllabic consonants in German.

50 The evidence for ambisyllabic consonants in German is divided. A study by Fischer-Jorgensen (1969) shows that an intervocalic consonant after a short vowel has the tendency to be longer than one after a long vowel. A recent study by Spiekerman (2000:66), however, shows the opposite pattern, namely, a slight tendency for consonants after long vowels to be longer than those after short ones.

51 There are some additional two-member onsets with various combinations of stops, fricatives, and affricates, but these occur only rarely: for example, *Xylophon* 'xylophone' /ksyːloːfoːn/, *Szene* 'scene' /stseːnə/.

52 This syllabification does pose a problem for analyses of German that assume that stops and fricatives are devoiced in coda position. Hall (1992:86) makes this assumption and thus argues for a rule of Resyllabification that yields the syllabifications *A.dlig* and *Han.dlung*, which are impervious to devoicing and thus lead to the desired pronunciation. Hall 2005, recognizing that such syllabifications are problematic because of the lack of word-initial *dl-* clusters, assumes the syllabifications in (100) and appeals to the notion of Paradigm Uniformity to account for the absence of devoicing in these forms.

53 Hall (1992:121) also includes the cluster /rtstʰ/ in *Arzt* 'doctor'. However, I analyze this as a three-consonant cluster with the affricate /ts/ as its second member.

54 Loudness (measured as "spectral balance" rather than simply as overall amplitude) has also been shown to be a correlate of stress in German (Claßen *et al.* 1998).

55 Note that neither the closed–penult restriction nor the final-schwa restriction account for the placement of stress in these words.

56 Notice that stress placement in *Nia'gara* is not accounted for by the closed-penult restriction or the final–schwa restriction.

57 Derivational suffixes are those that create new lexical items (words). The derivational suffix *-ung*, for example, creates nouns from verbs: *Deckung* 'cover' is derived from *decken* 'to cover'; *Meldung* 'report' is derived from *melden* 'to report'.

58 The suffix *-or* is somewhat unusual in that it does bear stress under certain circumstances: *Pro'fess-or* 'professor', *Pro'fess-or-s* 'professor's', *Pro'fess-or-chen* 'little professor'; but *Profe'ss-or-en* 'professors', *Profe'ss-or-in* 'female professor'. See Wiese 1996:293 for one possible explanation of the behavior of *-or*.

59 We follow the Duden grammar (Dudenredaktion 2005:699) and treat these forms as unstressed prefixes. However, they probably bear some degree of stress, since the tense vowels that some of them exhibit retain their length even though they do not bear primary stress: [y:]*ber'fischen* 'to overfish' and *w*[i:]*der'sprechen* 'to contradict' (Mangold 2005:794, 836).

60 Even those prefixes that are typically unstressed (those that do not contain schwa, e.g., *ent-*, *ver-*) bear secondary stress when followed by an unstressed syllable: ˌ*entmagneti'siert* 'demagnetized', ˌ*verbarrika'diert* 'barricaded' (Kiparsky 1966: 72).

61 The nominal prefix *ge-*, which has a schwa nucleus, is, of course, never stressed: *Ge-'äst* 'branches'. The prefixes of nouns derived from verbs with unstressed prefixes are also unstressed: *Ent'schuldigung* 'excuse' (from *ent'schuldigen* 'to excuse'); *Über'setzung* 'translation' (from *über'setzen* 'to translate').

62 Nominal *miss-* is sometimes unstressed. It is not clear, however, that there is a pattern to this behavior of *miss-*. Compare, for example, *Miss'handlung* 'maltreatment', derived from *miss'handeln* 'to maltreat', with *'Missdeutung* 'misinterpretation', derived from *miss'deuten* 'to misinterpret'. We also find conflicting information in standard reference works, which further obscures the behavior of *miss-*. For example, Mangold (2005:556) lists *'Missachtung* 'disregard'; Wahrig (2000:877), on the other hand, gives the form *Miss'achtung*.

63 The adjective prefix *un-* also occurs unstressed, but this change in stress is associated with a change in meaning. The word *'unglaublich*, for example, means 'not believable', whereas *un'glaublich* means 'enormous'; *'unmenschlich* means 'not human', but *un'menschlich* means 'tremendous'.

64 The stress patterns discussed here are for citation forms (forms given in dictionary entries).

65 The citation forms of phrasal verbs are stressed like subordinate compounds. Compare 'Rad fahren 'to pedal' and 'ausgehen 'to go out' with 'Haustür 'front door'. I treat items like *ausgehen* as phrasal verbs, not as compounds, because they do not behave syntactically as a single unit: *Wir gehen heute Abend aus* 'We're going out this evening.'

66 See also Giegerich 1985, Stötzer 1989, Kohler 1995, and Wiese 1996, among others, for further discussion of stress in compounds.

67 The sentence in (134), for example, contains four feet.

68 In German, a tag question is formed by adding words like *nicht* 'not', *nicht wahr* 'right', and *oder* 'or' to the end of a statement to form a question.

69 The intonational phrase is also called the intonation group (Fox 1984) and the tone group (C. Hall 2003).

70 The discussion here will focus on the nucleus, as this is the most important part of the intonational phrase. Other parts of the intonational phrase are the head, prehead, and tail (see, e.g., Fox 1984, C. Hall 2003, for further discussion).

71 Words that bear the main semantic content are lexical words (e.g., nouns, adjectives, main verbs). These contrast with function words (articles, pronouns, conjunctions, etc.), which have a grammatical function.

72 See Fox 1984 for discussion and examples of additional patterns. See also Féry 1993 for a more recent approach to German intonation.

73 Fox (1984:62–63) claims that it is "normal" for interrogative sentences with a question word to have a falling intonation pattern: *Was `machst du?* 'What are you doing?' *Wie `spät ist es?* 'How late is it?' According to Fox, the falling pattern "gives a fairly neutral implication, whereas the rise, with its element of 'appeal', may add a note of extra interest, often of friendliness or politeness": *Was ʹmachst du? Wie ʹspät ist es?*

2   Morphology

2.1   Introduction

The subfield of linguistics known as morphology deals with the structure of words. Although it typically is not difficult for literate speakers of a language to segment utterances into words when writing, for example, it is not an easy task to provide a precise definition of a word. The term "word" is ambiguous, which adds to the difficulty. To distinguish among the three main senses of "word," we will use the more specific terms "word form," "grammatical word," and "lexeme."

A word form is a minimal free form. It is the smallest stretch of speech that can occur in isolation. In the sentence in (1), there are five word forms: *sie*, *lacht*, *über*, *seine*, and *Witze*.

(1)   *Sie lacht über seine Witze.*
         'She laughs at his jokes.'

Witze 'jokes', for example, is a word form because it can occur in isolation, as the example below demonstrates.

(2)   *Was erzählt er?*
         'What is he telling?'
         Witze.
         'Jokes.'

Although a word like *ein* 'a' cannot occur in isolation in the way that *Witze* can, it can still be considered a free form because its position in a sentence is not entirely fixed. It can occur to the immediate left of a noun, but it can be separated from that noun by adverbs and adjectives.

(3)   *Ich habe {ein Problem/ein großes Problem/ein sehr großes Problem}.*
         'I have {a problem/a big problem/a very big problem}.'

A grammatical word is a word defined by its position in a paradigm. The word form *lacht* in (1), for example, represents the grammatical word 'third person singular present tense indicative of LACHEN'. In the sentence in (4),

54

the same word form, *lacht*, represents a different grammatical word, 'second person plural present tense indicative of LACHEN'.

(4)   *Ihr lacht über seine Witze.*
       'You laugh at his jokes.'

The grammatical word 'third person singular present tense subjunctive of GEWINNEN', on the other hand, is represented by two different word forms, *gewönne* and *gewänne*: (*gewönne* is from an earlier stage of the language; see the discussion of Subjunctive II forms in section 2.2.4.3 for further information).

(5)   *Wenn sie das Spiel {gewönne/gewänne} . . .*
       'If she were to win the game . . .'

When two different grammatical words are realized by the same word form, as in the example involving LACHEN (both 'third person singular . . .' and 'second person plural . . .' are realized by the word form *lacht*), we refer to this as syncretism. German exhibits numerous examples of syncretism, as we will see when we consider the morphology of nouns, determiners, verbs, and so on.

A lexeme (written using small capital letters) is an abstract unit of vocabulary that is realized by one or more word forms. The lexeme FRAU, for example, is realized by the word forms *Frau* and *Frauen*.

Words can be further analyzed as consisting of morphemes, the smallest units of language that bear meaning. Morphemes are abstract units, pairings of form and meaning. Morphemes are indicated in this book by enclosing them in curly brackets, {}. Morphemes are realized by morphs, the constituent parts of word forms. The word form *Frauen* 'women', for example, is made up of two morphs, /fraʊ̯/ and /ən/. The morph /fraʊ̯/ is a realization of the morpheme {frau}, which bears the meaning 'woman'; /ən/ is a realization of the plural morpheme {plural}, which has the meaning 'more than one'. The morpheme {plural} can also be realized as /n/: *Nase* /naːzə/ 'nose', *Nasen* /naːzə+n/ 'noses'. These two forms, /ən/ and /n/, are allomorphs of the morpheme {plural}.[1] Allomorphs are the variant realizations of a morpheme.

Some morphs can potentially be used on their own as word forms: *Hund* 'dog', *lauf* 'run', *durch* 'through', *nein* 'no'.[2] These are called potentially free morphs. Other morphs, obligatorily bound morphs, cannot occur alone as word forms, but must always be attached to other morphs. The morphs *-t* in the word form *komm+t* 'comes', *-ung* in *Wohn+ung* 'dwelling', and *un-* in *un+klar* 'unclear' are all examples of obligatorily bound morphs.

An obligatorily bound morph that cannot realize a lexeme is an affix. A root is that portion of a word form that is left when all affixes have been removed; it cannot be further analyzed into smaller morphs. In the word form *Hunde* 'dogs', for example, *Hund* is a root, and *-e* is an affix. In the word form *Verschiebung* 'postponement', *ver-* and *-ung* are affixes, and *schieb* is the root. A base is the form that an affix is attached to, whether a root or a form that is more than just a root. In the word form *Verschiebung*, the affix *-ung* is attached to the base *verschieb* 'postpone', which is made up of the root *schieb* 'push', to which the affix *-ver* has been added (*schieb* serves as the base for the affix *-ver*). A stem is a special kind of base; it is that portion of a word form that serves as a base for inflectional affixes. In the word form *Verschiebungen* 'postponements', *Verschiebung* is the stem, since it serves as the base for the plural affix *-en*, which is an inflectional affix.[3]

There are different kinds of affixes that are identified according to where they are attached to a base. The affix types that are relevant for German are prefix, suffix, and circumfix. A prefix is attached before a base; a suffix is attached after a base; a circumfix is a discontinuous affix that is attached around a base. The word *Urtext* 'original (text)' has the prefix *ur-*; *schuldig* 'guilty' has the suffix *-ig*; and past participles like *gekauft* 'bought' have the circumfix *ge . . . t*.[4]

2.2   Inflection

Inflection is the creation of different word forms of a lexeme, typically, although not always, through the addition of affixes. The different word forms that realize the lexeme HUND 'dog', for example, *Hund*, *Hund(e)s*, *Hunde*, and *Hunden*, are created by adding the affixes *-(e)s*, *-e*, and *-n* to the root *Hund*. Inflectional affixes do not change the part of speech of the base to which they are added. All the inflected word forms that realize the lexeme HUND, for example, are nouns. Inflectional affixes have a regular meaning. The *-(e)s* in *Hundes* means 'genitive singular' and has this same meaning when used to inflect other nouns.

A distinction can be made between two types of inflection: inherent and contextual. Inherent inflection is determined by the information that a speaker wishes to convey. The plural ending *-e* on the noun *Hunde* 'dogs', for example, is a case of inherent inflection. A speaker uses this ending to convey the meaning 'plural'. Tense marking on a verb is another example. Contextual inflection is determined (required) by the syntactic context in which a word form occurs. Case marking on a noun – the dative ending *-n* on *Hunden* 'dogs', for example – is an instance of contextual inflection. Person marking on a verb (which must agree with the person marking of the subject) is another example of contextual inflection. Inherent inflection typically precedes contextual inflection. We see this in the word form *Hund-e-n*, where the plural suffix *-e* precedes the dative case suffix *-n*.[5]

There are various ways in which inflection can be represented formally. The Item and Arrangement (IA) model of description views words as the "arrangement" (concatenation) of morphemes, each realized by a particular morph. Under this model, the word *Hunde* 'dogs' is represented as the sequence of the morphemes {Hund}, realized by the morph /hʊnt/, and {plural}, realized by the morph /ə/. This model is not ideal for German, however, since not all words in the language are inflected by affixation. The morpheme {plural}, for example, is not always realized as a suffix; it can also be realized by changing the vowel of the root (umlaut): *der Apfel* 'apple', *die Äpfel* 'apples'. The past tense forms of strong verbs are also formed by changing the vowel of the root (ablaut): *trinken* 'to drink', *trank* 'drank'.[6] Vowel-changing processes are in fact quite prevalent in the morphology of German.[7]

Under the Item and Process (IP) model, an inflectional rule takes a stem as input, alters it (through processes such as affixation, vowel change, etc.), and produces a word form as output. The IP model is better suited for dealing with vowel-changing processes like umlaut and ablaut than the IA model.

A third approach to inflection, the Word and Paradigm (WP) model, is similar to the IP model in that it views inflection as a process, but it differs from the IP model in various ways.[8] The WP approach takes the lexeme and its paradigm of word forms as its starting point; the different word forms in the paradigm are derived by processes or operations that apply to the lexeme. The WP model is particularly well suited for describing the inflectional morphology of languages like German. It is useful for treating portmanteau morphs (morphs that realize more than one morpheme, e.g., the morph /tʰ/ in *kommt* 'comes', which can be viewed as realizing the morphemes {third person}, {singular}, {present}, {indicative}). It is also useful for describing languages in which rules of affixation as well as vowel-changing rules (like umlaut and ablaut) are used for similar purposes.[9] To the extent that we formalize our description of the inflectional morphology of German, we will employ the WP model. In many cases we will exemplify inflection simply by using the relevant paradigms themselves.

2.2.1 The inflection of nouns

The morphosyntactic categories of gender, number, and case play a role in the inflection of nouns in German. Morphosyntactic categories are those categories that are referred to by rules in both morphology and syntax; these are the categories that play a role in the paradigm of a lexeme (Matthews 1991:38). The values for a category are features. For example, the relevant features for the category of number in German nouns are [singular] and [plural].

2.2.1.1 Gender Each noun in German has one of three features for the category of gender: feminine, masculine, or neuter. That is, each noun is assigned one of three grammatical genders. Grammatical gender is distinct from natural gender. Although the natural gender of an entity may coincide with the grammatical gender of the noun used to signify it (the grammatical gender of *Frau* 'woman' is feminine and the grammatical gender of *Mann* 'man' is masculine), this is not always the case (*Mädchen* 'girl' is neuter). Inanimate objects can have any of the three genders: *Erde* 'earth' is feminine, *Stein* 'stone' is masculine, and *Eisen* 'iron' is neuter. The citation form of a noun, the nominative singular form of the definite article together with the nominative singular form of the noun, signals its gender, since there are three different nominative singular forms of the definite article (*die, der, das*): *die Gabel* 'the fork' is feminine; *der Löffel* 'the spoon' is masculine; *das Messer* 'the knife' is neuter.

Although the assignment of gender in German may appear to be essentially arbitrary, the meaning and form of a noun can often be used to determine its gender. Airplanes are feminine, alcoholic drinks are typically masculine (an exception is *das Bier* 'beer'), and metals are most often neuter (Durrell 2002:2).

(6) a. Airplanes: *die Boeing 767, die Cessna, die Tu-154*
    b. Alcoholic drinks: *der Gin, der Schnaps, der Wein*
    c. Metals: *das Aluminium, das Gold, das Silber*

The suffix a noun ends in typically determines the gender of that noun. For example, nouns that end in *-ei*, *-heit*, and *-ung* are feminine; nouns that end in the suffixes *-ant*, *-ling*, and *-er* are masculine; nouns that end in *-chen*, *-lein*, and *-tum* are neuter.[10]

(7) a. *die Bäckerei* 'bakery', *die Freiheit* 'freedom', *die Leistung* 'achievement'
    b. *der Fabrikant* 'industrialist', *der Lehrling* 'apprentice', *der Fahrer* 'driver'
    c. *das Teilchen* 'particle', *das Büchlein* 'booklet', *das Heldentum* 'heroism'

Although nouns in German are not inflected for gender, gender does play a role in the inflection of a noun, as there is a correlation between the gender of a noun and the affixes that are used to inflect that noun.

2.2.1.2 Number   German nouns, like those in English, are inflected for number. In English, nouns typically add the suffix *-s* to signal the plural (*bed, beds; night, nights; house, houses*). Plural formation in German, however, is quite different. There are a number of different affixes that are used to signal the plural; the stem vowel of a noun can simply be umlauted or umlauted together with the addition of an affix; some nouns form their plurals without an overt affix. The complexity of plural formation in German has long fascinated linguists and resulted in numerous analyses over the years that have attempted to account for the systematicity that must underlie plural formation.[11]

Table 2.1 *Noun plurals*

		Masculine	Neuter	Feminine
1	-(e)	*der Fahrer* 'driver'	*das Muster* 'pattern'	
		der Tag 'day'	*das Jahr* 'year'	*die Mühsal* 'hardship'
2	-(e)n	*der Stachel* 'thorn'	*das Auge* 'eye'	*die Gabel* 'fork'
		der Staat 'state'	*das Ohr* 'ear'	*die Frau* 'woman'
3	¨(e)	*der Apfel* 'apple'	*das Kloster* 'cloister'	*die Mutter* 'mother'
		der Bach 'stream'	*das Floß* 'raft'	*die Nacht* 'night'
4	(¨)er	*der Mann* 'man'	*das Dach* 'roof'	
		der Leib 'body'	*das Kind* 'child'	
5	-s	*der Uhu* 'owl'	*das Auto* 'car'	*die Bar* 'bar'

The five plural classes in Table 2.1 capture the various possibilities for forming plurals in German.[12] We can account for the plural inflection of nouns formally within the WP model by positing rules like those in (8) and (9), where capital letters like *X*, *Y*, and *Z* are variables representing the phonological stem (or portions of the stem) of a noun, and *C* stands for a consonant.[13] The rules in (8) and (9) will account for the plural inflection of nouns in class 1.[14]

(8) $\begin{bmatrix} +\text{Noun} \\ +\text{plural} \\ +\text{class 1} \end{bmatrix}$

        /X/   = /Yə(C)/ → /X/

(9) $\begin{bmatrix} +\text{Noun} \\ +\text{plural} \\ +\text{class 1} \end{bmatrix}$

        /X/   → /Xə/

The rule in (8) says that a noun stem in class 1 that is marked [+plural] and ends in schwa followed (optionally) by a consonant will undergo no change. Rule (9) says that a noun stem in class 1 that is marked [+plural] should have /ə/ added after it. Notice that we need to make sure that the rule in (8) applies before the rule in (9) and that the rule in (9) applies only to those class 1 nouns that cannot serve as input to the rule in (8) (so that a schwa is not added to those nouns in class 1 that end in a schwa syllable). We can do this by means of the Elsewhere Principle (formulated by Anderson 1992:132):

(10)   Elsewhere Principle
        Application of a more specific rule blocks that of a later more
        general one.

The rule in (8) is more specific than the rule in (9) because it includes an extra specification about the phonological shape of the noun stems that it applies to.

If we order the rule in (9) after the rule in (8), the Elsewhere Principle will ensure that it does not apply to those noun stems to which (8) has already applied.

Rules that are similar to (8) and (9) will account for the plural forms of nouns in class 2. Nouns in class 2 that end in a schwa syllable will have the suffix -*n* in the plural; those that do not will have the suffix -*en*.[15]

The rule in (11) will account for the plural forms of those nouns in class 3 that end in a schwa syllable.

(11) $\begin{bmatrix} +\text{Noun} \\ +\text{plural} \\ +\text{class 3} \end{bmatrix}$
/X/   = /YVZ$_\partial$C/ $\rightarrow$ /YV̈Z$_\partial$C/

This rule says that a noun in class 3 that is [+plural] and ends in a schwa syllable will umlaut the main vowel of its stem. A class 3 word like *Vogel* 'bird', for example, will form its plural by umlauting /oː/: *Vögel* 'birds'. We can view the umlaut portion of the rule in (11), "V $\rightarrow$ V̈," as a shortcut way of expressing the vowel changes in (12).

(12)   /a/ $\rightarrow$ /ɛ/
         /aː/ $\rightarrow$ /ɛː/
         /o/ $\rightarrow$ /œ/
         /oː/ $\rightarrow$ /øː/
         /ʊ/ $\rightarrow$ /ʏ/
         /uː/ $\rightarrow$ /yː/
         /aʊ̯/ $\rightarrow$ /ɔɪ̯/

If we order the rule in (13) after the rule in (11), the Elsewhere Principle will ensure that it applies only to those nouns in class 3 that do not end in a schwa syllable.

(13) $\begin{bmatrix} +\text{Noun} \\ +\text{plural} \\ +\text{class 3} \end{bmatrix}$
/X/   = /YVZ/ $\rightarrow$ /YV̈Zə/

The rule in (14) accounts for the plural forms of nouns in class 4.

(14) $\begin{bmatrix} +\text{Noun} \\ +\text{plural} \\ +\text{class 4} \end{bmatrix}$
/X/   = /YVZ/ $\rightarrow$ /YV̈Zər/

We assume that the umlaut portion of this rule will apply only to those nouns in class 4 that have vowels that can be umlauted.

A rule similar to the rule in (9) will account for the plural forms of nouns in class 5. This rule adds the suffix *-s* to all nouns in this class.

A number of predictions can be made regarding the plural class membership of nouns, and there are also a number of probabilities for class membership based on gender assignment and form. That is, not all plural class membership needs to be learned on a lexeme-by-lexeme basis. Suffixed words, for example, can have fully predictable plural endings. Words with the suffixes *-e*, *-heit*, *-keit*, *-schaft*, and *-ung* have the plural ending *-(e)n* (they belong to class 2):

(15)   Singular   Plural
    die Brems+e 'brake'   *die Bremsen*
    die Schön+heit 'beauty'   *die Schönheiten*
    die Möglich+keit 'possibility'   *die Möglichkeiten*
    die Freund+schaft 'friendship'   *die Freundschaften*
    die Stör+ung 'disturbance'   *die Störungen*

Some probabilities based on gender and/or form are the following: Most masculine and neuter nouns that end in *-el*, *-en*, or *-er* form their plural without a suffix (they belong to class 1):

(16)   Singular   Plural
    der Beutel 'bag'   *die Beutel*
    der Wagen 'car'   *die Wagen*
    das Messer 'knife'   *die Messer*

There are exceptions to this generalization, however: *der Muskel* 'muscle', *die Muskeln* (class 2); *der Faden* 'thread', *die Fäden* (class 3); *das Kloster* 'cloister', *die Klöster* (class 3).

The great majority (90%) of all feminine nouns have the plural ending *-(e)n* (Durrell 2002:18) and thus belong to class 2: *die Blume* 'flower', *die Blumen*; *die Zeit* 'time', *die Zeiten*. About one quarter of monosyllabic feminine nouns have the ending *-e* and umlaut in the plural (Durrell 2002:18) and thus belong to class 3: *die Angst* 'fear', *die Ängste*; *die Maus* 'mouse', *die Mäuse*; *die Nuss* 'nut', *die Nüsse*.

Most (three quarters of) neuter nouns have the (class 1) plural ending *-e*. This includes most polysyllabic neuters (Durrell 2002:19): *das Bein* 'leg', *die Beine*; *das Verbot* 'ban', *die Verbote*; *das Zeugnis* 'witness', *die Zeugnisse*.[16]

One of the plural endings, *-s*, differs from the others in several ways. In particular, it is not limited to specific genders, like the "zero" ending and *-er*, which are used only with masculine and neuter nouns. Although the number of feminine plurals in *-s* is not large (Eisenberg 1998:159), this plural ending can occur with nouns of any gender: *der Scheck* 'check', *die Schecks*; *die Oma* 'grandma', *die Omas*; *das Auto* 'car', *die Autos*. In the recent literature, the -s plural is viewed as the unmarked member in the set of marked plural forms (Bornschein and Butt 1987) or as the regular or "default" plural ending (Clahsen *et al.* 1992; Marcus *et al.* 1995; Wiese 1996; Bartke 1998; Cahill and Gazdar 1999). Evidence in favor of this view includes overgeneralization of the -s plural in experimental studies with impaired and unimpaired monolingual German-speaking children (e.g., Clahsen *et al.* 1992; Bartke 1998).

Durrell (1999) questions the characterization of the -s plural as being "regular," as it is the least frequent plural marker (Janda 1991; Marcus *et al.* 1995). He also argues against a "default" ending analysis ("affix -s, all other things being equal"). In Durrell's view, the -s affix is no different from the other plural endings; like other plural endings, it occurs with a particular inflectional class of nouns.[17] However, because it is the affix that is the least restricted (it can occur with nouns of almost any phonological shape or nouns with any gender; Bartke 1998), he argues that it be viewed as a "last resort" ending ("affix -s if all else fails").[18] This "last resort" view would explain why -s is overgeneralized in first language acquisition (when a plural ending has not yet been learned) or when speakers deal with novel forms.

2.2.1.3 Case   German nouns are inflected for case.[19] There are four different cases in German (nominative, accusative, dative, genitive). Cases are used to signal, among other things, the role of a noun (phrase) in a sentence (subject, object, etc.). Not every case is realized by an affix. The vast majority of nouns have at most two suffixes that signal case. Masculine and neuter nouns (e.g., *der Tisch* 'table', *das Licht* 'light'), but not feminine (*die Tür* 'door'), add -*(e)s* in the singular to signal the genitive case:[20]

(17)

Singular	Masculine	Feminine	Neuter
Nominative	*der Tisch*	*die Tür*	*das Licht*
Genitive	*des Tisches*	*der Tür*	*des Licht(e)s*

All nouns add -*n* in the plural to signal the dative case (unless the plural stem ends in -*n* or -*s*, in which case no suffix is added):

(18)

Nominative Plural	Dative Plural
die Tische	*den Tischen*
die Lichter	*den Lichtern*
die Türen	*den Türen*
die Autos	*den Autos*

In an older stage of German, masculine and neuter nouns were inflected with the suffix -*e* in the dative singular. This ending is no longer common, although it can still be found in set phrases:

(19)   *auf dem Land(e)* 'in the country'
        im Grunde genommen 'basically'
        im Jahr(e) 2006 'in (the year) 2006'
        im Laufe des Gesprächs 'in the course of the conversation'
        zu Hause 'at home'

A small group of masculine nouns, commonly referred to as "weak" masculine nouns, which typically denote living beings (*der Junge* 'boy', *der Bauer* 'farmer', *der Held* 'hero'), are inflected differently.[21] They have the suffix *-(e)n* in all cases in the singular except the nominative.[22]

(20)   Masculine weak nouns

Nominative	*der Junge*	*der Bauer*	*der Held*
Accusative	*den Jungen*	*den Bauern*	*den Helden*
Dative	*dem Jungen*	*dem Bauern*	*dem Helden*
Genitive	*des Jungen*	*des Bauern*	*des Helden*

Many of these nouns end in *-e* in the nominative singular (*der Junge*, *der Affe* 'monkey', *der Franzose* 'Frenchman'). A large number can be identified by their suffixes. For example, nouns that end in *-ant*, *-ent*, *-ist*, and *-om* are weak masculine nouns (*der Emigrant* 'emigrant', *der Student* 'student', *der Linguist* 'linguist', *der Gastronom* 'restaurateur').

2.2.2   The inflection of determiners and pronouns

2.2.2.1 Determiners   Determiners are a closed set of words that co-occur with nouns and are used to express a variety of semantic contrasts. They help to make the meaning of a noun more precise. The definite article (e.g., *der* 'the') is one type of determiner. In German, a determiner occurs at the beginning of a noun phrase and is followed by an (optional) adjectival phrase and then a noun: *der sehr große Fisch* 'the very big fish'.

2.2.2.1.1 Definite articles   The definite article in German is inflected for gender, number, and case; it agrees in gender, number, and case with the noun with which it occurs. Gender is only relevant in the singular; the plural forms of the definite article are inflected for case only. Table 2.2 lists all the forms for the relevant gender, number, and case combinations of the definite article in German. Although there are sixteen different combinations, there are only six different forms of the definite article: *der*, *die*, *das*, *den*, *dem*, and *des*. Each of these forms occurs at least twice in the paradigm; two occur as many as four times. One of the most interesting forms is *der*, which can serve

Table 2.2 *The definite article*

	Masculine	Neuter	Feminine	Plural
Nominative	*der*	*das*	*die*	*die*
Accusative	*den*	*das*	*die*	*die*
Dative	*dem*	*dem*	*der*	*den*
Genitive	*des*	*des*	*der*	*der*

as the masculine nominative form, the feminine dative form, and the feminine and plural genitive forms. The definite article in German is a particularly good example of the syncretism that is prevalent in the language.[23]

In spoken German, the definite article is relatively unstressed, and reduced forms are not uncommon:

(21)   *Halts* (= *Halt das*) *Maul!* (Dudenredaktion 2005:301)
        'Shut your trap.'

When the forms *dem*, *den*, *das*, and *der* are only weakly stressed, they can be contracted with certain prepositions. For example, in place of *in dem* 'in the' one can use *im*, or instead of *zu der* 'to the' one can say *zur*. The contracted forms are most common in set phrases (*am Montag* 'on Monday', *zum Essen* 'for lunch/dinner') or idiomatic expressions (*jemanden hinters Licht führen* 'to pull the wool over somebody's eyes').

2.2.2.1.2 Demonstratives   Demonstratives are used to locate someone or something in relationship to the speaker, for example, or the addressee. Two relevant notions are proximal (close to the speaker) and distal (distant). The most frequent demonstrative determiner in spoken German, *der*, which is always stressed, can have both proximal ('this') and distal ('that') meaning (Durrell 2002:83):

(22)   *Ich mochte ein Stück von der* [teːɐ̯] *Wurst*.
        'I would like a piece of this/that sausage.'

The forms of the demonstrative determiner *der* are identical to those of the definite article (see Table 2.2).

The demonstrative *dieser* 'this' has proximal meaning and is similar to English *this*. Like the demonstrative *der*, *dieser* is inflected for gender, number, and case. The various forms of this demonstrative are made up of the root *dies-* 'this', to which suffixes are added that signal gender, case, and number. In Table 2.3, which lists all the forms of *dieser*, these suffixes are in bold face.

Table 2.3 *The demonstrative* dieser

	Masculine	Neuter	Feminine	Plural
Nominative	die*ser*	die*ses*	die*se*	die*se*
Accusative	die*sen*	die*ses*	die*se*	die*se*
Dative	die*sem*	die*sem*	die*ser*	die*sen*
Genitive	die*ses*	die*ses*	die*ser*	die*ser*

Table 2.4 *The indefinite article* ein *and negative* kein

	Masculine	Neuter	Feminine	Plural
Nominative	*(k)ein*	*(k)ein*	*(k)eine*	*keine*
Accusative	*(k)einen*	*(k)ein*	*(k)eine*	*keine*
Dative	*(k)einem*	*(k)einem*	*(k)einer*	*keinen*
Genitive	*(k)eines*	*(k)eines*	*(k)einer*	*keiner*

The distal counterpart to *dieser* is *jener* 'that'.

(23)   ***Jenes*** *Auto ist grün.* ***Dieses*** *Auto ist rot.*
       'That car is green. This car is red.'

The demonstrative *jener* is inflected like *dieser*; it takes the same endings as *dieser* (see Table 2.3).[24]

2.2.2.1.3 Indefinite articles   The indefinite article *ein* 'a' has no plural forms; indefinite plural nouns are simply used without an article:

(24)   *Teure Schuhe machen Jogging nicht sicherer.*
       'Expensive shoes don't make jogging safer.'

The negative indefinite article, *kein*, does have plural (as well as singular) forms: *keine Schuhe* 'no shoes'. Table 2.4 lists the forms of *ein* together with the forms of *kein*. The various forms of *ein* (and *kein*) are made up of the root *ein* 'a' (*kein* 'no'), to which endings that signal gender, number, and case are added. Notice that some forms have no endings: the masculine nominative form and the neuter nominative and accusative forms.

(25) a.   ***Ein*** *Lehrer* (masc. nom.) *kann* ***kein*** *Vaterersatz* (masc. nom.) *sein.*
          'A teacher can't be a father substitute.'
     b.   ***Ein*** *Kind* (neut. nom.) *hat* ***kein*** *Recht* (neut. acc.) *darauf.*
          'A child has no right to that.'

Table 2.5 *Possessive determiners (uninflected)*

	Personal pronoun	Possessive determiner
Singular	*ich* 'I'	*mein* 'my'
	du 'you'	*dein* 'your'
	Sie 'you' (polite)	*Ihr* 'your' (polite)
	er 'he'	*sein* 'his, its'
	sie 'she'	*ihr* 'her, its'
	es 'it'	*sein* 'its'
Plural	*wir* 'we'	*unser* 'our'
	ihr 'you'	*euer* 'your'
	Sie 'you' (polite)	*Ihr* 'your' (polite)
	sie 'they'	*ihr* 'their'

2.2.2.1.4 Possessives   The possessive determiners express notions like 'my', 'her', 'your', etc. Each personal pronoun in German has a corresponding possessive determiner, as shown in Table 2.5 (this table contains only the stems of the possessive determiners). Like other determiners, possessive determiners are inflected for gender, number, and case. They take the same endings as the indefinite article (see Table 2.4). Like the indefinite article, possessive determiners do not have endings in the masculine nominative and the neuter nominative and accusative.[25]

2.2.2.2 Pronouns   Pronouns are those words that can be used to substitute for a noun phrase. The pronoun *sie* 'she', for example, can be substituted for the noun phrase *die Frau* 'the woman' in (26a), yielding the sentence in (26b).

(26) a.   *Die Frau lächelte.*
           'The woman smiled.'
     b.   *Sie lächelte.*
           'She smiled.'

There are various kinds of pronouns: personal pronouns, relative pronouns, demonstrative pronouns, interrogative pronouns, possessive pronouns, and indefinite pronouns.

2.2.2.2.1 Personal pronouns   Personal pronouns are words like *I*, *you*, *he*, and *she*; they stand for a person or thing. In German, personal pronouns are inflected for person (first, second, third), number, gender (these are only relevant for the third person singular pronouns), and case.[26] Table 2.6 lists all the forms of the personal pronouns in German.[27]

Table 2.6 *Personal pronouns in German*

	Person		Nominative	Accusative	Dative	Genitive
	1st		*ich* 'I'	*mich*	*mir*	*meiner*
	2nd	familiar	*du* 'you'	*dich*	*dir*	*deiner*
Singular		polite	*Sie* 'you'	*Sie*	*Ihnen*	*Ihrer*
	3rd	masculine	*er* 'he'	*ihn*	*ihm*	*seiner*
		feminine	*sie* 'she'	*sie*	*ihr*	*ihrer*
		neuter	*es* 'it'	*es*	*ihm*	*seiner*
	1st		*wir* 'we'	*uns*	*uns*	*unser*
Plural	2nd	familiar	*ihr* 'you'	*euch*	*euch*	*euer*
		polite	*Sie* 'you'	*Sie*	*Ihnen*	*Ihrer*
	3rd		*sie* 'they'	*sie*	*ihnen*	*ihrer*

German, unlike English, makes a distinction between the familiar and the polite in second person pronominal forms. The familiar forms for 'you' are *du* (singular) and *ihr* (plural). There is one polite form, *Sie*, which can be singular or plural in meaning:[28]

(27) a. *Was meinen Sie damit, Frau Schneider?*
          'What do you mean by that, Mrs. Schneider?'
     b. *Sehr geehrte Damen und Herren, gestatten Sie mir bitte . . .*
          'Ladies and gentlemen, please allow me . . .'

The third person singular personal pronouns are inflected for gender and are used to refer to objects as well as people. In English, the "neuter" pronoun *it* can be used to refer to any object. In German, neuter *es* can only be used to refer to objects identified by neuter nouns. If a noun phrase with a masculine singular noun is replaced by a pronoun, the pronoun must be masculine. This holds for noun phrases with feminine singular nouns as well:

(28) a. *Ich habe den Film schon mehrmals gesehen.* **Er** *ist einer meiner Lieblingsfilme.*
          'I've already seen the film several times. It's one of my favorite films.'
     b. *Er nahm die Zeitung und brachte* **sie** *die Treppe runter.*
          'He took the newspaper and brought it down the stairs.'

Reflexive pronouns are personal pronouns that are used to refer back to the subject of a sentence or clause. In English, reflexive pronouns end in *-self* or *-selves*: *myself, yourself, themselves*, etc. In German, reflexive pronouns are identical in form to personal pronouns, with the exception of *sich*, which serves as the third person (and polite second person) reflexive in the accusative and

Table 2.7 *Reflexive pronouns in German*

	Person		Accusative	Dative	Genitive
Singular	1st		*mich* 'myself'	*mir*	*meiner*
	2nd	familiar	*dich* 'yourself'	*dir*	*deiner*
		polite	*sich* 'yourself'	*sich*	*Ihrer*
	3rd	masc., neut.	*sich* 'himself/itself'	*sich*	*seiner*
		feminine	*sich* 'herself'	*sich*	*ihrer*
Plural	1st		*uns* 'ourselves'	*uns*	*unser*
	2nd	familiar	*euch* 'yourselves'	*euch*	*euer*
		polite	*sich* 'yourselves'	*sich*	*Ihrer*
	3rd		*sich* 'themselves'	*sich*	*ihrer*

dative case. Compare the first person pronouns (personal and reflexive) in (29) with the third person pronouns in (30):

(29) a. *Er hat **mich** verteidigt.*
     'He defended me.'
   b. *Ich habe **mich** verteidigt.*
     'I defended myself.'

(30) a. *Er hat **ihn** verteidigt.*
     'He defended him.'
   b. *Er hat **sich** verteidigt.*
     'He defended himself.'

Table 2.7 lists the reflexive pronouns in German and highlights the forms that are distinct from their personal pronoun counterparts.[29] Because the third person genitive forms are potentially ambiguous, they are accompanied by *selbst* when a reflexive interpretation is intended:

(31)   *Er spottet seiner selbst.*
     'He is mocking himself.'

The form *selbst* (or *selber*) is also used without a reflexive and has the same function as the emphatic reflexive in English:[30]

(32) a. *Sie hat es selbst/selber gesagt.*
     'She said it herself.'
   b. *Sie selbst/selber hat es gesagt.*
     'She herself said it.'

2.2.2.2.2 Relative pronouns   A relative pronoun is a pronoun that is used at the beginning of a subordinate clause (relative clause) that describes a

Table 2.8 *The relative pronoun* der

	Masculine	Neuter	Feminine	Plural
Nominative	der	das	die	die
Accusative	den	das	die	die
Dative	dem	dem	der	denen
Genitive	dessen	dessen	deren	deren

preceding noun. The pronoun *der* 'who, which' is the most common relative pronoun in German.[31]

(33)   *Kennst du den Mann* (masc. acc.)*, **der** (masc. nom.) dort sitzt?*
        'Do you know the man who is sitting there?'

The relative pronoun *der* is inflected for gender, number, and case. It agrees with its antecedent in gender and number; its case is determined by its function in the relative clause. In (33), the relative pronoun is masculine because its antecedent, *Mann* 'man', is masculine. It is nominative because it functions as the subject of the relative clause. Table 2.8 lists the forms of the relative pronoun *der*. These forms are identical to the forms of the definite article, *der*, except in the genitive and dative plural. The forms of the relative pronoun *der* that differ from those of the definite article are highlighted in Table 2.8.

2.2.2.2.3 Pronominal use of determiners   As noted above, the forms of the relative pronoun *der* are very similar to those of the definite article *der* (see Table 2.2), a kind of determiner. It turns out that essentially all the determiners in German can also be used pronominally. Compare the demonstrative determiner in (34a) with the demonstrative pronoun in (34b):

(34) a.   **Den** *Ratschlag möchte er nicht annehmen.*
           'That bit of advice he doesn't want to take.'
     b.   **Den** *möchte er nicht annehmen.*
           'That he doesn't want to take.'

The demonstrative pronoun *der* is identical to the relative pronoun *der*, with the exception that the form *derer* can be used instead of *deren* in the genitive plural to refer forwards:

(35)   *In Israel und Palästina steigt die Zahl **deren/derer**, die nach einem Kompromiss suchen wollen.*
        'In Israel and Palestine, the number of those who want to search for a compromise is rising.'

The forms of the demonstrative pronoun *der* are listed in Table 2.9.

Table 2.9 *The demonstrative pronoun* der

	Masculine	Neuter	Feminine	Plural
Nominative	*der*	*das*	*die*	*die*
Accusative	*den*	*das*	*die*	*die*
Dative	*dem*	*dem*	*der*	*denen*
Genitive	*dessen*	*dessen*	*deren*	*deren/derer*

Table 2.10 *The indefinite pronoun* einer *and the negative pronoun* keiner

	Masculine	Neuter	Feminine	Plural
Nominative	*(k)einer*	*(k)eines*	*(k)eine*	*keine*
Accusative	*(k)einen*	*(k)eines*	*(k)eine*	*keine*
Dative	*(k)einem*	*(k)einem*	*(k)einer*	*keinen*
Genitive	*(k)eines*	*(k)eines*	*(k)einer*	*keiner*

The demonstrative pronoun *dieser* has the same set of endings as the demonstrative determiner *dieser* (see Table 2.3). That is, the inflection of *dieser* is the same whether it used as a determiner or a pronoun. This also holds for the demonstrative *jener* as well as other demonstratives and determiners that are inflected like *dieser*.

The indefinite article, *ein*, and all the other determiners that are inflected like it (*kein*, the possessives, *irgendein*), can also be used as pronouns. Recall that the masculine nominative and neuter nominative and accusative forms of these words have no endings when used as determiners (see Table 2.4). When used as pronouns, all the forms have endings. The pronominal ending of the masculine nominative form is *-er*; the neuter nominative and accusative endings are *-es*; otherwise the pronominal endings are identical to the determiner endings.

(36) a. ***Keiner*** (masc. nom.) *war da.*
      'Nobody was there.'
   b. *Ich möchte **eines*** (neut. acc.) *meiner Mopeds verkaufen.*
      'I would like to sell one of my mopeds.'

See Table 2.10, which lists the pronominal forms for *einer* and *keiner*.

2.2.3   The inflection of adjectives

There are two basic ways in which adjectives in German are inflected. They can be inflected for degree (positive, comparative, superlative). This type of inflection is an example of inherent inflection. When adjectives occur prenominally, they receive additional inflectional morphology. This type of inflection is contextual; it is dependent on the features of the syntactic environment in which the adjective occurs.

2.2.3.1 Degree forms   The positive degree form of an adjective is its basic stem. The comparative form is produced by adding the suffix *-er* to the stem; the superlative is formed by adding *-(e)st*:[32]

(37) a.   *schön* 'beautiful', *schöner* 'more beautiful', *schönst-* 'most beautiful'
      b.   *freundlich* 'friendly', *freundlicher* 'friendlier', *freundlichst-* 'friendliest'
      c.   *bunt* 'colorful', *bunter* 'more colorful', *buntest-* 'most colorful'

Contextually determined inflectional endings (see the following section for further details) are added after comparative and superlative endings.

(38) a.   *kein schön-er-er Tag* 'no more beautiful day'
      b.   *der schön-st-e Tag* 'the most beautiful day'

This is to be expected, since inflection for degree is a type of inherent inflection.
   A handful of monosyllabic adjectives with the root vowels *a*, *o*, and *u* umlaut these vowels in the comparative and superlative:

(39) a.   *alt* 'old', *älter* 'older', *ältest-* 'oldest'
      b.   *grob* 'coarse', *gröber* 'coarser', *gröbst-* 'coarsest'
      c.   *jung* 'young', *jünger* 'younger', *jüngst-* 'youngest'

As in English, some adjectives have irregular comparative and/or superlative forms:

(40) a.   *gut* 'good', *besser* 'better', *best-* 'best'
      b.   *hoch/hoh-* 'high', *höher* 'higher', *höchst-* 'highest'[33]
      c.   *nah* 'near', *näher* 'nearer', *nächst-* 'nearest'

The inflectional paradigm of the adjective *gut*, with comparative and superlative forms that are very different from its positive form, provides an excellent example of suppletion. We speak of suppletion when two forms in the paradigm of a lexeme show no phonological similarity.[34]

2.2.3.2 Prenominal inflection   When adjectives are used attributively (when they precede the noun they modify), they are inflected for gender, number, and case; they agree with the noun they modify in gender, number, and case. We will refer to the inflectional affixes on adjectives that indicate gender, number, and case as adjective endings. The adjective *toll* 'fantastic' is used attributively in (41a); it has the adjective ending *-es*. When adjectives are used predicatively (when they do not precede the noun they modify), they are not

Table 2.11 *The strong adjective endings*

	Masculine	Neuter	Feminine	Plural
Nominative	-er	-es	-e	-e
Accusative	-en	-es	-e	-e
Dative	-em	-em	-er	-en
Genitive	-en	-en	-er	-er

inflected for gender, number, or case; they receive no inflectional affixes beyond those indicating degree.[35] The adjective *toll* is used predicatively in (41b); it therefore has no adjective ending.

(41) a.   *Es war ein tolles Wochenende.*
           'It was a fantastic weekend.'
     b.   *Das Wochenende war toll.*
           'The weekend was fantastic.'

When an adjective is used attributively, it is also sensitive to the type (if any) of determiner that precedes it. For example, one says *der gute Mensch* 'the good person', with the adjective ending -*e*, but *ein guter Mensch* 'a good person', with the ending -*er*.

The traditional approach to adjective endings identifies three different paradigms of endings (Grebe 1973:244–246): strong endings (used when no determiner precedes the adjective); weak (used when the adjective is preceded by the definite article and determiners inflected like *dieser*); and mixed endings (adjective preceded by determiners inflected like *ein*, *kein*, etc.). Because each paradigm has sixteen relevant gender, number, and case combinations, this yields forty-eight different combinations. A somewhat simpler approach (with only thirty-two different combinations) identifies just two paradigms, strong and weak (e.g., Seymour 1959, Durrell 2002:126, Dudenredaktion 2005:368–369). This approach eliminates the mixed paradigm because it recognizes the overlap between the traditional strong and weak paradigms and the mixed paradigm. Under this approach, the strong endings (see Table 2.11) are used when the adjective is not preceded by a determiner or is preceded by an uninflected determiner (a determiner without a suffix); the weak endings (see Table 2.12) are used when the adjective is preceded by an inflected determiner.[36] Becaues both of these approaches present the adjective endings in paradigms, they obscure somewhat the fact that there are very few distinct endings: -*er*, -*es*, -*e*, -*en*, -*em*.[37]

More pedagogically oriented approaches to adjective endings, which endeavor to present the facts in the simplest way possible, capitalize on the small number of distinct endings and attempt to motivate any choice of ending

Table 2.12 *The weak adjective endings*

	Masculine	Neuter	Feminine	Plural
Nominative	-*e*	-*e*	-*e*	-*en*
Accusative	-*en*	-*e*	-*e*	-*en*
Dative	-*en*	-*en*	-*en*	-*en*
Genitive	-*en*	-*en*	-*en*	-*en*

for each combination of gender/number and case by considering the inflection of the noun phrase as a whole (see, for example, Dickens 1983, Barthel 1994).

Combining insights from the various approaches to adjective endings (including the more traditional approaches), the inflection of adjectives can be described in two steps, (a) and (b) below.[38]

(a) The adjective ending supplies the same gender, case, and number information that the endings of *dieser* supply if there is nothing in the noun phrase that already supplies this information. For example, if there is no determiner in the noun phrase and the noun itself is not inflected for case, the adjective will take the ending that *dieser* would have. This is demonstrated by the nominative singular and plural noun phrases in (42).

(42) a. *dieser Wein* 'this wine'
    billiger Wein 'cheap wine'
  b. *dieses Bier* 'this beer'
    gutes Bier 'good beer'
  c. *diese Suppe* 'this soup'
    warme Suppe 'warm soup'
  d. *diese Äpfel* 'these apples'
    rote Äpfel 'red apples'

If there is a determiner but it does not have an ending, the adjective will take the ending that *dieser* would have. This situation occurs with masculine nouns in the nominative and neuter nouns in the nominative or accusative, as shown in (43).

(43) a. *dieser Wein* 'this wine'
    ein billiger Wein 'a cheap wine'
  b. *dieses Bier* 'this beer'
    ein gutes Bier 'a good beer'

This first step in our account of the inflection of adjectives capitalizes on the fact that the strong adjective endings (see Table 2.11) are virtually identical to the endings of the determiner *dieser* (see Table 2.3). The only difference between the two sets of endings is in the masculine and neuter genitive singular, where *dieser* has the ending *-es* and a strong adjective has the ending *-en*. This difference is noted by highlighting the masculine and neuter genitive singular endings in Table 2.11; these endings are accounted for by step (b) below.

(b) If something in the noun phrase already supplies the gender, case, and number information that the endings of *dieser* supply, the adjective takes the ending *-e* when it occurs in a noun phrase in its citation (canonical) form, otherwise it takes *-en*.[39] The citation form of a noun phrase is the nominative singular form, or any form that is identical to the nominative singular (the accusative singular for neuter and feminine nouns). For example, in the phrase *der billige Wein*, the definite article, *der*, supplies the same gender, case, and number information that the corresponding form of *dieser* would, and the noun phrase is in its citation form (nominative singular); therefore the adjective ending on *billig* is *-e*; see (44a). In the noun phrase *die roten Äpfel* 'the red apples', the definite article, *die*, supplies the same gender, case, and number information that the corresponding form of *dieser* would (*diese*), but the noun is not in its citation form, so the adjective ending is *-en* instead of *-e*; see (44b).[40]

(44) a.   *dieser Wein* 'this wine'
             der billige Wein 'the cheap wine'
       b.   *diese Äpfel* 'the apples'
             die roten Äpfel 'the red apples'

If a masculine or neuter noun is in the genitive singular and not preceded by a determiner, the adjective modifying it will receive the ending *-en*, because the noun phrase *does* contain the information that an ending of *dieser* would supply – these nouns are inflected with the ending *-(e)s* – and the noun phrase is not in its canonical form:

(45) a.   *die Tasse schwarzen Kaffees* (masc. gen.) 'the cup of black coffee'
       b.   *das Stück harten Brotes* (neut. gen.) 'the piece of hard bread'

This second step in our account of the inflection of adjectives motivates the weak endings in the masculine and neuter genitive singular (the endings in Table 2.11 that differ from the corresponding endings of *dieser*), and explains the relatively "uninformative" and undifferentiated weak adjective endings (see Table 2.12).

Support for this approach to the inflection of adjectives comes from adjectives that modify weak masculine nouns. Recall that weak masculine nouns are inflected with the ending *-en* in the genitive singular, not with the *-(e)s* ending of "strong" masculine nouns: Compare *dieses Studenten* 'of this student' (weak noun) with *dieses Mannes* 'of this man' (strong noun). If a weak masculine noun in the genitive singular is modified by an adjective not preceded by a determiner, the adjective ending is not *-en* (the ending for an adjective modifying a strong noun), but *-es*, the ending that *dieser* would have, since this ending does not occur elsewhere in the noun phrase. Compare the inflection of the adjective and weak masculine noun in (46a) (from Durrell 2002:126) with the inflection of the adjective and strong masculine noun in (46b).[41]

(46) a. *der Gesuch obiges Adressanten* 'the request of the above sender'
    b. *im Sinne obigen Punktes* 'in the sense of the point above'

For further details of adjectival inflection, see, for example, Durrell 2002, Dudenredaktion 2001, and Dudenredaktion 2005.

2.2.4   The inflection of verbs

Verbs in German are inflected for the morphosyntactic categories person, number, tense, mood, participle, and infinitive.[42] The citation (dictionary) form of a verb is the infinitive, a form that ends in *-(e)n*: *lieb-en* 'to love', *sammel-n* 'to collect', *zitter-n* 'to tremble'. The stem of a verb is the infinitive without the *-(e)n* suffix. Verbs are inflected by attaching affixes to the stem and/or by changing the root vowel of the stem. For example, *liebt* 'loves' (from *lieben* 'to love') is formed with an affix; *trank* 'drank' (from *trinken* 'to drink') is formed by changing the root vowel; and *trankst* 'drank' (second person singular) is formed by changing the root vowel and adding an affix. The way in which a verb is inflected is determined by the class of verb to which it belongs. There are two main classes, weak and strong. There is also a small mixed class, made up of verbs that have features of both weak and strong verbs; a small class that includes the modals (verbs like *können* 'to be able to' and *müssen* 'to have to'); and some irregular verbs (e.g., *sein* 'to be').

The majority of German verbs are weak. Weak verbs are regular; they form their past and past participle forms with a *-t* suffix: *lieben* 'to love', *liebte* 'loved', *geliebt* 'loved'. There are many fewer strong verbs than weak verbs. According to the Duden grammar, there are roughly 170 simple (non-derived) strong verbs in German (Dudenredaktion 2005:456). Strong verbs form their principal parts (infinitive, past, past participle) by alternating the vowel of the root: *trinken* 'to drink', *trank* 'drank', *getrunken* 'drunk'. This vowel alternation is known as ablaut, and it can be seen in irregular verbs in English like *drink* (*drink, drank, drunk*). Although there are a number of different ablaut patterns that must be learned in German, the strong verbs appear to be able to resist pressure to become regular (weak), in spite of their small numbers. Many strong verbs in German, like their strong (irregular) counterparts in English, are very common (they belong to the basic vocabulary and are used frequently) and are thus relatively stable as strong verbs.

Table 2.13 *Present tense forms*

Number	Person	Present tense	
Singular	1st	*ich lieb-e*	'I love'
	2nd	*du lieb-st*	'you love'
	3rd	*er/sie/es lieb-t*	'he/she/it loves'
Plural	1st	*wir lieb-en*	'we love'
	2nd	*ihr lieb-t*	'you love'
	3rd	*sie lieb-en*	'they love'

2.2.4.1 Person and number   Verbs in German agree with their sub-jects in person and number. The person and number of the subject of a verb determine the affix that is attached to that verb. Any form of a verb that is inflected for person and number is a finite form.[43] A form that is not inflected for person and number is a non-finite form. Non-finite forms are the infinitive (*lieben* 'to love'); the present participle (*liebend* 'loving'); and the past participle (*geliebt* 'loved', *getrunken* 'drunk'). See section 2.2.4.4 for a discussion of the inflection of these forms.

The relevant person distinctions (features) are first, second, and third (person); the relevant number distinctions are singular and plural. Table 2.13 illustrates the different person and number affixes for the present tense (indicative) forms of the verb *lieben* 'to love'.[44] Not included in this chart (or any other verb charts) are the polite second person forms, since these are identical with the third person plural forms: compare *Sie lieben* 'you (polite) love' and *sie lieben* 'they love'.

Notice that it does not make sense to try to identify a unique affix for each of the person and number distinctions in German. For example, given the three different affixes on present tense singular forms, -*e*, -*st*, and -*t*, one would be hard pressed to find a single affix with the feature [singular]. Similarly, given the singular and plural third person affixes, -*t* and -*en*, it would not be particularly productive to search for a single affix with the feature [third person]. Verbal affixes in German are portmanteau morphs, morphs that realize more than one morpheme. The -*t* affix on *liebt* in *sie liebt* 'she loves', for example, can be viewed as realizing the morphemes {third person} and {singular} as well as the morphemes {present} and {indicative}.

2.2.4.2 Tense   Tense is a morphosyntactic category of the verb that is used to express the time at which the action denoted by the verb takes place. There are two features for the category of tense in German, [+past] and [−past]: finite verbs in German (those inflected for person and number) are either [+past] or [−past]. We use the feature [−past] instead of the feature [present] to capture the fact that verb forms like *besuche* in (47) express more than just present-time meaning.

(47)   *Ich besuche ihn.*
        I visit([−past]) him
        'I'm visiting him.'/'I'll visit him.'

The verb form *besuche* in (47) can have present-time or future-time meaning.

In this discussion of tense we will consider the various forms of the verb that are inflected for the category of tense. In chapter 4 (section 4.3) we will discuss the semantics of these verb forms as well as the semantics of the periphrastic tense forms. Periphrastic tense forms are those that are made up of more than one word (periphrasis is the use of a multi-word expression in place of a single word). German present perfect forms, for example (see [48a] and [49a] below), are periphrastic.[45] They are made up of a present tense form of an auxiliary verb (*haben* 'to have' or *sein* 'to be') and the past participle of the main (lexical) verb. Like past tense forms, present perfect forms are used to locate events in time.

(48) a.   *Sie **hat** lange **geschlafen**.* (present perfect)
            'She {slept/has slept} for a long time.'
     b.   *Sie **schlief** lange.* (past)
            'She slept for a long time.'

(49) a.   *Sie **ist** nach Hause **gefahren**.* (present perfect)
            'She {drove/has driven} home.'
     b.   *Sie **fuhr** nach Hause.* (past)
            'She drove home.'

However, we do not include the present perfect forms of a verb (the auxiliary together with the past participle) in the inflectional paradigm of that verb; we only include the past participle, the portion of the verb that is used in the formation of the present perfect.[46] This discussion of the inflection of verbs for the category of tense will therefore not deal with present perfect tense forms. It will also exclude discussion of other periphrastic tense forms (the past perfect, double past perfect, and the so-called future and future perfect). When we discuss the semantics of these forms in chapter 4, we will touch briefly on their structure.

2.2.4.2.1 The present tense   When we speak here of the "present tense," we mean those verb forms that realize the feature [−past]. These are the forms that textbooks and grammars typically refer to as the "present tense." As mentioned above, Table 2.13 presents the different present tense forms for the verb *lieben* 'to love'. The verb *lieben* is a weak verb; the present tense of weak verbs is formed by adding the appropriate person and number endings to the stem of the verb. Some present tense forms involve the epenthesis of -e-:[47]

(50)   e-Epenthesis
         If a verbal base ends in -d, -t, or in an obstruent followed by a nasal, -e- is added before the endings -st and -t.

We find e-Epenthesis with a verb like *arbeiten* 'to work', which has a stem that ends in -t, and with a verb like *öffnen* 'to open', which has a stem that ends in a fricative followed by *n*:

(51) a. *du liebst* 'you love'
         du arbeitest 'you work', *du öffnest* 'you open'
     b. *sie liebt* 'she loves'
         sie arbeitet 'she works', *sie öffnet* 'she opens'
     c. *ihr liebt* 'you love'
         ihr arbeitet 'you work', *ihr öffnet* 'you open'

The strong verbs and verbs belonging to the mixed class take the same endings in the present as the weak verbs. Some strong verbs, however, also change the root vowel in second and third person singular forms. Most strong verbs with -e- ([eː] or [ɛ]) in the root change this to -ie- or -i- ([iː] or [ɪ]) in the second and third person singular forms:

(52) a. *lesen* 'to read':   *du liest, sie liest*
     b. *sprechen* 'to speak': *du sprichst, sie spricht*

Most strong verbs with -a- or -au- in the root umlaut these vowels in the second and third person singular forms:[48]

(53) a. *fahren* 'to drive': *du fährst, sie fährt*
     b. *laufen* 'to run':   *du läufst, sie läuft*

If the root of a strong verb with a vowel change ends in -t, no -e- is added before the ending -st in the second person singular (e-Epenthesis does not apply), and no ending is added in the third person singular:[49]

(54) a. *gelten* 'to be worth': *du giltst, sie gilt*
     b. *halten* 'to hold':   *du hältst, sie hält*

The verbs in the class that includes the modals are inflected quite differently from their strong and weak counterparts. The root vowel of the singular is typically different from the root vowel of the infinitive (and plural). In addition, the first and third person singular forms have no endings. Table 2.14 lists the present tense forms of the modals (*dürfen* 'to be allowed to', *können* 'to be able to', *mögen* 'to like to', *müssen* 'to have to', *sollen* 'to be to', *wollen* 'to want to') and *wissen* 'to know'. Historically, these were past forms with past meaning. They are now past forms with present meaning.[50]

Table 2.14 *Present tense forms of the modal verbs and* wissen *'to know'*

	dürfen	*können*	*mögen*	*müssen*	*sollen*	*wollen*	*wissen*
ich	darf	kann	mag	muss	soll	will	weiß
du	darfst	kannst	magst	musst	sollst	willst	weißt
er/sie/es	darf	kann	mag	muss	soll	will	weiß
wir	dürfen	können	mögen	müssen	sollen	wollen	wissen
ihr	dürft	könnt	mögt	müsst	sollt	wollt	wisst
sie	dürfen	können	mögen	müssen	sollen	wollen	wissen

Table 2.15 *The past of weak verbs*

	lieben	*arbeiten*	*öffnen*
ich	liebt-e	arbeitet-e	öffnet-e
du	liebt-est	arbeitet-est	öffnet-est
er/sie/es	liebt-e	arbeitet-e	öffnet-e
wir	liebt-en	arbeitet-en	öffnet-en
ihr	liebt-et	arbeitet-et	öffnet-et
sie	liebt-en	arbeitet-en	öffnet-en

2.2.4.2.2 The past tense   Past tense forms are those finite verb forms in German that realize the feature [+past].[51] Weak verbs form the past by simply adding -*t* to the stem (which yields what we will call the past stem) and then the endings for person and number. The person and number endings in the past of weak verbs are identical to the person and number endings in the present – with the exception that the third person singular ending is -*e* (rather than -*t*, as in the present). The rule of *e*-Epenthesis applies in the formation of the past stem for those verbs that end in -*d*, -*t*, or in an obstruent followed by a nasal, since the past ending is -*t*. In addition, because the past stem ends in -*t*, -*e*- must be also be added before the person/number endings -*st* and -*t*. Table 2.15 lists the past forms for the weak verbs *lieben* 'to love', *arbeiten* 'to work' (which has a stem that ends in -*t*), and *öffnen* 'to open' (which has a stem that ends in a fricative followed by *n*). The instances of -*e*- that are produced by *e*-Epenthesis are in bold face in this table.

The past of strong verbs is formed by changing the root vowel and adding endings for person and number. The past endings of strong verbs differ from those of weak verbs, however. In fact, the first and third person singular forms of strong verbs in the past have no endings. Table 2.16 lists the past forms for the strong verbs *trinken* 'to drink' and *halten* 'to hold'. As Table 2.16 shows, *e*-Epenthesis applies only optionally before the second person singular ending -*st* with strong verbs like *halten* (which ends in -*t*); it is mandatory before

Table 2.16 *The past of strong verbs*

	trinken	*halten*
ich	*trank*	*hielt*
du	*trank-st*	*hielt(e)st*
er/sie/es	*trank*	*hielt*
wir	*trank-en*	*hielt-en*
ihr	*trank-t*	*hielt-et*
sie	*trank-en*	*hielt-en*

Table 2.17 *Ablaut classes in German*

			Infinitive	Past	Past participle	Meaning
ei	*ie*	*ie*	*schreiben*	*schrieb*	*geschrieben*	'to write'
ei	*i*	*i*	*beißen*	*biss*	*gebissen*	'to bite'
i	*a*	*u*	*trinken*	*trank*	*getrunken*	'to drink'
i	*a*	*o*	*beginnen*	*begann*	*begonnen*	'to begin'
ie	*o*	*o*	*fliegen*	*flog*	*geflogen*	'to fly'
e	*a*	*o*	*helfen*	*half*	*geholfen*	'to help'
e	*a*	*e*	*lesen*	*las*	*gelesen*	'to read'
e	*o*	*o*	*heben*	*hob*	*gehoben*	'to lift'
a	*u*	*a*	*fahren*	*fuhr*	*gefahren*	'to drive'
a	*ie*	*a*	*fallen*	*fiel*	*gefallen*	'to fall'

the second person plural ending -*t*. The epenthesized -*e*- is in bold face in Table 2.16.

There are a number of different ablaut classes (subclasses of strong verbs) that can be identified on the basis of the vowel changes in their principal parts (infinitive, past, past participle).[52] According to Durrell (2002:234), most of the strong verbs belong to one of ten different ablaut classes. These ten classes are given in Table 2.17. In some classes, the vowel of the past participle is identical with the vowel of the infinitive; in others, the vowel of the past participle is identical with the vowel of the past. In no class, however, is the vowel of the past identical with the vowel of the infinitive.

Verbs that belong to the mixed class form the past by changing the root vowel, like strong verbs, but they also add -*t* to the stem and then the person and number endings of the weak past. The past participle of verbs in the mixed class also has characteristics of both strong and weak verbs. It has the same vowel as in the past (a vowel that differs from the vowel of the infinitive), but it ends in -*t*, like the past participle of weak verbs. Table 2.18 lists representative verbs that belong to the mixed class. Notice that *bringen* 'to bring' has consonant as well

Table 2.18 *Principal parts of verbs in the mixed class*

Infinitive	Past	Past participle	Meaning
bringen	*brachte*	*gebracht*	'to bring'
brennen	*brannte*	*gebrannt*	'to burn'
denken	*dachte*	*gedacht*	'to think'
senden	*sandte*	*gesandt*	'to send'

Table 2.19 *Principal parts of the modals and* wissen *'to know'*

Infinitive	Past	Past participle	Meaning
dürfen	*durfte*	*gedurft*	'to be allowed to'
können	*konnte*	*gekonnt*	'to be able to'
mögen	*mochte*	*gemocht*	'to like to'
müssen	*musste*	*gemusst*	'to have to'
sollen	*sollte*	*gesollt*	'to be to'
wollen	*wollte*	*gewollt*	'to want to'
wissen	*wusste*	*gewusst*	'to know'

as vowel changes: *brachte* 'brought'. The remaining verbs all have the same vowel changes, but *denken* 'to think' also involves a consonant change (*dachte* 'thought'), and *senden*, which ends in *-d*, does not require *e*-Epenthesis.[53]

The modal verbs (and *wissen* 'to know') form their past very much like verbs in the mixed class. The only significant special feature of the modals is the vowel change:[54] The vowel in the infinitive, if umlauted, appears without umlaut in the past and past participle. The two modals without umlaut, *sollen* 'to be to' and *wollen* 'to want to', do not involve a vowel change in the past (or past participle) and are thus like weak verbs. The verb *wissen* changes the infinitive vowel to *u* in the past and past participle. Table 2.19 lists the principal parts of the modals and *wissen*.

The verbs *haben*, *sein*, and *werden* (which are used as auxiliary verbs in periphrastic tense forms) are irregular in that they do not fit neatly into any one of the major verb classes. The present and past forms of these verbs, as well as their past participles, are given in Table 2.20. The verb *sein* is particularly interesting because it provides a classic example of suppletion. The forms (*ich*) *bin* '(I) am', (*sie*) *sind* '(they) are', and (*er*) *war* '(he) was', for example, are all suppletive (they show no phonological similarity).[55]

2.2.4.3 Mood There are three moods in German: the indicative, the subjunctive, and the imperative. The indicative is the unmarked mood; it is

Table 2.20 *Inflection of* haben *'to have'*, sein *'to be', and* werden *'to become'*

Infinitive	haben	sein	werden
Present tense	ich habe	ich bin	ich werde
	du hast	du bist	du wirst
	er/sie/es hat	er/sie/es ist	er/sie/es wird
	wir haben	wir sind	wir werden
	ihr habt	ihr seid	ihr werdet
	sie haben	sie sind	sie werden
Past	ich hatte	ich war	ich wurde
	du hattest	du warst	du wurdest
	er/sie/es hatte	er/sie/es war	er/sie/es wurde
	wir hatten	wir waren	wir wurden
	ihr hattet	ihr wart	ihr wurdet
	sie hatten	sie waren	sie wurden
Past Participle	gehabt	gewesen	geworden

used to express statements of fact and questions. The discussion of tense in the preceding section focused solely on indicative forms. The following section deals with the formation of the subjunctive. Section 2.2.4.3.2 treats the imperative.

2.2.4.3.1 The subjunctive   Whereas the indicative is used to express statements of fact, the main role of the subjunctive is to mark a clause as expressing something other than a statement of what is certain. In German, there are two sets of subjunctive forms, which we will call Subjunctive I and Subjunctive II.[56] Each set has simple as well as periphrastic forms. The simple forms bear the tense feature [−past]; the periphrastic forms bear the feature [+past]. Subjunctive I forms are used primarily for indirect speech, to report what someone said, asked, or commanded. The sentence in (55a) contains a direct quote, an example of direct speech. (55b) is an example of indirect speech, a report of what was said in the direct quote.

(55) a. *Er sagte: "Ich lese* (present indicative) *die Zeitung."*
          'He said, "I'm reading the newspaper."'
     b. *Er sagte, dass er die Zeitung lese* (Subjunctive I).
          'He said that he was reading the newspaper.'

Subjunctive II forms are used, for example, in conditional sentences that express unreal conditions, conditions that are contrary to fact.[57]

Table 2.21 *Present Subjunctive I forms*

	lieben	haben	sein	können
ich	liebe	habe	sei	könne
du	liebest	habest	sei(e)st	könnest
er/sie/es	liebe	habe	sei	könne
wir	lieben	haben	seien	können
ihr	liebet	habet	seiet	könnet
sie	lieben	haben	seien	können

(56)   *Wenn ich genug Geld hätte* (Subjunctive II)*, wäre* (Subjunctive II)
       ich schon längst weg.
       'If I had enough money, I would be long gone.'

There are two sets of Subjunctive I forms: present and past. Present Subjunctive I forms are marked [−past]; like their indicative counterparts (present tense indicative forms), they are used to refer to non-past (present or future) situations.

(57)   *Sie sagte, dass sie ihn besuche* (present Subjunctive I).
       'She said that she {was visiting/would visit} him.'

We refer to these forms as present Subjunctive I forms to highlight this similarity.

With the exception of the verb *sein* 'to be', present Subjunctive I forms are completely regular; they are formed by adding the subjunctive person and number endings to the stem of the infinitive, the first principal part of the verb (hence the terminology "Subjunctive I"). Present Subjunctive I forms for the verb *lieben* 'to love' are presented in Table 2.21. This table also includes the present Subjunctive I forms for *sein*, some of which are irregular, as well as those for *haben* 'to have' (which, like *sein*, is used as an auxiliary in forming past Subjunctive I forms) and *können* 'to be able to', a representative modal.

Many present Subjunctive I forms are identical to present indicative forms. For example, with the exception of *sein*, the first and third person plural present Subjunctive I forms are identical to present indicative forms; both are formed by adding *-en* to the stem of the infinitive. Only third person singular present Subjunctive I forms (which have the ending *-e*) are consistently distinct from their present tense indicative counterparts (which have the ending *-t* or, if a modal, no ending). Because of the overlap between present Subjunctive I and present indicative forms, present Subjunctive I forms other than those in the third person singular are typically avoided.[58]

The past Subjunctive I is periphrastic. It is constructed using the past participle of a verb together with the present Subjunctive I of *haben* or *sein*:

(58) a.   *Er erzählte uns, dass er **verschlafen habe**.*
        'He told us that he had overslept.'
     b.   *Sie antwortete, dass ihr Onkel **gestorben sei**.*
        'She answered that her uncle had died.'

Although the past Subjunctive I is made up of two-word forms, we include it in the inflectional paradigm of a verb, since it fills a gap in the paradigm. This is illustrated in (59) for the third person singular form of the verb *lieben* 'to love':

(59)   [indicative]   [subjunctive I]
     [−past]   *liebt*   *liebe*
     [+past]   *liebte*   [*habe geliebt*]

See Haspelmath 2000 for arguments in favor of allowing periphrastic forms as members of a paradigm in cases such as this.[59]

There are two Subjunctive II forms: the present and past. Like present Subjunctive I forms, the present Subjunctive II is marked [−past]; it is used to refer to non-past situations.

(60)   *Wenn jetzt Bundestagswahl **wäre**, **bekäme** die SPD nur noch 31 Prozent der Wählerstimmen.*
        'If there were to be a federal parliamentary election now, the SPD would get only 31 percent of the vote.'

The present Subjunctive II is based on the stem of the past indicative, the second principal part of a verb (hence the terminology "Subjunctive II").[60] For weak verbs, the present Subjunctive II is identical to the past indicative. The present Subjunctive II of the mixed verbs and modals is formed by taking the past indicative and umlauting the root vowel.[61] The present Subjunctive II of strong verbs is constructed by using the stem of the past indicative, umlauting the root vowel if possible, and adding the subjunctive endings (the same endings used for present Subjunctive I forms). Table 2.22 presents the present Subjunctive II forms for a representative verb from each of these groups: *lieben* 'to love' (weak); *bringen* 'to bring' (mixed); *können* 'to be able to' (modal); *trinken* 'to drink' (strong).

Some strong verbs have a special present Subjunctive II vowel, a vowel that is different from the umlauted vowel of the past indicative. Others have two Subjunctive II forms: one that is formed "regularly" (by umlauting the vowel of the past indicative), and another that is formed with a different vowel.[62]

Table 2.22 *Present Subjunctive II forms*

	lieben	bringen	können	trinken
ich	liebte	brächte	könnte	tränke
du	liebtest	brächtest	könntest	tränkest
er/sie/es	liebte	brächte	könnte	tränke
wir	liebten	brächten	könnten	tränken
ihr	liebtet	brächtet	könntet	tränket
sie	liebten	brächten	könnten	tränken

Table 2.23 *Present Subjunctive II forms of*
auxiliary verbs

	haben	sein
ich	hätte	wäre
du	hättest	wärest
er/sie/es	hätte	wäre
wir	hätten	wären
ihr	hättet	wäret
sie	hätten	wären

(61)	Infinitive	Past indicative	Subjunctive II
a.	*sterben* 'to die'	*starb*	*stürbe*
b.	*werfen* 'to throw'	*warf*	*würfe*
c.	*beginnen* 'to begin'	*begann*	*begänne (begönne)*
d.	*befehlen* 'to order'	*befahl*	*befähle/beföhle*
e.	*stehen* 'to stand'	*stand*	*(stände) stünde*

These unexpected Subjunctive II forms reflect an earlier stage of the language.

The past Subjunctive II forms use the past participle of a verb together with the present Subjunctive II forms of the auxiliaries *haben* or *sein*. (Table 2.23 lists the present Subjunctive II forms of these auxiliary verbs.)

(62) a. *Gestern habe ich ein Kleid gesehen, das ich gerne für die Hochzeit meines Bruders **gekauft hätte**.*
'Yesterday I saw a dress that I gladly would have bought for my brother's wedding.'

  b. *Wir glaubten, sie **wäre gestorben**.*
'We thought she had died.'

Because past Subjunctive II forms fill a gap in the verbal paradigm in the same way as past Subjunctive I forms do, as illustrated for the third person singular form of the verb *trinken* 'to drink' in (63), we include them in the inflectional paradigm of a verb.

(63)   [indicative]   [Subjunctive II]
       [−past]   *trinkt*   *tränke*
       [+past]   *trank*   [*hätte getrunken*]

There is another periphrastic subjunctive form that we do not include in the inflectional paradigm of a verb, the *würde*-construction. The *würde*-form of a verb is formed using a present Subjunctive II form of *werden* together with the infinitive of that verb.

(64)   *So ein Album **würde** ich nie **kaufen**.*
        'I would never buy such an album.'

We do not include the *würde*-construction in the inflectional paradigm of a verb because it does not fill a gap in a paradigm, like the other periphrastic subjunctive forms. It is an alternative to the present Subjunctive II. It is often used instead of the present Subjunctive II of weak verbs (identical to the past indicative forms of these verbs) in order to avoid ambiguity. For example, if *kaufte* were used instead of the *würde*-form (*würde kaufen*) in (64), the sentence would be ambiguous (*kaufen* 'to buy' is a weak verb). It could mean 'I never bought such an album' or 'I would never buy such an album.'[63]

2.2.4.3.2 The imperative   The imperative mood is used to express commands and requests. There is only one form that is distinctly imperative (different from a present tense indicative form): the second person singular form.

(65)   *Anna, **hol** mir bitte ein Glas!*
        'Anna, please get me a glass.'

The second person singular imperative form is simply the stem of the infinitive. (For those strong verbs that change the *-e-* of the infinitive to *-ie-* or *-i-* in the present, the imperative uses the stem of the second person singular form.) Verbs with stems that end in *-ig*, *-d*, *-t*, or an obstruent followed by a nasal must also add an *-e* to the stem. Strong verbs that change the root vowel in the imperative do not add an *-e* to the stem. All other verbs may add an *-e* optionally. The optional *-e* is typically dropped in the spoken language, but common in written German. One exception to these rules is the verb *werden* 'to become'. Although the formation of the present involves a change from *-e-* to *-i-* in second and third person singular forms, the imperative stem retains *-e-* (and the ending *-e* is added because the stem ends in *-d*). Table 2.24 lists the second person singular imperative forms for a number of representative verbs.

Table 2.24 *Imperative forms*

Infinitive	Imperative	Infinitive	Imperative	Infinitive	Imperative
fahren	*fahr(e)!*	*arbeiten*	*arbeite!*	*empfehlen*	*empfiehl!*
glauben	*glaub(e)!*	*atmen*	*atme!*	*essen*	*iss!*
haben	*hab(e)!*	*binden*	*binde!*	*lesen*	*lies!*
kaufen	*kauf(e)!*	*erledigen*	*erledige!*	*nehmen*	*nimm!*
laufen	*lauf(e)!*	*öffnen*	*öffne!*	*sein*	*sei!*
stoßen	*stoß(e)!*	*werden*	*werde!*	*werben*	*wirb!*

The remaining imperative forms, which are identical with present tense indicative forms, are the following: second person plural, second person polite, and first person plural forms.

(66) a. *Kinder,* **putzt** *euch die Zähne!*
'Kids, brush your teeth!'
b. **Kommen** *Sie bitte in meine Sprechstunde.*
'Please come to my office hours.'
c. **Gehen** *wir heute Abend ins Kino!*
'Let's go to the movies tonight.'

Notice that only the polite second person and first person plural forms are accompanied by a personal pronoun (*Sie*; *wir*).

The infinitive is also used with imperative force in official situations and instructions.

(67) a. *Bitte* **einsteigen***!*
'All aboard!'
b. *Die Torte 20 bis 30 Minuten* **backen***.*
'Bake the cake for 20 to 30 minutes.'

2.2.4.4 Non-finite verb forms   The three non-finite verb forms are the infinitive, the present participle, and the past participle.

(68) a. infinitive
Ich kann das nicht mehr **ertragen***.*
'I can no longer bear that.'
b. present participle
Vor dem Flughafen auf den Bus **wartend***, beobachtet sie die Menschen um sich herum.*
'Waiting for the bus in front of the airport, she observes the people around her.'

c. past participle
*Ihr Haus wurde **zerstört**.*
'Her house was destroyed.'

The infinitive is formed with the basic stem and the suffix *-(e)n*. If a verb stem ends in /əl/ or /ər/, the infinitive ending is *-n* (/n/); otherwise it is *-en* (/ən/).

(69) a. *sammel**n*** 'to collect'
    b. *wander**n*** 'to hike'
    c. *lieb**en*** 'to love'

One exception is the verb *tun* 'to do', which has the infinitive ending *-n* rather than the expected *-en*, which we find with other verbs whose stems end in a vowel.

(70) a. *tu**n*** /tʰuːn/ 'to do'
    b. *seh**en*** /zeːən/ 'to see'
    c. *flieh**en*** /fliːən/ 'to flee'

The present participle is formed using the verbal stem and the suffix *-(e)nd*. As with the infinitive ending, those verb stems that end in /əl/ or /ər/ use the suffix variant without schwa; all others use the variant with schwa.

(71) a. *sammel**nd*** 'collecting'
    b. *wander**nd*** 'hiking'
    c. *lieb**end*** 'loving'

The formation of the past participle is sensitive to the class to which a verb belongs (weak, strong, etc.). The past participles of weak verbs are formed by attaching the circumfix *ge . . . t* around the base. As the past participles of verbs like *arbeiten* 'to work' and *öffnen* 'to open' show, *e*-Epenthesis applies in the formation of past participles of weak verbs.

(72) a. *lieben* 'to love'   *geliebt* 'loved'
    b. *arbeiten* 'to work'   *gearbeitet* 'worked'
    c. *öffnen* 'to open'   *geöffnet* 'opened'

The past participles of strong verbs are formed by attaching a slightly different circumfix around the base, *ge . . . en*. The formation of the past participle of many strong verbs also involves a change in the root vowel: *singen* 'to sing', *gesungen* 'sung'; *helfen* 'to help', *geholfen* 'helped'. In a number of ablaut classes, however, there is no vowel change; the root vowel of the past participle is identical to that of the infinitive: *lesen* 'to read', *gelesen* 'read', *fahren* 'to drive', *gefahren* 'driven'. Compare the infinitives and past participles in Table 2.17. The past participles of verbs in the mixed class (Table 2.18) and the class that includes the modals (Table 2.19) are formed by attaching the weak circumfix, *ge . . . t*, around the stem and (with the exception of *sollen* and *wollen*) changing the root vowel (the vowels of the past participles of these verbs are identical to the vowels of the past).

If a verb begins with an unstressed syllable, the *ge-* portion of the circumfix is dropped. This holds for verbs in all classes.

(73) a. *stu'dieren* 'to study'   *stu'diert* 'studied'
     b. *ver'kaufen* 'to sell'   *ver'kauft* 'bought'
     c. *ver'bringen* 'to spend'   *ver'bracht* 'spent'
     d. *ver'mögen* 'to be able to'   *ver'mocht* 'been able to'
     e. *zer'reißen* 'to tear up'   *zer'rissen* 'torn up'

Although written as single orthographic words, phrasal verbs like *ausführen* 'to carry out' and *wegfahren* 'to drive away', which are made up of an adverb plus a verb, behave syntactically like the phrasal verbs *Rad fahren* 'to ride a bike' and *Schlittschuh laufen* 'to ice-skate', which are made up of a noun plus a verb. For example, as the sentences in (74) show, the non-verbal elements of phrasal verbs (whether adverbs, nouns, or members of another category) appear at the end of a main clause, separated from the finite forms of the verbal elements, which occur in the second position of the clause.

(74) a. *Sie führt den Plan aus.*
         'She's carrying out the plan.'
     b. *Das Kind fährt schnell Rad.*
         'The kid pedals quickly.'

The past participles of phrasal verbs like *ausführen* and *wegfahren* behave no differently from the past participles of other phrasal verbs (e.g., *Rad fahren* and *Schlittschuh laufen*). In all types of phrasal verbs, the *ge-* portion of the past participle circumfix is attached to a verbal element of the phrase.

(75) a. *ausführen* 'to carry out'   *ausgeführt* 'carried out'
     b. *wegfahren* 'to drive away'   *weggefahren* 'driven away'

(76) a. *Rad fahren* 'to pedal'   *Rad gefahren* 'pedaled'
     b. *Schlittschuh laufen* 'to ice-skate'   *Schlittschuh gelaufen* 'ice-skated'

2.3   Derivation

Derivation is a word-formation process that creates a new lexeme, typically by adding an affix to a base. This process may or may not change the class to which a word belongs. For example, the verb *beschreiben* 'to describe' is derived by attaching the prefix *be-* to the verbal base *schreib-* 'write'. Although *beschreiben* and *schreiben* are two different lexemes with two different meanings, both belong to the same word class (verb). Thus the derivational process that creates *beschreiben* does not change the word class. The suffix *-ung*, on the other hand, does change the class to which a word belongs. This suffix typically changes verbs into nouns: *binden* 'to tie, bind' > *Bindung* 'tie, bond'.[64]

The status of *be-* and *-ung* as derivational affixes is not at all controversial. However, it is not always easy to determine whether a particular affix is inflectional or derivational. For example, do we want to treat the *-end* suffix on present participles (*schreibend* 'writing') as inflectional (as is done here; see 2.2.4.4), or should it be considered derivational? Donalies (2002:132), for example, analyses all forms like *schreibend* as adjectives derived from the verbal stem with the derivational suffix *-end*.[65] For further discussion of some of the difficulties in distinguishing inflection from derivation, see, for example, Bauer 2003:91–107.

The following sections discuss four productive derivational processes in German: prefixation, suffixation, circumfixation, and conversion. The process of implicit derivation, which is no longer productive in German, is also briefly discussed.

2.3.1   Prefixation

Derivational prefixation is the process of attaching prefixes to a base to create a new lexeme. While prefixation plays a role in the derivation of German nouns and adjectives, it is particularly important in the formation of verbs. Section 2.3.1.1 discusses nominal and adjectival prefixation; section 2.3.1.2 treats verbal prefixation.

2.3.1.1 Nominal and adjectival prefixation   The number of native nominal and adjectival prefixes is relatively small; those that are productive are *erz-*, *Ge-*, *miss-*, *un-*, and *ur-*. With the exception of *Ge-*, these prefixes do not change the class to which a word belongs.

(77) a.   *der Feind* 'enemy' > *der Erzfeind* 'archenemy'
            konservativ 'conservative' > *erzkonservativ* 'ultraconservative'
    b.   *der Busch* 'bush' > *das Gebüsch* 'bushes'
            bellen 'to bark' > *das Gebell* 'barking'
    c.   *der Griff* 'grip, grasp' > *der Missgriff* 'mistake'
            verständlich 'understandable' > *missverständlich* 'unclear'
    d.   *der Dank* 'thanks' > *der Undank* 'ingratitude'
            frei 'free' > *unfrei* 'not free'
    e.   *der Text* 'text' > *Urtext* 'original text'
            alt 'old' > *uralt* 'ancient'

These prefixes clearly change the meaning of the bases to which they are attached. Several distinct meanings can often be assigned to each prefix. The prefix *un-*, for example, can mean something like 'not': *die Lust* 'desire' >

die Unlust 'reluctance (lack of desire)'; *die Logik* 'logic' > *die Unlogik* 'illogicality'. This prefix can also be used as an intensifier meaning 'very large': *die Menge* 'amount' > *die Unmenge* 'vast amount'; *die Zahl* 'number' > *die Unzahl* 'vast number'.

The prefix *Ge-* is particularly interesting because it has suffix-like characteristics. Like nominal suffixes (and unlike other nominal prefixes), it can bring about a change in word class; compare *das Gebell* (< *bellen*) with *die Wohnung* 'dwelling' (< *wohnen* 'to live'). It can also bring about a change in gender; compare *das Gebüsch* (< *der Busch*) with *die Arbeiterschaft* 'workforce' (< *der Arbeiter* 'worker'). Notice that prefixation with *Ge-* can also involve umlauting the vowel of the base (*die Mauer* 'wall' > *das Gemäuer* 'masonry').[66]

A number of nominal and adjectival prefixes of foreign origin are productive in German, for example, *anti-*, *ex-*, *hyper-*, *inter-*, *neo-*, *non-*, *post-*, *prä-*, *super-*, *trans-*, and *ultra-*. Like native nominal and adjectival prefixes, many of these fit into the meaning categories 'opposite' ('negation') and 'graduation' (Fleischer and Barz 1995:204; Klosa 1996; Kinne 2000; Eisenberg 1998:240): *der Antiheld* 'antihero', *der Nonkonformist* 'non-conformist'; *hyperkorrekt* 'hypercorrect', *superklug* 'super smart', *ultraschön* 'ultra-beautiful'.

2.3.1.2 Verbal prefixation   New verbs in German are derived primarily through prefixation (Fleischer and Barz 1995:316). The traditional approach (e.g., Fleischer and Barz 1995) to verbal prefixation recognizes three types of prefixes: inseparable (prefixes like *be-* in *beschreiben* 'to describe'), separable (forms like *aus-* in *ausgehen* 'to go out'), and variable (forms like *über-* in *über'setzen* 'to translate' and *'übersetzen* 'to take across'). Only those forms that are never stressed or separated from the verbal base are recognized here as prefixes. These include *be-*, *ent-*, *er-*, *miss-*, *ver-*, and *zer-* (traditionally known as inseparable prefixes) and unstressed *durch-*, *über-*, *um-*, *unter-*, and *wider-* (the unstressed occurrences of the "variable prefixes"). Because the so-called separable prefixes and stressed variable prefixes can be separated from their verbal bases, they are treated here not as prefixes, but as elements of phrasal verbs, like *Rad* 'bike, wheel' in *Rad fahren* 'to pedal' and *Schlittschuh* 'ice skate' in *Schlittschuh laufen* 'to ice-skate'.[67]

(78) a. *Ich laufe gern Schlittschuh.*
           'I like to ice-skate.'
      b. *Wir gehen heute Abend aus.*
           'We're going out this evening.'
      c. *Der Fährmann setzte ihn über.*
           'The ferryman took him across.'

Prefixed verbs can be denominal, that is, formed by attaching a prefix to a noun: *Fleck* 'stain' > *beflecken* 'to stain'. They can also be deadjectival: *frei* 'free' > *befreien* 'to free'. The majority of prefixed verbs, however, are deverbal: *lügen* 'to lie' > *belügen* 'to lie to'. Prefixation of a verbal base not only changes the meaning of the base, it can also change its valency, the number and type of arguments that occur with it. For example, the verb *lügen* is intransitive. It only requires a subject noun phrase (NP). The verb *belügen*, on the other hand, is transitive; it requires an object NP as well as a subject.

(79) a. *Mein Freund lügt.*
         'My friend lies.'
     b. *Mein Freund belügt mich.*
         'My friend lies to me.'

The verb *lachen* 'to laugh' can have a prepositional object: *über jemanden/etwas lachen* 'to laugh at someone/something'. The verb *belachen* expresses the prepositional object of *lachen* as a direct (accusative) object: *jemanden/etwas belachen* 'to laugh at someone/something'.

Verbs derived through *be-* prefixation are essentially all transitive; they have a direct object in the accusative case. Prefixation with *be-* can take an intransitive verb and make it transitive, as is the case with *belügen* and *belachen*. It can also "shift" an object. For example, the verb *liefern* has a dative object (person) and an accusative object (thing): *jemandem* (dative) *etwas* (accusative) *liefern* 'to supply something to someone'. The verb *beliefern* has an accusative object (person) and a prepositional object (thing): *jemanden* (accusative) *mit etwas beliefern* 'to supply someone with something'. The dative person of *liefern* is shifted to the accusative person of *beliefern*; the accusative thing of *liefern* is shifted to the prepositional thing of *beliefern*. Prefixation with *be-* can simply have a semantic effect, intensifying the action of the unprefixed verb. Compare *fühlen* 'to feel' and *befühlen* 'to run one's hands over'; *fragen* 'to ask' and *befragen* 'to question, examine'.

The prefix *be-* is used here to exemplify some of the general characteristics of verbal prefixation in German. This prefix can be characterized as the most productive among the prefixes *be-*, *ent-*, *er-*, *ver-*, and *zer-* (Eisenberg 1998:250).[68] All of these prefixes developed historically from prepositions or adverbs, although they no longer have prepositional or adverbial counterparts. They are an older set of prefixes in comparison to the group that includes *durch* and *über*, for example, which do have prepositional counterparts.

(80) a. verbal prefix
         Ich übersetze einen Roman.
         'I'm translating a novel.'

b. preposition
   Er hängt das Bild über das Sofa.
   'He is hanging the picture above the sofa.'

The prepositional counterparts of these prefixes all occur as elements of phrasal verbs; see, for example, (78c). For further information on *be-* and the other verbal prefixes in German, see, for example, Fleischer and Barz 1995, Eisenberg 1998, Durrell 2002, and Donalies 2002.

2.3.2   *Suffixation*

Whereas prefixation plays a particularly important role in verbal derivation in comparison to nominal and adjectival derivation, suffixation plays a major role in nominal and adjectival derivation and only a limited role in the formation of verbs.

2.3.2.1 Nominal and adjectival suffixation   Derivational suffixes are especially important in the formation of nouns because of the grammatical effect they have on their output. In the vast majority of cases, each suffix assigns a specific gender to the noun it is used to create, and each suffix is associated with a specific plural ending. The suffix *-er*, for example, which is highly productive, is used to derive masculine nouns, primarily from verbs: *fahren* 'to drive' > *der Fahrer* 'driver'; *rauchen* 'to smoke' > *der Raucher* 'smoker'; *entsaften* 'to juice' > *der Entsafter* 'juicer'. These nouns typically designate the entity (person or instrument) that carries out the activity characterized by the verb. The suffix *-ung*, next to *-er* the most productive suffix in German (Fleischer and Barz 1995:172), is used to derive feminine nouns, primarily from verbs: *spalten* 'to split' > *die Spaltung* 'splitting'; *landen* 'to land' > *die Landung* 'landing'. Nouns derived from verbs using the *-ung* suffix refer to the action of the verb. Because there is such a close relationship between the meaning of a verb and the meaning of its *-ung* derivative, suffixation with *-ung* can be viewed as a means for making verbs useful syntactically as nouns (Donalies 2002:107).

Suffixes can be used to derive nouns from words other than verbs. The suffix *-ling*, for example, can be used to derive nouns from verbs, nouns, and adjectives: *prüfen* 'to examine' > *der Prüfling* 'examinee'; *die Lust* 'desire' > *der Lüstling* 'lecher'; *frech* 'impudent' > *der Frechling* 'impudent person'. Derived as well as simple words can be used as a base for suffixation. For example, the verb *verkaufen* 'to sell', which is derived from the verb *kaufen* 'to buy', can serve as a base for the *-er* noun *der Verkäufer* 'seller'. Phrasal verbs can also serve as a base for suffixation: *angeben* 'to show off' > *der Angeber* 'show-off'.

Some common, productive native suffixes in addition to -er, -ling, and -ung that are used to derive nouns are the following:

(81) a. -chen   die Idee 'idea' > das Ideechen 'little idea'
    b. -heit   blind 'blind' > die Blindheit 'blindness'
    c. -in   der Jogger 'jogger' > die Joggerin 'female jogger'
    d. -nis   bitter 'bitter' > die Bitternis 'bitterness'
    e. -schaft   der Leser 'reader' > die Leserschaft 'readership'

There are many words of foreign origin in German that have identifiable suffixes. For example, words like der Dirigent 'director', der Konkurrent 'competitor', and der Student 'student' all end in -ent, which is used primarily to form nouns from verbs that end in -ieren (dirigieren 'to direct'; konkurrieren 'to compete'; studieren 'to study'). Because suffixes of foreign origin rarely take native words as their base, the productivity of suffixation with foreign suffixes is very restricted (Fleischer and Barz 1995:185). Some common foreign suffixes that are found in nouns are the following:

(82) a. -age   die Spionage 'espionage'
    b. -enz   die Konferenz 'conference'
    c. -erie   die Drogerie 'drugstore'
    d. -ik   die Dramatik 'drama'
    e. -är   der Millionär 'millionaire'
    f. -eur   der Friseur 'barber'
    g. -ismus   der Kapitalismus 'capitalism'

There are a number of native suffixes that are used in the derivation of adjectives. Like suffixes that are used to derive nouns, adjectival suffixes can be attached to bases from a variety of word classes. Common native German suffixes include the following:

(83) a. -bar   lesen 'to read' > lesbar 'legible; readable'
    b. -haft   der Held 'hero' > heldenhaft 'heroic'
    c. -ig   die Frucht 'fruit' > fruchtig 'fruity'
    d. -isch   das Kind 'child' > kindisch 'childish'
    e. -lich   klein 'little' > kleinlich 'petty'
    f. -los   der Bart 'beard' > bartlos 'beardless'
    g. -sam   biegen 'to bend' > biegsam 'flexible'

There are also several common adjectival suffixes of foreign origin.

(84) a. -abel   akzeptabel 'acceptable'
    b. -esk   kafkaesk 'Kafkaesque'
    c. -ös   nervös 'nervous'

2.3.2.2 *Verbal suffixation*   Verbal suffixation is much more limited than nominal suffixation. The most common suffix, *-ieren* (and its variants *-isieren* and *-ifizieren*), is attached primarily to words (bases) of foreign origin.

(85) a. *aktivieren* 'to activate', *finanzieren* 'to finance'
     b. *characterisieren* 'to characterize', *pulverisieren* 'to pulverize'
     c. *falsifizieren* 'to falsify', *identifizieren* 'to identify'

There are a few examples, though, where *-ieren* is attached to a native base: *buchstabieren* 'to spell' (< *Buchstabe* 'letter'); *hausieren* 'to hawk, peddle' (< *Haus* 'house').

    The number of verbs derived with the suffix *-el* is relatively small, although the suffix is productive (Durrell 2002:519).

(86) a. *Stück* 'piece' > *stückeln* 'to patch'
     b. *streichen* 'to stroke' > *streicheln* 'to caress'
     c. *alt* 'old' > *älteln* 'to begin to get old'

As the examples above illustrate, nouns, verbs, and adjectives can serve as the base for *-el* suffixation.

2.3.3   *Circumfixation*

A minor type of affixation in German is circumfixation. The only circumfix used to derive nouns is *Ge . . . e*, which is attached to a verbal base to form a noun that expresses the repeated activity of the verb, often with a pejorative connotation (incessant, annoying, etc.).

(87) a. *klopfen* 'to knock' > *das Geklopfe* 'knocking'
     b. *pfeifen* 'to whistle' > *das Gepfeife* 'whistling'
     c. *anbrüllen* 'to bellow' > *das Angebrülle* 'bellowing'

Notice that the circumfix is attached around the verbal base with phrasal verbs (*anbrüllen*) as well as with simple verbs (*klopfen*, *pfeifen*). Verbs with prefixes and those derived with the suffix *-ieren* do not allow circumfixation with *Ge . . . e* (an asterisk before a word indicates that the form is unacceptable).[69]

(88) a. *besuchen* 'to visit' > *das *Gebesuche* 'visiting'
     b. *telefonieren* 'to telephone' > *das *Getelefoniere* 'telephoning'

    Recall that there is a simple prefix *Ge-* that can be used to derive nouns. Because verbs can be used as the basis for prefixation with *Ge-*, there is the potential for doublets.

(89) a. *bellen* 'to bark' > *das Gebell/Gebelle* 'barking'
     b. *schreien* 'to shout' > *das Geschrei/Geschreie* 'shouting'

The difference between the two forms is the pejorative connotation that is associated with the circumfix *Ge . . . e* (Fleischer and Barz 1995:208).

The single adjectival circumfix is *ge . . . ig*, which is not productive and can be found in only a handful of adjectives: *gefügig* 'submissive', *gehässig* 'spiteful', *geläufig* 'common', *gelehrig* 'quick to learn' (Donalies 2002:116).

The main verbal circumfix is *be . . . ig*, which is used to form verbs from noun and adjective bases.

(90) a.   *die Erde* 'earth' > *beerdigen* 'to bury'
     b.   *sanft* 'gentle' > *besänftigen* 'to soothe'

Some verbs occur only with the suffix *-ig*, yet have the same semantic effect as circumfixation with *be . . . ig*.

(91) a.   *die Angst* 'fear' > *ängstigen* 'to frighten'
     b.   *die Pein* 'agony' > *peinigen* 'to torture'

Compare *steinigen* 'to stone' (< *der Stein* 'stone') with *belobigen* 'to praise' (< *der Lob* 'praise').

2.3.4   Conversion

Conversion, also known as zero-derivation, is the creation of a new lexeme by changing the word class of an existing lexeme without the use of affixation. For example, the creation of the noun *der Kauf* 'sale' from the verb *kauf-* 'to sell' is an example of conversion. The creation of *fischen* 'to fish' from *der Fisch* 'fish' is also an example of conversion (the *-en* suffix in *fischen* is an inflectional suffix, not a derivational suffix).

Nominal conversion in German is productive. Most word classes can be converted into nouns, although deverbal conversion is probably the most common.[70]

(92) a.   *lauf-* '(to) run' > *der Lauf* 'run'
     b.   *laufen* 'to run' > *das Laufen* 'running'
     c.   *biss* 'bit' (past of *beißen* 'to bite') > *der Biss* 'bite'
     d.   *ernst* 'serious' > *der Ernst* 'seriousness'
     e.   *ich* 'I' > *das Ich* 'self'

Even phrases can be converted into nouns (Donalies 2002:130).

(93) a.   *die kleine Todeskapsel des **Für-alle-Fälle***
          the small death-capsule of just-in-case
     b.   *ein rotes Bisschen **Vergissmichschnell***
          a red bit of forget-me-quickly

Conversion is less common in the derivation of adjectives than in the derivation of nouns. There are some examples of denominal adjectives: *die Angst* 'fear' > *angst* 'afraid'; *die Schuld* 'guilt, blame' > *schuld* 'at fault'. These adjectives are limited syntactically, however; they can only be used predicatively: *Ihr wurde angst* 'She became worried'. Most common is the conversion of participles to adjectives.

(94) a. *schreiend* (present participle) 'shouting, screaming, screeching' >
         schreiend (adjective): *die schreienden Kinder* 'the screaming kids'
     b. *verloren* (past participle) 'lost' > *verloren* (adjective): *die*
         verlorene Ehre 'the lost honor'

These deverbal adjectives often acquire figurative or special meanings. The present participle *glänzend* 'shining, gleaming', for example, can have the figurative meaning 'brilliant' when used as an adjective: *eine glänzende Idee* 'a brilliant idea'.

Conversion can be used to change both nouns and adjectives into verbs. As Donalies (2002:133) points out, just about any noun can be converted into a verb.

(95) a. animal names: *der Tiger* 'tiger' > *tigern* 'to mooch'
     b. proper names: *W. C. Röntgen* (physicist) > *röntgen* 'to X-ray'
     c. musical instruments: *die Geige* 'violin' > *geigen* 'play the violin'
     d. substances: *das Salz* 'salt' > *salzen* 'to salt'
     e. professions: *der Gärtner* 'gardener' > *gärtnern* 'to garden'

Although there are many verbs that have been derived from adjectives by conversion, it is debatable whether this process is productive (Donalies 2002: 134).

(96) a. *faul* 'rotten' > *faulen* 'to rot'
     b. *grün* 'green' > *grünen* 'to turn green'
     c. *süß* 'sweet' > *süßen* 'to sweeten'

Complex adjectives are only rarely converted into verbs: *kräftig* 'strong' > *kräftigen* 'to build up (somebody's) strength'; compare *niedlich* 'cute and small' > **niedlichen, verniedlichen* 'to trivialize' (Fleischer and Barz 1995:314; Donalies 2002:135). This is not the case with verbs converted from nouns (Donalies 2002:135): *brutpflegen* 'to care for the brood' (< *die Brutpflege* 'care of the brood'), *langfingern* 'to pickpocket' (< *der Langfinger* 'pickpocket'), *schriftstellern* 'to try one's hand as an author' (< *der Schriftsteller* 'author').

2.3.5 Implicit derivation

Implicit derivation makes use of ablaut to create new lexemes.[71] This (now unproductive) process forms causatives, verbs that mean 'to cause someone/something to do something'.

(97) a. *fallen* 'to fall' > *fällen* 'to fell (cause to fall)'
    b. *sinken* 'to sink' > *senken* 'to sink (someone/something)'
    c. *trinken* 'to drink' > *tränken* 'to water'

Following Donalies (2002), words like *der Schritt* 'step' are not considered here to be the product of implicit derivation (from the verb *schreiten* 'to stride').[72] Instead, they are derived through conversion from the past stem *schritt* 'strode'.

2.4   Compounding

Compounding is the creation of a new word (lexeme) by adjoining two or more words. For example, the words *Haus* 'house' and *Tür* 'door' can be joined to form the compound *Haustür* 'front door'. Two types of compounds are recognized here, subordinate compounds and copulative compounds. *Haustür* is an example of a subordinate compound. The first element in this compound modifies the second element. A *Haustür* is a kind of *Tür*; the element *Haus* tells what kind of a *Tür* it is. In copulative compounds, on the other hand, each member of the compound is equal. One member does not modify another. The compound adjective *schwarzweiß* 'black and white', for example, is a copulative compound. If something is *schwarzweiß*, it is both black and white.

All subordinate compounds in German are binary in structure, even if they are made up of more than two elements. The compound *die Nudelsauce* 'noodle sauce', which is made up of two words, *Nudel* and *Sauce*, is formed by joining these two words together. The compound *Nudelsaucenrezept* 'noodle sauce recipe', which is made up of a total of three words, is also formed by joining two words together, *Nudelsauce* (itself a compound) and *Rezept*. Similarly, *Nudelsaucenrezeptsammler* 'noodle sauce recipe collector' is made up of a total of four words, but is formed by adjoining two, *Nudelsaucenrezept* (a compound) and *Sammler*.[73]

There are sometimes "extra" segments between the members of a compound:

(98) a. *der Frau-en-sport* 'women's sport', *der Kind-er-wagen* 'baby carriage', *der Schwein-e-braten* 'roast pork'
    b. *die Tag-es-temperatur* 'daytime temperature'
    c. *der Wohnung-s-markt* 'housing market'

Sometimes these segments are identical to the plural ending of the first element in the compound, as in (98a), where the *-en-* in *Frauensport*, for example, is the plural ending of *Frau* 'woman'. In other compounds, these segments are identical to the genitive ending of the first member; in (98b), *-es-* is the genitive singular ending of *Tag* 'day'. In some compounds, however, these extra segments have no connection at all to the first member of the compound. The *-s-* in *Wohnungsmarkt*, for example, is not an inflectional ending of *Wohnung*. The word is feminine and thus has no genitive singular ending; its plural form is *Wohnungen*.

Those extra elements that are identical to plural endings are treated here as inflectional affixes (e.g., *-e*, *-en*, *-er*). Note that it is necessary to acknowledge the presence of inflected words in compounds, given compounds like *Mütterberatungsstelle* 'advisory center for (pregnant and nursing) mothers', where *Mütter* is the plural form of *Mutter* 'mother'. The *-(e)s-* that occurs in compounds is not treated as an inflectional affix, however, but simply as a "linking element,"[74] even if it could be considered a genitive ending in some compounds (e.g., in *Tagestemperatur*).[75]

Compounding is particularly important in modern German. It is a highly productive source of new words, and the extensive use of compounds is a typical feature of the language. For example, the first two sentences in a randomly chosen newspaper article yield the following compounds: *Bundeskabinett* 'federal cabinet', *Gesundheitsreform* 'health reform', *Wechselfrist* 'usance', and *Krankenversicherung* 'health insurance'. German is also notorious for the potential length of its compounds. In an essay on "The Awful German Language," Mark Twain remarked that "some German words are so long that they have a perspective," and listed compounds like *Waffenstillstandsunterhandlungen* 'cease-fire negotiations' and *Wiederherstellungsbestrebungen* 'restoration attempts' as examples (Twain 1996:611–612). Although the length and complexity of the following (attested) compound is not characteristic of a typical compound, it does demonstrate the potential of compounding in German (Donalies 2002:62):

(99)   *Australienlangstreckendirektflugstopoverspezialisten*
         Australia-long-distance-direct-flight-stop-over-specialists

It is not always easy to distinguish between the processes of compounding and derivation, both of which create new lexemes. For example, are *Astwerk* 'branches', *Buschwerk* 'bushes', and *Laubwerk* 'foliage' compounds formed with the noun *Werk* 'work', or are they nouns derived using the suffix *-werk*? Historically, affixes can develop from lexemes. The affix *-schaft* in *Freundshaft* 'friendship', for example, developed from the Old High German word *scaf* 'nature', which no longer exists as a lexeme.[76] Some linguists use the term "affixoid" to identify affix-like morphemes like *-werk* that differ somewhat in meaning from their corresponding lexemes (*Werk* 'work'). Others argue against recognizing an additional type of morphological unit (Schmidt 1987, Fleischer and Barz 1995:27–28; Eisenberg 1998:210).

2.4.1   Nominal compounds

The majority of nominal compounds are subordinate compounds. Although nominal copulative compounds exist, they are not common. Many compounds that have been identified as copulative compounds in the literature can also be analyzed as subordinate compounds:

(100) a. *Hosenrock* 'pant skirt'
     b. *Radiowecker* 'radio alarm clock'
     c. *Kinocafé* 'cinema café'
     d. *Dichterkomponist* 'author composer'

For example, a *Kinocafé* can be interpreted as a cinema and café (copulative compound) or as a type of café that shows films (subordinate compound). One example of a compound that is unambiguously a copulative compound is *Schleswig-Holstein* 'Schleswig-Holstein', one of the current German states made up of Schleswig and Holstein. As all these compounds demonstrate, the individual members of copulative compounds are (necessarily) nouns.

Although the final element of a nominal subordinate compound will always be a noun, a variety of elements can serve as the first element.[77]

(101) a. noun: *die Bühnenmusik* 'incidental (stage) music'
     b. adjective: *die Blindlandung* 'blind landing'
     c. verb: *die Stehkneipe* 'stand-up bar'[78]
     d. adverb: die *Jetztzeit* 'present (now time)'
     e. preposition: *der Mitstudent* 'fellow (with) student'
     f. pronoun: *der Ich-Roman* 'first person novel'
     g. phrase: *die Ohne-mich-Haltung* 'without-me attitude'
     h. sentence: *der Ich-mach-aus-dir-Hackfleisch-Blick*
                          'I'll-make-mincemeat-out-of-you-look'

The most common (two-member) nominal compounds are those with nouns, adjectives, or verbs as first members. Although other word types are possible as first members, they are less common.

2.4.2   Adjectival compounds

Adjectival copulative compounds are the most common type of copulative compound. Although adjectival subordinate compounds are more numerous than their copulative counterparts, adjectival copulative compounds are not uncommon (Donalies 2002:87).[79]

(102) a. *deutsch-armenische Beziehungen* 'German–Armenian relations'
b. *eine krummgelbe Banane* 'a bent-yellow banana'
c. *Armeniens rot-blau-aprikosenfarbene Flagge* 'Armenia's red-blue-apricot flag'

Adjectival compounds are typically made up of just two elements, although more complex compounds are possible, as the following subordinate compound demonstrates: *stachelbeerstrauchbraun* 'gooseberry bush brown' (Donalies 2002:78).

Two-member adjectival subordinate compounds can have a variety of elements as their first member.

(103) a. noun: *farbenblind* 'color-blind'
b. adjective: *altklug* 'precocious (old-clever)'
c. verb: *fahrtüchtig* 'roadworthy'
d. preposition: *mitschuldig* 'complicit'
e. phrase: *zweibibeldick* 'two-bible thick'

The most common adjectival subordinate compounds are those with nouns as their first element.

2.4.3   Other compounds

Compounding is a very minor process in the formation of verbs in German. Only those verbs whose first elements are words that are never separated from the rest of the verb are considered compounds. Verbal compounds with verbs as their first element are typically found in technical language and sometimes in fictional works.

(104) a. *presspolieren* 'to press-polish', *schleifpolieren* 'to sand-polish'
b. *grinskeuchen* 'to grin-pant', *knirschkauen* 'to grind-chew'

Compound verbs with nouns and adjectives as their first element are probably less common than those with verbs as first elements.[80]

(105) a. *nachtwandeln* 'to sleepwalk', *lobpreisen* 'to praise'
b. *liebäugeln* 'to ogle', *frohlocken* 'to rejoice', *vollenden* 'to finish'

The use of nouns and adjectives to form verbal compounds is not a productive process in German; the examples above are well-established verbal compounds.

Adverbial compounds, on the other hand, are not uncommon, and relatively new compounds attest to the productive nature of this method of deriving adverbs (Donalies 2002:87).

(106) a. *tagsüber* 'during the day': *jahrsüber* 'during the year'
     b. *bergauf* 'uphill': *strumpfauf* 'up-stocking', *wandauf* 'up-wall'

Nominal compounds, however, are by far the most productive and numerous type of compound in German.

2.5   Reductions

Reductions (*Kurzwörter*) are nouns that are simply shortened versions of complex nouns (or phrases) that already exist in the language. For example, *die Demo* 'demonstration' is a reduction of *die Demonstration*. Both the original long form and the reduction co exist. There is typically no difference in meaning between the long form and its reduced counterpart, although there may be stylistic differences. The reduction *die Demo*, for example, is more casual than *die Demonstration*. The reduced form may or may not be inflected like its long counterpart. The plural forms of both *Ober* 'waiter' and *Oberkellner* 'head waiter' are identical to their singular forms. However, the plural ending of *Demo* is -*s*, whereas the plural ending of its long form is -*en*: *Demos*; *Demonstrationen*. The *s*-plural is in fact a typical plural ending for reductions. Reductions typically have the same gender as their full forms: *der Bus, der Autobus* 'bus'; *die Kripo, die Kriminalpolizei* 'criminal investigation department'; *das Abi, das Abitur* (school-leaving exam). Exceptions are rare: *das Foto, die Fotografie* 'photograph'; *das Litho, die Lithographie* 'lithograph' (Dudenredaktion 2005:745).

Acronyms (*AOK, Lkw, TÜV*) are included in the class of reductions, but not abbreviations (*ca., dgl., km*). Acronyms are pronounced according to how they are written. Either the individual letters are named (*AOK, Lkw*) or they are pronounced using the sounds that their individual letters would signify (*TÜV* [tʰʏf]). Abbreviations, on the other hand, are pronounced exactly like their unabbreviated forms: *ca.* and *circa* 'circa' are both pronounced [tsɪɐ̯kʰa].

The formation of reductions in German is quite productive. The creation of acronyms, in particular, is a popular process. The names of new organizations, companies, publications, etc. are in fact often created with the goal of producing a particular acronym. Many such names have acronyms that are identical to words or names that are already established (Donalies 2002:150): *Junge Liberale* 'Young Liberals' > *JULI* (*Juli* 'July'); *Osnabrücker Beiträge zur Sprachtheorie* 'Osnabrück Contributions to Language Theory' > *OBST* (*Obst* 'fruit').

Not until recently have reductions been given more than a marginal place in the discussion of word-formation processes in German – derivation and compounding (concatenative processes) being viewed as the central means of deriving new lexical items (Wiese 2001). In the past twenty years, reductions have begun to capture the attention of linguists, as evidenced by an increase in descriptive studies (e.g., Greule 1983, 1996; Kobler-Trill 1994) and theoretically oriented studies (e.g., Neef 1996; Féry 1997; Itô and Mester 1997; Wiese 2001; Grüter 2003).

2.5.1   A typology of reduction types

Three basic types of reductions can be identified: clippings, multi-segmental reductions, and partial reductions. Clippings and multi-segmental reductions can be divided into further subtypes.

A clipping is created by "clipping" off part of an existing word. Most clippings are created by deleting the last part of a word. The portion that is deleted can be anything from a syllable to a word (in a compound word):

(107) a. *das Abitur* (school-leaving exam) > *das Abi*
       b. *die Demonstration* 'demonstration' > *die Demo*
       c. *der Oberkellner* 'head waiter' > *der Ober*

Much less common are clippings that are created by deleting the first portion of a word.

(108) a. *das Violoncello* 'violoncello' > *das Cello*
       b. *der Omnibus* 'omnibus' > *der Bus*

According to Kobler-Trill (1994:66), *Cello* and *Bus* are the only examples of such clippings.[81] Clippings that delete the first and last portions of a word are extremely rare, and appear to be possible only with proper names.

(109) a. *Elizabeth > Liza*
       b. *Sebastian > Basti*
       c. *Theresia > Resi*

A multi-segmental reduction is a pronounceable word that is formed from the initial letters and/or syllables of the words in a compound or phrase. There are three basic types of multi-segmental reductions: acronyms, syllable reductions, and mixed reductions. Acronyms are formed by taking the initial letters of a compound or phrase and pronouncing them as a word.

(110) a. *der **Last**kraftwagen* 'truck' > *der Lkw*
       b. *Institut für **D**eutsche **S**prache* > IDS

Syllable reductions are formed by taking the initial syllables (or parts of syllables) of a compound or phrase and pronouncing them as a word.

(111) a. *die **Schutz**polizei* 'police force' > *die Schupo*
b. ***Ju**nge **Li**berale* 'young liberals' > *JULI* (Donalies 2002:150)

Mixed reductions are created by using both initial letters and syllables (parts of syllables) of a compound or phrase to create a pronounceable word.

(112) a. ***A**us**zu**bildender* 'trainee' > *Azubi*
b. ***B**undes**a**usbildungs**fö**rderungs**g**esetz* (law regarding grants for higher education) > *BAFöG*
c. ***A**rbeitspapiere und **Ma**terialien zur **de**utschen **S**prache* 'working papers and materials on the German language' > *amades* (Donalies 2002:148)

Partial reductions are created by reducing part of an established compound or phrase.

(113) a. ***Schoko**ladenbonbon* 'chocolate candy' > *Schokobonbon*
b. ***O**rangensaft* 'orange juice' > *O-Saft*
c. ***Vo**rne-**ku**rz-**hi**nten-**la**ng-Frisur* 'short-in-front-long-in-back-haircut (mullet)' > *Vokuhila-Frisur* (Donalies 2002:147)
d. ***h**altbare Milch* 'long-life milk' > *H-Milch*

Although the portion of the compound or phrase that is reduced typically ends up as a single letter or an acronym (*O-Saft*, *H-Milch*, *UV-Strahlen* 'UV rays'), the reduced portion can also be a clipping (*Schoko* < ***Schoko**lade* in *Schokoladenbonbon*) or a syllable reduction (*Schuko* < ***Schu**tz**ko**ntakt* in *Schukostecker* 'safety plug').

2.5.2   Reductions in word formation

Several suffixes in German are used together with reductions to create new lexical items: *-ler*, *-i*, and *-o*. The suffix *-ler* is typically added to acronyms to create nouns that designate people.

(114) a. *CDUler* 'CDU member'
b. *FKKler* 'nudist'
c. *IBMler* 'IBMers'

The suffixes *-i* and *-o* are added to clippings.

(115) a. *Pulli* 'pullover' (< *Pullover*)
b. *Anarcho* 'anarchist' (< *Anarchist*)

Suffixation and clipping can be viewed as happening simultaneously (the forms *Pull and *Anarch do not exist independently). Words derived by suffixing -i and -o to clippings typically designate people, but they can also designate objects: *der Trabbi* (name of East German car) < *Trabant*.

The *i*-suffix is particularly productive and often adds a special nuance to the meaning of the derived word. It can add a hypocoristic sense.

(116) a. *Omi* < *Oma* 'grandma'
 b. *Riki* < *Ulrike*
 c. *Susi* < *Susanne*

It can also add a slightly pejorative sense.

(117) a. *der Alki* < *der Alkoholiker* 'alcoholic'
 b. *der Drogi* 'druggie' < *der Drogensüchtige* 'drug addict'
 c. *der Ami* < *der Amerikaner* 'American'

Not all reductions that end in an -*i* are products of reduction and suffixation. The following words are simply clippings that happen to end in an -*i*:

(118) a. *die Uni* 'university' < *die Universität*
 b. *der Krimi* 'crime novel' < *der Kriminalroman*
 c. *der Chauvi* 'chauvinist' < *der Chauvinist*

Reductions play a particularly active role in the creation of compounds. They typically occur as the first member of a compound.

(119) a. *CIA-Agent* 'CIA agent'
 b. *VW-Fahrer* 'VW driver'
 c. *Zivi-Stelle* 'position for a person doing alternative service'

Though less common, they can also appear in other positions in a compound.

(120) a. *Reality-TV*
 b. *Fußball-WM* 'soccer world championship'

Reductions can also be used together to form a compound.

(121) a. *CD-ROM*
 b. *BASF-Azubi* 'BASF trainee'

Some compounds formed with reductions are in fact redundant (but generally not perceived as such), which suggests that the reductions are on their way to becoming lexical items independent of their long forms (Dudenredaktion 2005:742).

(122) a. *die PIN-Nummer* 'PIN number' < *die persönliche
Identifikationsnummer-Nummer 'personal identification number
number'
b. *die ABM-Maßnahme* < *die
Arbeitsbeschaffungsmaßnahme-Maßnahme 'job creation
measure measure'

2.5.3   Other reduction types and related word-formation processes

Two less common word-formation processes in German that are similar to
the process of reduction are blending and reduplication. Blends are new
lexical items that are created by reducing and then fusing together two
words.

(123) a. *Ameropa* (name of a travel agency) < ***Amer**ika* and *Eu**ropa***
b. *jein* 'yes and no' < *j**a*** and *n**ein***

The two words used to form a blend may have one or more segments in
common; the common segments occur only once in the blend.

(124) a. *Jobst* (name of a company) < ***Jo**ghurt* 'yogurt' and *Obst* 'fruit'
b. *Kurlaub* 'spa vacation' < ***Kur*** 'health cure' and *Urlaub* 'vacation'

Blends are similar to reductions in that both involve the deletion of portions
of words. They differ from reductions, however, in that they do not have
corresponding long forms. Blending creates a new lexical item; the process of
reduction creates an alternative (shortened) form of a lexical item that already
exists in the lexicon.

Reduplication is a process of affixation that makes use of an affix created by
repeating part (or all) of the base to which it is attached.

(125) a. *die Pinkepinke* 'dough' < *Pinke* 'money'
b. *der/die Schickimicki* 'member of the in-crowd' < *schick* 'chic'

Reduplication is a limited means of creating new lexical items in modern
German. According to the Duden grammar, there are only approximately one
hundred reduplicated forms in German (nouns, verbs, adjectives, adverbs, and
interjections); many of these belong to non-standard varieties of German or are
common in child language.

Many reduplicated forms in German involve more than just simple repetition
of segments.

(126) a. simple repetition: *das Blabla* 'empty talk'
     b. rhyming repetition: *der Heckmeck* 'nonsense' (< *meckern* 'to grump, gripe')
     c. ablauting repetition: *das Tingeltangel* 'second-rate night-club' (< *tingeln* 'to appear in small night-clubs')

As forms like *Schickimicki* and those below demonstrate, reduplicated forms in German often contain the segment *-i*, a feature they have in common with reductions (clippings) that happen to end in *-i* (*Krimi* 'crime novel') as well as those that involve reduction and *i*-suffixation (*Drogi* 'druggie').

(127) a. *das Larifari* 'nonsense'
     b. *das Wischiwaschi* 'drivel'
     c. *das Remmidemmi* 'rumpus'

Wiese 2001 in fact provides arguments (from phonology, morphology, semantics, and usage) that reduction and reduplication are two variants of the same phenomenon. He argues that reductions are basically reduplicative constructions in which prosodic wellformedness conditions prevent the double realization of the material.

Exercises

1. Write rules like those in (8) and (9), for example, to account for the following:
   (a) the plural inflection of nouns ending in *-lein* (*das Büchlein* 'little book', *das Wörtlein* 'little word'), a subclass of class 1 nouns
   (b) the plural inflection of class 2 nouns (those that end in a schwa syllable have the suffix *-n*; those that do not have the suffix *-en*)
   (c) the plural inflection of the class 2 words *der Konsul* 'counsel' and *der Ungar* 'Hungarian', which do *not* end in a schwa syllable but nevertheless have the plural suffix *-n* (they end in an unstressed vowel followed by a liquid, /l/ or /r/).
2. Identify the prefixes, suffixes, circumfixes, roots, and stems in the following word forms: (a) *Lesern* 'readers' (b) *fragliche* 'questionable' (c) *Schuldigkeit* 'duty' (d) *zertreten* 'to crush' (e) *gekauft* 'bought' (f) *partnerschaftliches* 'based on partnership' (g) *ultramoderne* 'ultra modern' (h) *unglücklich* 'unhappy' (i) *Gequatsche* 'gabbing' (j) *mutterlose* 'motherless'
3. Identify the suffixes in the following words and determine whether they are inflectional or derivational.

(a) *Krankheiten* 'diseases' (b) *schönerer* 'more beautiful' (c) *Studentinnen* 'students' (d) *studieren* 'to study' (e) *Brüderchen* 'little brother' (f) *Schreiberlingen* 'pen-pushers' (g) *Verhältnisse* 'relationships' (h) *Arbeiterschaft* 'work force' (i) *zauberhafte* 'enchanting' (j) *Humoristen* 'humorists'

4. Identify the word-formation process(es) used in the formation of the following words (affixation, conversion, compounding, reduction). Note that some words are the result of more than one process.

   (a) *Freundin* 'female friend' (b) *salzen* 'to salt' (*Salz* 'salt') (c) *Info* 'handout' (*Informationsblatt* 'handout') (d) *Fundi* 'fundamentalist' (*Fundamentalist* 'fundamentalist') (e) *hypermodern* 'ultra modern' (f) *Teekanne* 'tea pot' (g) *Kita* '(children's) day-care center' (*Kindertagesstätte* 'day-care center') (h) *süßlich* 'sweetish' (i) *Süßwein* 'dessert wine' (j) *süßen* 'to sweeten'

5. Identify the following as subordinate or copulative compounds: (a) *schwarzrot-gold* 'black-red-and-gold' (b) *Butterfett* 'butterfat' (c) *Sojabohne* 'soybean' (d) *Schreibtisch* 'desk' (e) *Kneeschützer* 'knee pad' (f) *Hotelkasino* 'hotel casino' (g) *Frühlingsfest* 'spring festival' (h) *alkoholarm* 'low in alcohol' (i) *süßsauer* 'sweet and sour' (j) *hellblau* 'light blue'

6. Identify the following reductions as clippings, multi-segmental reductions, or partial reductions.

   (a) *Dia* 'slide' (*Diapositiv*) (b) *A-Saft* 'apple juice' (*Apfelsaft*) (c) *CDU* 'Christian Democratic Union' (*Christlich-Demokratische Union*) (d) *Schiri* 'ref' (*Schiedsrichter* 'referee') (e) *Spezi* 'pal' (*spezieller Freund* 'special friend') (f) *SB-Laden* 'self-service store' (*Selbstbedienungsladen*) (g) *VW* 'VW' (*Volkswagen*) (h) *Frust* 'frustration' (*Frustration*) (i) *Kadewe* (*Kaufhaus des Westens* [name of a department store in Berlin]) (j) *D-Zug* 'fast train' (*Durchgangszug*) (k) *Sani* 'medical orderly' (*Sanitäter*)

NOTES

1 See section 2.2.1.2 for a discussion of the other plural allomorphs in German.

2 Morphs will be cited from now on using conventional orthography rather than phonemic representations unless such representations are necessary for the discussion.

3 Inflectional affixes are used to create the different word forms of a lexeme. These contrast with derivational affixes, which are used to create new lexemes. See sections 2.2 and 2.3 for further discussion of the properties of inflectional and derivational affixes.

4 The participle *gekauft* could be viewed as containing the prefix *ge-* and the suffix *-t* rather than the circumfix *ge . . . t*. However, *gekauft* never occurs without the *ge-* or the *-t*; there is no *gekauf* or *kauft* meaning 'bought'. (See Bauer 2003:28 and Donalies 2002:33 for arguments to this effect.)

5 See Bauer 2003 for further discussion of the characteristics of inflection and properties of inflectional affixes.

6 Strong verbs are one of the inflectional classes of verbs in German. See section 2.2.4 for further discussion.

7 See sections 2.2.1.2 and 2.2.4.2 for further discussion of umlaut and ablaut.

8 See Bauer 2003:236 and Booij 2005:117–118 for a discussion of some of the differences.

9 See Bauer 2003:210 for a discussion of additional features that can be accounted for in a straightforward way under the WP model.

10 See Corbett 1991 for a survey of the role of gender in language in general as well as information on gender in German. Durrell 2002 presents common generalizations about gender assignment in German. See also Köpcke 1982, Köpcke and Zubin 1984, and Steinmetz 1986.

11 See, for example, Bech 1963, Carstairs 1986, and Wurzel 1994. More recent studies have investigated German noun plurals in the context of developing models of the mental representation of grammar (e.g., Clahsen *et al.* 1992, Marcus *et al.* 1995, Bartke 1998).

12 The first four classes are based on Bech's (1963) four plural classes (Bech does not treat the *s*-plural). There are also words of foreign origin that have unusual plural forms: *das Museum* 'museum', *die Museen*; *der Organismus* 'organism', *die Organismen*; *die Skala* 'scale', *die Skalen*. These plurals are not treated here. See Durrell 2002:21–22 for further examples and discussion of these plural forms.

13 The formalization in this presentation of plural inflection is based on the formalization used by Bauer in his treatment of the inflection of neuter nouns in German (2003:200–209). This presentation differs from Bauer's approach in the number of noun classes recognized and the number and content of the rules used to account for plural inflection.

14 An additional rule that is similar to the rule in (8) is also needed to account for nouns that end in the diminutive suffix -*lein*, since these do not add an affix in the formation of the plural: *Büchlein* 'little book', *Büchlein* 'little books'. This rule is addressed in the exercises to this chapter.

15 There are a few exceptions to this generalization. The words *der Konsul* 'counsel' and *der Ungar* 'Hungarian', for example, do not end in a schwa syllable, but they do not take the variant with schwa to form their plurals: *Konsuln* 'counsels', *Ungarn* 'Hungarians'. These exceptions are addressed in the exercises to this chapter.

16 The doubling of the *s* before the plural ending in nouns with the suffix -*nis* is simply a spelling convention; the doubled consonant indicates that the preceding vowel, *i*, is short.

17 This is the view of the *s*-plural that we present here. See Bauer 2003:208 for a WP formulation of the *s*-plural rule that views -*s* as the default plural affix in German.

18 Although Pinker (1999:222) argues that the *s*-plural is "regular" and serves as the "default," he characterizes this as "acting whenever memory retrieval comes up empty-handed." This view appears not to contradict Durrell's position. Pinker also notes van Dam's (1940) characterization of the *s*-plural as the *Notpluralending*

'emergency plural ending', "which nicely captures the key trait of regularity in the psychological sense."

19 We can provide a formal WP account of the inflection of nouns for case by positing rules like those formulated to account for the inflection of nouns for number. We leave it to the reader to work out the details of such an account.

20 The full form, -es, is used if a noun ends in /s/, /z/, /ts/, /ʃ/, or /stʰ/: des Flusses 'river', des Glases 'glass', des Sitzes 'seat', des Busches 'bush', des Zwistes 'discord'. The shorter form is used, for example, if a word ends in an unstressed syllable: des Wagens 'car', des Königs 'king'. See Dudenredaktion 2001:358–360 for further details regarding the distribution of -es and -s.

21 These nouns are a subset of those masculine nouns that form their plural with the suffix -(e)n (class 2).

22 If a weak masculine noun ends in a schwa syllable (-e or -er) in the nominative singular, the ending is -n for all other cases in the singular; if it does not end in a schwa syllable, the ending is -en. A very small set of masculine nouns, which end in -e and do not denote animate beings, are inflected like the weak masculine nouns, with the one difference that they have the genitive singular ending -ens rather than -en: der Buchstabe 'letter of the alphabet', des Buchstabens; der Name 'name', des Namens.

23 Recall that syncretism is the realization of two (or more) grammatical words by homonymous word forms.

24 There are a number of additional determiners in German that are inflected like dieser. Some of the common ones are aller 'all (the)', jeder 'each', mancher 'some, many a', and welcher 'which'.

25 The determiner irgendein 'some (or other)' is another determiner that is inflected like ein.

26 While the nominative, accusative, and dative forms of the personal pronouns are common in all stylistic levels of the language, the genitive forms occur only in formal situations.

27 Table 2.6 is a modified version of Durrell's personal pronoun table (2002:49).

28 See chapter 7 (7.3) for a brief history and analysis of the German address system.

29 There are no nominative reflexive forms.

30 The form selbst belongs more to the standard language, whereas selber belongs more to everyday speech (Dudenredaktion 2001:767).

31 In formal written German, the relative pronoun welcher is also used. See Durrell 2002:98–99 for details on the forms and use of welcher. German also makes use of uninflected relative pronouns like was 'what' and wo 'where' (Durrell 2002:99–103).

32 An -e- is added to the superlative ending -st when an adjective ends in an alveolar obstruent (-d, -t, -s, etc.), -sk, or -sch. See Dudenredaktion 2005:374 for examples.

33 The form hoch 'high' is used predicatively (e.g., when it is a complement to a noun that is the subject of a verb, as in der Preis ist hoch 'the price is high'); hoh- is used attributively (when it occurs in a noun phrase before the noun it modifies, as in der hohe Preis 'the high price').

34 We can explain the difference in the various forms of gut if we consider their history. The positive form derives historically from the Indo-European root *ghedh-;

the comparative and superlative forms derive from the root *bhad-*. See chapter 5 for a discussion of Indo-European, an ancestor of English as well as German.

35 An exception is the superlative degree form of an adjective, which is always inflected. If used predicatively, it occurs in a prepositional phrase: *Hamburg ist am schönsten* 'Hamburg is the most beautiful.'

36 All forms of the definite article (*der* 'the') are considered to be inflected.

37 The adjective endings are another good example of the syncretism that can be found in German.

38 We can formalize this account within a WP approach to inflectional morphology along the lines suggested by Booij's (2002:43–44) treatment of prenominal adjectives in Dutch: The relevant features of the determiners and nouns in a noun phrase will "percolate" to the top node of the noun phrase and then downward to the prenominal adjective. The particular combination of these features that are associated with an adjectival stem will determine the shape of the affix that is realized on that stem.

39 This use of "citation" form (for noun phrases) is inspired by Dickens's (1983) use of "standard" form (for determiners).

40 The endings of *dieser* (*dies*[ɐ]) can be viewed as phonetically reduced forms of the "endings" of the definite article *der* (d[eːɐ̯]). (Compare the forms of *dies-er* in Table 2.3 with the forms of *d-er* in Table 2.2.) The forms of the definite article *der* thus supply the same gender, case, and number information that the forms of *dieser* supply.

41 According to Durrell (2002:126), the *-es* ending in a phrase like *obiges Adressanten* 'of the above sender' occurs only rarely.

42 I follow Booij (2002:19) and use the categories "participle" and "infinitive" to account for the non-finite forms of verbs in German.

43 Finite verb forms in German are also inflected for tense and mood.

44 The indicative is the unmarked mood, the mood used to express statements of fact and questions. See section 2.2.4.3 for further discussion of mood.

45 We can also say that the present perfect is analytic (expressed using separate words), in comparison to the past, which is synthetic (expressed using a single, inflected word). The terms "analytic" and "synthetic" are also used to refer to languages themselves. Languages in which grammatical distinctions are realized by separate words are known as analytic; those in which grammatical distinctions are realized by inflections are characterized as synthetic. See chapter 5 for further discussion of the terms "analytic" and "synthetic."

46 But see Haspelmath 2000. Haspelmath identifies three different types of periphrastic forms (one of which is exemplified by the periphrastic tense forms in German) and argues that all three types may be included in inflectional paradigms.

47 The epenthesis of *-e-* is in part pronunciation-driven. It allows one to avoid forms like *öffnst* and *öffnt*, which are impossible to pronounce (unless the *n* is syllabic). It also allows the *-t* ending to be articulated following *-d* or *-t*; compare *arbeitet* [aʁbaɪtʰətʰ] 'works' with *arbeitt* [aʁbaɪtʰ]. The Duden grammar (Dudenredaktion 2005:449) argues that epenthesis in forms like *arbeitet* is also governed by the principle of morpheme constancy (*Morphemkonstanz*), which ensures that the verbal stem and ending do not coalesce. Verbs that end in [s] do not lend themselves well to either

explanation (pronunciation; morpheme constancy), since these verbs do not require epenthesis and thus allow the -s- of the second person singular ending -st to coalesce phonetically as well as graphemically with the stem: *reißen* 'to rip', *du reißt* 'you rip'.

48 See Durrell 2002:240–241 for examples of some less common vowel alternations in the present tense of strong verbs.

49 The verb *laden* 'load', which has a vowel change and a root that ends in a -d, does not add -e- before the ending -st in the second person singular. However, it adds a -t rather than no ending in the third person singular: *sie lädt* 'she loads'. The pronunciation of this form is [lɛːtʰ], which would also be the pronunciation if no ending were added.

50 Compare the forms of these verbs with the forms of strong verbs in the past in Table 2.16.

51 Textbooks and grammars use various terms to refer to this form of the verb: past, preterite, imperfect.

52 For further information on the formation of the infinitive and the past participle, see section 2.2.4.4.

53 The verb *senden*, as well as *wenden*, which both belong to the mixed class, are also inflected like weak verbs (e.g., *senden, sendete, gesendet*). However, the difference in inflection is also associated with a difference in meaning (Dudenredaktion 2001).

54 The verb *mögen* 'to like to' has a consonant change as well as a vowel change: *mochte* 'liked to'.

55 Historically, these forms derive from three different Indo-European roots, **bheuə-*, **es-*, and **wes-*.

56 German grammars and textbooks refer to these two sets of forms as *Konjunktiv I* and *Konjunktiv II*.

57 See Durrell 2002 and Dudenredaktion 2005 for additional uses of Subjunctive I and II forms.

58 Present Subjunctive II forms, which are always distinct from present tense indicative forms, are used instead.

59 The paradigm is no longer a purely morphological notion if one admits periphrastic forms as members. Haspelmath argues, however, that it is not possible to separate morphology and syntax neatly anyway.

60 The choice of terminology is a difficult issue when dealing with Subjunctive II forms. The simple forms (which we call "present Subjunctive II" forms) are based on past indicative forms, but have [−past] meaning. The trick is to keep in mind that the "present" portion of the term "present Subjunctive II" reflects meaning, whereas the second portion of the term reflects form (stem of second principal part).

61 The modals *sollen* 'to be to' and *wollen* 'to want to' are an exception; the vowels of their past indicative stems are not umlauted to form the present Subjunctive II. The present Subjunctive II of *wollen*, for example, is *wollte* 'would want to'. Verbs in the mixed class, like *kennen* 'to know' and *brennen* 'to burn', indicate umlaut in present Subjunctive II forms using the orthographic symbol <e> instead of <ä>. For example, the past indicative form of *kennen* is *kannte* 'knew'; the present Subjunctive II is *kennte* 'would know'.

62 The Subjunctive II forms in (61) that are in parentheses are less common (Dudenredaktion 2005:462).

63 See Durrell 2002:328–330 for further details on the use of the *würde*-construction.

64 The symbol ">" means 'becomes' or 'changes to'; "<" means '(comes) from' or '(is) derived from'.

65 We treat only those forms that occur prenominally as adjectives (*ein schreibendes Kind* 'a writing child'). We argue that these adjectival forms are derived from their verbal counterparts via conversion (see section 2.3.4 for further discussion). The verbal forms are created by inflection using the inflectional affix *-end*.

66 Umlaut was brought about by a *-j* suffix that fronted the vowel of the base; this suffix eventually disappeared.

67 The Duden grammar (Dudenredaktion 2005:677) treats these elements as "verb particles," recognizing several particle types, including verb particles with homonym prepositions (*an*, *auf*, *aus*) and verb particles with homonym nouns (*preis*, *stand*). It is not necessary, however, to recognize a new word class, "particle," to account for these forms. They are simply prepositions, nouns, etc. that participate in the formation of phrasal verbs.

68 The prefix *be-* has been the focus of numerous studies. See, for example, Günther 1974, 1987, Eroms 1980, Braun 1982, and Kim 1983.

69 This is similar to the constraint that "deletes" the *ge-* portion of the past participle circumfix of verbs that begin with an unstressed syllable (*gebesucht* 'visited'; *getelefoniert* 'telephoned').

70 Notice that verb forms (infinitives, past forms, etc.) as well as verbal stems can be converted into nouns.

71 Historically, these forms are derived by ablaut and suffixation: *legen* 'to lay (cause to lie)' < *lag-jan*. The *-jan* suffix then brought about umlaut of the root vowel. (See chapter 5 for discussion of umlaut as a phonological process.)

72 Fleischer and Barz (1995), for example, view such words as the product of implicit derivation. As Donalies points out, with words like *Schritt*, implicit derivation would require first the process of ablaut (to produce the past stem) and then the process of conversion.

73 The example *Nudelsaucenrezeptsammler* is from Donalies 2002:64.

74 Various terms that have been used in the literature in addition to "linking element" (*Fugenelement*) are interfix, empty morph, and *Fugenmorphem* 'linking morpheme'. Terms like "morph," "morpheme," and "interfix" (a type of affix) all imply that these segments are associated with meaning, which they are not. The term "linking element" is neutral in this respect.

75 As Wiese notes, linking *-(e)s-* behaves very differently from genitive *-(e)s*. The optionality of schwa in the genitive ending does not extend to the schwa of the linking element: *das Mann-es-alter/*Mann-s-alter* 'manhood'.

76 Old High German is the stage of the German language that was spoken from roughly 750 to 1050 A.D. See chapter 5 for further details.

77 The examples in (g) and (h) are from Donalies 2002:75–77.

78 The infinitive stem is typically used as the verbal portion of verb–noun compounds. Exceptions are finite forms of modal and auxiliary verbs: *die Muss-Vorgaben* 'requirements' (must-guidelines); *der Ist-Zustand* 'the way things are' (is-state) (Donalies 2002:73).

79 Pümpel-Mader *et al.* (1992:43) estimate that one fourth of the adjectival compounds in their corpus are copulative.

80 Many noun-plus-verb and adjective-plus-verb combinations that are identified in the literature as compounds are actually phrasal verbs (the noun or adjective portion can be separated from the verb portion): *standhalten* 'to stand firm' (*er hält stand* 'he's standing firm'); *gesundstoßen* 'to grow fat' (*Investor stößt sich gesund* 'investor grows fat').

81 Words like *Rad* 'bike' (< *Fahrrad* 'bicycle') and *Platte* 'record' (< *Schallplatte*) are considered by some authors to be examples of reductions created by clipping the first portion of a word (e.g., Fleischer and Barz 1995:220). Donalies (2002:145–146), taking Kobler-Trill's lead, views such forms not as true reductions, but as compounds with the modifying portion of the compound left unexpressed.

3   Syntax

3.1   Introduction

The subfield of linguistics known as syntax is concerned with the structure of sentences. It deals with categories of words and the rules for combining these categories to form the sentences of a language. The system of rules that underlies sentence formation in any language allows speakers to produce as well as recognize and comprehend the grammatical sentences of that language. This knowledge of their language (this system of rules) allows speakers to determine whether any given sentence in their language is grammatical without ever having heard the sentence before. For example, speakers of German will characterize the sentence in (1a) as grammatical, that is, as a possible sentence of German. They will characterize the sentence in (1b) as ungrammatical.[1]

(1) a.   *Dort hat ein großer Löwe auf mich gewartet.*
          there has a large lion for me waited
          'A large lion waited for me there.'
     b.   **Ein großer Löwe hat gewartet auf mich dort.*
          a large lion has waited for me there

Various models are used to account for the system of rules that underlie native-speaker competence in any given language. The model that will be used here is a simple version of generative-transformational syntax.[2] Before we look specifically at the syntax of German, we will consider briefly the common categories of words that can be found in the world's languages, the types of phrases that can be formed using these categories, and the ways in which the generation and structure of these phrases can be expressed formally.

The words of a language can be grouped together into a relatively small number of classes, known as syntactic categories. This classification of words takes into account the semantics (meaning), morphological characteristics (e.g., types of inflectional affixes), and syntactic distribution of words in identifying the central syntactic categories. Four important categories, known as lexical categories, are noun (N), verb (V), adjective (A), and preposition (P). An additional lexical category, adverb (Adv), is similar in many ways to the category of adjective. In English, most adverbs are derived from adjectives (*quickly* < *quick*). In German, adverbs and adjectives are often morphologically identical (*Sie fährt gut* 'She drives well'; *Das Foto ist gut* 'The photograph is good'). Languages may also have non-lexical or functional categories, which include determiners (Det), auxiliary verbs (Aux), and conjunctions (Con). Functional categories typically have meanings that are harder to characterize than the meanings of lexical categories. Compare, for example, the meaning of a noun like *Tisch* 'table' with that of a determiner like *das* 'the'.

Sentences are not simply strings of words; they have a hierarchical structure, in which words are grouped together into increasingly larger units. The units that are formed around the lexical categories N, V, A, Adv, and P, for example, are noun phrases (NPs), verb phrases (VPs), adjective phrases (APs), adverb phrases (AdvPs), and prepositional phrases (PPs). The element around which each phrase is built (the obligatory element in the phrase) is the head of that phrase. The head of NP is N, the head of VP is V, and so on.[3] Phrases can consist solely of a head: [NP *Kinder*] 'children'; [AP *sicher*] 'certain'. They can also contain specifiers, words that make the meanings of their heads more precise: [NP *meine Kinder*] 'my children'; [AP *sehr sicher*] 'very certain'. The specifier *meine* (a determiner) in the NP *meine Kinder*, for example, indicates which children are meant; the specifier *sehr* (an adverb) in the AP *sehr sicher* indicates the degree of certainty. Specifiers also have a syntactic function; they typically mark a phrase boundary. In the AP *sehr sicher*, the specifier *sehr* marks the left boundary of the AP. Phrases can also contain complements. Complements in English are attached to the right of their heads, whereas specifiers are attached to the left.[4] For example, in the NP *the backpack on the chair*, which has the noun *backpack* as its head, the specifier, *the*, is to the left of the head; the complement, *on the chair*, is to the right. Complements are themselves phrases. The complement in *the backpack on the chair* is a PP. The complement in the VP *always read the labels* is an NP, *the labels*; in the PP *on the moon* (which does not have a specifier), the complement is also an NP, *the moon*.

The structure of phrases can be represented as tree diagrams. For example, the NP *der Rucksack auf dem Stuhl* 'the backpack on the chair' can be represented as the tree diagram in (2). In (2), the top NP node dominates all the other nodes in the tree:[5] it is higher in the tree than all these nodes and connected to them by continuous downward-branching lines. The top NP node immediately dominates the Det, N, and PP nodes, since no other nodes intervene.[6]

(2)

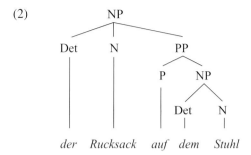

der   Rucksack   auf   dem   Stuhl

Phrase structure can also be represented with labeled bracketing, which pro-vides the same information as a tree, but does so linearly:

(3)   [NP [Det *der*] [N *Rucksack*] [PP [P *auf*] [NP [Det *dem*] [N *Stuhl*]]]]

The well-formed phrases in any given language are generated by phrase structure rules (PS-rules). The phrase structure rule in (4), for example, gener-ates PPs in German like *auf dem Stuhl* 'on the chair' or *vor der Tür* 'in front of the door'.

(4)   PP → P NP

The arrow in this rule can be read as "consists of": a prepositional phrase consists of a preposition followed by a noun phrase.

The lexical entries of the words in a language will contain subcategorization frames, which indicate the kinds of lexical categories and phrases with which these words can occur.[7] For example, the lexical entry of the preposition *auf* 'on' will indicate that it can occur before an NP.

(5)   *auf*: _____ NP

Although PS-rules may not be a necessary component of a grammar, since the information contained in them can potentially come from other sources, includ-ing the subcategorization frames of lexical items, PS-rules are a convenient way of expressing generalizations about the phrase structure of a language.

3.2   Noun phrases

3.2.1   NP structure

The following are examples of typical NPs in German. All have a head N and one or more of the categories Det, AP, and PP, except (h), which only has a head.

(6) a.   *die sehr kleinen Kinder auf dem Spielplatz* 'the very small children on the playground'
     b.   *die sehr kleinen Kinder* 'the very small children'
     c.   *die Kinder auf dem Spielplatz* 'the children on the playground'
     d.   *sehr kleine Kinder auf dem Spielplatz* 'very small children on the playground'
     e.   *die Kinder* 'the children'
     f.   *sehr kleine Kinder* 'very small children'
     g.   *Kinder auf dem Spielplatz* 'children on the playground'
     h.   *Kinder* 'children'

All NPs with the same structure as those above can be generated by the following PS-rule (where parentheses indicate that an element is optional):

(7)   NP → (Det) (AP) N (PP)

In addition to PPs, various types of phrases can serve as the complement of N: NPs, AdvPs, and CPs (complementizer phrases; e.g., relative clauses, *dass*-clauses, etc.).

(8) a.   *der erste Tag **des Monats*** 'the first day of the month'[8]
     b.   *der Baum **dort*** 'the tree there'
     c.   *das Buch, **das er mir geschenkt hat*** 'the book that he has given me'

We can substitute NP, AdvP, or CP for PP in the PS-rule above, which will yield PS-rules that generate NPs like those in (8):

(9) a.   NP → (Det) (AP) N (NP)
     b.   NP → (Det) (AP) N (AdvP)
     c.   NP → (Det) (AP) N (CP)

The four PS-rules in (7) and (9) can be collapsed into one by putting PP, NP, AdvP, and CP in curly brackets, indicating that either PP, NP, AdvP, or CP can optionally follow N:

(10)   NP → (Det) (AP) N $\left(\left\{ \begin{matrix} PP \\ NP \\ AdvP \\ CP \end{matrix} \right\} \right)$

The following rule is also necessary in order to generate NPs that are realized as pronouns (*ich* 'I', *er* 'he', *uns* 'us', etc.).

(11)   NP → Pro

Strictly speaking, pronouns should be called pro-NPs, since they occur in NP rather than N positions. The pronoun *sie* 'she' in (12b), for example, replaces the entire NP *die Mutter* 'the mother' in (12a), not just the N *Mutter*:[9]

(12) a. [NP [Det *die*] [N *Mutter*]] *weckt* [NP [Det *den*] [N *Sohn*]]. 'The mother wakes the son.'

 b. [NP *Sie*] *weckt* [NP *ihn*]. 'She wakes him.'

3.2.2   Case

German NPs are marked for case, which signals the role of the NP in a phrase (e.g., sentential subject, direct object, nominal complement, etc.). Although an entire NP will bear a particular case, it is typically the determiner (or adjective) in the NP rather than the N itself that is inflected for case.

(13)		Singular	Plural
	Nominative	*der Tag* 'the day'	*die Tage* 'the days'
	Accusative	*den Tag*	*die Tage*
	Dative	*dem Tag*	*den Tagen*
	Genitive	*des Tages*	*der Tage*

Recall from the discussion in section 2.2.1.3 that (with the exception of the weak masculine nouns) only singular masculine and neuter nouns in the genitive and plural nouns in the dative are inflected for case.

3.2.2.1 Nominative   The main function of the nominative case is to mark the subject of the finite verb in a clause.

(14)   *Gestern fiel **der Unterricht** aus.*
 'Instruction was cancelled yesterday.'

Because subject NPs in German are marked for case, they are syntactically freer than subjects in English. As the example above shows, German subjects are not required to precede the verb, unlike subjects in English (**Yesterday was cancelled instruction*).

 The nominative is used to mark the NP complement (predicate complement) of copulative verbs like *sein* 'to be', *werden* 'to become', and *bleiben* 'to remain'.[10]

(15)   *Er ist **der beste Bond**.* 'He is the best Bond.'

It is also used to mark NPs in isolation and for NPs used to address people.

(16) a. *Und **dein Mann**? Was sagt der dazu?* 'And your husband? What does he say about it?'

 b. *Guten Morgen, **Herr Schmidt**.* 'Good morning, Mr. Schmidt.'

The sentence in (16a) suggests that nominative is the default case in German. In English, on the other hand, the default case appears to be accusative (non-nominative). If we substitute a pronoun for *your husband* in the English translation of (16a), it appears in the accusative: *And him? What does he say about it?*

3.2.2.2 Accusative   The main function of the accusative case is to mark the direct object of a transitive verb.

(17) a.   *Der Spieler schlägt* **den Ball** *über das Netz.* 'The player hits the ball over the net.'

b.   *Mein Bruder hat mir* **den Tipp** *gegeben.* 'My brother gave me the tip.'

Greetings like *guten Morgen* 'good morning' and wishes like *herzlichen Glückwunsch* 'congratulations', which can be viewed as direct objects of an unexpressed verb like *wünschen* 'to wish', are in the accusative.

Some adjectives (e.g., *los* 'rid of', *gewohnt* 'used to') have NP complements in the accusative:

(18) a.   *Nach Chemotherapie ist sie* **den Krebs** *los.* 'After chemotherapy she's rid of cancer.'

b.   *Sie ist* **den Lärm** *gewohnt.* 'She's used to the noise.'

Various types of NPs used adverbially are in the accusative:

(19) a.   definite expressions of time: *Dort waren wir* **den ganzen Abend**. 'We were there the whole evening.'

b.   measurement: *Meine Tochter ist jetzt* **einen Monat** *alt.* 'My daughter is a month old now.'

NP complements of certain prepositions are in the accusative:

(20) a.   *Millionen arbeiten täglich für* **den Frieden**. 'Millions work daily for peace.'

b.   *Künstler gegen* **den Krieg** 'artists against the war'

3.2.2.3 Dative   The dative case has a broad range of uses.[11] The indirect objects of ditransitive verbs (verbs with two objects) are typically in the dative.

(21) a.   *Ich habe* **meiner Tochter** *einen Hund geschenkt.* 'I have given my daughter a dog.'

b.   *Er zeigte* **seinem Freund** *das neue Fahrrad.* 'He showed his friend the new bike.'

Although the majority of monotransitive verbs (verbs taking a single object) have accusative objects, a number have dative objects.

(22) a. *Ich habe **ihm** nie richtig gedankt.* 'I've never thanked him properly.'
   b. *Wir haben **ihr** gratuliert.* 'We congratulated her.'

The dative is also used to mark an optional NP that is affected in some way (positively or negatively) by the action of the verb.

(23) a. *Er hat **mir** einen Kuchen gebacken.* 'He baked me a cake.'
   b. *Sein Handy is **ihm** kaputt gegangen.* 'His cell phone broke on him.'

The dative can also indicate possession, particularly when it is used with parts of the body. As the following examples show, a possessive determiner is typically used in English when a dative of possession is used in German.

(24) a. *Du hast **ihm** die Hände gewaschen.* 'You washed his hands.'
   b. ***Ihr** schmerzt das Knie.* 'Her knee hurts.'

The dative is the most common case assigned by adjectives to their NP complements (Durrell 2002:137).[12]

(25) a. *Das kommt **mir** bekannt vor.* 'That seems familiar to me.'
   b. *Die Wohnung ist **ihr** zu teuer.* 'The apartment is too expensive for her.'

A number of prepositions govern the dative case.

(26) a. *Mit **dem Weihnachtsgeschäft** ist der deutsche Einzelhandel sehr zufrieden.* 'The German retail industry is very satisfied with the Christmas trade.'
   b. *Nach **dem Krieg** hat sich ihr Leben schnell verändert.* 'After the war, her life changed quickly.'

3.2.2.4 Genitive   One of the main uses of the genitive is to mark NP attributes of nouns. As the following examples show, the genitive is used to express much more than a possessive relationship between the head noun and its NP attribute.

(27) a. *der Wagen **meines Vaters*** 'my father's car'
   b. *der Beginn **der Behandlung*** 'the beginning of the treatment'
   c. *die Tür **der Schlosskirche*** 'the door of the castle church'
   d. *die Untersuchung **seines Todes*** 'the investigation of his death'

A prepositional phrase with *von* 'from' (which governs the dative case) is often used in colloquial speech in place of the genitive.[13]

(28) a.   *der Wagen **von meinem Vater*** 'my father's car'
     b.   *der Beginn **von der Behandlung*** 'the beginning of the treatment'

If genitive nouns are proper names, they may precede the head of an NP (in which case they function as determiners).

(29) a.   ***Theos/sein** bester Freund* 'Theo's/his best friend'
     b.   ***Frau Müllers** neuer Wagen* 'Frau Müller's new car'

A handful of verbs take an object in the genitive case.

(30) a.   *Sechs Patienten bedurften **einer psychiatrischen Behandlung**.* 'Six patients needed psychiatric treatment.'
     b.   *Ich ermangelte nicht gänzlich **der Erfahrung**.* 'I wasn't entirely lacking in experience.'

A small number of set expressions can serve as a genitive NP complement of the verb *sein* 'to be'.

(31) a.   *Ich bin **der Meinung**, dass . . .* 'I am of the opinion that . . .'
     b.   *Er ist **schlechter Laune**.* 'He's in a bad mood.'
     c.   *Die Namen sind **deutschen Ursprungs**.* 'The names are of German origin.'

Some NPs used adverbially are in the genitive. For example, NPs that express indefinite time or have a habitual meaning are in the genitive.

(32) a.   *eines Tages* 'one day'
     b.   *abends* 'in the evening'
     c.   *freitags* 'on Fridays'

Other genitive NPs, with a variety of meanings, are also used adverbially.

(33) a.   *meines Erachtens* 'in my opinion'
     b.   *schweren Herzens* 'with a heavy heart'
     c.   *letzten Endes* 'after all'

A number of adjectives that occur in formal German take genitive NP complements.

(34) a.   *Das ist **höchster Bewunderung** wert.* 'It is worthy of the highest admiration.'
     b.   *Er ist **seines Erfolges** überdrüssig.* 'He is weary of his success.'

A number of prepositions also govern the genitive case. Several are common and are often used with the dative case in colloquial German.

(35) a. *Trotz {des Regens/dem Regen}ist es angenehm warm.* 'In spite of the rain, it's comfortably warm.'

   b. *Wegen {seines Jobs/seinem Job}ziehen wir alle drei bis vier Jahre um.* 'Because of his job, we move every three to four years.'

A large number of genitive prepositions are limited to formal written German typically used in official and commercial contexts (see Durrell 2002:462–464 for further examples).

(36) a. *Er ist dann kraft seines Amtes ein Stellvertreter des Präsidenten.* 'He is then by virtue of his office a proxy of the president.'

   b. *fehlende Akzeptanz seitens der Verbraucher* 'lacking acceptance on the part of consumers'

3.3 Prepositional phrases

A typical PP in German is simply a preposition followed by an NP.

(37) a. *durch die Luft* 'through the air'
   b. *mit einem Kompromiss* 'with a compromise'
   c. *außerhalb des Sonnensystems* 'outside the solar system'

That is, in a typical PP, the head, P, precedes its complement. However, some prepositions can follow their complements, in which case they are more accurately characterized as postpositions.[14]

(38) a. *dem Artikel nach* 'according to the article'
   b. *die Straße entlang* 'along the street'
   c. *der Umwelt zuliebe* 'for the sake of the environment'

Several appear in two parts, which surround the complement, and thus can be identified as circumpositions.

(39) a. *um der Liebe willen* 'for the sake of love'
   b. *von diesem Tag an* 'from this day on'

Although the cover term for prepositions, postpositions, and circumpositions is adposition, the term "preposition" will be used here, since these are the most common in German.

NPs are probably the most common complement in a PP. APs, AdvPs, and PPs, however, can also serve as prepositional complements.

(40) a. *Ich halte ihn* [$_{PP}$ *für* [$_{AP}$ *sehr klug*]]. 'I take him for very intelligent.'
   b. [$_{PP}$ *von* [$_{AdvP}$ *unten*]] 'from below'
   c. [$_{PP}$ *von* [$_{PP}$ *vor dem Krieg*]] 'from before the war'

In English, prepositional complements can be optional.

(41)   *She went in (the shop).*

In German, however, prepositional complements are obligatory.[15]

(42) a.   *Sie ging in den Laden.* 'She went in the shop.'
     b.   **Sie ging in.* 'She went in.'

The NP complement in a PP may be replaced by a pronoun if it refers to an animate being (person or animal); if it refers to a thing, a prepositional adverb must replace the entire PP.

(43) a.   *Er spricht mit {seinem Vorgesetzen/ihm}.* 'He's speaking with {his boss/him}.'
     b.   *Sie arbeitet {an dem Problem/daran}.* 'She's working {on the problem/on it}.'

NPs and AdvPs can function (optionally) as the specifier of P.[16]

(44) a.   *Sie stehen* [PP [NP *einen Schritt*] *vor dem Abgrund*]. 'They're a step from disaster.'
     b.   *Sie stehen vor dem Abgrund.* 'They're facing (standing in front of) disaster.'

(45) a.   [PP [AdvP *Kurz*] *nach seinem Tod*] *erschien sein Hauptwerk.* 'Shortly after his death, his main work appeared.'
     b.   *Nach seinem Tod erschien sein Hauptwerk.* 'After his death, his main work appeared.'

3.4   Adjective phrases

AdvPs occur optionally in APs as specifiers; they precede the adjective they modify.

(46) a.   *eine* [AP [AdvP *besonders schnell*] *laufende*] *Kellnerin*
           a particularly quickly running waitress
     b.   *die* [AP *beste*] *Kellnerin* 'the best waitress'

APs can also contain complements; these occur as the first element in APs that are used attributively.[17] That is, attributive APs are head-final. In the following example, the PP complement occurs first in the AP; it is followed by the AdvP specifier, which immediately precedes the adjective:

(47)   *die* [AP [PP *mit den Ergebnissen*] [AdvP *sehr*] *zufriedenen*] *Fachleute*
        the with the results very satisfied experts (Dudenredaktion 2005:845)

APs used predicatively allow more freedom of word order. NP complements typically precede the adjective in predicative APs.[18]

(48) a. *Das ist* [$_{AP}$ [$_{NP}$ *dem Leser*] *bekannt*]. 'That is known to the reader.'
  b. **Das ist bekannt dem Leser.*

PP complements, on the other hand, can precede or follow the adjective.

(49) a. *Wir sind* [$_{AP}$ [$_{PP}$ *mit dem Weihnachtsgeschäft*] *sehr zufrieden*].
    'We're very satisfied with the Christmas trade.'
  b. *Wir sind* [$_{AP}$ *sehr zufrieden* [$_{PP}$ *mit dem Weihnachtsgeschäft*]].

A striking characteristic of German attributive APs is their potential length and complexity. For example, adjectives derived by conversion from present and past participles can occur in APs along with their (formerly verbal) complements.

(50) a. *das* [$_{AP}$ [$_{NP}$ *sich*] [$_{AdvP}$ *täglich*] *steigernde*] *Verstehen der Sprache*
    the REFL daily increasing understanding of language
  b. *eine* [$_{AP}$ [$_{NP}$ *dem Vater*] [$_{NP}$ *den Vorrang*] *einräumenden*] *Regelung*
    a to-the father the priority giving provision
  c. *ein* [$_{AP}$ [$_{PP}$ *in der amerikanischen und europäischen Wirtschaft*]
    [$_{AdvP}$ *inzwischen*] [$_{AdvP}$ *weit*] *verbreitetes*] *Instrument*
    an in the American and European economy meanwhile widely
    spread instrument

These "extended" APs ("extended adjective constructions"), which are often best translated in English as relative clauses, can be viewed as being derived, in a sense, from relative clauses. Compare the AP in the (b)-example above with the relative clause (CP) in the following example:

(51)   *eine Regelung,* [$_{CP}$ *die dem Vater den Vorrang einräumt*] 'a provision
    that gives priority to the father'

Although extended APs are typically formed using participial adjectives, they also occur with other adjectives, as the example in (47) above demonstrates. Extended APs are typically found in formal written German (e.g., journalistic and scientific prose); they are not common in everyday speech (Durrell 2002:282).[19]

3.5   Adverb phrases

In German, the category of adverb refers to a heterogeneous group of words that are often, but by no means always, used to characterize the action of the verb. In addition to verbs, adverbs can modify adjectives and other adverbs; they can even modify sentences. Different subclasses of adverbs can be identified according to meaning. For example, some of the semantically defined subclasses of adverbs are locational (*hier* 'here', *dorthin* 'thither'), temporal (*jetzt* 'now', *gestern* 'yesterday'), modal (*gern* 'gladly', *brieflich* 'by letter'), and degree adverbs (*sehr* 'very', *fast* 'almost'). Adverbs can also be classified according to their distributional characteristics. Sentence-adverbs, for example, which express the speaker's opinion of the content of a sentence (e.g., *leider* 'unfortunately', *vielleicht* 'maybe'), cannot be questioned, unlike adverbs that modify verbs (e.g., *sofort* 'immediately', *kaum* 'barely').

(52)   *Sie hat das leider/sofort gesehen.* 'She unfortunately/immediately saw that.'

(53) a.   *Wie hat sie das gesehen? *Leider.* 'How did she see that? Unfortunately.'
     b.   *Wann hat sie das gesehen? Sofort.* 'When did she see that? Immediately.'

AdvPs are typically not complex. They can optionally contain adverbs as specifiers.

(54) a.   *Es ging* [AdvP [Adv *sehr*] *schnell*]. 'It went very quickly.'
     b.   *Sie ging* [AdvP *oft*] *ins Kino.* 'She often went to the movies.'

NPs can serve optionally as complements. As the following examples demonstrate, AdvPs are head-final; that is, adverbs are preceded by their complements.

(55) a.   *Fahren Sie* [AdvP [NP *den Berg*] *hinauf*]. 'Drive up the mountain.'
     b.   *Fahren Sie* [AdvP *hinauf*]. 'Drive up.'

(56) a.   *Sie kommen die Treppe herunter.* 'They come down the stairs.'
     b.   *Sie kommen herunter.* 'They come down.'

Not all adverbs can occur in AdvPs with specifiers and/or complements. The subclass to which an adverb belongs plays a role in determining whether and how it can be further modified. Directional adverbs like *hinauf* and *herunter* allow NP complements, but not positional adverbs like *hier* 'here' and *dort* 'there'.

(57) a.   *Wir wohnen hier/dort.* 'We live here/there.'
     b.   **Wir wohnen die Stadt hier/dort.* 'We live the city here/there.'

3.6   Verb phrases

Verbal complements in German can, on the surface, both precede and follow the verb.

(58) a. *Ich **gab** ihm einen Kuss.* 'I gave him a kiss.'
    b. *. . . dass ich ihm einen Kuss **gab**.*
        that I him a kiss gave (' . . . that I gave him a kiss.')

However, the verb precedes its complements only when it is in a finite form in a main clause, as in the (a)-sentence above. If it is in a subordinate clause, as in the (b)-example above, or if it is in a non-finite form (infinitive; past participle), as in the examples below, it follows its complements.

(59) a. *Ich möchte ihm einen Kuss **geben**.* 'I'd like to give him a kiss.'
    b. *Ich habe ihm einen Kuss **gegeben**.* 'I've given him a kiss.'

To account for the order of verbs and their complements, we can assume that VPs in German are head-final in underlying structure (the structure generated by PS-rules).[20] For example, to generate VPs with verbs like *geben* 'to give' (those with two NP complements), we posit the following PS-rule:

(60)   VP → (NP) (NP) V

Because the NP complements in this rule are optional, the rule generates VPs with verbs that require only one NP complement (*putzen* 'to clean': *Ich putze das Zimmer* 'I'm cleaning the room') and those that do not require any (*schlafen* 'to sleep': *Sie schlafen* 'They're sleeping') in addition to those that require two. This rule will yield the correct placement of the verb in relation to its complements in all sentences except main clauses when the verb is finite – the one instance when the verb precedes its complements. A movement rule (see section 3.7.1.2) will account for this particular order of constituents.[21]

The PS-rule above does not exhaust the possible combinations and types of verbal complements. For example, some verbs require PP complements, others require NP and PP complements.

(61) a. *Sie hat* [PP *auf ihre Mutter*] *gewartet.* 'She waited for her mother.'
    b. *Ich habe* [NP *ihn*] [PP *für einen Freund*] *gehalten.* 'I regarded him as a friend.'

A PS-rule like the following will generate the proper VP structure to account for these kinds of verbs:

(62)   VP → (NP) PP V

Additional PS-rules will be needed to generate the structures for other verbal complement patterns.

The subcategorization frame of any given verb will indicate the kind of VP in which it can occur. For example, the subcategorization frame for *geben* 'to give' will indicate that it occurs following two NP complements; the subcategorization frame for *warten* 'to wait for' will indicate that it occurs following a PP complement (and that the P must be *auf* 'for').

(63) a. *geben*: NP NP _____
     b. *warten*: [PP *auf* NP] _____

Not all NPs and PPs that occur with a verb are complements; some are adjuncts, elements that are always optional. The (non-subject) NPs and PPs that occur with a verb like *arbeiten* 'to work', for example, are adjuncts. The NP that occurs with a verb like *verteidigen* 'to defend' and the PP that occurs with a verb like *liegen* 'to be located' are complements.

(64) a. *Sie arbeitet* [NP *jeden Tag*]. 'She works every day.'
     b. *Sie arbeitet* [PP *zu Hause*]. 'She works at home.'
     c. *Sie arbeitet*. 'She works.'

(65) a. *Er verteidigt* [NP *seinen Standpunkt*]. 'He defends his position.'
     b. **Er verteidigt*. 'He defends.'

(66) a. *Das Museum liegt* [PP *am Main*]. 'The museum is located on the Main.'
     b. **Das Museum liegt*. 'The museum is located.'

Although complements are often obligatory, adjuncts never are (as noted above). Verbs are subcategorized with respect to their complements, but not with respect to the optional adjuncts with which they can occur. Typical adjuncts in the VP are PPs and AdvPs that express the time of the verbal action (*am Montag* 'on Monday', *gestern* 'yesterday'), the location of the verbal action (*in der Stadt* 'in the city', *dort* 'there'), the instrument with which the verbal action is carried out (*mit dem Korkenzieher* 'with the corkscrew'), and so on.

Verbal complements typically occur closer to their heads than do adjuncts (*I bought the book yesterday*/**I bought yesterday the book*). If the VP in German is head-final (as is assumed here) and the VP in English is head-initial, we should expect to find the opposite order of adjuncts, complements, and verbs in the two languages.[22] This prediction is borne out, as the following examples (from Kirkwood 1969:87) demonstrate.[23]

(67) a. *Ich habe mich (auf der Sitzung) auf deine Unterstützug verlassen.*
         I have REFL at the meeting on your support relied
     b. *I was relying on your support (at the meeting).*

These sentences contain the optional PP adjuncts *auf der Sitzung* and *at the meeting*, and the obligatory PP complements *auf deine Unterstützung* and *on your support*. In the German sentence we find the order adjunct–complement–head; in English the order is head–complement–adjunct.

3.7   Sentential phrases

3.7.1   Sentences

3.7.1.1 IP and CP   The PS-rules that generate VPs do not account for auxiliary verbs (e.g., finite modal verbs, finite forms of *sein* 'to be' and *haben* 'to have' when used with past participles, finite forms of *werden* 'to become' when used with infinitives, etc.). These PS-rules only account for main verbs. If we compare the distribution of auxiliary verbs with that of main verbs, we see a striking similarity. Finite auxiliary verbs, like finite main verbs, occur as the second constituent in a main (declarative) clause and as the final constituent in a subordinate clause.

(68) a. *Ich **gab** ihm einen Kuss.* 'I gave him a kiss.'
     b. *Ich **habe** ihm einen Kuss gegeben.* 'I have given him a kiss.'

(69) a. *. . . dass ich ihm einen Kuss gab*. ' . . . that I gave him a kiss.'
     b. *. . . dass ich ihm einen Kuss gegeben **habe***. ' . . . that I have given him a kiss.'

Auxiliary verbs are considered to be a realization of the abstract category Infl, short for "inflection" (auxiliary verbs are inflected for tense, among other things). Infl is viewed as the head of a sentence, an Infl-phrase (IP). An IP has an NP (the subject) as its specifier and a VP as its complement. Given the similarity in distribution between main verbs and auxiliary verbs in German, we assume that German IPs, like VPs, are head-final:

(70)   IP → (NP) VP Infl

The Infl position can be occupied by abstract features for finiteness ([+tense], [−tense]) and tense ([+past], [−past]).[24]

(71) a. [$_{IP}$ [$_{NP}$ *ich*] [$_{VP}$ *ihm einen Kuss gab*] [$_{Infl}$ [+tense, +past]]]
         I him a kiss gave
     b. [$_{IP}$ [$_{NP}$ PRO] [$_{VP}$ *ihm einen Kuss zu geben*] [$_{Infl}$ [−tense]]] him a kiss
         to give

It can also be occupied by inflected auxiliary verbs, actual words.

(72)   [$_{IP}$ [$_{NP}$ *ich*] [$_{VP}$ *ihm einen Kuss gegeben*] [$_{Infl}$ *habe*]]
         I him a kiss given have

Notice that the NP in a German IP is optional. This accounts for the fact that some sentences in German do not have subjects. For example, impersonal passives (passives formed from verbs without accusative objects) do not have subjects. The first impersonal passive below does not even exhibit an NP.

Although the second one has an NP, it does not have the characteristics of a subject; it does not bear nominative case and also does not participate in subject–verb agreement.

(73) a. *Nachher wurde getanzt.*
      afterwards was danced 'There was dancing afterwards.'
   b. *Ihnen wurde geholfen.*
      them-DATIVE was helped. 'They were helped.'

Impersonal verbs also lack subject NPs (nominative NPs that control subject-verb agreement).

(74) a. *Mich hungert.*
      me-ACCUSATIVE hungers 'I'm hungry.'
   b. *Mir ist kalt.*
      me-DATIVE is cold 'I'm cold.'

In order to generate subordinate clauses (e.g., *dass*-clauses, indirect questions, relative clauses) – as well as main clauses – we need to establish the structure of CPs, complementizer phrases. Complementizers are words like *dass* 'that', *weil* 'because', *ob* 'whether', and *um* 'in order [to]'. The complementizer constituent (COMP; C) is the head of CP; IP is the complement of C; and Spec will represent the specifier position of CP.

(75)   CP → (Spec) C IP

CPs with complementizers like *dass* 'that' or *um* 'in order' in the C position will have the kind of structure illustrated in the following examples:

(76) a. [CP [C *dass*] [IP *ich ihm einen Kuss gegeben habe*]]
      that I him a kiss given have
   b. [CP [C *um*] [IP PRO *ihm einen Kuss zu geben*]]
      in-order him a kiss to give

Main clauses are also CPs. For example, the main clause in (68b), *Ich habe ihm einen Kuss gegeben* 'I have given him a kiss', has the underlying structure illustrated below:

(77)   [CP [Spec] [C] [IP [NP *ich*] [VP *ihm einen Kuss gegeben*] [Infl *habe*]]]

In the underlying representation of this clause, Spec is empty and so is C. To account for the surface (actual) word order of this clause, we assume two movement rules.[25]

3.7.1.2 Movement rules One movement rule, Verb Movement, moves the finite verb into the C position.[26] The other, Topicalization,[27] moves the subject NP, *ich* 'I', into the Spec position.[28]

(78)   Verb Movement
        Move the finite verb into the C position.

(79)   Topicalization
        Move an XP that is an immediate constituent of IP or VP into the
        Spec position in CP (Spec-CP).[29]

These two rules, applied to the (underlying) structure in (77), yield the following
(surface) structure.

(80)   [$_{CP}$ [$_{Spec}$ [$_{NP}$ *ich*$_2$]] [$_C$ [$_{Infl}$ *habe*$_1$]] [$_{IP}$ [$_{NP}$ t$_2$] [$_{VP}$ *ihm einen Kuss*
        gegeben] [$_{Infl}$ t$_1$]]]

An element that is moved does not change its category. For example, the finite
verb, *habe*, retains its Infl label even though it is moved into the C position.
Movement also does not change the structure created by the PS-rules. The Infl
position occupied by *habe* before movement is not eliminated. Constituents
that are moved leave behind a co-indexed trace (t). This trace indicates the
position in the sentence where the moved element originated. A trace is simply
a formal means of marking the place that a constituent held before it was
moved.

The two movement rules, together with the PS-rules of German, will also
generate main clauses like (68a), *Ich gab ihm einen Kuss* 'I gave him a kiss',
that is, clauses in which a verb precedes its complements. PS-rules generate
the underlying structure in (81a); movement rules yield the surface structure in
(81b).

(81) a. [$_{CP}$ [$_{Spec}$] [$_C$] [$_{IP}$ [$_{NP}$ *ich*] [$_{VP}$ *ihm einen Kuss* [$_V$ *gab*]] [$_{Infl}$ PAST]]]
     b. [$_{CP}$ [$_{Spec}$ [$_{NP}$ *ich*$_2$]] [$_C$ [$_V$ *gab*$_1$]] [$_{IP}$ [$_{NP}$ t$_2$] [$_{VP}$ *ihm einen Kuss* [$_V$ t$_1$]]
         [$_{Infl}$ PAST]]]

Note that it is not only subject NPs that can move into Spec-CP. Object NPs,
PPs, AdvPs – even the VP – can move into this position.

(82) a. ***Seinem Sohn** hat er das Elternhaus geschenkt.*
         his son-DATIVE has he the parents-home given 'To his son he gave
         the parental home.'
     b. ***Mit seiner Frau** hat er einen Ehevertrag geschlossen.*
         with his wife has he a prenuptial-agreement closed 'He entered into
         a prenuptial agreement with his wife.'
     c. ***Sehr oft** haben sie Sommersprossen.*
         very often have they freckles 'Very often they have freckles.'
     d. ***Fußball spielen** wollte er.*
         soccer to-play wanted he 'He wanted to play soccer.'

Wh-phrases (question words/phrases) can also move into Spec-CP, yielding wh-questions.[30]

(83) a. ***Wann** hat sie Geburtstag?*
when has she birthday 'When is her birthday?'

b. ***Welchen Wagen** würdest du empfehlen?*
which car would you recommend 'Which car would you recommend?'

c. ***Mit wem** ist sie verheiratet?*
with whom is she married 'To whom is she married?'

It turns out that portions of the VP that do not appear to be XPs can also occur in the Spec CP position in main clauses. For example, non-finite Vs and non-finite Vs with only one of their complements can occur in this position.

(84) a. ***Gelesen** hat das Buch keiner.*
read has the book-ACCUSATIVE no-one-NOMINATIVE 'No-one has read the book.'

b. ***Ein Buch gegeben** hat die Claudia dem Peter.* (Müller 1998:3)
a book-ACCUSATIVE given has the Claudia-NOMINATIVE the Peter-DATIVE 'Claudia has given Peter a book.'

Müller (1998) argues that these fronted elements are nevertheless XPs, namely, VPs. According to Müller (1998:2), the sentence in (84a), for example, involves two instances of movement. First, the direct object, *das Buch*, is "scrambled" out of the VP and adjoined to IP in front of the subject (leaving behind a trace, t_1).[31] Second, the remnant VP is topicalized (also leaving behind a trace, t_2).[32]

(85)   [$_{VP}$ t_1 *gelesen*]$_2$ *hat* [$_{IP}$ [$_{NP}$ *das Buch*]$_1$ [$_{IP}$ *keiner* t_2]]

In main clauses, which are CPs, Verb Movement is obligatory. C is the head of CP and thus must be filled with some element. If the Spec-CP position is not generated (Spec is optional in CP), this yields a verb-first clause, which can be realized as a yes/no-question, a command, or an exclamation.[33]

(86) a. [$_{CP}$ [$_C$ *hat*$_1$] [$_{IP}$ *keiner das Buch gelesen* t_1]]
has no-one the book read 'Has no-one read the book?'

b. [$_{CP}$ [$_C$ *lies*$_1$] [$_{IP}$ *das Buch* t_1 [$_{Infl}$ IMPERATIVE]]]
read the book 'Read the book!'

c. [$_{CP}$ [$_C$ *hast*$_1$] [$_{IP}$ *du aber einen schönen Hund* t_1 [$_{Infl}$ PRESENT]]]
have you but a lovely dog 'You have a really lovely dog!'

If Spec-CP is generated, it must be filled. There is a constraint in German, the Verb-Second Constraint, which requires main declarative clauses to be verb-second. If there is no element that can be moved to Spec-CP, the place-holder *es* 'it' is inserted in this position. In impersonal passives, for example, which do not have subjects, *es* is inserted into the Spec-CP position to satisfy the Verb-Second Constraint and prevent the sentence from being ungrammatical – if no other element can occupy this position.[34]

(87) a.   **Wurde getanzt.*
          was danced 'Was dancing.'
    b.   *Überall wurde getanzt.*
          everywhere was danced 'There was dancing everywhere.'
    c.   *Es wurde getanzt.*
          it was danced 'There was dancing.'

Sentences with subjects can also contain place-holder *es*. For example, when a subject is new information (and for discourse reasons must occur as far to the right in the sentence as possible), place-holder *es* is inserted so that discourse requirements can be satisfied without violating the Verb-Second Constraint.

(88) a.   *Es war einmal eine Müllerin.*
          it was once a miller's-wife 'Once upon a time there was a miller's wife.'
    b.   *Es kamen die Franzosen.*
          it came the French 'The French came.'

In embedded clauses – CPs embedded in a higher (matrix) clause or phrase – Verb Movement typically does not apply. In embedded CPs that contain an overt complementizer (e.g., *dass* 'that', *ob* 'whether', *um* 'in order', *ohne* 'without'), the finite verb cannot move to C, since this position is already occupied by the complementizer.

(89) a.   [$_{CP}$ [$_C$ *ob*] [$_{IP}$ *ich ihm einen Kuss gegeben habe*]]
          whether I him a kiss given have 'whether I have given him a kiss'
    b.   [$_{CP}$ [$_C$ *um*] [$_{IP}$ PRO *ihm einen Kuss zu geben*]]
          in-order him a kiss to give 'in order to give him a kiss'

In embedded wh-questions, the finite verb also cannot move to C.

(90)   *Sie wusste,* [$_{CP}$ [$_{Spec}$ [$_{NP}$ *welchen Preis*]$_1$] [$_C$ [+wh]] [$_{IP}$ *ich* t$_1$ *dafür zahlen musste*]]
       she knew which price I for-it pay had-to 'She knew what price I had to pay for it.'

In this type of clause, the embedded CP is selected by the matrix verb (the verb *wissen* 'to know' in the example here); it is a complement of the matrix verb. Thus the head of this CP, C, must contain the feature [+wh] in order to satisfy the subcategorization requirements of the matrix verb. The finite verb in the embedded CP cannot move to C because C is already filled with the feature [+wh] (Vikner 1995:49–50). The wh-phrase moves to the Spec-CP position from its underlying position in IP.

Although one might be tempted to rule out Verb Movement in embedded wh-questions by assuming that the wh-phrase moves to C rather than Spec-CP, there are arguments that can be made on theoretical as well as empirical grounds against such an analysis. The following sentences, for example (from Dudenredaktion 2005:878), provide empirical evidence that the moved wh-phrase does not occupy the C position. In these sentences, found in non-standard German, particularly in the southern portion of the German-speaking area, a wh-phrase (*mit wem* 'with whom'; *wann* 'when') can appear in an embedded wh-question together with the complementizer *dass* 'that'. The wh-phrase thus cannot occur in C, which is occupied by *dass*.

(91) a. *Kommt drauf an, mit wem dass sie zu tun haben.*
comes on-it on with whom that they to do have 'It depends who they're dealing with.'

   b. *Jetzt bleibt nur noch abzuwarten, wann dass genügend Software für Palm OS5 verfügbar sein wird.*
now remains only still to-wait when that enough software for Palm OS5 available be will 'Now it just remains to be seen when enough software will be available for the Palm OS5.'

The structure of relative clauses (CPs that are embedded in NPs) is identical to that of embedded wh-questions.

(92)   *der Mantel,* [$_{CP}$ [Spec [$_{NP}$ *den*]$_1$] [$_C$ [+wh]] [$_{IP}$ *ich* t$_1$ *gekauft habe*]]
the coat that I bought have 'the coat that I bought'

The relative pronoun (a wh-element) moves to the Spec-CP position from its underlying position in IP. The finite verb remains in its underlying position; it cannot move to C, which is occupied by the feature [+wh].

Although embedded clauses are typically verb-final clauses (e.g., *dass*-clauses, embedded questions, relative clauses), some verbs select verb-second clauses. For example, verbs like *antworten* 'to answer', *behaupten* 'to claim', and *berichten* 'to report', which select verb-final complements, also select verb-second complements.

(93) a. *Er behauptet, dass er es zur Post gebracht hat.*
he claims that he it to-the post-office brought has 'He claims that he took it to the post office.'

   b. *Er behauptet, er hat es zur Post gebracht.*
'He claims he took it to the post office.'

As the example in the (b)-sentence shows, verb-second clauses in German are not limited to main clauses. Verb Movement and Topicalization apply in embedded verb-second clauses in the same way as they apply in main clauses.

If, as we assume here, verbal complements occur to the left of the verb in underlying structure, we need to account for the position of sentence (CP) complements that occur to the right of the verb in sentences like the following:

(94)   *Ich muss* [VP t₁ *feststellen*], [CP *was geschehen ist*]₁
        I must determine what happened is 'I have to determine what has happened.'

In this example, the CP *was geschehen ist* is the object of the verb *feststellen*. Subject CPs as well as adverbial CPs can also appear in the same position as this object CP.

(95) a. *Mir ist* [IP t₁ *aufgefallen*], [CP *dass viele dasselbe Problem hatten*]₁
         me is struck that many the-same problem had 'It struck me that many had the same problem.'
     b. *Ich werde* [VP *dir* t₁ *helfen*], [CP *sobald ich Zeit habe*]₁ [35]
         I will you help as-soon-as I time have 'I'll help you as soon as I have time.'

Although adverbial CPs are acceptable in their underlying position inside the matrix clause, subject and object CPs are not (Dudenredaktion 2005:1062).

(96) a. ?*Ich muss, was geschehen ist, feststellen.*
     b. ?*Mir ist, dass viele dasselbe Problem hatten, aufgefallen.*
     c. *Ich werde dir, sobald ich Zeit habe, helfen.*

Subject and object CPs must either move to the end of the matrix clause or to the Spec-CP position of the matrix clause (via Topicalization).

(97) a. *Was geschehen ist, muss ich feststellen.*
     b. *Dass viele dasselbe Problem hatten, ist mir aufgefallen.*
     c. *Sobald ich Zeit habe, werde ich dir helfen.*

The movement rule necessary to account for the rightward movement of CPs is Extraposition. Unlike Verb Movement and Topicalization, which are substitution rules, Extraposition is a rule of adjunction. Adjunction is an operation on a phrase structure tree that creates a new position for a moved element. As illustrated in (98), it adjoins this element (YP) to a node, XP, by making a copy of the XP node immediately above it and attaching the moved element to the higher XP node.

(98)   Adjunction

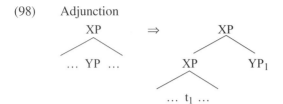

In the case of Extrapostion, an IP-internal CP is adjoined to the CP in which it is contained.

(99)   Extraposition
        Right-adjoin an embedded CP to the CP in which it is contained.

We can illustrate Extraposition with the tree structures in (100).

(100)

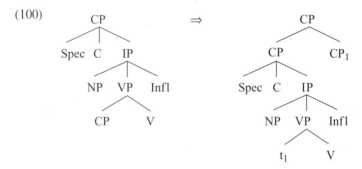

Given the underlying structure in (101a), for example, Extraposition, together with Verb Movement and Topicalization, will yield the surface structure in (101b).[36]

(101) a. [cp [Spec] [c] [IP [NP *ich*] [VP [CP *was geschehen ist*] [V *feststellen*]]
         [Infl *muss*]]]
      b. [CP [CP [Spec [NP *ich₂*]] [C *muss₁*] [IP [NP t₂] [VP t₃ [V *feststellen*]]
         [Infl t₁]]] [CP *was geschehen ist*]₃]
         'I have to determine what has happened.'

Extraposition is not limited to subject, object, and adverbial clauses like those above; it can also apply to relative clauses.

(102) a. [CP [CP *Ich hatte damals einen* [NP *BMW* t₃] *im Auge,*] [CP *den ich kaufen wollte*]₃]

I had then a BMW in-the eye that I buy wanted 'I had at that time a BMW in mind that I wanted to buy.'

b. [CP [CP *Später ist noch* [NP *ein Freund* t₃] *aufgetaucht,*] [CP *der DJ ist*]₃]

later is yet a friend appeared who DJ is 'Later yet another friend appeared, who is a DJ.'

The extraposition of relative clauses is not mandatory; they can remain in the NP with the noun they modify.

(103) a. *Er hat sich* [NP *den Film,* [CP *den er von Anja empfohlen bekam*]], *angesehen.*

he has REFL the film that he by Anja recommended got seen 'He has seen the film that was recommended to him by Anja.'

b. *Einmal hat* [NP *ein Freund,* [CP *der mich häufig besuchte*]], *sogar gesagt, dass . . .*

once has a friend who me often visited actually said that 'Once a friend who often visited me actually said that . . .'

The extraposition of CPs is an optional movement rule. Subject, object, and adverbial CPs, for example, can move to the left via Topicalization instead of to the right via Extraposition. Relative clause CPs do not have to move at all; they can remain inside the NP in which they appear in underlying structure. However, speakers appear to prefer sentences with moved CPs over sentences with CPs that remain in their original position. According to Durrell (2002:492), while both sentences below are acceptable, the second sentence (which contains an embedded CP that has not been moved) is regarded as clumsier.

(104) a. *Ich konnte den Gedanken nicht loswerden,* **dass wir ihn betrogen hatten**.

I could the thought not shed that we him deceived had 'I couldn't get rid of the thought that we had deceived him.'

b. *Ich konnte den Gedanken,* **dass wir ihn betrogen hatten,** *nicht loswerden.*

This preference can help to explain why sentences with subject and object CPs that have not been topicalized or extraposed (see [96a] and [96b]) are less acceptable than sentences with those that have. Why should sentences with adverbial CPs that have not been moved be different (see [96c])? Recall that adverbial CPs are optional elements, unlike subject and object CPs. When these CPs are not moved from their underlying position, they behave much like parenthetical statements, which are also CPs that are not required by the matrix clause. Compare (96c), for example, with the sentence below.

(105)   *Das Kind hat – was doch wirklich erstaunlich ist – den Absturz*
         überlebt. (Dudenredaktion 2005:1063)
         the child has what however really amazing is the fall survived 'The
         child has – and this is really amazing – survived the fall.'

3.7.2   The topological model

A traditional approach to German sentence structure is the topological model, which divides a sentence up into fields. There are three fields (*Felder*): the *Vorfeld* 'first field', the *Mittelfeld* 'central field', and the *Nachfeld* 'final field'. These fields are separated from each other by the sentence bracket (*Satzklammer*). In main clauses, the left bracket (*linke Satzklammer*) contains the finite verb and the right bracket (*rechte Satzklammer*) contains the remaining verb forms. In subordinate clauses, the left bracket contains complementizers, and the right bracket contains all verb forms.

The topological model is useful for mapping out the three types of clauses that can be identified by the position of the finite verb: verb-first, verb-second, and verb-final clauses.

(106)   verb-first clauses
         a. **Hat** *er dich gestern angerufen?* 'Did he call you yesterday?'
         b. **Ruf** *mich mogen an!* 'Call me tomorrow!'

(107)   verb-second clauses
         a. *Er **hat** dich gestern nicht angerufen, weil er dich nicht stören wollte.*
            'He didn't call you yesterday because he didn't want to disturb you.'
         b. *Sobald er Zeit hat, **wird** er dich anrufen.* 'As soon as he has time,
            he'll call you.'

(108)   verb-final clauses
         a. . . . *dass er dich gestern nicht angerufen **hat*** 'that he didn't call you
            yesterday'
         b. . . . *wer dich gestern angerufen **hat*** 'who called you yesterday'

Table 3.1 shows how these three types of clauses fit into the topological model format.

Notice how this view of sentence structure corresponds to the analysis presented above in section 3.7.1. The Vorfeld corresponds to Spec-CP. Like Spec-CP, the Vorfeld is occupied by an XP constituent in main clauses and a wh-word in embedded clauses. The left bracket corresponds to C: it is occupied by the finite verb in main clauses and complementizers in embedded clauses. The Mittelfeld and the right bracket together correspond to IP. The right bracket

Table 3.1 *The topological model of sentence structure*

Vorfeld	Linke Satzklammer	Mittelfeld	Rechte Satzklammer	Nachfeld
	Hat	*er dich gestern*	*angerufen?*	
	Ruf	*mich morgen*	*an!*	
Er	*hat*	*dich gestern nicht*	*angerufen,*	*weil er dich nicht stören wollte.*
Sobald er Zeit hat,	*wird*	*er dich*	*anrufen.*	
	dass	*er dich gestern nicht*	*angerufen hat*	
wer		*dich gestern*	*angerufen hat*	

by itself does not correspond to a single constituent in IP, however. The right bracket contains both non-finite verb forms, which appear in VP, and finite verb forms, which appear in VP (if main verbs) or Infl (if auxiliary verbs). The Nachfeld corresponds to the CP position created by Extraposition. For example, the Nachfeld in the third example in Table 3.1 is filled by the extraposed CP *weil er dich nicht stören wollte* 'because he didn't want to disturb you'. The structure of this CP can be analyzed according to the topological model, as the last line in Table 3.1 shows. Any CP, whether a matrix CP or an embedded CP, can be analyzed according to the topological model.

The use of sentence brackets in the topological model highlights a salient feature of German syntax that sets it apart from English, namely the split verb.

(109) a. *Ich **habe** ihnen einen Brief **geschrieben**.*
    b. *I **have written** them a letter.*

This model also brings out the essentially fixed position of verb forms (these are limited to positions in the sentence brackets), in contrast to the much freer distribution of non-verbal constituents, which can occupy any of the three fields (subject, of course, to pragmatic restrictions, among others).[37] The following section addresses in more detail the freedom of German word order as well as the constraints.

3.7.3   Word order constraints and freedom

Because German has a relatively "strong" case system, with four cases to signal grammatical functions like subject, direct object, and indirect object, word order can be used to a certain extent for pragmatic purposes. In particular, word order can be used to distinguish between theme (old information) and rheme (new information).[38] In languages with pragmatic (as opposed to syntactically determined) word order, the general order of elements is theme before rheme (old information before new information). This pragmatic word order can be seen in the following example from Russian (Comrie 1979:95), where the rheme (*Maksim*, the answer to the question 'Who defends Viktor?') is to the right of the theme (*Viktor*), even though this results in the object preceding the subject.

(110) a. *Któ zaščiščájet Víktora?*
'Who defends Viktor?'
b. *Víktora zaščiščájet Maksím.*
Viktor-THEME defends Maksim-RHEME
'Maksim defends Viktor.'

Word order in German is governed partly by syntactic constraints, partly by semantic and pragmatic considerations. For example, as Lenerz (1977) argues, the unmarked order of non pronominal NPs in German is indirect object (IO) < direct object (DO).[39] This order can be reversed if the indirect object is the rheme, as in (111b).[40]

(111)   *Wem hast du das Geld gegeben?* 'To whom did you give the money?'
a. *Ich habe dem Ka'ssierer das Geld gegeben.*
I have the teller-IO the money-DO given
b. *Ich habe das Geld dem Ka'ssierer gegeben.*
I have the money-DO the teller-IO given

If the direct object precedes the indirect object, and the indirect object is not the rheme, as in (112b), the sentence is not acceptable.

(112)   *Was hast du dem Kassierer gegeben?* 'What did you give to the clerk?'
a. *Ich habe dem Kassierer das 'Geld gegeben.*
I have the teller-IO the money-DO given
b. ?**Ich habe das 'Geld dem Kassierer gegeben.*
I have the money-DO the teller-IO given

In short, the unmarked order, indirect object < direct object, can be overridden only if pragmatic restrictions are not violated. Other unmarked orders of constituents are subject (SUB) < object (when these are all non-pronominal NPs in the Mittelfeld); and direct object < prepositional object (PO).[41]

(113) a. *Ich glaube, dass der Kranke das Medikament braucht.*
I think that the sick-man-SUB the medicine-DO needs.
'I think that the sick man needs the medicine.'
b. *Ich habe ein Bild an den Kleiderhaken gehängt.*
I have a picture-DO on the coat-hook-PO hung
'I hung a picture on the coat hook.'

A semantic restriction on German word order involves the definiteness of an NP. For example, semantically definite objects can appear to the right or left of a sentential adverb; indefinite objects can only appear to the right (Webelhuth 1992:197–198).

(114) a. *weil er wohl das Buch gelesen hat*
　　　　because he probably the book read has
　　　　'because he has probably read the book'
　　　b. *weil er das Buch wohl gelesen hat*

(115) a. *weil er wohl ein Buch gelesen hat*
　　　　because he probably a book read has
　　　　'because he has probably read a book'
　　　b. **weil er ein Buch wohl gelesen hat*

A constraint on German word order that can be viewed as pragmatically driven is the requirement that pronouns occur before non-pronominal NPs. Pronouns are essentially old information; they are used in place of NPs that have already been mentioned in the discourse. This constraint explains the acceptability judgments of the word order in the following examples:

(116) a. **Er hat dem Lehrer es gegeben.*
　　　　he has the teacher-IO it-DO given
　　　　'He gave the teacher it.'
　　　b. *Er hat es dem Lehrer gegeben.*
　　　　he has it-DO the teacher-IO given
　　　　'He gave it to the teacher.'

If all the NPs in a sentence have been pronominalized and appear in the Mittelfeld, they must occur in the sequence nominative (nom.) < accusative (acc.) < dative (dat.).

(117)　　... *dass er es ihr geben wird.*
　　　　that he-nom. it-acc. her-dat. give will
　　　　' ... that he will give it to her.'

This constraint on the order of pronouns can be viewed as essentially syntactically governed. For example, there is no apparent pragmatically driven reason for the order of pronominal objects (DO < IO), which is the opposite of the unmarked order for non-pronominal objects (IO < DO).

If we assume that constituents are generated in the VP in their unmarked positions (e.g., IO < DO, DO < PO, etc.), we need a movement rule to account for surface orders that differ from unmarked orders. This type of movement is known as scrambling. In German, scrambling is to the left, and can be viewed as left-adjunction of a phrase to VP or IP (Webelhuth 1992, Müller 1998, Choi 1999).

(118)   Scrambling
Left-adjoin an XP dominated by VP to VP or IP.

In the example in (85), repeated here for convenience, the object *das Buch* has been scrambled (left-adjoined) to IP.

(85)   [$_{VP}$ t$_1$ *gelesen*]$_2$ *hat* [$_{IP}$ [$_{NP}$ *das Buch*]$_1$ [$_{IP}$ *keiner* t$_2$]]

The scrambled element is subject to certain semantic and pragmatic constraints: the Definiteness Constraint and the Focus Constraint. The Definiteness Constraint requires scrambled elements to be semantically definite. For example, direct objects must be definite in order to be scrambled to the left of sentential adverbs, as the examples in (114) and (115) demonstrate. The Focus Constraint requires that scrambled elements be unfocused (Webelhuth 1992:194). An element is focused if it contains new information (if it is the rheme of an utterance). For example, a direct object cannot be scrambled to the left of an indirect object if it is focused, as in (112b).

Much has been written on the syntactic, semantic, and pragmatic (discourse) factors that influence word order in German. For further details and discussion, see, for example, Boost 1955, Lenerz 1977, Hoberg 1981, Lötscher 1981, Höhle 1982, and Eroms 1986.

3.7.4   *Distribution of pronominal elements*

The distribution of anaphors (reflexive and reciprocal pronouns) in comparison to pronouns has played an important role in the development of generative grammar.[42] The distribution of anaphors and pronouns is particularly interesting because of cross-linguistic variation. For example, whereas Icelandic allows the reflexive *sig* 'himself' to be co-referential with (refer to the same entity as) the subject of the matrix clause in a sentence like (119a), English does not, as (119b) demonstrates.[43]

(119) a. *Pétur*$_i$ *bað Jens um að raka sig*$_i$.
    Peter asked Jens for to shave REFL
    'Peter asked Jens to shave him.'
  b. **Peter*$_i$ *asked Jens to shave himself*$_i$.
    'Peter asked Jens to shave him.'

In the following we will look at some of the salient characteristics of the distribution of anaphors and pronouns in German. To avoid confusion, we will refer to these using the theory-neutral terms "reflexive pronoun" and "non-reflexive pronoun."[44]

In German, a reflexive pronoun is used after a preposition to signal co-reference with the subject of a clause.[45]

(120) a. *Die Frau$_i$ hatte mehrere tausend Dollar bei sich$_i$.*
    'The woman had several thousand dollars on her.'
  b. *Sie$_i$ schloss die Tür leise hinter sich$_i$.*
    'She closed the door quietly behind her/herself.'

Notice the variation in the corresponding English sentences. English requires a non-reflexive pronoun instead of a reflexive in (120a), but allows both in (120b). In some expressions, only a reflexive pronoun is allowed following a preposition when co-reference with the subject is intended.

(121) a. *She$_i$ looked at herself$_i$.*
  b. **She$_i$ looked at her$_i$.*

If a reflexive pronoun occurs in an NP$_j$ it is co-referential with the nearest "subject." The nearest subject in (122a) is the sentential subject; the nearest subject in (122b) is in the NP itself.[46]

(122) a. *Maria$_i$ hat [den Stolz auf sich$_i$] nie verloren.*
    'Maria has never lost pride in herself.'
  b. *Maria$_i$ hat [Peters$_j$ Stolz auf sich$_{j/*i}$] nie verstanden.*
    'Maria has never understood Peter's pride in himself.'

In A.c.I. (Accusative and Infinitive) constructions, a reflexive pronoun refers back to the object of the finite verb; a non-reflexive pronoun refers back to the subject (Durrell 2002:52).

(123) a. *Er ließ seinen Vater$_i$ sich$_i$ in der Villa verstecken.*
    'He had his father hide himself in the villa.'
  b. *Er$_i$ ließ seinen Vater ihn$_i$ in der Villa verstecken.*
    'He had his father hide him in the villa.'

If the reflexive is the object of a preposition in an A.c.I. construction, it refers back to the subject of the finite verb.

(124)   *Er$_i$ ließ mich bei sich$_i$ arbeiten.*
    'He let me work at his place.'

In infinitive clauses with *zu* 'to', the referent of the embedded pronoun (reflexive or non-reflexive) depends on the referent of the understood subject of the infinitive, PRO. The referent of PRO is itself dependent on the type of verb in the matrix clause. If the matrix verb is a verb of subject control (e.g., *versprechen* 'to promise'), PRO is co-referential with the subject of the matrix verb. In an infinitive clause embedded under a verb with subject control, a reflexive pronoun is co-referential with the subject of the matrix verb; a non-reflexive pronoun is co-referential with the object of the matrix verb.[47]

(125) a. *Karl$_i$ versprach Peter$_j$, [PRO$_i$ sich$_i$ zu entschuldigen].*
Karl promised Peter REFL to excuse
(Karl promised to apologize.)
   b. *Karl$_i$ versprach Peter$_j$, [PRO$_i$ ihn$_j$ zu entschuldigen].*
Karl promised Peter him to excuse
(Karl promised to excuse Peter.)

If the matrix verb is a verb of object control (e.g., *bitten* 'to ask'), PRO is co-referential with the object of the matrix verb. In an infinitive clause embedded under a verb with object control, a reflexive pronoun is co-referential with the object of the matrix verb; a non-reflexive pronoun is co-referential with the subject of the matrix verb.

(126) a. *Karl$_i$ bat Peter$_j$, [PRO$_j$ sich$_j$ zu entschuldigen].*
Karl asked Peter REFL to excuse
'Karl asked Peter to apologize.'
(Peter was asked to apologize.)
   b. *Karl$_i$ bat Peter$_j$, [PRO$_j$ ihn$_i$ zu entschuldigen].*
Karl asked Peter him to excuse
'Karl asked Peter to excuse him.'
(Peter was asked to excuse Karl.)

Notice that even though the reflexive in (126a) is referential with *Peter*, the object of the matrix clause, it is co-referential with a subject, namely, the subject of the embedded clause, PRO.

Exercises

1. Indicate the category of each word in the following sentences: N(oun), V(erb), A(djective), Adv(erb), P(reposition), Det(erminer), Aux(iliary), Pro(noun), Con(junction).
   (a) *Welches Auto passt zu Ihrer Persönlichkeit?*
   (b) *Sie haben plötzlich großen Hunger und gehen in ein Lokal.*
   (c) *Ich muss mich leider mit einer Beschwerde an sie wenden.*
   (d) *Ich glaube, dass das das Buch ist, das du brauchst.*
   (e) *Das Haus verfügt über einen schön angelegten Garten.*
2. Draw phrase-structure trees for the following phrases (NP, PP, VP, AP, AdvP):
   (a) *ihr größtes Schiff*
   (b) *erstaunlich klein*
   (c) *mit ihrer Freundin*
   (d) *ein Buch über Tischtennis*
   (e) *auf dem langen Weg nach Italien*

(f) *sehr glücklich über deinen Besuch*

(g) *einen Roman schreiben*

(h) *die Verurteilung des Angeklagten*

(i) *selten lachen*

(j) *bei seinem Freund übernachten*

3. Write one PS-rule for each of the following sets of phrases:

   (a) *durch den Park; für sehr lustig; nach oben; von vor dem Start*

   (b) *zufrieden; sehr zufrieden; mit ihren Mitarbeitern zufrieden; mit ihren Mitarbeitern sehr zufrieden*

   (c) *hinauf; den Berg hinauf; langsam hinauf; den Berg langsam hinauf*

4. Use labeled bracketing to indicate the structure of the following IPs and CPs.

   (a) *meine Schwester den Roman gelesen hat*

   (b) *dass meine Schwester den Roman gelesen hat*

   (c) *Claudia nach Berlin fahren wollte*

   (d) *ob Claudia nach Berlin fahren wollte*

   (e) *ich einen Kaffee trank*

   (f) *während ich einen Kaffee trank*

5. Use labeled bracketing and co-indexed traces to indicate the structure of the following CPs.

   (a) *Meine Schwester hat den Roman gelesen.*

   (b) *Den Roman hat meine Schwester gelesen.*

   (c) *Hat deine Schester den Roman gelesen?*

   (d) *(Sie wollte wissen,) welchen Roman meine Schwester gelesen hat.*

   (e) *(der Roman,) den meine Schwester gelesen hat*

NOTES

1 An asterisk before a sentence indicates that the sentence is unacceptable.

2 Generative-transformational grammar is a version of generative grammar that recognizes a "transformational component" that mediates between the underlying structure of sentences (a more abstract level of representation) and their surface structure (a level that corresponds to the spoken language). The transformational component contains movement rules (transformations) that can change the order of constituents in underlying structure. See section 3.7.1.2 for a discussion of movement rules in German.

3 For the view that noun phrases are headed by determiners and should therefore be referred to as determiner phrases (DPs), see Abney 1987.

4 Cross-linguistically, specifiers do not always occur to the left of their heads – nor do complements always occur to the right. As argued in section 3.6, for example, verbal complements in German occur to the left of their heads.

5 A node is any point connected by a line in a tree diagram.

6 For the sake of simplicity, a relatively flat phrase structure is assumed here. In the NP in (2), for example, the NP node immediately dominates Det, N, and PP. A more

articulated view of phrase structure recognizes a level of structure between the word level and the phrase level. In an NP, this level would be N' (N-bar). In the NP in (2), NP would immediately dominate Det and N', and N' would immediately dominate N and PP.

7 Subcategorization is the assignment of a lexical item to a subclass (subcategory) of the syntactic category to which it belongs, typically with respect to the types of phrases with which it can occur. A subcategorization frame is that part of the lexical entry for a word that indicates the details of its subcategory.

8 Although genitive NP complements are most common, accusative NPs are also possible: *die Sitzung **letzten Montag*** 'the meeting last month' (Dudenredaktion 2005:814).

9 Pronouns cannot be preceded by determiners, which is further evidence that they do not occur in N positions: *[NP [Det *die*] [N *sie*]].

10 A copula or "linking verb" is a verb like English *be* whose main function is to link the subject of a sentence with the predicate. In the sentence *She is a doctor*, the copula *is* links the subject, *she*, with the predicate complement, *a doctor*.

11 In general, NPs that bear the semantic roles of GOAL, SOURCE, and BENEFICIARY are typically in the dative case. This holds for bare NPs; those NPs that are the objects of prepositions bear a wider range of semantic roles. For example, many prepositions assign the dative case to NPs that bear the role LOCATION. See chapter 4, section 4.5, for a discussion of semantic (thematic) roles.

12 See Durrell 2002:137 for a list of frequent adjectives that govern the dative.

13 See Durrell 2002:39–41 for further discussion of the use of *von* instead of the genitive.

14 Some can function both as prepositions and postpositions (*gegenüber dem Hotel/dem Hotel gegenüber* 'across from the hotel').

15 The word *hinein* in a sentence like *Sie ging hinein* 'She went in' is an adverb.

16 The exercises to this chapter address the PS-rules that capture the generalizations about the structure of PPs in German, as well as the structure of APs and AdvPs.

17 An AP is used attributively when it precedes the noun it modifies (*das* [AP *sehr kleine*] *Kind* 'the very small child'). An AP is used predicatively when it follows a copulative verb like *sein* 'to be' (*Das Kind ist* [AP *sehr klein*] 'The child is very small').

18 Only a few adjectives used predicatively (e.g., *treu* 'true to') can precede as well as follow their NP complements: *treu seinen Grundsätzen/seinen Grundsätzen treu* 'true to his principles'.

19 Wipf (2004:144) argues that the use of extended modifiers in spoken German is increasing. He notes that extended modifiers of various lengths are currently used routinely in German newscasts. He also observes that the spontaneous use of extended attributes by interviewees in response to impromptu questions from reporters is rather common.

20 It is widely assumed that German is an SOV language, that is, that German word order is underlyingly Subject–Object–Verb. Classic arguments for this view can be found in Koster 1975 (Koster's arguments for Dutch can be applied to German).

21 A constituent is one or more words that make up a syntactic unit. The NP *einen Kuss* 'a kiss', for example, is a constituent of the sentence *Ich gab ihm einen Kuss* 'I gave him a kiss.'

22 This prediction involves the basic (underlying) word order of the two languages. As discussed in sections 3.7.1 and 3.7.3, various syntactic and pragmatic requirements can alter this basic order.

23 Note that we can explain this difference in word order in English and German if we assume that German VPs are underlyingly head-final. This assumption also allows us to maintain the generalization that complements occur closer to their heads than do adjuncts.

24 PRO in (71b) is the "empty" (understood) subject found in infinitival clauses. In a sentence like *Sie weigerte sich,* PRO *ihm einen Kuss zu geben* 'She refused to give him a kiss', PRO is co-referential with the subject of the main clause in which the infinitival clause is embedded (it refers to the same person to which the pronoun *sie* 'she' refers).

25 Under the model of grammar used here, PS-rules generate the underlying representations of clauses (their underlying structure), and movement rules modify these structures to yield the surface representations of clauses (their surface structure). Surface structure represents the actual word order of a sentence as it is spoken.

26 See Vikner 1995:42–46 for arguments in support of the assumption that the finite verb occupies the C-position in main clauses. For an alternative view – that the finite verb occupies the C-position in main clauses only in inversion constructions (main clauses that are not subject-initial) – see Zwart 1997 (Zwart's arguments for Dutch can be extended to German).

27 The term "topicalization" (which we adopt here) is commonly used to identify this movement rule because the constituent that it moves to the Spec position of CP is often a topic (also "theme"), that is, what the sentence is about. See section 3.7.3 for further discussion of the notion of "theme."

28 Drach (1940) is credited with first formulating the rule that every major clausal constituent (*Satzglied*), with the exception of the finite verb, can occupy the first position in a main clause (Uszkoreit 1987:24).

29 An immediate constituent is one of the parts into which a linguistic unit is immediately divisible. The XPs (phrases) that are immediate constituents of IP are NP and VP. The XPs that are immediate constituents of VP are all the XP adjuncts and complements of the V.

30 If a clause contains a wh-phrase, but that phrase remains in its underlying position and another phrase moves to Spec-CP, this yields an echo question.

    (i) *Ich soll was auf den Tisch legen?* (Dudenredaktion 2005:905)
       I should what on the table lay 'I should put what on the table?'

31 See section 3.7.3 for a discussion of scrambling.

32 See Müller 1998:3–20 for arguments in favor of this analysis.

33 As the example in (86b) demonstrates, abstract features for mood – as well as abstract features for tense – can appear in Infl.

34 The *es* that appears in impersonal passives is not a subject. Whereas subjects in German are not limited to the Spec-CP position, place-holder *es* is: **Überall wurde es getanzt* 'Everywhere was there dancing.'

35 This sentence, as well as the versions below with the adverbial CP in sentence-initial and sentence-internal position, are from Dudenredaktion 2005:1062.

36 Although not indicated in (101b), Topicalization also applies in the embedded CP to move *was* into the Spec position of that CP.

37 Pragmatic restrictions are those that are determined by the context in which an utterance is expressed.

38 The terms "theme" and "rheme" stem from work on the information structure of sentences that was first begun by Mathesius (e.g., 1929) and further advanced by linguists such as Firbas (e.g., 1964) and others in the Prague School of Linguistics. These terms are used here informally as labels for old information and new information.

39 The symbol < can be read here as "before." Lenerz defines the unmarked order of constituents as the one that is not subject to any constraints.

40 The sentences in (111) and (112) and the grammaticality judgments are from Lenerz (1977:43). In (111), the indirect object is the answer to the question posed and hence the rheme (it contains the nucleus of the utterance). In (112), the direct object is the rheme.

41 The sentences in (113) are from Lenerz (1977:68; 101).

42 Binding Theory, a subtheory of the Government and Binding version of generative grammar, deals with the distribution of nominal elements like anaphors and pronouns in relation to their antecedents. For an overview of some of the theoretical issues involved in dealing with the distribution of these elements, see, for example, Harbert 1995.

43 The Icelandic example is cited in Harbert 1995:193.

44 We will not consider the distribution of reciprocal pronouns.

45 Co-reference is indicated by co-indexation. Items that bear the same index are co-referential.

46 The examples in (122) are from Wöllstein-Leisten *et al.* 1997:114.

47 The sentences on which the examples in (125) and (126) are based are from Durrell (2002:53).

4 Semantics

4.1 Introduction

Semantics is the subfield of linguistics that deals with meaning in human language. It is concerned with the meaning of words and sentences. This chapter deals primarily with issues in sentence-level semantics: tense and aspect, modality, and voice. Word-level semantics is treated briefly.

4.2 Lexical semantics

Lexical semantics deals with the meaning of words. One area of lexical semantics involves the semantic relationships among words. The relationships we will discuss here are synonymy, antonymy, hyponymy, and meronymy.

4.2.1 Synonymy

Synonyms are words that have the same meaning in some or all contexts. Examples of synonyms in German are *Anschrift/Adresse* 'address', *Abendessen/Abendbrot* 'supper', *zwei/zwo* 'two', and *erhalten/bekommen/kriegen* 'to get'. Although these pairs (triplets) can be exchanged in most contexts without causing a change in meaning and are therefore synonyms, as the examples below demonstrate, they differ in various non-semantic ways.

(1) a. *Man muss seinen Namen und seine **Anschrift** angeben.*
    b. *Man muss seinen Namen und seine **Adresse** angeben.*
       'One has to give one's name and address.'

For example, *Adresse* is a loanword from French, and *Anschrift* is the "German" word created by Philipp von Zesen to replace it during the seventeenth-century efforts to rid the language of foreign elements.[1] Both words live on in the language today, like many other pairs of synonyms with a similar history. *Abendbrot* is a northern German synonym of Standard German *Abendessen* 'supper'; it exemplifies the existence of regional synonyms. The word *zwo* is the historically feminine form of the word for 'two'; *zwei* is the historically neuter form. *Zwo* is used colloquially instead of *zwei*, especially on the telephone, to ensure clarity (*zwei* has the same diphthong as *eins* and *drei*; *zwo* does not). The verbs for 'get' (like *zwo* and *zwei*) differ in style: *erhalten* is formal, *bekommen* is neutral, and *kriegen* is colloquial.

4.2.2   Antonymy

Antonymy is the relationship of oppositeness. There are various types of opposites. The terms used here to refer to three of the most common types of opposites are complementary pairs (complementaries), gradable antonyms, and converses. Examples of complementary pairs are *lebendig* 'alive' and *tot* 'dead', *richtig* 'correct' and *falsch* 'incorrect', and *offen* 'open' and *geschlossen* 'closed'. The relationship between complementaries is such that the negative of one implies the positive of the other. If a plant, for example, is not *lebendig*, then it is *tot*. If a door is not *offen*, then it is *geschlossen*.

Gradable antonyms are pairs like *groß* 'large' and *klein* 'small', *heiß* 'hot' and *kalt* 'cold', and *lang* 'long' and *kurz* 'short'. Gradable antonyms differ from complementaries in that the negative of one does not necessarily imply the positive of the other. If a house is not *groß*, this does not necessarily mean that it is *klein*. If it is not *heiß* outside, this does not imply that it is *kalt* – it could be *warm*. Gradable antonyms can be viewed as being two terms at the opposite ends of a scale that includes intermediate terms. For example, the scale with *kalt* at one end and *heiß* at the other includes *kühl* 'cool', *lauwarm* 'tepid', and *warm*.

Cruse (1986) identifies at least three different types of gradable antonyms: polar, overlapping, and equipollent antonyms. This distinction is of particular interest because it highlights a difference between two pairs of gradable antonyms in German and English: *gut* and *schlecht* versus *good* and *bad*.

The notions "pseudo-comparative" and "true comparative" are useful in distinguishing Cruse's three subtypes of gradable antonyms. The comparative form *heavier*, for example, does not mean 'heavy to a greater degree', but 'of greater weight', as the following sentences show;[2] it is therefore the pseudo-comparative of *heavy*.[3]

(2) a.   ?*This box is light, but it's heavy.*
    b.   *This box is light, but it's heavier than that one.*

The word *hotter*, however, does mean 'hot to a greater degree'; *hotter* is the true comparative of *hot*:

(3) a.   ?*It's cold today, but it's hot.*
    b.   ?*It's cold today, but it's hotter than yesterday.*

Two antonyms are polar antonyms if there is a pseudo-comparative corresponding to each member of a pair. The antonyms *light* and *heavy* are polar antonyms, as are the antonyms *long* and *short*.

(4) a. *It's long, but it's shorter than the other one.*
   b. *It's short, but it's longer than the other one.*

Antonyms are overlapping antonyms if there is a pseudo-comparative corresponding to one member of the pair, but the other member has a true comparative.

(5) a. *John's a dull lad, but he's cleverer than Bill.*
   b. *?Bill's a clever lad, but he's duller than John.*

Both members of a pair of equipollent antonyms have true comparatives.

(6) a. *?It's hot, but it's colder than yesterday.*
   b. *?It's cold, but it's hotter than yesterday.*

If we compare the terms for 'good' and 'bad' in German with the corresponding terms in English, we see that they do not belong to the same subgroup of antonyms. German *gut* and *schlecht* appear to be polar antonyms.

(7) a. *Es ist gut, aber es ist schlechter als das andere.*
   b. *Es ist schlecht, aber es ist besser als das andere.*

English *good* and *bad*, on the other hand, are overlapping:

(8) a. *?It's good, but it's worse than the other one.*
   b. *It's bad, but it's better than the other one.*

There is a certain amount of variation among speakers in their judgments of gradable antonyms. According to Cruse (1986:219), *good* and *bad* are polar antonyms for a minority of English speakers.[4]

Converses are the final type of opposite to be discussed here. Examples of converses are *Eltern* 'parents' and *Kinder* 'children', *ärmer* 'poorer' and *reicher* 'richer', and *hinter* 'behind' and *vor* 'in front of'. Two terms, A and B, are converses if they relate two entities, x and y, in such a way that x A y is equivalent to y B x. Using this "formula," we can show that *hinter* and *vor*, for example, are converses. In the following sentences, *hinter* and *vor* are A and B; *Stuhl* and *Tisch* are x and y.

(9) a. *Der Stuhl ist hinter dem Tisch.*
      'The chair is behind the table.'
   b. *Der Tisch ist vor dem Stuhl.*
      'The table is in front of the chair.'

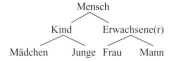

Figure 4.1 Lexical taxonomy for *Mensch*

Because the two sentences are equivalent when we switch the order of *Stuhl* and *Tisch* and substitute *vor* for *hinter*, we can say that *hinter* and *vor* are converses. Other examples of converses are *besitzen* 'to own' and *gehören* 'to belong to', *Arbeitgeber* 'employer' and *Arbeitnehmer* 'employee', and *Ehemann* 'husband' and *Ehefrau* 'wife'.

4.2.3   Hyponymy

Hyponymy is the relation between two lexical items in which the meaning of the first is included in the meaning of the second. Because a *Rose* 'rose' is a type of *Blume* 'flower', we can say that *Rose* is a hyponym of *Blume*. *Blume* is the superordinate (more general) term. *Nelke* 'carnation', like *Rose*, is a hyponym of *Blume*; thus both are co-hyponyms of *Blume*.

Lexical taxonomies like the one illustrated in Figure 4.1 can be constructed on the basis of hyponymy. *Kind* 'child' and *Erwachsene(r)* 'grown-up' are co-hyponyms of *Mensch* 'human being'; *Mädchen* 'girl' and *Junge* 'boy' are co-hyponyms of *Kind*; and so on. If we try to construct similar taxonomies for animals, it is not unusual to find lexical gaps.[5] Whereas the superordinate *Pferd* 'horse' has the female and male co-hyponyms *Stute* 'mare' and *Hengst* 'stallion', the superordinate *Hund* 'dog' only has a uniquely female hyponym, *Hündin* 'bitch'.[6] The superordinate *Katze* 'cat' only has a uniquely male hyponym, *Kater* 'male cat'.[7]

If we compare lexical taxonomies in German with their counterparts in English, differences are not difficult to find. For example, English *hang*, *lay*, *set*, and *stand* are all co-hyponyms of *put*. Although German has the corresponding co-hyponyms *hängen* 'to hang', *legen* 'to lay', *setzen* 'to set', and *stellen* 'to stand', there is no superordinate term corresponding to *put*. In German, one must choose from among the different verbs used to express the notion 'put', whereas in English it is perfectly acceptable to use the general term instead of a more specific one. Hawkins (1986:28–29) argues that German regularly forces a semantic distinction where English uses a broader, undifferentiated term. Some additional examples that support his claim are English *know* versus German *kennen*, *wissen*, and *können*; *leave* versus *lassen*, *verlassen*, *überlassen*, *abreisen, abfahren, gehen*; and *stop* versus *aufhören, halten, stehenbleiben, aufhalten, innehalten, anhalten*, and *unterlassen*.

There are of course examples of lexical differences between German and English where English has several terms that correspond to a single term in German. For example, English *slug* and *snail* correspond to German *Schnecke* (with or without a *Gehäuse* 'shell'). English has *watch* and *clock*, whereas German simply has *Uhr*. If we look at these examples in terms of taxonomies, we can say that English lacks a superordinate term for *slug* and *snail* as well as one for *watch* and *clock*. Although German does have hyponyms for *Schnecke* and *Uhr*, these are expressed differently than in English. In German, the terms *slug* and *snail* are expressed with a phrase rather than with a simple word: *Schnecke ohne Gehäuse* 'slug', *Schnecke mit Gehäuse* 'snail'. Hyponyms for *Uhr* are typically expressed using compound nouns: *Armbanduhr* 'watch', *Wanduhr* 'wall clock', *Tischuhr* 'table clock'.

4.2.4 Meronymy

The term "meronymy" is used to refer to a part–whole relationship. For example, *Finger* 'finger' is a meronym of *Hand* 'hand', since a finger is a part of a hand. *Türklinke* 'doorknob' is a meronym of *Tür* 'door'. *Kinnstütze* 'chinrest', *Saitenhalter* 'tailpiece', *Steg* 'bridge', and *Schnecke* 'scroll' are all meronyms of *Geige* 'violin'.

An interesting example of meronymy in German that has no exact counterpart in English is the relationship between the meronyms *Messer* 'knife', *Gabel* 'fork', and *Löffel* 'spoon' and the term that refers to them collectively, *Besteck* 'eating implements for one person'. Although the term *cutlery* in English might appear to correspond to *Besteck*, it is quite different. As Cruse (1986:97) points out, *cutlery* is a mass noun that refers to eating implements in general. Cruse characterizes *cutlery* as a "quasi-superordinate" of the "quasi-hyponyms" *knife, fork*, and *spoon*. That is, the relationship is one of hyponymy, not meronymy. *Besteck*, on the other hand, is a count noun. It is made up of a *Messer, Gabel*, and *Löffel*, and each of these can be said to be a part of a *Besteck* (Durrell 1988:233).[8]

4.3   Tense and aspect

Tense is a morphosyntactic category used in the description of verbs that allows speakers to locate an event or situation in time. Aspect is a category that allows speakers to express the internal temporal contour of an event or situation in various ways. The perfective aspect views an event or situation as a whole; the imperfective aspect, on the other hand, views the internal structure of an event or situation. There are various types of imperfective aspects: habitual, progressive, etc.[9]

In sections 4.3.1 through 4.3.4, we will look at the semantics of the different tenses in German (present, past, present perfect, etc.). It is important to note that terms like "present tense" and "past tense," when applied to verbs in German, refer to different *forms* of the verb. As we will see, these forms can express more than just tense. For example, they also express notions that can be categorized as aspect. In section 4.3.5, we will consider one aspect, the progressive, and consider the explicit ways in which progressive meaning is expressed in German.

4.3.1   The present tense

The basic meaning of the present tense in German is 'non-past' (Vater 1994:62). The present is thus used to express events that occur (or situations that obtain) at the moment of speaking, those that take place after the moment of speaking (future events), habitual events, and timeless "truths."

(10) a. *Meine Freundin sitzt gerade auf dem Sitz neben mir.*
        'My girlfriend is sitting right now on the seat next to me.'
    b. *Ich fahre morgen nach Berlin.*
        'I'm going to Berlin tomorrow.'
    c. *Sie kauft täglich ein.*
        'She shops daily.'
    d. *Vier minus zwei ist zwei.*
        'Four minus two is two.'

In German, the present tense must be used to express an event that is happening at the moment of speaking – even if the event began in the past. This explains why the present in German can correspond to the perfect in English.

(11) a. *Steffi und Peter **wohnen** seit zwei Jahren in ihrem neuen Heim.*
        Steffi and Peter live since two years in their new home
    b. *Steffi and Peter **have lived** in their new home for two years.*

In the German example, the present is used because Steffi and Peter are still living in their new home. The prepositional phrase *seit zwei Jahren* 'for two years' indicates that they began to live there two years ago.[10]

The use of the present to depict purely past events, the "historic present," is a stylistic device that has the effect of making the past event more alive and immediate. It is used in narrative fiction and newspaper headlines, and is often found in colloquial speech (Durrell 2002:295).

(12) a. *Die Stille ringsum war groß. Und aus einem kleinen Tor, das . . . sich*
plötzlich aufgetan hatte, bricht – ich wähle hier die Gegenwartsform,
weil das Ereignis mir so sehr gegenwärtig ist – etwas Elementares
hervor, rennend, der Stier. (attested; Vater 1994:65)
'The silence all around was huge. And out of a small gate that had
suddenly opened bursts out – I choose here the present because the
event is so present to me – something elemental, running, the bull.'

b. *Radfahrer bedroht Frau*
'Bicyclist threatens woman'

c. *Gestern gehe ich wie immer an den Briefkasten und . . .*
'Yesterday I go like always to the mailbox and . . .'

As Vater notes (1994:65), the present is not required in these situations. It is
clear from the context that a past event is being described. The present can
therefore be used to bring the past event alive for the reader/listener.

The present in German can be translated in various ways into English, as the
following example demonstrates.

(13)   *Sie läuft nach Hause.*
a.   'She runs home.'
b.   'She is running home.'

The present tense in (13a) has two interpretations, both of which are potential
interpretations of the sentence in German. It can describe a one-time event
('She runs home, opens the door, and . . . ') or it can describe a habitual action
('She runs home every day after work'). The German sentence can also have
progressive meaning, as in (13b). Context can help to distinguish between these
different readings of the German present; the addition of adverbial phrases can
also help.

(14) a. *Sie läuft nach Hause, öffnet die Tür . . .*
'She runs home, opens the door . . .'

b. *Sie läuft jeden Tag nach Hause.*
'She runs home every day.'

c. *Sie läuft eben nach Hause.*
'She's running home.'

As these examples demonstrate, present tense verb forms in German can convey
aspectual information as well as tense.

4.3.2   The past and the present perfect

Both the past and the present perfect are used in German to describe past
events.[11]

(15) a. *Er wohnte in Berlin.*
         'He lived in Berlin.'
     b. *Er hat in Berlin gewohnt.*
         'He lived/has lived in Berlin.'

An essential difference between the two is their relationship to the moment of speaking. The past typically does not have a close relationship to the present; the present perfect does. This difference can be made explicit by distinguishing among three different times: event time (E), speech time (S), and reference time (R). Event time is the time at which an event (situation) that is being described takes place; speech time is the time of an utterance; and reference time is the time "from which an event is seen" (Reichenbach 1947:289). Using the notions of event time, speech time, and reference time, Vater (1994:69; see also Erich and Vater 1989) characterizes the past as specifying that event time and reference time are simultaneous (E,R) and that reference time precedes speech time (R < S). The present perfect, on the other hand, specifies that event time precedes reference time (E < R) and that speech time and reference time are simultaneous (S,R). The major difference between the two tenses is the location of reference time. With the past, it is simultaneous with event time (which is prior to speech time); with the present perfect, it is simultaneous with speech time. The following diagrams illustrate this difference concretely.[12]

(16) a. past
              E,R   S

         ⎯⎯⎯⎯|⎯⎯⎯⎯|⟶

     b. present perfect
              E   S,R

         ⎯⎯⎯⎯|⎯⎯⎯⎯|⟶

This characterization of the past and present perfect explains the difference in acceptability between the past and the present perfect in the following example.[13]

(17)   *Ist dein Onkel zu Hause?* 'Is your uncle at home?'
     a. ? – *Nein, leider nicht, er **fuhr** nach Mainz.*
         'No, unfortunately not; he went to Mainz.'
     b. – *Nein, leider nicht, er **ist** nach Mainz **gefahren**.*
         'No, unfortunately not; he's gone to Mainz.'

In this example, reference time is simultaneous with speech time; the question is whether the addressee's uncle is home at the time the question is posed. An answer to this question that uses the past is odd because the reference time for the past is prior to speech time. An answer in the present perfect, however, is completely appropriate because the reference time for the present perfect is identical to speech time.

The past in German is appropriate for narration. It has the effect of transporting the listener/reader to the scene of the past action. A passage from Frisch's *Homo Faber* demonstrates this.

(18)   *Ich erinnere mich genau an jene Zeit, Parteitag in Nürnberg, wir saßen*
         vor dem Radio, Verkündung der deutschen Rassengesetze. Im Grunde
         war es Hanna, die damals nicht heiraten wollte; ich war bereit dazu.
         (Frisch 1957:55)
         'I remember that time exactly, party congress in Nuremberg, we sat in
         front of the radio, announcement of the German race laws. Basically
         it was Hanna who didn't want to get married then; I was ready to.'

In this passage, the narrator, using the present tense, says that he remembers a particular time in the past. He then switches to the past tense to take the reader back to that time.

The past is primarily used in written German, a medium that is typical for narrative discourse. The present perfect, on the other hand, is characteristic of the spoken language. Any past action that is relevant to the moment of speaking will be conveyed in the present perfect, since the reference time for the present perfect is located in the moment of speaking. Of course the past can occur in speech, and the present perfect in the written language. An example of the past in the spoken language can be found in a passage from Dürrenmatt's *Der Richter und sein Henker* ('The judge and his hangman'). In this passage, Inspector Bärlach relates the last pieces of the puzzle as he explains to the murderer exactly how the murder was carried out (Dürrenmatt 1952:140).

(19)   *"Das weitere ist einfach: du fuhrst über Ligerz nach Schernelz und*
         ließest den Wagen im Twannbachwald stehen . . . Bei den Felsen
         wartetest du Schmied ab, er erkannte dich und stoppte verwundert.
         Er öffnete die Türe, und dann hast du ihn getötet. Du hast es mir ja
         selbst erzählt."
         'The rest is simple: you drove via Ligerz to Schernelz and left the
         car in the forest near Twann . . . You waited for Schmied at the
         cliffs, he recognized you and stopped, surprised. He opened the
         door, and then you killed him. You've told me so yourself.'

Bärlach introduces the narrative by using the present tense, "The rest is simple." He then tells the story using the past (*fuhrst* 'drove', *ließest* 'left', etc.) until the moment before the murder was committed. At this point Bärlach switches to the present perfect and says, "and then you killed him" (*und dann **hast** du ihn **getötet***). When Bärlach switches to the present perfect, he ends the narrative and brings the conversation back to the present. By switching to the present perfect, Bärlach looks back at what happened from the perspective of the present. He and the murderer are no longer reliving the events of the past.

Although there are similarities between the past and present perfect in German and the past and present perfect in English, they are by no means identical. Compare the tenses used in the following two English sentences with the tenses used in their German equivalents.

(20) a.   *Anna **went** to France twice.*
          *Anna **ist** zweimal nach Frankreich **gefahren**.*
     b.   *Anna **has been** to France twice.*
          *Anna **ist** schon zweimal nach Frankreich **gefahren**.*

In the English sentence in (20a), the use of the past tense conveys that Anna will not go to France again; it describes a closed-ended situation. The present perfect in the English sentence in (20b) leaves open the possibility that Anna will go to France again sometime; it describes an open-ended situation. The present perfect is used in both of the German sentences, since they are expressed from the perspective of the present. The speaker looks back from the moment of speaking over the past and determines how many times a particular event has occurred. The closed-ended versus open-ended meanings conveyed by the past and present perfect in English are conveyed in German not by a difference in tense, but by simple adverbial phrases (*zweimal* 'twice', *nie* 'never') versus ones that contain *schon* or *noch* (*schon zweimal* 'already twice', *noch nie* 'never yet').

The generalizations related here concerning the past versus the present perfect in German apply to the standard language. In spoken colloquial German, the present perfect is gaining ground over the past. This development is the most pronounced in southern German dialects, where the present perfect serves essentially as the single tense with which to convey past events. Past forms are still used (by some speakers) only with *sein* 'to be', the modal verbs, and some high-frequency main verbs (Dudenredaktion 2005:520).

4.3.3   The future tenses

Vater (1975, 1994) argues that German does not have a future tense. According to Vater, the temporal meaning of so-called "future" forms (*werden* + infinitive/perfect infinitive) is only secondary.[14]

(21) a.   *Er **wird** nicht **heiraten**.* (future)
          'He will not marry.'
     b.   *Jemand **wird** ihn **gesehen haben**.* (future perfect)
          'Someone will have seen him.'

Semantically, *werden* behaves like a modal verb. Like other modals (*können* 'to be able to', *müssen* 'to have to', etc.), *werden* has both inferential and non-inferential meaning. In its inferential use (indicating that what is said is based on inference), *werden* expresses a degree of probability that lies between the degree expressed by *müssen* (strong) and *können* (weak).[15]

(22) a. *Peter muss zuhause sein.* (Peter is definitely at home.)
    b. *Peter wird zuhause sein.* (Peter is probably at home.)
    c. *Peter kann zuhause sein.* (Peter is possibly at home.)

In its non-inferential use, *werden* expresses an intention of the subject or an expectation of the speaker (Vater 1994:74).

(23) a. *"Ich werde alles veranlassen", sagte der Intendant.* (attested; Vater 1975.120)
        '"I will initiate everything," the manager said.'
    b. *Paul wird tun, was ich gesagt habe.* (Vater 1975:124)
        'Paul will do what I said.'

According to Vater, it has a purely temporal future meaning in this use, a meaning that can also be found with other modal verbs:

(24) a. *Es will regnen.*
        it wants to-rain
        'It will rain.'
    b. *Der Tunnel soll 1993 fertig sein.*
        the tunnel should 1993 finished be
        'The tunnel is to be finished in 1993.'

A strong argument for treating the meaning of *werden* as primarily modal rather than temporal comes from its inability to change the temporal meaning of the main verb with which it occurs (Vater 1994:74). In the following examples, the addition of *werden* in the (b)-sentences does not change the present, past, or future reference of the (a)-sentences.

(25) a. *Es ist zehn Uhr.* 'It's ten o'clock.'
    b. *Es wird zehn Uhr sein.* 'It'll be ten o'clock.'

(26) a. *Paul hat das Buch gelesen.* 'Paul has read the book.'
    b. *Paul wird das Buch gelesen haben.* 'Paul will have read the book.'

(27) a. *Paul hat das Buch (bis) morgen gelesen.*
        'Paul will have read the book by tomorrow.'
    b. *Paul wird das Buch (bis) morden gelesen haben.*
        'Paul will have read the book by tomorrow.'

The factor that remains constant in these pairs of sentences is the time reference; the factor that changes is the addition of modality with the addition of *werden*.

Vater (1994:74–75) argues that the strongest evidence against treating the *werden* construction as one that expresses the future comes from the observation that a modality-free future can only be expressed with the present tense.

(28) a.   *Morgen ist Dienstag.* 'Tomorrow is Tuesday.'
     b.   *Morgen wird Dienstag sein.*
          tomorrow will Tuesday be

According to Vater, (28b) is possible only with a modal interpretation: 'Tomorrow is probably Tuesday.'

4.3.4   The past perfect

The past perfect in German locates a past event prior to another point in time in the past.[16] That is, the past perfect specifies that event time is prior to reference time (E < R) which is prior to speech time (R < S). In the following example, reference time is the point at which Hanna arrived at the train station.[17]

(29)   *Kurz nachdem der Zug abgefahren war, kam Hanna am Bahnhof an.*
       'Shortly after the train had left, Hanna arrived at the train station.'

Notice that the past is used to express the event that coincides with reference time. The past perfect has a close relationship to the past, a relationship that mirrors the relationship between the present perfect and the present. As Schipporeit and Strothmann argue (1970:29), there are two parallel sets of tenses in German: the past perfect and the past, the set used in storytelling (*die erzählte Welt* 'the world of narration'); and the present perfect and the present, the set used in conversation (*die besprochene Welt* 'the world of conversation').[18] The sentence in (29) contains the set for narration; the following sentence contains the set used in conversation.

(30)   *Kurz nachdem der Zug abgefahren ist, kommt der Schaffner und kontrolliert die Fahrscheine.*
       'Shortly after the train has left, the conductor comes and checks the tickets.'

There is an additional past perfect tense, the double past perfect (formed with the past perfect of the auxiliary together with the participle of the main verb), which is used to describe an event in the past that happened before an event that one would describe using the past perfect. The following example, with past, past perfect, and double past perfect forms, illustrates the relationship between the tenses.

(31)   ... *aber als sie ankamen, war der Platz leer. Old Firehand*
         untersuchte ihn genau. Es waren inzwischen neue Scharen von
         Tramps angekommen gewesen; die Flüchtigen hatten sich mit diesen
         vereinigt und waren dann ohne Verweilen in nördlicher Richtung
         davongeritten (attested; Litvinov and Radčenko 1998:203)
         ' ... but when they arrived, the place was empty. Old Firehand
         checked it out thoroughly. New hordes of tramps had arrived in the
         meantime; the transients had banded together with them and had then
         ridden away, without lingering, in a northerly direction'

In this example, the arrival of the new hordes of tramps is expressed using the
double past perfect (*waren... angekommen gewesen*) because it precedes the
event of the transients banding together with them and riding away, which is
conveyed using the past perfect (*hatten... vereinigt*; *waren... davongeritten*).
These events are in the past perfect since they precede the point in time when
the place was empty, expressed with a past tense form (*war*).

Those southern German speakers who do not have past forms in their speech
also do not have past perfect forms, since the past perfect is made up of the
past tense form of *haben* 'to have' or *sein* 'to be' and the past participle of the
main verb. In order to express a past event that precedes another past event,
these speakers use the double present perfect (formed with the present perfect
of the auxiliary together with the participle of the main verb).

(32)   *Und wie sie mich gefunden haben,* **bin** *ich* **angefroren gewesen.**
         (attested; Litvinov and Radčenko 1998:203)
         'And when they found me, I had started to freeze.'

Although the double present perfect is not considered "correct" in written
Standard German (Dudenredaktion 2005:521), it can be found in the spoken
language and in written texts that have a spoken character.[19]

4.3.5 Progressive meaning

The German past, like the present (see section 4.3.1), can have progressive as
well as non-progressive meaning.

(33)   *Ich las das Buch.*
   a.   'I read the book.'
   b.   'I was reading the book.'

Although there is no progressive in German that corresponds to the progressive
in English, there are a number of ways to make progressive meaning explicit
in German. For example, the progressive reading of (33) can be made explicit
by saying *im Buch* 'in the book' instead of *das Buch* 'the book'.

(34)   *Ich las im Buch.* 'I was reading the book.'

Other examples of this strategy of using a noun in a prepositional phrase are the following (Durrell 2002:305):

(35) a.   *Meine Mutter ist an der Arbeit.* 'My mother is working.'
     b.   *Ich strickte an einem Pulli.* 'I was knitting a pullover.'

Another strategy is to use adverbs like *eben* 'just' or *gerade* 'just' (Durrell 2002:304).

(36) a.   *Du liest eben den Anfang.* 'You're reading the beginning.'
     b.   *Er schläft gerade hier im Wohnzimmer in seinem Laufgitter.*
        'He's sleeping here in the living room in his playpen.'

In addition to these two strategies, there are two constructions that can be used to make progressive meaning explicit. The first progressive construction is *am/beim/im* + nominalized infinitive + *sein*.

(37) a.   *Während die Piraten noch auf einer Insel **am Feiern sind**, läuft die "Neptun" mit den alten und neuen Herren wieder aus mit Kurs auf Spanien.* (attested; Zifonun *et al.* 1997:1877)
        'While the pirates are still celebrating on an island, the *Neptune* goes out again with the old and new gentlemen, heading for Spain.'
     b.   *Auch Familie Schwarz **ist beim Aufräumen**.* (attested; Krause 2002:45)
        'The Schwarz family is also tidying up.'
     c.   *Einfache Arbeiten im gewerblichen Sektor **sind im Schwinden**.* (attested; Krause 2002:118)
        'Simple jobs in the industrial sector are dwindling.'

This progressive construction is more common in the spoken language than in the written standard (Dudenredaktion 2005:434). Forms with *beim* and *im* are less common than those with *am* (Krause 2002:88).

The second progressive construction is *dabei sein* + infinitival clause. According to Krause (2002:88), this construction is roughly as common as the progressive formed with *am* + *sein*. Literally, the *dabei sein* construction means 'to be in the process of doing something'.

(38)   *Eintöpfe mit viel Geschmack und wenig Fett sind auch denjenigen zu empfehlen, die gerade dabei sind, überflüssige Pfunde loszuwerden.* (attested; Krause 2002:131)
    'Stews with a lot of flavor and little fat can be recommended to those who are getting rid of spare pounds.'

Not all examples of *dabei sein* + infinitival clause, however, have progressive meaning, as the following example demonstrates.

(39)   *Der Kurzstreckenläufer ist gerade dabei, das Ziel zu erreichen.*
         'The sprinter is about to reach the finish line.'

In this example, *dabei sein* means 'to be about to' rather than 'to be in the process of'. The interpretation of *dabei sein* is dependent on the meaning of the infinitive. If the verb is punctual, as in (39), *dabei sein* is interpreted as meaning 'to be about to'. If the verb depicts an action that is punctual but can be iterated, *dabei sein* can have progressive meaning:

(40)   *Sie seien dabei gewesen, Wild zu fotografieren.* (attested; Krause
         2002:201)
         'They were apparently taking pictures of game animals.'

In general, verbs that depict non-iterative punctual actions (e.g., *jemanden erkennen* 'to recognize someone', *etwas finden* 'to find something') are not compatible with the progressive. These verbs are known as "achievements" in Vendler's (1967) classification of verbs. States (e.g., *wissen* 'to know', *ähneln* 'to resemble') are also incompatible with the progressive. The progressive has internal temporal structure (Comrie 1976:24), whereas achievements and states do not. Achievements are instantaneous; they lack duration. Although states have duration, they are stable situations that lack internal structure (Smith 1997:32). The following sentences demonstrate the incompatibility of states with the progressive in German:[20]

(41) a.   **Er ist am Amerikanersein.* 'He is being an American.'
     b.   **Er ist dabei, einen BMW zu besitzen.* 'He is owning a BMW.'

The following attested example with *sterben* 'to die', which is typically classified as an achievement, might appear to be a counterexample to the incompatibility of achievements and the progressive:

(42)   *Die nächste Patientin Nadolnys ist dabei zu sterben.* (attested;
         Krause 2002:200)
         'Nadolny's next patient is dying.'

However, as Krause points out (2002:199), this use of *sterben* focuses on the process that leads to death, not the actual moment of death itself. A verb that describes a process that has an end point (an "accomplishment" in Vendler's typology) is perfectly acceptable in the progressive.

(43)   *Ein Fernsehteam des NDR war gerade dabeigewesen, . . . eine
         Reportage . . . zu drehen, als . . .* (attested; Krause 2002:103)
         'A television team of the NDR had been filming a reportage when . . .'

For further discussion of progressive constructions in German see, for example, Zifonun *et al.* 1997:1877–1880 and Krause 2002.

4.4   Modality and evidentiality

Modality refers to the various means by which speakers express different attitudes towards or degrees of commitment to a proposition (Saeed 2003:135–136).[21] For example, a speaker can use an adverb or a modal verb, as shown in (45), to express a high degree of certainty in the truth of the proposition in (44).

(44)   *Jürgen ist krank.* 'Jürgen is sick.'

(45) a.   *Jürgen ist bestimmt krank.* 'Jürgen is definitely sick.'
    b.   *Jürgen muss krank sein.* 'Jürgen must be sick.'

In this discussion of modality in German, we will focus on the types of modality expressed by the modal verbs. There are many terms in the literature for different types of modality. We will distinguish here between two major types of modality, epistemic and root. We will also look at the evidential use of modals in German, since this is related to the epistemic use. As we will see, the modals in German have a range of meanings. In general, they can be used to express root modality as well as either epistemic modality or evidentiality.

4.4.1   Epistemic modality

Epistemic modality involves the speaker's assumptions or assessment of possibilities and indicates the speaker's degree of confidence in the truth of the proposition expressed (Coates 1983:18). In uttering the sentence in (45b), for example, the speaker uses the modal *müssen* 'to have to' to conclude, on the basis of available evidence, that the proposition *Jürgen ist krank* 'Jürgen is sick' is extremely likely to be true. The verbs *dürfen, können, mögen, müssen,* and *werden* can all be used to express epistemic meaning. They differ in the degree of certainty they express in the likelihood that a proposition is true. They are arranged here from strongest to weakest (Buscha *et al.* 1993:21; Durrell 2002:302).[22]

(46) a.   *Das muss ein Tippfehler sein.*
       'That has to be a typo.'
    b.   *Das dürfte ein Tippfehler sein.*
       'That's probably a typo.'
    c.   *Das wird wohl ein Tippfehler sein.*
       'That's probably a typo.'
    d.   *Das mag ein Tippfehler sein.*
       'That's possibly a typo.'
    e.   *Das kann ein Tippfehler sein.*
       'That may be a typo.'
    f.   *Das könnte ein Tippfehler sein.*
       'That might be a typo.'

When the modal *können* is used in its Subjunctive II form, as in (46f), it expresses a weaker degree of certainty than when it occurs in its indicative form, as in (46e).

When modals are used epistemically, they are subject to various restrictions. The infinitives they occur with are also subject to restrictions. The modal *dürfen*, for example, must occur in a Subjunctive II form in order to be interpreted epistemically. The following sentence, with the indicative form *darf*, can only have a non-epistemic interpretation.

(47) *Er darf zu Hause sein.*
      'He's allowed to be at home.'
      *'He's probably at home.'

Epistemic modals typically occur in the present or past indicative. The most common tense for epistemic modals is the present, but the past is used when necessitated by narration.

(48) *Hinter ihnen stand Elisabeth, und der Herr neben ihr mußte, wenn nicht alles täuschte, Professor Mertens sein, der Chirurg, Annas Mann.*
      'Elisabeth was standing behind them and it seemed that the gentleman next to her had to be Professor Mertens, the surgeon, Anna's husband.' (attested; Laetz 1969:5)

In this example, the past form *musste* is used in keeping with the narrative mode (the verbs *stand* and *täuschte* are past forms).

Epistemic modals can appear in the Subjunctive I.

(49) *Er entsann sich der Stellung, in welcher der Wagen auf der Landstraße gestanden hatte, und schloß daraus, daß die Fahrt in östlicher Richtung . . . gehen müsse.* (attested; Laetz 1969:79)
      'He recalled the position in which the wagon had stood on the country road and concluded that the direction of travel must be eastwards.'

Subjunctive I forms, however (*müsse* in the example here), are used to indicate indirect speech. Subjunctive I plays no role in the interpretation of the modal. In short, epistemic modals occur in the present indicative, unless the conventions of narration or indirect speech require the past or Subjunctive I.[23]

In general, the infinitive that appears with an epistemic modal is stative (it expresses a state or condition). Fullerton (1977) claims that German modals do not naturally have an epistemic reading unless the infinitive is stative. Brünner and Redder (1983:60) claim that an epistemic reading is more likely with stative verbs than with non-statives. Verbs that mean essentially 'to be' are typically found with epistemic modals, for example, *herrschen* 'to prevail', *liegen* 'to be situated', *sein* 'to be', and *vorliegen* 'to be'. The following sentences provide examples of epistemic modals with infinitives that have a variety of stative meanings:[24]

(50) a.   *Ziemlich abgegriffen ist das Blatt. Folglich muß es zu einem oft gelesenen Buch **gehören**.* (attested; Welke 1965:74)
'The page is rather well worn. It must therefore belong to a book that was read often.'

   b.   *Das muss eine Menge **gekostet** haben.* 'That must have cost a lot.'

   c.   *Die Anhöhe hatte eine leichte Senke, und hinter der Senke mußten die Amerikaner **liegen**.* (attested; Laetz 1969:75)
'The hill had a slight valley, and the Americans had to be lying behind the valley.'

   d.   *Er muss es ja **wissen**.* 'He has to know.'

As the (b)-sentence above shows, perfect infinitives (*gekostet haben* 'have cost') can occur with epistemic modals. Although the presence of a perfect infinitive often signals epistemic meaning, root modals may also occur with perfect infinitives.

4.4.2   Root modality

Root modality is essentially non-epistemic modality. Because modals can have both root and epistemic meaning, as the following sentence demonstrates, sentences with modals are potentially ambiguous.

(51)   *Er muss mindestens 1,80 m sein.* (Heine 1995:21)
   a.   root: '(They are looking for a new goalkeeper;) he has to be at least six feet tall.'
   b.   epistemic: '(On the basis of the available evidence I am led to conclude that) he must be at least six feet tall.'

In general, the context of an utterance can help to disambiguate it. The context can be extra-linguistic and involve facts that are known or observable. The context can also be linguistic. As mentioned in the previous section, stative predicates tend to favor epistemic modality. Verbs of action and telic verbs (verbs with a clear end point, e.g., *build a house, write a novel*), on the other hand, are associated primarily with root modality (Heine 1995:25).[25] Tense can also help to disambiguate. Whereas epistemic modality is essentially limited to modals in the present and past, a root interpretation is possible with modals regardless of tense. A modal in the perfect will thus have an unambiguous root interpretation.

(52)   *Auf einmal ist mir schlecht geworden, da **habe** ich schnell*
       *hinausgehen **müssen**, dann bin ich gleich ins Bett gegangen.*
       (attested; Laetz 1969:46)
       'Suddenly it made me ill so I had to go outside quickly, then I went
       to bed immediately.'

Root modality includes a number of different meanings. Some of the core
notions are obligation, permission, and ability.

(53)   obligation
   a. *Fußgänger **müssen** sich an Verkehrsregeln halten.*
       'Pedestrians must observe traffic rules.'
   b. *Ich **soll** nicht so viel fernsehen.* 'I'm not supposed to watch so much TV.'

(54)   permission
   a. *Sie **dürfen** hier parken.* 'You can park here.'
   b. *Du **kannst** herein kommen.* 'You can come in.'

(55)   ability
       *Du **kannst** gut schwimmen.* 'You can swim well.'

Root modality also includes a notion of possibility that is distinct from the
epistemic notion of possibility. Compare the epistemic use of *können* in (46e),
repeated here for convenience, and the root interpretation of *können* in (56).

(46) e. *Das **kann** ein Tippfehler sein.*
        'That may be a typo.'

(56)   possibility
       *Wir **können** heute baden gehen, es ist warm genug.* (Buscha *et al.*
       1993:15)
       'We can go swimming today, it's warm enough.'

Notice that the sentence in (56) contains an action verb (*baden gehen* 'to go
swimming'), the type of verb found with root interpretations of modals, whereas
the epistemic use in (46e) contains the stative verb *sein* 'to be'.
   Another type of root modality is prediction.

(57) a. *Das fehlende Stück der Autobahn **soll** bald gebaut werden.* 'The
        missing piece of highway is to be built soon.'
   b. *Morgen **wird** es bestimmt regnen.* 'Tomorrow it is definitely going to
       rain.'
   c. *Er **will** es nicht zugeben.* 'He won't admit it.' (Durrell 2002:363)

Buscha *et al.* (1993:20), as well as Durrell (2002:363), while acknowledging a
"future" reading of *wollen* in sentences like (56c), also note a difference between

this use of *wollen* and the use of *werden* in the same sentence. According to Buscha *et al.*, for example, *wollen*, unlike werden, retains a weak sense of its basic meaning (volition, intent).

The final type of root modality is volition.

(58)   volition
    a.   *Ich **werde** es heute Abend noch erledigen.* 'I am going to finish it tonight.' (Durrell 2002:301)
    b.   *Er **will** das Buch kaufen.* 'He intends to buy the book.'
    c.   ***Willst** du mir helfen? – Ja, ich **will** dir helfen.*
       'Will you help me? – Yes, I will help you.' (Durrell 2002:363)

The first two examples here clearly express the idea of intent, which can be subsumed under the notion of volition. The third example demonstrates another sense of *wollen*, that of willingness, which can also be included under the notion of volition. According to Durrell (2002:363), *werden* does not convey this sense of willingness.

4.4.3   Evidentiality

Evidentiality is a semantic category that is similar to epistemic modality. Whereas epistemic modality allows a speaker to indicate different attitudes towards the truth of a given proposition, evidentiality allows a speaker to indicate an attitude towards the source of the information in the proposition. According to Palmer (1990:12), "both judgment [epistemic] and evidential systems present speakers with the means of indicating that they do not guarantee the truth of their statements, so that, if the statements proved to be untrue, they cannot be accused of lying." In both English and German, a speaker can use a separate clause or an adverbial expression to indicate the source of an assertion. For example, some of the ways in which one can qualify the assertion *She was sick* (*Sie war krank*) are the following.

(59) a. *I heard that she was sick.*
    b. *I'm told that she was sick.*
    c. *She was supposedly sick.*

(60) a. *Man behauptet, sie sei krank gewesen.* 'They claim she was sick.'
    b. *Sie war angeblich krank.* 'She was supposedly sick.'
    c. *Sie war vermutlich krank.* 'She was presumably sick.'

In German, unlike English, modals can be used with evidential meaning. The evidential use of modals, however, is limited to *sollen* and *wollen*. The modal *sollen* allows a speaker to indicate that the source of the assertion is an entity other than the speaker.

(61)   *Sie soll krank gewesen sein.* 'She was supposedly sick'; 'I hear that
         she was sick'; etc.

The modal *wollen* indicates that the subject itself is the source of the assertion.

(62)   *Sie will krank gewesen sein.* 'She claims to have been sick.'

   The evidential use of modals is sometimes treated as a type of epistemic
modality (Zifonun *et al.* 1997:1897; Dudenredaktion 2005:565, 567). However,
the evidential use of modals differs in several ways from the epistemic use. For
example, evidential modals are not limited to the present or past, like epistemic
modals; they can also occur in the present perfect.

(63) a.   *Er hat krank sein sollen.*
          'They claimed that he was sick.'
   b.   *man hat später wissen wollen, daß* . . . (attested; Leirbukt 1988:178)
          'one later claimed to know that . . .'

This and additional evidence support an analysis that treats the evidential use
of modals as distinct from the epistemic use.[26]

4.5   Thematic roles

Thematic roles are the semantic roles that are played by the entities involved
in a situation or event.[27] For example, in the sentence in (64), *Gabi* plays the
role of AGENT, *Päckchen* is the THEME, and *Post* is the GOAL.

(64)   *Gabi hat das Päckchen zur Post gebracht.*
         'Gabi (AGENT) has taken the package (THEME) to the post office
         (GOAL).'

An AGENT is defined as the entity that initiates or carries out an action and is
capable of volition. A THEME is the entity that is moved by an action or whose
location is described. A GOAL is the entity towards which a motion takes place.
   In (64), the THEME is a direct object. In (65), it is a subject.

(65)   *Gestern bin ich von Berlin nach Müchen geflogen.*
         'Yesterday I (THEME) flew from Berlin (SOURCE) to Munich (GOAL).

The sentence in (65) also contains a SOURCE, the entity from which a motion
takes place, as well as a GOAL.
   Two additional thematic roles are illustrated in (66), INSTRUMENT (the entity
with which an action is performed) and PATIENT (the entity that undergoes an
action and often a change of state).

(66)   *Mit einem Messer hat der Junge seinen Onkel lebensgefährlich*
         verletzt.
         'The boy (AGENT) critically injured his uncle (PATIENT) with a knife
         (INSTRUMENT).'

The three final thematic roles that will be identified here are EXPERIENCER,
PERCEPT, and LOCATION. An EXPERIENCER feels or perceives something; a
PERCEPT is the entity that is felt or perceived.

(67)   *Mein Sohn hat ein Geräusch gehört.*
         'My son (EXPERIENCER) heard a sound (PERCEPT).'

A LOCATION is the place where something is located or takes place.

(68)   *Er lag auf dem Sofa.*
         'He (THEME) lay on the sofa (LOCATION).'

Thematic roles are useful in discussing issues that range from the relationship between the active and the passive (see the discussion in 4.6) to the
identification of verb classes based on systematic linkings between thematic
roles and grammatical relations. For example, the so-called *spray/load* verbs
in English have the characteristic that they can map the THEME or the GOAL
onto the grammatical function of direct object (Foley and Van Valin 1984:57;
Rappaport and Levin 1988:50–53).[28]

(69) a.   *Helen* (AGENT) *sprayed paint* (THEME) *on the wall* (GOAL).
     b.   *Helen* (AGENT) *sprayed the wall* (GOAL) *with paint* (THEME).

The *clear* verbs can map the THEME or the SOURCE onto the direct object.

(70) a.   *Mark* (AGENT) *cleared the dishes* (THEME) *from the table* (SOURCE).
     b.   *Mark* (AGENT) *cleared the table* (SOURCE) *of dishes* (THEME).

In the remainder of this discussion of thematic roles, we will look briefly at the
ways in which German and English map thematic roles onto the grammatical
relation of subject.

Both German and English allow the thematic roles AGENT, EXPERIENCER,
THEME, PATIENT, and GOAL to be realized as subjects.

(71) a.   *Sie ohrfeigte ihn.* 'She (AGENT) slapped him.'
     b.   *She slapped him.*

(72) a.   *Sie sah den Zettel in meiner Hand.* 'She (EXPERIENCER) saw the
          note in my hand.'
     b.   *She saw the note in my hand.*

(73) a. *Ein Apfel fiel vom Baum.* 'An apple (THEME) fell from the tree.'
    b. *An apple fell from the tree.*

(74) a. *Der Schnee zerschmilzt.* 'The snow (PATIENT) is melting.'
    b. *The snow is melting.*

(75) a. *Ich bekam einen Strafzettel.* 'I (GOAL) got a ticket (penalty notice).'
    b. *I got a ticket.*

EXPERIENCER subjects are the norm in English, whereas in German they are often realized as accusative or dative NPs.

(76) a. *I'm freezing.*
    b. *I'm hot.*
    c. *I really like the film.*

(77) a. *Mich friert.*
      me-acc. freezes 'I'm freezing.'
    b. *Mir ist heiß.*
      me-dat. is hot 'I'm hot.'
    c. *Mir gefällt der Film sehr.*
      me-dat. pleases the film very 'I really like the film.'

In addition, whereas English allows the roles INSTRUMENT and LOCATION to function as subjects, German typically does not (König and Nickel 1970:74–76).[29]

(78) a. **Vor einigen Jahren kaufte ein Pfennig zwei bis drei Stecknadeln.*
      'A few years ago a pfennig (INSTRUMENT) would buy two or three pins.'
    b. *A few years ago a pfennig would buy two or three pins.*

(79) a. **Dieses Zelt schläft vier.* 'This tent (LOCATION) sleeps four.'
    b. *This tent sleeps four.*

In German, INSTRUMENT and LOCATION are typically expressed as objects of prepositions.

(80) a. *Mit Geld kann man nicht alles kaufen.* (König and Nickel 1970:75)
      with money (INSTRUMENT) can one not everything buy
      'One can't buy everything with money.'
    b. *In diesem Zelt können vier Personen schlafen.* (König and Nickel 1970:76)
      in this tent (LOCATION) can four people sleep
      'Four people can sleep in this tent.'

In general, subjects in German are semantically more restricted than those in English. However, one of the restrictions noted in Rohdenburg 1974 (a study based on a large corpus and large numbers of native speakers) and discussed further in Hawkins 1986:56–61 may have since become more relaxed. For example, the following sentences (from Hawkins 1986:58) suggest that whereas *hotel* can function as the subject of English *forbid*, *Hotel* cannot function as the subject of its German counterpart, *verbieten* 'to forbid'.

(81) a.   *This hotel forbids dogs.*
     b.   **Dieses Hotel verbietet Hunde.*

An on-line search, however, yields examples like the following:

(82) a.   *Hotel verbietet Kinder* 'Hotel forbids children'
          (www.abendblatt.de [October 13, 2005])
     b.   *Das Hotel verbietet Getränke von außerhalb.*
          'The hotel forbids drinks from outside.'
          (http://reisen.ciao.de [October 4, 2007])

In general, though, it is the case that "non-agentive roles are converted to subjects significantly less frequently [in German] than they are in English, and . . . English subjects correspond regularly to prepositional phrases (or dative-marked NPs) in German" (Hawkins 1986:58).[30]

4.6   Voice

Voice is a grammatical category that allows a speaker to alter the pairing of thematic roles with grammatical functions. A transitive verb like *beschädigen* 'to damage' in the active voice realizes the AGENT as a subject and the PATIENT as a direct object. In the passive voice, the PATIENT is realized as the subject and the AGENT is either left unspecified or appears in a prepositional phrase.

(83) a.   active voice
          Er beschädigte das Auto.
          'He (AGENT) damaged the car (PATIENT).'
     b.   passive voice
          Das Auto wurde (von ihm) beschädigt.
          'The car (PATIENT) was damaged (by him [AGENT]).'

Notice that the passive in German is periphrastic: it is formed using the past participle of a verb (*beschädigt* 'damaged' in the example above) together with a form of *werden* as an auxiliary (*wurde* 'was' in the example above).[31]

In addition to the *werden*-passive, German also has a *sein*-passive. These two passive types differ in their semantics as well as in their auxiliaries.

(84) a. *Das Auto wird gewaschen.* (*werden*-passive)
         'The car is being washed.'
     b. *Das Auto ist gewaschen.* (*sein*-passive)
         'The car is washed.'

The *werden*-passive expresses a process, for example, the process of washing a car, as in (84a). The *sein*-passive expresses a state that results from a process, for example, the state resulting from having been washed, as in (84b).

In German (as well as in English) there is also a middle construction, which has characteristics of both active and passive clauses. The verb in the middle construction in (85c), for example, has active morphology, like the verb in the active sentence in (85a). The subject of the middle, however, is a PATIENT, and is thus similar to the PATIENT subject of the passive in (85b).

(85) a. active
         Er liest das Buch.
         'He (AGENT) reads the book (PATIENT).'
     b. passive
         Das Buch wird gelesen.
         'The book (PATIENT) is being read.'
     c. middle
         Das Buch liest sich leicht.
         the book reads REFL easily 'The book (PATIENT) reads easily.'

In the following section (4.6.1) we will look at the semantics of the passive, and in section 4.6.2 we will look at the semantics of the middle.

4.6.1   The passive

We will focus this discussion on the semantic restrictions on *werden*-passives. There are two types of *werden* passives: personal, which are formed from verbs with accusative objects in the active, as in (86); and impersonal, which are formed from verbs without accusative objects, as in (87).[32]

(86) a. *Er zerreißt den Zettel.*
         he tears-up the note-acc. 'He tears up the note.'
     b. *Der Zettel wird zerrissen.* 'The note is torn up.'

(87) a. *Sie tanzen überall.* 'They're dancing everywhere.'
     b. *Überall wird getanzt.* 'There's dancing everywhere.'

Not all verbs with accusative objects can be used to form personal passives. Those verbs that most closely fit the transitive prototype (action predicates with agentive subjects and totally affected objects) form the most acceptable personal passives (Shannon 1987; Dudenredaktion 2005:553) – verbs like *zerreißen* 'to tear up', for example.[33] Verbs that fit this prototype less closely are less acceptable in the passive. For example, passives formed from verbs like *haben* 'to have', *besitzen* 'to own', *wissen* 'to know', *enthalten* 'to contain', and *umfassen* 'to include', which are stative and have non-agentive subjects, are unacceptable.

(88)   *Ein BMW wird von mir gehabt/besessen.*
        'A BMW is had/owned by me.'

Verbs like *erhalten* 'to receive', *bekommen* 'to receive', and *kriegen* 'to get', which have GOAL subjects, do not form good passives.

(89)   *Ein Brief wurde von ihm erhalten/bekommen.*
        'A letter was received by him.'

Verbs with objects that are a part of the subject's body do not form good passives (Drosdowski 1984:182).

(90) a.   *Er schüttelt den Kopf.* 'He shakes his head.'
     b.   *Der Kopf wird von ihm geschüttelt.* 'The head is shaken by him.'

The (active) subject in (90a) does not fit the transitive prototype because it is not separate from the PATIENT and not unaffected by the action (Shannon 1987); hence the unacceptability of the passive in (90b). A passive with a verb like *schütteln* 'to shake' is perfectly acceptable, however, if the entity being shaken is not a part of the subject's body.

(91)   *Das Fass wurde geschüttelt.* 'The barrel was shaken.'

Intransitive verbs like *tanzen* 'to dance' and *feiern* 'to celebrate' may be used to form passives in German. Although these verbs do not fit the transitive prototype, since they lack objects, they are acceptable in passive clauses because they have highly agentive subjects. Intransitive verbs with subjects that are not agentive do not form good passives. In the following example (from Zifonun *et al.* 1997:1806), the underlying subject is not animate and hence not agentive.

(92) a.   *Der Baum fiel.* 'The tree fell.'
     b.   *Hier wurde (von dem Baum) gefallen.* 'Here it was fallen (by the tree).'

The passive in (93) is acceptable, but only if it is understood as referring to a noise made by a human subject; it cannot refer to noise being made by a door.

(93)   *Es wurde laut gequietscht.* (Zifonun *et al.* 1997:1805)
        'There was loud squeaking.'

The verbs *bluten* 'to bleed' and *sterben* 'to die', typically classified as non-agentive predicates, should not be acceptable in impersonal passives. However, if these verbs are understood as describing volitional acts, as in the following (attested) example, impersonal passives are fine:

(94)   *Für den lieben König und Herrn wird alles getan, wird treulich*
         *gekämpft, **wird** willig **geblutet**, wird freudig in den Tod gegangen,*
         *für ihn **wird** mehr als **gestorben**.* (attested; Curme 1960:338)
         'Everything is done for the beloved king and lord, battle is loyally
         fought, blood is willingly shed, death is entered happily, more is
         done for him than simply die.'

In the example here, *bluten* means something like 'to shed blood for one's country' and *sterben* means 'to die for one's country'.

A prototype approach to the semantics of the passive, as outlined here briefly, is useful for accounting for the interaction of the passive with a range of predicates. It takes into account not just the basic meaning of a verb, but its extended meanings as well. It also focuses on the semantic properties of the arguments that occur with a verb.[34]

4.6.2   The middle

The term "middle voice" has been used in the linguistic literature to refer to a wide range of phenomena, from an inflectional category of the verb in languages like Greek to reflexive verbs in German like *sich verbeugen* 'to bow' and *sich fürchten* 'to be afraid'.[35] We use the term "middle" here to refer to sentences like those in (95b) and (96b). The middle in (95b) is a personal middle, formed from a transitive verb (a verb with an accusative object). The middle in (96b) is impersonal; it is formed from a verb that does not have an accusative object.

(95) a. *Meine Frau fährt dieses Rad.*
         'My wife rides this bike.'
     b. *Dieses Rad fährt sich leicht.*
         this bike rides REFL easily 'This bike rides easily.'

(96) a. *Sie singt im Chor.*
         'She sings in the choir.'
     b. *Es singt sich leichter im Chor.*
         it sings REFL more-easily in-the choir
         'It's easier to sing in the choir.'

Both types of middles contain a reflexive pronoun. The subject of a personal middle corresponds to the (accusative) object of its active counterpart; compare (95a) and (95b). The subject of an impersonal middle is *es* 'it'. It is a syntactic subject, not a place-holder, since it can occur in other than sentence-initial position.

(97)   *Hier sitzt **es** sich bequem.*
        'You can sit here comfortably.'

Both personal and impersonal middles describe a property of some entity. The middle in (95b) describes a property of a particular bicycle; the middle in (96b) describes a property of a location (in the choir). Because they describe properties, middles are stative rather than eventive. Both types of middle also have an understood AGENT. A common paraphrase of the middle is an active clause with *man* 'one' as subject, an overt realization of this understood AGENT. The middle in (96b), for example, can be paraphrased as in (98). Notice that this paraphrase contains the modal verb *kann* 'can', reflecting the modal notion of ability or possibility inherent in middles.

(98)   *Man kann leichter im Chor singen.*
        'One can sing more easily in the choir.'

The understood AGENT in a middle, unlike its passive counterpart, cannot appear overtly.

(99)   **Dieses Rad fährt sich von {einem/den meisten Fahrern} leicht.*
        'This bike rides by {one/most riders} easily.'

In general, middles require an adverbial modifier. This holds for middles in English as well as those in German.

(100)   *This book reads.

(101) a. **Das Buch liest sich.*
         'The book reads.'
      b. **Es singt sich im Chor.*
         'It sings in the choir.'

Goldberg and Ackerman (2001) account for obligatory adverbials in middles by appealing to pragmatics.[36] Without an adverbial modifier, middles like those in (100) and (101) are anomalous because they are uninformative. A middle that asserts that a book can be read, for example, conveys no new information, because it is a given that books can be read. A middle that claims that a book can be read easily, on the other hand, is acceptable, because it conveys new information. As Goldberg and Ackerman point out, their pragmatic explanation for obligatory adverbials allows them to account for middles that are acceptable without such expressions.

(102)   *It snaps/It zips/ It buttons.* (Goldberg and Ackerman 2001:806)

If uttered in response to a question like *How do you close this purse?*, the middles in (102) are acceptable. They are informative in this context because the predicates themselves (*snap*, *zip*, *button*) are informative, and no adverbial is necessary.[37]

Exercises

1. Are the following word pairs examples of synonymy, complementary opposites, gradable antonyms, converses, hyponymy, or meronymy?
   (a) *Eigelb, Hühnerei*; (b) *Verb, Zeitwort*; (c) *volljährig, minderjährig*; (d) *Hund, Schnauzer*; (e) *Verkäufer, Kunde*; (f) *über, unter*; (g) *größer, kleiner*; (h) *Tomate, Paradeiser*; (i) *laut, leise*; (j) *Brille, Brillenglas*

2. What do the present tense forms express in the following examples? Do they describe an event that occurs at the moment of speaking, before the moment of speaking (the historical present), or after the moment of speaking – or do they express habitual events or timeless truths?
   (a) *Sie **liest** jeden Abend zwei Stunden vor dem Einschlafen.*
   (b) *Wir **essen** gleich.*
   (c) *Waschbären **sind** Säugetiere.*
   (d) *Die Maschine **landet** in einer Stunde.*
   (e) *Ich **sitze** gestern in der Mensa, als sich drei Personen an meinen Tisch **setzen**.*
   (f) *Wir **sind** gerade beim Abendessen.*
   (g) *Der Rhein **ist** der größte Nordseezufluss.*
   (h) *Ich **rufe** dich heute Abend an.*

3. Present perfect or past? Translate the following sentences into English.
   (a) *Ich bin schon zweimal nach Österreich geflogen.*
   (b) *Letztes Jahr bin ich zweimal unter 2:09 gelaufen.*
   (c) *Noch nie habe ich ihn ohne seine Einkaufstüte gesehen.*
   (d) *Sie hat nie geraucht.*
   (e) *Das habe ich dir schon hundertmal gesagt.*
   (f) *Sein schönes Büro hat er nur einmal benutzt.*
   (g) *Ich habe schon oft vor Gericht gelogen.*
   (h) *Wir sind auch einmal jung gewesen.*

4. Do the modals in the following sentences express epistemic modality, root modality, or do they express evidential meaning?
   (a) *Ich **kann** nicht verstehen, warum sie so reagiert hat.*
   (b) *Ich **soll** dieses Motorrad angeblich vor 6 Tagen gekauft haben.*
   (c) *Er **dürfte** darüber etwas verstimmt sein.*
   (d) *Der Baum **könnte** krank gewesen sein und daher morsch.*
   (e) *Es wird ihr langsam klar, dass es Sabotage gewesen sein **muss**.*
   (f) *Die Pressefreiheit **darf** nicht missbraucht werden.*

(g) *Wir **sollten** nicht vergessen, dass ein langer und schwieriger Weg vor uns liegt.*

(h) *Er hat für die Tatzeit ein Alibi: Während des Vorfalls **will** er mit einem Freund in einer Diskothek gewesen sein.*

5. Identify the thematic roles of the NPs in bold in the following sentences (AGENT, PATIENT, THEME, EXPERIENCER, INSTRUMENT, LOCATION, GOAL, SOURCE, PERCEPT).

(a) *Ich spüre **den Rauch** in **meiner Lunge**.*

(b) ***Die Katze** sprang von **meinem Arm** direkt auf **Annas**.*

(c) ***Das Kind** hat **ihn** mit **einem Stock** geschlagen.*

(d) ***Ein Frosch** sitzt auf **einem Stein**.*

(e) ***Wir** sehen **einen Schatten** in **der Dunkelheit**.*

(f) *In **Italien** isst **man** **Nudeln** mit **einer Gabel**.*

(g) ***Das Gepäck** wird vom **Hotel** direkt zum **Bahnhof** gebracht.*

(h) ***Die Schokolade** zerschmilzt auf **meiner Zunge**.*

NOTES

1 Philipp von Zesen (1619–1689) was a member of *die Fruchtbringende Gesellschaft*, the first and most famous of the seventeenth-century German language societies that were dedicated to the preservation and purification of the German language. See chapter 5 (section 5.5) for further discussion of these language societies.

2 If *heavier* meant 'heavy to a greater degree', then (2b) would mean 'This box is light, but it's heavy to a greater degree than that one', in which case it would be as marginally acceptable as (2a).

3 The examples in (2) through (6) are from Cruse (1986:207).

4 Durrell notes (1988:236) that his tests with native informants confirm Cruse's claim that *gut* and *schlecht* are polar antonyms, but that Bierwisch's analyses (1967, 1987:230–237) suggest that *gut* and *schlecht* are of the overlapping type, like English *good* and *bad*.

5 Gaps in lexical taxonomies are, in general, not uncommon.

6 The term *Rüde* refers to male dogs, wolves, foxes, and members of the marten family.

7 There is likely a correlation between these hyponymic facts and grammatical gender. For example, the superordinate that has only a uniquely female hyponym is grammatically masculine (*der Hund*); the superordinate that has only a uniquely male hyponym is grammatically feminine (*die Katze*).

8 For additional examples of differences between German and English in the area of lexical semantics, see, for example, Leisi 1967, Hawkins 1986, and Durrell 1988.

9 For further discussion of tense and aspect, see, for example, Comrie 1976, 1985.

10 Schipporeit and Strothmann (1970) classify phrases with *seit* as up-to-now (UTN) phrases, phrases that refer to periods of time that begin somewhere in the past and reach up to the moment of speaking.

11 As mentioned in chapter 2 (section 2.2.4.2), the present perfect is formed using the past participle and *haben* 'to have' or *sein* 'to be' (in the present tense) as an

auxiliary. The choice between *haben* and *sein* is governed by a verb's transitivity and semantics. If a verb is intransitive (if it does not have an accusative object) and it expresses a change of location or state, it will select the auxiliary *sein*; otherwise, it will select *haben*. For example, intransitive *fahren* 'to drive' expresses a change of location and thus selects the auxiliary *sein*: *Er ist nach Berlin gefahren* 'He has driven to Berlin.' Transitive *fahren* 'to drive (someone or something)', on the other hand, selects *haben*: *Er **hat** den Wagen nach Berlin gefahren* 'He has driven the car to Berlin.'

12 Reichenbach (1947:290) uses diagrams like these to characterize the difference between the past and the present perfect in English. They also apply to Vater's characterization of the past and present perfect in German.

13 This example is based on one in Trier 1965:18.

14 The future is formed with a present tense form of the auxiliary *werden* 'to become' and the infinitive of the main verb. The future perfect is formed with a present tense form of *werden* and the perfect infinitive of the main verb. The perfect infinitive is formed using the past participle of the main verb followed by the infinitive of the auxiliary it requires in the perfect tenses, *haben* or *sein*.

15 These and the remaining German examples in this section, but not the glosses or translations, are from Vater 1994:74–75, unless indicated otherwise.

16 The past perfect is formed with a *past* form of *haben* 'to have' or *sein* 'to be' as an auxiliary and the past participle of a verb: *hatte gekauft* 'had bought'; *war gegangen* 'had gone'.

17 Reference time does not have to be stated explicitly; it can be implicit, as in the following example (Vater 1994:71): *Ich hatte geträumt* 'I had dreamed.'

18 See Weinrich 1964 and Weinrich 1993:198–222 for further discussion of *die erzählte Welt* and *die besprochene Welt*.

19 For further discussion of the double present perfect and double past perfect, see Breuer and Dorow 1996, Litvinov and Radčenko 1998, and Dudenredaktion 2005:520–521.

20 The English translations of these sentences are also unacceptable and provide further evidence for the incompatibility of states with the progressive.

21 When modality distinctions are marked on the verb, these distinctions are traditionally called moods (Lyons 1995:327). See chapter 2, section 2.2.4.3 for a discussion of the three moods in German: the indicative, the subjunctive, and the imperative.

22 According to Durrell (2002:302), a sentence with epistemic *dürfen* means much the same as one with the "future" (*werden* + infinitive) and *wohl* 'probably'.

23 See Fagan 2001 for an explanation for why the default form of epistemic modals is essentially the present indicative.

24 See Fagan 1996 for an explanation for the correlation between epistemic modality and stative infinitives.

25 Verbs that are accomplishments (*make a cake*) or achievements (*win the race*) in Vendler's (1967) classification are telic.

26 See Fagan 2001:225–226 for further discussion.

27 There are many terms that are used to refer to these semantic roles: for example, thematic relations (Gruber 1965, Jackendoff 1972), participant roles (Allan 1986), thematic roles (Dowty 1986), and semantic roles (Gívon 1990). We use the term "thematic role," since it is widely used in the literature. There is also a certain

amount of variation in the terms for, definitions of, and number of thematic roles that have been identified. The thematic roles presented here largely those proposed by Jackendoff (1972, 1987).

28 Foley and Van Valin as well as Rappaport and Levin have somewhat different labels for the thematic roles that are identified here as GOAL and SOURCE.

29 The examples in (78) and (79) are from Hawkins 1986:58–59. Many examples in Hawkins's discussion of the semantic range of subjects in German and English are from Rohdenburg 1974.

30 See König and Nickel 1970, Rohdenburg 1974, and Hawkins 1986:57–61 for further discussion and examples.

31 The passive in German has essentially the same range of tenses and moods as the active voice; these are indicated by the different forms of the passive auxiliary. See Durrell 2002:308 for details.

32 If a verb has a dative object (e.g., *helfen* 'to help'), this object stays in the dative case in the passive, and the verb is in its "default" form, the third person singular: *Den Kindern* (dative plural) *wird* (third person singular) *geholfen, traumatische Erfahrungen zu überwinden* 'The children are being helped to overcome traumatic experiences.'

33 See Hopper and Thompson 1980 for a discussion of the properties that contribute to the transitivity of a clause.

34 For further discussion of restrictions on the *werden* passive in German, see, for example, Shannon 1987, Zifonun *et al.* 1997:1796–1808, and Dudenredaktion 2002:553–554.

35 Verbs like *sich verbeugen* 'to bow' and *sich fürchten* 'to be afraid' are inherently reflexive: they must and can only be used with a reflexive pronoun. Compare *Er verbeugte sich* 'He bowed' with *Er verbeugte ihn* 'He bowed him.' This use of the reflexive, while widespread in German, is not common in English.

36 Fagan (1992) argues that adverbial phrases in German and English middles are required by the rule of Middle Formation. Goldberg and Ackerman's (2001) account provides an explanation for the presence of these expressions.

37 For further discussion of middle constructions in German, as well as additional references, see Fagan 1992.

5   History of the language

All languages change over time, phonologically, morphologically, lexically, syntactically, and semantically. The example in (1a), a form of German from the ninth century (Old High German), differs significantly from its modern German glosses and its modern German translation in (1b).

(1) a.   *Fater unsēr, thu in himilom bist, giuuīhit sī namo thīn.* (Braune *et al.* 1994:34)
       Vater unser du in Himmel bist geweiht sei Name dein
    b.   *Vater unser, der du bist im Himmel. Geheiligt werde dein Name.* (Waterman 1991:81)
       father our who you are in-the heaven sacred become your name
       'Our Father who art in heaven, hallowed be thy Name.'

We see differences in pronunciation (*thu/du*),[1] differences in morphology (*himil-om/Himmel*), lexical/semantic differences (*giuuīhit/geheiligt*), and differences in word order (*namo thīn/dein Name*).[2] The various changes that German has undergone throughout its history can be used to identify the major periods of the language that precede the modern period: Old High German (750–1050); Middle High German (1050–1350); Early New High German (1350–1650); and New High German (1650–1900). In this chapter we will look at the important phonological, morphological, and syntactic characteristics of three of these periods, Old High German, Middle High German, and Early New High German, and briefly describe developments in the New High German period. We will begin with a discussion of the prehistoric period and provide a brief description of German's ancestors, Proto-Indo-European and Germanic.

5.1   The prehistoric period

5.1.1   Proto-Indo-European

The languages of the world can be classified genetically, that is, according to their development from common ancestors. The ancestor can be an attested

Table 5.1 *PIE stops (from Fortson 2004:51)*

	labial	dental	palatal	velar	labiovelar
voiceless	p	t	k̂	k	kʷ
voiced	b	d	ĝ	g	gʷ
voiced aspirated	bh	dh	ĝh	gh	gʷh

language (a language with extant texts); or it can be a reconstructed proto-language for which no texts exist. For example, the ancestor of Spanish and French is Latin, a language that is attested. The ancestor of English and German, Germanic, is not attested.[3] Latin and Germanic are themselves genetically related; the ancestor they have in common is Proto-Indo-European (PIE).

PIE is the parent language of the family of languages known as Indo-European (IE), which are spoken in the area extending from (and including) Europe in the west up to the southern portion of the Indian subcontinent in the east. The branches of PIE that still have living descendents are Celtic, Germanic, Italic, Albanian, Greek, Balto-Slavic, Armenian, and Indo-Iranian. Two branches that are now extinct are Anatolian (which includes Hittite) and Tocharian.

A salient characteristic of PIE phonology is its wealth of stops. Table 5.1 lists the fifteen stops reconstructed for PIE.[4] In contrast, PIE has a single fricative, **s*.[5] PIE also had the liquids **l* and **r*, and the nasals **n* and **m*.[6] PIE vowels include short **i*, **e*, **u*, **o*, and **a*, and long **ē*, **ō*, and **ā*. Although the inventory of PIE sounds is more extensive than presented here, this simplified picture is sufficient for tracing the development of PIE sounds in Germanic.

Stress (accent) is an important feature of PIE phonology that ultimately plays an important/defining role in the history of German. As noted in chapter 1, a stressed syllable is one that is perceived as more prominent than neighboring syllables. A language that uses greater volume as the primary signal of promi-nence is a stress-accent language. One that primarily uses a difference in pitch to signal prominence is a pitch-accent language. It is generally agreed that PIE was a pitch-accent language. Vedic Sanskrit and Ancient Greek, for exam-ple, are among the IE languages with pitch-accent systems (Fortson 2004:62). Another feature of the accent in PIE is its mobility; the position of the accent was not predictable, and it could be used to signal differences in meaning. Compare Russian *pisál* 'he was writing' with *písal* 'he was peeing' (Fortson 2004:62).

PIE was a highly inflected language; words typically consisted of a root (which carried the basic meaning of the word) plus one or more (derivational) suffixes plus an (inflectional) ending. For example, the word *mn̥-téi-s 'of thought' was made up of the root *_men-_ 'think', followed by the suffix *-_t(e)i-_, used to form abstract nouns, followed by the genitive case ending *-_s_ 'of' (Fortson 2004:77). Nouns were inflected for number (singular, dual, plural), case (eight), and gender (masculine, feminine, neuter).[7] Verbs were inflected for person (first, second, third), number (singular, dual, plural), tense (present, imperfect, aorist),[8] voice (active, middle), and mood (indicative, imperative, subjunctive, optative).[9] The various grammatical categories of the verb yielded many different inflected forms for each verb – a much more complicated system of verbal inflection than we find in modern English and even in modern German.

PIE is generally held to be an SOV (subject–object–verb) language, with verb-final the "default" in most of the earlier IE languages (Fortson 2004:142, Watkins 1998:68). In Hittite, for example, the verb is clause-final; the only exception to this basic order is when the verb is moved to clause-initial position by the process of topicalization (Fortson 2004:142, 144). Various movement processes have the effect of altering the basic order of elements in a clause. Topicalization is used to front a constituent – not just a verb – for purposes of emphasis or contrast.[10] (Fronting is the movement of an element to the beginning of a sentence.) Another type of fronting, wh-movement, moves elements like interrogatives ('who', 'what'), relative pronouns, and subordinating conjunctions to the complementizer position. In the older IE languages, the landing site for topicalization was to the left of the complementizer position (Hale 1987). We see this in the following example (from Fortson 2004:145), where the topicalized element is underlined and the complementizer is boldfaced:

(2)   Latin
       <u>_fēstō diē_</u> **_sī_** _quid prodēgeris_
       '**if** you splurge a bit <u>on a holiday</u>'

An important feature of the syntax of older IE languages, discovered by Jacob Wackernagel (1892), is known as Wackernagel's Law, the tendency of clitics to appear in the "second position" in a clause.[11] In the following Gothic example (from Fortson 2004:146), the clitic is underlined.

(3)   Gothic
       fram-<u>uh</u> þamma sokida Peilatus fraletan ina
       at-and this sought Pilate release him
       'And at this Pilate sought to release him.'

Hale (1987) shows that several independent processes lead to clitics appearing in the "Wackernagel position."[12]

Table 5.2 *Grimm's Law*

Stage I	Stage II	Stage III
*$p > f$	*$b > p$	*$bh > b$
*$t > þ$	*$d > t$	*$dh > $ d
*$k > x (> h)$	*$g > k$	*$gh > g$

5.1.2   Germanic

5.1.2.1 Introduction   The Germanic languages are traditionally divided into three branches: East Germanic (now extinct), made up of Gothic (Goth.) and the languages of the Vandals and Burgundians; North Germanic, made up of Old Norse, the ancestor of the modern Scandinavian languages, Icelandic, Faroese, Norwegian, Danish, and Swedish; and West Germanic, made up of Old High German, Old Saxon (ancestor of Low German), Old Low Franconian (earliest attestation of what is now the Dutch linguistic area), Old Frisian, and Old English (OE).

The earliest speakers of Germanic lived in northern Europe during the first half of the first millennium BC, mainly in southern Scandinavia and along the shores of the North and Baltic seas. By 500 BC they had migrated beyond the Rhine in the west, to the Vistula River in the east, and had occupied the Low German plain in the south (Ramat 1998).

The Germanic tribes came into contact with speakers of various languages. Germanic (Gmc.) borrowings in Russian point to contact with Balto-Slavic in the east: Russian *xleb* 'bread' < Gmc. *$hlaibaz$ (> OE *hlāf* > Eng. *loaf*).[13] Germanic borrowings in Finnish, a non-IE language, are particularly intriguing, since the modern forms of these words are very similar to forms that have been reconstructed for Germanic: Finnish *kuningas* 'king' < Gmc. *$kuningaz$ (> Old Saxon *cuning*, OHG *kuning* 'king'). Borrowings like these provide evidence for syllables that have been lost in the daughter languages because of an important innovation in the phonology of Germanic, the accent shift. In the following section we will look at this as well as other important features of the phonology of Germanic.

5.1.2.2 Phonology   Grimm's Law is the name given to one of the major innovations in the phonology of Germanic that sets it apart from the other branches of IE.[14] This sound change, also known as the First Sound Shift (*Die erste Lautverschiebung*), involves a shift (or a series of shifts) in the articulation of the PIE stops. In Germanic, the voiceless stops are changed to voiceless fricatives, the voiced stops become voiceless stops, and then voiced aspirated stops become plain voiced stops,[15] as shown in Table 5.2.[16] The forms in (4) through (6) illustrate these changes.

(4)   Stage I
       *p > f   Lat. *pater*   Eng. *father*
       *t > þ   Lat. *trēs*   Eng. *three*
       *k > x (> h)   Lat. *cornū*   Eng. *horn*

(5)   Stage II
       *b > p   Lat. *labium*   Eng. *lip*
       *d > t   Lat. *duo*   Eng. *two*
       *g > k   Lat. *ego*   OE *ic* (= Eng. *I*)

(6)   Stage III[17]
       *bh > b   Sk. *bhar-*   Eng. *bear*
       *dh > d   Sk. *dhā-* 'put'   Eng. *do*
       *gh > g   Sk. *maghám* 'wealth' German *mag* 'am able'

The Germanic reflexes of the PIE voiced aspirated stops are treated as voiced stop phonemes with two types of allophones. In initial position, these phonemes are realized as simple voiced stops; intervocalically they appear as voiced fricatives. We see this in the English word *give* (< OE *giefan*), which derives from the PIE root **ghabh-* (Pokorny 1959–1969:407–408). The voiced fricatives became voiced stops in many of the Germanic languages (German *geben* 'to give', for example, corresponds to Eng. *give*).

There were various exceptions to Grimm's Law. For example, PIE voiceless stops did not shift if they followed an *s*. Compare Lat. *stella* 'star' with Eng. *star*, which retains an unshifted PIE **t* following **s*.[18] Another set of exceptions, also involving the PIE voiceless stops, was explained by the Danish scholar Karl Verner. Verner discovered that the PIE accent was responsible for the voiced fricatives that sometimes appeared instead of the expected voiceless fricatives *f, þ, h* (< PIE **p, *t, *k*). According to Verner's Law, if PIE **p, *t*, and **k* occurred word-internally and were not immediately preceded by a stressed syllable, they became voiced fricatives, not the voiceless fricatives one would expect given Grimm's Law. We see this in (7a), where the syllable preceding PIE **t* is not stressed. In (7b), on the other hand, the syllable before PIE **t* is stressed, Verner's Law does not apply, and we find the voiceless fricative predicted by Grimm's Law.[19]

(7) a.   PIE **ph₂tér*   > Gmc. **fadér* 'father'
     b.   PIE **bhrā́ter-*   > Gmc. **brṓþer-* 'brother'

Verner's Law also affected PIE **s*, which became **z* when in word-internal position and not preceded by a stressed syllable: PIE *k̑asón* > Gmc. *hazón* 'hare' > German *Hase* (Fortson 2004:303).

Because stress in PIE and early Germanic was mobile and could appear on different syllables in different forms of a given word, Verner's Law resulted in alternations between voiced and voiceless fricatives within a single paradigm. Jacob Grimm, who noticed these alternations but could not explain them, termed them "Grammatischer Wechsel." Although some of these alternations have been leveled out over time, we still find examples, particularly in the forms of strong verbs and words derived from these forms. Because of subsequent sound changes, these alternations appear in Modern German as alternations between *f* and *b*; *d* and *t*; *h* and *g*; and *s* and *r*:[20]

(8) a. *Hefe* 'yeast'   *heben* 'to lift'
    b. *schneiden* 'to cut'   *geschnitten* 'cut'
    c. *ziehen* 'to pull'   *zog* 'pulled'
    d. *Verlust* 'loss'   *verloren* 'lost'

Various changes in the PIE vowels took place before or in Germanic. Two significant changes were the merger of short **a* and **o* to *a* and the merger of long **ā* and **ō* to *ō*:[21]

(9) a. PIE **oḱtō(u)* > German *acht* 'eight'
    b. PIE **bhrātēr* > Goth. *broþar* 'brother'[22]

After the changes brought about by Verner's Law had taken place, the accent, which was mobile in PIE and early Germanic, became fixed on the initial syllable of the root. Certain prefixes remained unstressed (e.g., *be'kommen* 'to receive', *ge'bären* 'to bear', *ver'geben* 'to forgive'). In addition, the pitch accent found in PIE had evolved into stress accent: prominent syllables in Germanic were signaled not by a difference in pitch, but by greater muscular energy used in their production.

5.1.2.3 Morphology and syntax   The morphology of Germanic can be characterized as much simpler than that of PIE. In the declension of nouns, the eight cases found in PIE are reduced to six: nominative, vocative,[23] accusative, dative, genitive, and instrumental (Fortson 2004:304).[24] The three numbers (singular, dual, plural) are reduced to two in nouns: singular, plural (the dual is retained only in pronouns and verbs). The three grammatical genders of PIE (masculine, feminine, neuter), however, are preserved.

The Germanic verbal system is also much simpler than the verbal system in PIE. Only the present and perfect stems remain; the perfect becomes a simple past tense called the preterite (= the past of Modern German). The optative becomes the Germanic subjunctive. The middle survives as the passive only in Gothic.[25]

An important feature of the verbal system in Germanic is the distinction between the "strong" and "weak" conjugations.[26] The strong conjugation continues and extends the IE system of ablaut (alternation of the root vowel) to make past-tense forms (the preterite and past participle): *trinken* 'to drink', *trank* 'drank', *getrunken* 'drunk'. The weak conjugation, an innovation in Germanic, uses a dental suffix for past tense forms: *danken* 'to thank', *dankte* 'thanked', *gedankt* 'thanked'.[27]

Germanic, like its ancestor PIE, is generally considered to be an SOV language. Because it is still a relatively heavily inflected language, sentence constituents are to a great extent free syntactically and can be used to convey pragmatic information. There is thus a good deal of variation in surface (actual) word order, as demonstrated by the oldest runic inscriptions (Ramat 1998:386, 410–411):[28]

(10) a. SOV
        ek hlewagastiz holtijaz horna tawido
        I Hlewagastiz of-Holt horn made
     b. SVO
        hAþuwolAfA sAte stAbA þria
        Haþ. set staves three
     c. OVS
        hAidR runoronu fAlAh-Ak
        bright runes-sequence hid-I

Other features, however, suggest an underlying SOV order for Germanic. For example, we find the Determiner + Determined order that is characteristic of OV languages (Ramat 1998:411):

(11) a. genitive + noun
        hariwulfs stainaz (Runic inscription)
        Hariwulf's stones
     b. adjective + noun
        afar ni managans dagans (Gothic)
        after not many days

Although Germanic is still a highly synthetic (inflecting) language, we see the beginnings of features of analytic languages.[29] For example, meanings that were expressed with case inflections in PIE began to be expressed by prepositions when these cases were lost. Some of the prepositions that can be attributed to Germanic are the following (Ramat 1998:408): **frama* 'from' (> Goth. *fram*), **med̄(i)* 'with' (> Goth. *miþ*), **under* 'under' (Goth. *undar*), **to*, **ta* 'towards' (> OE *tō*), **ūt* 'out of' (> Goth. *ūt*).

5.2   Old High German

5.2.1   Introduction

Old High German (OHG), the earliest stage of the German language for which there are extensive written documents, spans the period from roughly 750 to 1050 AD. The term "High" identifies the area in which much of the language

Table 5.3 *The High German Consonant Shift*

West Germanic	English		Old High German
*p-	**p**ath	pf	**pf**ad
*t-	**t**ide	ts	*zīt* (= *Zeit* 'time')
*k-	**c**orn	kx	**ch**orn
*pp	a**pp**le	pf	a**ph**ul
*tt	se**t** (OE se**tt**an)	ts	se**tz**an
*kk	wa**k**e (OE we**cc**ean)	kx	we**ch**en
*-p	shi**p**	f	sci**f**
*-t	foo**t**	s	fuo**z**
*-k	boo**k**	x	buo**ch**

was spoken, the mountainous region in the southern portion of the territory occupied by the West-Germanic languages, and distinguishes it from the "Low German" spoken in the lowlands in the north. There was no standard or suprare-gional variety of OHG; OHG consisted rather of a number of different dialects. There was also no literary standard that united the dialects. Most of the OHG lit-erature was produced in monasteries and consisted primarily of religious texts, many of which were translations from Latin. The oldest surviving "book" in German is *Der Abrogans* (c. 765), a Latin–OHG synonym dictionary, named after the first entry, Lat. *abrogans* (OHG *dheomodi* 'humble'). Other transla-tions of Latin texts include the Lord's Prayer, the Rule of St. Benedict, the Psalms, and the Gospels. Notker Labeo (c. 950–1022), a Benedictine monk, translated works by Boethius and Aristotle, among others. Some OHG works are original compositions, for example, Otfrid von Weissenburg's *Evangelien-buch* (863–871), a gospel harmony in rhyming couplets. There is very little extant non-Christian original OHG material. One important work is the *Hilde-brandslied*, a fragment (sixty-eight lines) of an epic poem in alliterative verse in an unusual mixture of OHG and Old Saxon, found on the first and last leaves of a manuscript dating from the early part of the ninth century. The *Merseburger Zaubersprüche* (magic spells), generally held to be of pagan origin, were dis-covered in a religious manuscript in Fulda from the ninth or tenth century.

5.2.2   Phonology

The most important sound change that distinguishes OHG from all other West Germanic languages is known as the Second Sound Shift (*Die zweite Lautver-schiebung*) or the High German Consonant Shift. In OHG, the West Germanic voiceless stops *p *t *k became the affricates *pf ts kx* when in initial position, medially following a consonant, or geminated (*pp *tt *kk); elsewhere they became the fricatives *f s x*. Table 5.3 provides examples from English and OHG that illustrate this sound change. The English words contain unshifted *p t k*; their OHG cognates contain the affricates and fricatives that resulted from the sound shift.[30] Because there was no standard orthography, the sounds that resulted from the Old High German Consonant Shift were not represented consistently. Examples (12) and (13) illustrate the typical ways in which the affricates and fricatives resulting from *$*p$ *$*t$ *$*k$ were represented orthographically in OHG texts.

(12) a. *pf*   <pf> or <ph>
 b. *ts*   <z> or <tz>
 c. *kx*   <kh> or <ch>

(13) a. *f*   <ff> or <f>
 b. *s*   <zz> or <z>
 c. *x*   <hh> or <ch> (in later texts)

Notice that the orthography was often ambiguous: <z> could represent the affricate *ts* as well as the fricative *s*; <ch> could represent the affricate *kx* or the fricative *x*.

One consistent exception to the High German Consonant Shift involved the sound *$*s$. West Germanic *$*p$ *$*t$ *$*k$ were not shifted when they followed *$*s$.[31]

(14) a. OHG **sp***innan* 'to spin'
 b. OHG *ga**st*** 'guest'
 c. OHG **sc***uoh* 'shoe'

The High German Consonant Shift began in the southern portion of the German-speaking territory and eventually petered out by the time it reached the Low German area. We in fact find the affricate *kx* only in the south, in the Alemannic (Swiss German) area; elsewhere West Germanic *$*k$ (initial, post-consonantal, and geminate) remains unshifted. In OHG dialects that have unshifted *$*k$ we find, for example, *korn* 'grain' and *wecken* 'to wake' instead of *chorn* and *wechen*. In OHG dialects closer to the Low German area we also find unshifted*$*p$- and *$*t$-. In Rhenish Franconian (Frankfurt, Mainz), for example, West Germanic *$*p$- frequently remains unshifted (Waterman 1991:58). As we will see in the discussion of Modern German dialects in chapter 6, the extent to which a given dialect participated in the High German Consonant Shift determines whether the dialect is classified as being Upper, Central, or Low German.

Two additional sound changes that are characteristic of OHG are the change from *$*d$ to *t* and the change from *$*þ$ to *d*.

(15) a. *$*d > t*   Eng. **deep**   OHG **t***iof* (= *tief*)
 b. *$*þ > d*   Eng. **th***ing*   OHG **d***ing*

These changes are usually viewed as a chain reaction. After *t* had become *ts* and *s* (as a result of the High German Consonant Shift), *d* became *t*, allowing *þ* to become *d*. The change from *þ* to *d* affected Dutch (Dutch *ding* 'thing') and eventually spread to Low German, although Old Saxon, the ancestor of Low German, did not yet show the change (Old Saxon *thing* 'thing').

Two important features of the OHG vowel system are umlaut and the retention of full vowels in unaccented syllables. Prior to the OHG period, West Germanic *e* had been raised to *i* preceding an *i* or *j* (a non-syllabic *i*) in a following syllable. This change, known as West Germanic *i*-Umlaut, is an example of assimilation, a sound change where one sound acquires one or more features of a neighboring sound. In this example, the mid vowel *e* becomes the high vowel *i* (it acquires the feature [+high]) when it precedes the high vowel *i*. We see this change in the third person singular form of the present tense of strong verbs like OHG *geban* 'to give'. We also see it in etymologically related words.

(16)   West Germanic *i*-Umlaut
   a.   OHG *geban* 'to give', *er gibit* 'he gives' (< *gebit*)
   b.   OHG *erda* 'earth', *irdisc* 'earthly' (< *erdisk*)

Primary Umlaut, the change from (short) *a* to *e* before an *i* or *j* in a following syllable, took place at the beginning of the OHG period.[32] We see this change in the present tense of strong verbs, in comparative forms of adjectives, and in the plurals of nouns.

(17)   Primary Umlaut
   a.   OHG *faran* 'to drive', *er ferit* 'he drives' (< *farit*)
   b.   OHG *lang* 'long', *lengiro* 'longer' (< *langiro*)
   c.   OHG *gast* 'guest', *gesti* 'guests' (< *gasti*)

In Modern German, Primary Umlaut is typically represented orthographically by <ä>.

West Germanic *i*-Umlaut and Primary Umlaut, which were both a type of *i*-umlaut (*i* influenced a vowel in a preceding syllable), yielded sounds that already existed in the language, *i* and *e*. Secondary Umlaut, also a type of *i*-umlaut, yielded sounds that were new to the language. It is assumed that Secondary Umlaut took place during the OHG period, but was not indicated orthographically with regularity until later, during the Middle High German (MHG) period, because of the difficulty of representing these sounds with the letters available in the Latin alphabet. Secondary Umlaut is illustrated here using MHG words with the "normalized" orthography that is typically used for MHG texts.

(18)   Secondary Umlaut
  a.   *ā > æ*   OHG *māri*   MHG *mære* 'news'
  b.   *o > ö*   OHG *mohti*   MHG *möhte* 'would like'
  c.   *ō > æ*   OHG *scōni*   MHG *schæne* 'beautiful'
  d.   *u > ü*   OHG *ubir*   MHG *über* 'over'
  e.   *ū > iu* [y:]   OHG *hūsir*   MHG *hiuser* 'houses'

The umlaut symbol used today to indicate umlauted vowels originated in the
MHG practice of writing <e> or <i> over the vowels <a>, <o>, and <u>.

   The vocalism of unaccented syllables in OHG is another important feature
of the language – one in particular that distinguishes it from the language of the
MHG period. In OHG, unaccented syllables still retain full vowels. Although
some syllables have been lost because of the Germanic accent shift (Gmc.
*kuningaz > OHG *kuning* 'king'), the vowels in the remaining unaccented
syllables have not yet been reduced to schwa.[33] Compare the endings in the
following OHG words with those of their MHG counterparts (where <e> in
word-final syllables represents [ə]).

(19) a.   OHG *hirti*   MHG *hirte* 'shepherd'
     b.   OHG *habēn*   MHG *haben* 'to have'
     c.   OHG *zunga*   MHG *zunge* 'tongue'
     d.   OHG *boto*   MHG *bote* 'messenger'
     e.   OHG (*ih*) *nimu*   MHG (*ich*) *nime* '(I) take'

As we will see in the next section, the presence of full vowels in unaccented
syllables in the OHG period is of significance for the morphology and syntax
of the language.

5.2.3   Morphology and syntax

Because the vowels of inflectional endings are still rather strongly differenti-
ated in the OHG period, grammatical distinctions can still be made to a large
extent synthetically (through inflection rather than through the use of independent words). There are some changes in the inflection of nouns and pronouns,
however. Of the six cases found in Germanic, essentially only four remain:
nominative, accusative, dative, and genitive. The function of the vocative has
been taken over by the nominative. Vestiges of the instrumental remain, but
only in early OHG in the strong nouns and pronouns: OHG *tagu* 'day' (masculine singular instrumental); OHG *diu* 'the' (masculine singular instrumental).
Unlike Gothic, OHG no longer distinguishes between the dual and plural in the
pronouns.[34]

   In addition to these changes in nominal inflection, we also see some changes
in verbal inflection. In OHG verbs, the two tenses of Germanic remain: the

present, which can also be used to express the future, and the preterite, which is the general tense for the past.[35] The three moods of Germanic remain: active, subjunctive, and imperative. Passive voice, however, which is only partially retained in Gothic, can no longer be found in OHG in synthetic form. Passive meaning is expressed analytically in OHG, with an inflected form of *wesan* 'to be' or *werdan* 'to become' and a past participle, for example, *ist ginoman* or *wirdit ginoman* 'is taken' (Braune 2004:256).

Although OHG is still largely a synthetic language, we see further evidence of movement towards the use of analytic structures. In addition to the expression of mood (the passive) by analytic means, we also find the analytic expression of tense. For example, although the present is generally used to express the future, there are a few examples of an analytic future, most using the auxiliary *sculan* (*sollen*) 'shall', some using *wellen* (*wollen*) 'to intend' (Braune 2004:256). A periphrastic perfect (with the auxiliaries *habēn* 'to have', *eigan* 'to have', or *wesan* 'to be') is used in translations of the Latin perfect, although the preterite is also used for this purpose.

Because many of the extant OHG texts are translations of Latin, it is often difficult to gain a clear picture of OHG syntax. For example, if the use of a feature in OHG does not deviate from the use of that feature in the Latin original, it is impossible to determine whether the feature can be attributed to OHG or whether it simply reflects a feature of Latin. Other factors that contribute to the difficulty in determining the characteristics of OHG syntax include the diverseness of the various German-speaking regions, the large time span covered by the OHG period, and the possible influence of meter and rhyme on the language of the OHG texts (Schrodt 2004:vii). In spite of these difficulties, there are some generalizations that can be made about the syntactic characteristics of the language.

With increasing frequency, the subject of a sentence is realized pronominally even when it can be determined through context or by linguistic means (Meineke and Schwerdt 2001:312). The eventual loss of distinctive inflectional endings on the verb may have contributed to the increase in the use of subject pronouns. However, we find examples where subject pronouns are used (possibly for emphasis) when the Latin original lacks them and when the verbal endings in OHG are unambiguous (Meineke and Schwerdt 2001:313).

(20)   OHG *Dhu minnōdes reht* 'you loved justice'
        Lat. *dilexisti iustitiam*

This suggests that the loss of distinct inflections cannot have been the sole factor that contributed to the rise in the use of subject pronouns.

OHG continues the development of a definite article from a demonstrative pronoun. The definite article is particularly common in Otfrid's writings, and most nouns in Notker's translations from Latin are preceded by a definite article (Meineke and Schwerdt 2001:314–315).

(21)   *zu **dero** uuiti **dero** euuigheite* (Notker, cited in Schrodt 2004:25)
         to the vastness of-the eternity

The position of the finite verb in OHG is a particularly difficult topic, given the potential influence of Latin, the effects of meter, and the role of stylistic factors (e.g., extraposition), all of which have to be taken into account.[36] Although there is a good deal of variation and many sentences are difficult to analyze unequivocally, some generalizations about the position of the finite verb can be made (Schrodt 2004:197–208). Verb-final position, inherited from IE, has become a feature typical of subordinate clauses (adverbial elements can be extraposed to the right of the finite verb, however).

(22) a. *daz uuir des dikkēm* (Braune *et al.* 1994:34)
          that we for-it ask
     b. extraposition: *daz zistōrit ist durh unsre suntan* (Braune *et al.* 1994:81)
          that destroyed is through our sins

Verb-second or middle position is an innovation in OHG, as in the other Germanic languages, and is the norm in declarative sentences.

(23)   *Anna hiaz ein wib thar* (Otfrid, cited in Schrodt 2004:200)
         Anna was-called a woman there

Verb-first position, which has the emphatic and discourse-connective function found in IE, also has the Modern German function of marking imperatives, interrogatives, and wishes.

(24) a. emphatic: *yrforahtun tho thie liuti thio wuntarlichun dati* (Otfrid, cited in Schrodt 2004:198)
          feared then the people the marvelous deed
     b. interrogative: *pechennest tu mih?* (Notker, cited in Schrodt 2004:200)
          recognize you me

Although the finite verb appears in various positions on the surface (first, second, last, etc.), we can assume that OHG still has underlying SOV word order. In spite of Latin influence on OHG translations, we find, for example, the adjective + noun word order that is characteristic of OV languages, not the noun + adjective order that is characteristic of Latin. As a rule, attributive adjectives precede the noun they modify (Schrodt 2004:37).

(25)   *fohem uuortum*; *friuntlaos man* (*Hildebrandslied*, Braune *et al.*
1994:84)
few words (dative plural); friendless man

5.3   Middle High German

5.3.1   Introduction

Middle High German (MHG) was spoken from roughly 1050 to 1350.[37] During the MHG period we see the development of the first "standard language" (*Gemeinsprache*) in the German-speaking area, the literary language of the court poets during the golden age of chivalric poetry (1170–1250). This language, also known as "Classic Middle High German" (*das klassische Mittelhochdeutsch*), is relatively uniform, but less so than would appear from the modern editions of MHG texts, which employ a normalized orthography.[38] The uniformity of this literary language has its origins in the desire of MHG poets to achieve as broad a circulation of their work as possible. They avoided words and pronunciations that were perceived as strongly dialectal. They also made an effort to use words that would rhyme in any dialect. In general, the manuscripts of the courtly literature exhibit a mixture of Alemannic and East Franconian phonology (Paul 1998:14).

Whereas the literature of the OHG period was used primarily for religious/didactic purposes, the literature of the MHG period, especially that of "Classic MHG," was intended as entertainment for the knightly class (*Ritterstand*). The main genres of this period are the courtly epic and lyric poetry. A famous epic, the *Nibelungenlied*, is the work of an anonymous poet from roughly 1200. Important MHG authors of epic poetry include Hartmann von Aue (c. 1168–1210), who wrote *Erec* and *Iwein*; Wolfram von Eschenbach (c. 1170–1220), author of *Parzival*; and Gottfried von Straßburg (c. 1200), author of *Tristan und Isolde*. Lyric poetry included the *Minnesang* 'minnesong', the song of courtly love. Perhaps the greatest lyric poet of the MHG period was Walther von der Vogelweide (c. 1170–1230), who composed political verse as well as *Minnelieder*.

The prestige of French culture was strong during the MHG period, and many borrowings found their way into the German language during this period through contact with French speakers. In addition to loanwords like MHG *âventiure* (*Abenteuer*) 'adventure' (< Old French *aventure*) and MHG *rîm* 'rhyme' (< Old French *rime*), we find loan translations such as MHG *hovesch* 'courtly' (French *courtois*) and MHG *ritter* 'knight' (French *chevalier*). French suffixes also found their way into the language. They first appeared in loanwords and then became productive and were used to create new lexical items with

German stems. The suffix *-ei* in words like *Bäckerei* 'bakery' and the verbal suffix *-ieren* in words like *buchstabieren* 'to spell' were introduced into the language in this way (*-ei* through words like MHG *partîe* 'part' and *-ieren* through words like MHG *parlieren* 'to speak').

With the demise of the knightly class came the end of the influence of the literary language on the development of a German standard. During the next several hundred years, the language of the chanceries, dialectally less neutral than the language of court poets, played an important role in shaping the standard language that emerged during the Early New High German period.

5.3.2   Phonology

One of the most salient features of MHG phonology is the weakening of unstressed syllables. Recall from the discussion in section 5.2.2 that the full vowels in the unaccented (typically inflectional) syllables of OHG are replaced in MHG by schwa (<e>). The famous opening lines of the first *âventiure* 'adventure' of the *Nibelungenlied* show this clearly.

(26)   *Das Nibelungenlied* (First Adventure)
        Uns ist in alten mæren   wunders vil geseit
        von helden lobebæren,   von grôzer arebeit,
        von fröuden, hôchgezîten,   von weinen und von klagen,
        von küener recken strîten   muget ir nu wunder hæren sagen.
        (de Boor 1988:3)

        Wondrous things are told in ancient tales
        Of famous men and bold, of great travails,
        Of joy and festive life, of woe and tears,
        Of warriors met in strife – the wonder shall fill your ears!
        (Ryder 1962:43)

All the inflectional syllables in this text contain schwa (e.g., the adjective ending of *alten* 'old' < OHG *altēn*, the infinitive ending on the verb *weinen* 'to cry' < OHG *weinōn*, etc.). The weakening of unstressed vowels is presumed to be a result of the accent shift in Germanic. The fixing of the accent on the initial syllable of the root and, in particular, the change from a pitch accent to a stress accent led to the weakening (and loss) of unstressed syllables, as these were articulated with less force than accented syllables.

Another important feature of MHG, Secondary Umlaut, can also be seen in the first lines of the *Nibelungenlied*. The words *mæren, küener,* and *hæren* all contain vowels that were fronted by an *i* in a following syllable. The word *mære*, for example, was *māri* in OHG. After the *ā* assimilated to *i* and became *æ*, the *i* was weakened to schwa. As mentioned in section 5.2.2, it is assumed that Secondary Umlaut took place during the OHG period, but was not represented orthographically until MHG times. When the conditioning factor for umlaut was lost (when *i* was reduced to schwa), the new sounds, *æ ö œ ü iu* [yː], acquired the status of phonemes. The sound *æ*, for example, was no longer an allophone of the phoneme *ā* (the realization of *ā* when it occurred before *i* in a following syllable); it was a phoneme in its own right.

In OHG, when the consonant clusters *ht, hs,* and *rw* occurred between *a* and *i*, or when *i* appeared two syllables away from *a*, Primary Umlaut did not take place. These barriers to umlaut were overcome in MHG, and this later fronting of short *a*, represented orthographically with the symbol *ä*, is subsumed under Secondary Umlaut. In OHG we find, for example, *mahtig* 'powerful' and *magadi* 'virgins'; in MHG these appear as *mahtec* and *magede*.

Two important changes can be seen in the consonants of MHG, Palatalization and Final Fortition (*Auslautverhärtung*). Several lines from Walter von der Vogelweide's "Under der linden" contain examples of both changes.

(27) a. **sch**ône sanc diu nahtegal
        beautifully sang the nightingale
    b. *seht wie rôt mir ist der munt*
        see how red me is the mouth

Palatalization refers to the development of a new phoneme, /ʃ/, from the consonant cluster *sk*. For example, OHG *scif* 'ship' > MHG *schif*. In the example in (27a), we find MHG *schöne* 'beautifully', which developed from OHG *scōni*. We find this same change in English, where *ship* corresponds to German *Schiff* and *fish* to German *Fisch* (< OHG *fisc*). In late MHG, *s* is palatalized (> /ʃ/) when it occurs before other consonants (*l, m, n, p, t, w*).

(28) a. OHG *slahan* 'to hit' > *schlagen*
    b. OHG *smal* 'small' > *schmal*
    c. OHG *snē* 'snow' > *Schnee*

This change began in the Upper German dialects in the south and spread northward, but did not reach all of the northern dialects. It is not represented consistently in the orthography of Modern German (*spitz* 'pointed', *Stein* 'stone'), and in the modern colloquial language of northern Germany, speakers retain the old (unpalatalized) pronunciation before *p* and *t*: [s]*pitz,* [s]*tein.*

Final Fortition affected *b, d,* and *g,* which became *p, t,* and *c* when in syllable-final position. Although Final Fortition is predictable, it is represented orthographically in MHG texts, as we see in the words *sanc* 'sang' and *munt* 'mouth' in (27). The effects of Final Fortition are particularly clear if we compare words with and without inflectional endings.

Table 5.4 *The declension of OHG* tag *'day' and MHG* tac *'day'*

		OHG	MHG
Singular	Nominative	*tag*	*tac*
	Accusative	*tag*	*tac*
	Dative	*tage*	*tage*
	Genitive	*tages*	*tages*
	Instrumental	*tagu*	
Plural	Nominative	*taga*	*tage*
	Accusative	*taga*	*tage*
	Dative	*tagum*	*tagen*
	Genitive	*tago*	*tage*

(29) a. *stoubes, stoup* 'dust'
     b. *kindes, kint* 'child'
     c. *tages, tac* 'day'

See Mihm 2004 for a discussion of the history of Final Fortition and the relationship between Final Fortion in MHG and the modern Fortition found in the standard language.

As we will see in the following section, the changes in phonology that are evident in the MHG period, in particular the weakening of unstressed vowels, were to have far-reaching effects on the make-up of the language.

5.3.3 Morphology and syntax

If we compare the OHG paradigm for the noun *tag* 'day' with the paradigm for its counterpart in MHG, *tac*, we see how the weakening of unstressed syllables has led to a simplification in the inflectional endings of MHG (see Table 5.4). In the OHG paradigm there are seven different endings (including the zero-ending in the nominative and accusative singular). In the MHG paradigm there are four different endings. A comparison of the OHG and MHG paradigms for the preterite indicative of the strong verb *nehmen* 'to take' also reveals a simplification in inflectional endings (see Table 5.5). The first and third person plural endings, which are distinct in OHG, are identical in MHG. The various functions of these inflectional endings (the signaling of case, person and number distinctions, etc.) is increasingly carried out by analytic means in the MHG period – through the use of articles with nouns, personal pronouns with verbs, prepositions, and auxiliary verbs (Paul 1998:21).

Table 5.5 *The preterite indicative of* nehmen
'to take' in OHG and MHG

		OHG	MHG
Singular	1st person	*nam*	*nam*
	2nd person	*nāmi*	*næme*
	3rd person	*nam*	*nam*
Plural	1st person	*nāmum*	*nâmen*
	2nd person	*nāmut*	*nâmet*
	3rd person	*nāmun*	*nâmen*

In MHG we see an increase in the number of different tense forms through the use of analytic tenses. In addition to the present and the preterite, we also see a present perfect and a past perfect. The present perfect is made up of a present form of *haben* 'to have' or *sîn* 'to be' and a past participle.

(30)   *er sprach: 'dâ **hân** ich freude vil **verlorn'** (Parzival,* cited in Paul 1998:294)
he spoke there have I joy much lost

The past perfect is formed using a preterite form of *haben* or *sîn* and a past participle.

(31)   *er (got) hie3 in (Abraham) da3 er tate, also in sin wib **gebeten hete*** (Paul 1998:294)
he (God) commanded him (Abraham) that he do as him his wife had asked

In OHG, the preterite was used to express past perfect meaning and could also be used to express present perfect meaning (analytic means were used as well; see the discussion in section 5.2.3).

Although the present tense is used in MHG to express future meaning, an analytic future is also used: *sol* 'shall', *wil* 'intend', or *muo3* 'must' + infinitive.

(32)   *und dâ nâch sol ich schouwen die schœnen juncvrouwen* (Paul 1998:296)
and there after shall I see the beautiful virgins

This analytic future can convey modal as well as temporal information. A periphrastic future with *werden* 'to become' + infinitive is not yet common. In MHG *werden* is used with a present participle to express inchoative meaning.

(33)   *Pinte schire vliende wart* (Paul 1998:311)
'Pinte suddenly began to flee.'

Because of the increased use of articles, subject pronouns, prepositions, and auxiliary verbs during the MHG period, the language in general can be characterized as increasingly analytic, thus carrying on the trend begun in Germanic. The syntax of the language is becoming more stable (Paul 1998:22), with an increasing tendency for verb-second word order in main declarative clauses and verb-final order in embedded clauses (Roelcke 1997:148).

(34) a. *Sîn name* **was** *erkennelich: er* **hiez** *der herre Heinrich* (Hartmann von Aue, cited in Schmidt 2000:292)
         his name was well-known he was-called the Herr Heinrich
     b. *daz wir ir niemer vergessen* **mügen** (Schmidt 2000:293)
         that we them never forget can

In OHG, the clitic *ni* 'not' was used preverbally to negate a sentence, either alone or with a negative indefinite pronoun.

(35) a. **ni** *mag ther man iouuiht intphahen* (Schrodt 2004:136)
         not can the man something receive
     b. **nioman nist** *in thinemo cunne* (Schrodt 2004:136)
         no-one not-is in your family

In MHG, the use of *ne* (< OHG *ni*) by itself becomes less common; *ne* (*en* when cliticized onto the front of a word) together with *niht* (< *ni wiht* 'not something'), originally used for emphasis, becomes the regular means of expressing negation (Paul 1998:338–339).

(36)   *des* **en**mac diu schœne **niht** getuon (Schmidt 2000:295)
         it not-can the beauty not do

In MHG, sentences can in fact contain multiple expressions of negation. These do not cancel each other out, however; the sentence remains negated.

(37)   *daz iu* **nieman niht en**tuot (Paul 1998:400)
         that you no-one not not-do 'that no-one do it to you'

Eventually, *niht* takes over the function of negation from *en* (Paul 1998:398).

5.4   Early New High German

5.4.1   Introduction

Early New High German (ENHG) is generally held to span the period from 1350 to 1650. During this period we see the beginning of the development of a German standard language. German was used with greater frequency as the language of the legal documents produced in the chanceries (*Kanzleien*) during this period. Although each chancery had its local writing practices, scribes in the larger chanceries attempted to avoid dialectal characteristics that were strongly local. Two widely used written languages with roots in chancery languages emerged during the ENHG period: *Das Gemeine Deutsch*, the Upper German literary dialect from the imperial chancery in Vienna, which served as the standard written language of southern Germany and Austria; and *Ostmitteldeutsch*, the language of the Saxon chancery, which had its roots in the lingua franca that had developed from the various dialects of the speakers who had migrated to the east between 1150 and 1350. *Ostmitteldeutsch* served as the basis for Martin Luther's German and ultimately for the German standard language.

Two important developments hastened the emergence of a standard language: the substitution of paper for the more expensive parchment at the end of the fourteenth century; and the invention of printing with moveable type (by Johannes Gutenberg) in the middle of the fifteenth century. These developments made the printed word affordable and widely available, whereas the written word had once been accessible to only a privileged few. The first books printed in Germany were in Latin, but towards the end of the seventeenth century, German overtook Latin as the dominant language. Printers of German books developed local printing languages (*Druckersprachen*) and over time sought to avoid sounds and expressions that were considered strongly dialectal in an effort to increase their readership in other dialect areas. Printers turned to the language of the larger chanceries, which already had wide appeal. The language of the imperial chancery, *das Gemeine Deutsch*, was popular early on: all fourteen of the pre-Luther German Bibles followed the writing practices of *das Gemeine Deutsch* (Waterman 1991:128). Luther's successful translation of the Bible, however, resulted in the increase in prestige of the language of the Saxon chancery, on which it was based. A third literary dialect, Swiss German, enjoyed wide appeal and retained its independence through the ENHG period. Luther's German was rejected in Switzerland for religious reasons (many Swiss were followers of Calvin and Zwingli), and the language of the imperial chancery was rejected for political reasons, although Swiss printers did adopt the "new" Bavarian diphthongs (see the discussion in section 5.4.2) in an effort to increase their readership.

Although we cannot view Martin Luther (1483–1546) as the creator of New High German, his translation of the Bible had a major impact on the language. He sought to create a translation that was idiomatic, natural, and accessible to ordinary people. As he explains in his "Sendbrief vom Dolmetschen" ('Circular letter on translation'), his goal in translating was to reproduce the sense of the text clearly and vividly (Schmidt 2000:114–115). It is estimated that Hans Lufft's press in Wittenberg sold over 100,000 copies of his Bible between 1534 and 1583 (Waterman 1991:130). In part because Luther's Bible was so widely read and accepted, the language on which it was based, *Ostmitteldeutsch*, came to serve as the basis for the modern standard.

5.4.2   Phonology

The phonological differences between MHG and ENHG lie primarily in the vowels. The two major phonological changes are Diphthongization and Monophthongization.

Diphthongization changed the MHG long vowels *î*, *û*, and *iu* [y:] to the diphthongs *ei* (*ai*), *au*, and *eu* (*äu*).

(38)   MHG   NHG
   a.   *î > ei*   *zît*   *Zeit*
   b.   *û > au*   *mûs*   *Maus*
   c.   *iu* [y:] *> eu*   *diutsch*   *Deutsch*

This process began in the twelfth century in the Bavarian dialect area and spread northward to include the Central German dialects; the Alemannic dialect area did not undergo this change (in Swiss German one pronounces *auf Schweizerdeutsch* as [u:]*f Schw*[i:]*zerd*[y:]*tsch*). Diphthongization is also absent in Low German. The three new High German diphthongs eventually merge in pronunciation with the old MHG diphthongs, *ei*, *ou*, and *öu*, which were inherited from Germanic. Thus only the MHG forms of the words in which these diphthongs appear reveal their differing histories.

(39) a.   MHG *wîȝ* (*weiß*) 'white'   MHG *weiȝ* (*weiß*) '(I) know'
    b.   MHG *ûf* (*auf*) 'on'   MHG *loufen* (*laufen*) 'to run'
    c.   MHG *liuten* (*läuten*) 'to ring'   MHG *vröude* (*Freude*) 'joy'

A mnemonic for remembering ENHG Diphthongization is the MHG phrase *mîn niuweȝ hûs*, which is *mein neues Haus* 'my new house' in modern German.

The second major phonological development in ENHG, Monophthongization, affected the central dialects.[39] The MHG diphthongs *ie*, *uo*, and *üe* were monophthongized to the long vowels [i:] (still spelled *ie*), [u:], and [y:].

(40)   MHG   NHG
   a.   *ie > [i:]*   *lieb*   *lieb* 'kind'
   b.   *uo > [u:]*   *buoch*   *Buch* 'book'
   c.   *üe > [y:]*   *süeȝe*   *süß* 'sweet'

Monophthongization began in the early twelfth century. It did not affect the Upper German dialects; instead of *lieb* 'kind' and *gut* 'good', one finds *liab* and *guat* in Bavarian, and *lieb* and *guet* in Alemannic (Stedje 2001:135). Low German dialects had other vowels from the beginning: Middle Low German *lēf*, *gōt* (Stedje 2001:135). A mnemonic for remembering ENHG Monophthongization is the MHG phrase *lieben guoten brüeder*, which is *liebe gute Brüder* 'dear good brothers' in modern German.

Table 5.6 *The declension of ENHG*
tag *'day'*

		ENHG
Singular	Nominative	*t*[a]*g*
	Accusative	*t*[a]*g*
	Dative	*t*[aː]*ge*
	Genitive	*t*[aː]*ges*
Plural	Nominative	*t*[aː]*ge*
	Accusative	*t*[aː]*ge*
	Dative	*t*[aː]*gen*
	Genitive	*t*[aː]*ge*

A third important phonological change, which had morphological ramifications, particularly in nominal paradigms, was the lengthening of short vowels in open syllables (syllables that end in a vowel).[40]

(41)   MHG (short vowel)   NHG (long vowel)
   a. *fa.ren*   *fah.ren* 'to drive'
   b. *ne.men*   *neh.men* 'to take'
   c. *si.ben*   *sie.ben* 'seven'

In the paradigm of a noun like *tag* 'day', for example, vowel lengthening led to some forms with a short vowel in the stem, others with a long vowel, as shown in Table 5.6. This kind of variation within the stem of a noun was ultimately eliminated. In the paradigm of Modern German *Tag*, we find a long vowel in the stem in all forms, even in the closed syllables of the forms of the singular without inflectional endings.

Before we turn to the morphology of ENHG, a few words about the orthography of the language are in order. Spelling during the ENHG period was highly inconsistent; in Waterman's words, it was "flagrantly haphazard" (1991:106). A single text could reveal orthographic variants of a given word. Long vowels were indicated by several means, by the doubling of the vowel or by a following *h, e, i,* or *y,* although sometimes no indication of length was given.

(42) a. *seer* 'very', *spraach* 'spoke', *froo* 'glad'
     b. *ehre* 'honor', *raht* 'advice', *verlohren* 'lost'
     c. *broeder* 'brother', *jair* 'year'

After the MHG diphthong *ie* (<ie>) had become monophthongized (to [iː]), the <e> was free to be used as a symbol of length. This explains its continued use in words like *lieb* 'dear' and its appearance in words like *jaer* (*Jahr*) 'year'. Modern German also continues to use <h> (*ihn* 'him', *Floh* 'flea', *Ehe*

Table 5.7 *The declension of "weak" feminine nouns*

		MHG	NHG
Singular	Nominative	*zunge*	*Zunge*
	Accusative	*zungen*	*Zunge*
	Dative	*zungen*	*Zunge*
	Genitive	*zungen*	*Zunge*
Plural	Nominative	*zungen*	*Zungen*
	Accusative	*zungen*	*Zungen*
	Dative	*zungen*	*Zungen*
	Genitive	*zungen*	*Zungen*

'marriage') and doubled vowels (*Paar* 'pair', *Meer* 'ocean', *Boot* 'boat') to signal length.

A particularly salient feature of ENHG orthography was the decorative doubling or tripling of consonants (*Konsonantenhäufung*): *pffenning* 'penny', *auff* 'on', *czeytten* (*Zeiten*) 'times', *funffczig* 'fifty', *wherdenn* 'to become'. In addition to <ʃʃ> and <ss>, one could also often find <ʃs>: *saʃs* 'sat', *groʃs* 'large'. Later the spelling <ʃz> took hold (Schmidt 2000:305), out of which the *β*-ligature developed (from a "long" *s* and following *z*).[41]

By the sixteenth century, the use of a capital letter for the first word of a sentence is a common practice. Earlier (in OHG and MHG times), capital letters were only used for the beginning of a text or a section of text. During the course of the ENHG period, the capitalization of nouns took hold. One can see this development in Luther's writings. In his "Sendbrief vom Dolmetschen" (1530), only those nouns that have a special status or emphasis are capitalized (*Christus* 'Christ', *Deutsch* 'German', *Esel* 'ass') – in addition to proper names and nouns in sentence-initial position; in 1540, roughly eighty percent of those nouns that are not proper nouns are also capitalized (Schmidt 2000:307).

5.4.3   Morphology and syntax

The differences in morphology between MHG and ENHG are the result of analogical change (generalization of a regularity), unlike the differences between OHG and MHG morphology, which were the result of phonological changes (e.g., the weakening of unstressed vowels).

In MHG, the "weak" feminine nouns had two different forms in the singular (all but the nominative singular forms ended in -*n*) and one in the plural (all ended in -*n*). In ENHG, all singular forms in this declension were identical: the form of the nominative singular spread to all forms of the singular (see Table 5.7). Similarly, *i*-stem nouns had forms with and without umlaut in the

Table 5.8 *The declension of* i-*stem nouns*

		MHG	NHG
Singular	Nominative	*kraft*	*Kraft*
	Accusative	*kraft*	*Kraft*
	Dative	*krefte*	*Kraft*
	Genitive	*krefte*	*Kraft*
Plural	Nominative	*krefte*	*Kräfte*
	Accusative	*krefte*	*Kräfte*
	Dative	*kreften*	*Kräften*
	Genitive	*krefte*	*Kräfte*

Table 5.9 *Principal parts of selected strong verbs in MHG*

Infinitive	Preterite Singular	Preterite Plural	Past Participle
grîfen 'to grasp'	*greif*	*griffen*	*gegriffen*
biegen 'to bend'	*bouc*	*bugen*	*gebogen*
binden 'to tie'	*bant*	*bunden*	*gebunden*
helfen 'to help'	*half*	*hulfen*	*geholfen*

singular in MHG (because of an *i* following the root in OHG times). The umlauted forms were replaced in the singular in ENHG (see Table 5.8); thus umlaut, which occurred only in plural forms, came to be viewed as a marker of the plural. The function of umlaut as a plural marker spread to nouns that did not originally have an *i* following the root in OHG: *Gärten* 'gardens', *Höfe* 'courts', *Läden* 'shops', *Schäden* 'damages'. In MHG, a small number of neuter nouns formed their plural with an -*er* suffix and umlaut of the root (MHG *lamp* 'lamb', *lember* 'lambs'). This class of nouns was expanded in ENHG, and included masculine as well as neuter nouns that historically had not formed their plurals in this way: *Haus* 'house', *Häuser* 'houses'; *Mann* 'man', *Männer* 'men'; *Wald* 'forest', *Wälder* 'forests'.

Analogical change brought simplification to ENHG verbal paradigms. The preterite in MHG exhibited two different stems, one for the singular and one for the plural, as Table 5.9 shows.[42] The vowel of the preterite was leveled during the ENHG period, sometimes in favor of the singular (*bot* 'offered', *band* 'tied', *half* 'helped'), sometimes in favor of the plural (*griff* 'grasped'). We find relics of the old preterite stems in some older Subjunctive II forms (*hülfe* 'would help', *stürbe* 'would die'), in the archaic past form *ward* 'became', and in the following proverb (with *sungen* instead of *sangen* 'sang'): *Wie die Alten **sungen**, so zwitschern auch die Jungen* 'Like father, like son.'

Personal endings become more uniform in ENHG. The third person plural present indicative ending *-ent* was replaced by *-en*, which was the third person plural ending in the present subjunctive and preterite indicative and subjunctive.[43]

(43)   MHG *sie gebent* > NHG *sie geben* 'they give'

The ending of the second person singular preterite indicative form, *-e*, was replaced by *-st* (the second person singular ending elsewhere), and the root vowel of this form, which had been the umlauted form of the root vowel of the plural stem, was replaced by the root vowel of the other singular forms.

(44)   MHG *du gæbe* > NHG *du gabst* 'you took'

Some salient characteristics of ENHG word order are the following. Verb-second word order in main declarative clauses is the norm.[44]

(45)   *das sah si niht allein* (Ebert *et al.* 1993:432)
         that saw she not alone

In subordinate clauses, several different word order patterns can be found involving finite and non-finite verb forms. For example, the finite verb can precede the past participle and be followed by an extraposed element.

(46)   *daz du virtzig wochen **pist gelegen** unter meim meitlichen hertzen*
         (Ebert *et al.* 1993:438)
         that you forty weeks are lain under my maiden heart

The finite verb can also follow the past participle.

(47)   *von der grozzen heilikeit die wir hie **funden haben*** (Ebert *et al.*
         1993:438)
         from the great holiness that we here found have

Both of these orders are also possible with material between the finite and non-finite verb forms.

(48)   *wo jhr euch nicht **wolt** dero unwürdig **machen*** (Ebert *et al.*
         1993:438)
         where you yourself not want of-it unworthy make

The frequency of the modern German order, non-finite verb + finite verb, which we see in (47), increases during the ENHG period, and by 1600 it is the most common order by far.

As in MHG, two or more negation words in a sentence do not cancel each other out.

(49)   *Vorgisse **nymmer nicht** dez strengen gerichtes unsers herren.* (Ebert
        et al. 1993:427)
        forget never not the rigorous judgment of-our lord
        'Never forget the rigorous judgment of our Lord.'

The use of multiple negation decreases significantly in the seventeenth century.

5.5   New High German

New High German (NHG), which covers the time from 1650 to 1900, can be characterized as a period focused on the standardization of the language. At the beginning of this period there were essentially two forms of the written language, *Ostmitteldeutsch* and *das Gemeine Deutsch*, but by the end of the eighteenth century, the south had adopted the writing practices of *Ostmitteldeutsch*.[45]

Language societies (*Sprachgesellschaften*), whose members included grammarians and prominent authors, endeavored to create a standard literary language free of foreign influences. The first and most famous German language society, *die Fruchtbringende Gesellschaft*, modeled on the Italian *Accademia della Crusca*, was founded in Weimar in 1617, and included such authors as Andreas Gryphius, Martin Opitz, and Philipp von Zesen in its membership. During the "alamode era," the period following the Thirty Years' War (1618–1648), the influence of French on German was particularly great, and many loanwords found their way into the language, roughly half of which remain in it to this day (Stedje 2001:143): *Mode* 'fashion', *Parfüm* 'perfume', *Serviette* 'napkin', *Tasse* 'cup', *Balkon* 'balcony', *Hotel* 'hotel', *Cousin* 'cousin', etc. In an attempt to rid the language of foreign words, members of the *Sprachgesellschaften* created new German replacements. The list in Table 5.10 contains some of the successful (lasting) creations and the loanwords they were meant to replace. Among the neologisms that were felt to be extreme and did not survive the test of time were *Zitterweh* 'shiver ache' for *Fieber* 'fever' and *Gesichtserker* 'face projection' for *Nase* 'nose' (which was incorrectly thought to be a loanword).

A number of grammarians from this period contributed to the development of a standard language. Justus Georg Schottel's *Ausführliche Arbeit von der Teutschen Haubt Sprache* (1663) included rules for word formation, spelling, inflection, and syntax. Johann Christoph Gottsched promoted *Ostmitteldeutsch* as the ideal model for a literary standard in his *Grundlegung einer deutschen Sprachkunst, Nach dem Muster der besten Schriftsteller des vorigen und itzigen Jahrhunderts aufgestellet* (1748). Johann Christoph Adelung's works included a five-volume dictionary, a book on orthography, and a school grammar. Like

Table 5.10 *German replacements of French loanwords*

Loanword	German replacement
Adresse 'address'	*Anschrift*
Akt 'act'	*Aufzug*
Autor 'author'	*Verfasser*
Dialekt 'dialect'	*Mundart*
Korrespondenz 'correspondence'	*Briefwechsel*
Nekrolog 'obituary'	*Nachruf*
observieren 'to observe'	*beobachten*
Teleskop 'telescope'	*Fernglas*
Tragödie 'tragedy'	*Trauerspiel*

Gottsched, Adelung stressed the importance of usage in determining the grammatical norm.

Great poets and writers of the eighteenth century not only contributed to the establishment of German as a literary language, they also provided support for *Ostmitteldeutsch* as the standard. Klopstock, Lessing, Herder, Wieland, Goethe, and Schiller all used *Ostmitteldeutsch* in their works (Chambers and Wilkie 1970:50).

Much attention was given to the standardization of spelling. Schools sought spelling guides, but could not use the printed word as a model. Publishing practices were not uniform, and individual publishers were inconsistent. For example, Gustav Freytag's *Die Geschwister*, published by S. Hirzel in Leipzig in 1878, contains variant spellings like the following: *Schooß/Schoß* 'lap', *Der Tod/der Tot* 'death'; *töten/tödten* 'to kill' (Wells 1985:349). Various attempts at reform were made in the schools, but results did not come until after the unification of Germany in 1871.

One of the issues treated in attempts to standardize German orthography was whether one should spell phonetically or etymologically (historically). Jacob Grimm favored an etymological approach, whereby etymologically related words would be related orthographically. For example, he promoted the spellings *gäste* 'guests' and *hände* 'hands' rather than *geste* and *hende* (as in MHG), so that these plurals could easily be related to their singular forms, *gast* and *hand*. He argued (unsuccessfully) for the use of *ß* for those *s*-sounds that developed from Germanic *t* (through the High German Consonant shift): e.g., *Waßer* (Eng. *water*), *Haß* (Eng. *hate*). He also argued unsuccessfully against the capitalization of nouns.

Conferences on spelling reform were held in Berlin – in 1876 and again in 1901. Konrad Duden, a headmaster who had published a pamphlet of spelling conventions for his grammar school in Schleiz, was invited to the conference in 1876 (Wells 1985:350). In 1880 he published his *Vollständiges orthographisches Wörterbuch für die Schule. Nach den amtlichen Regeln der neuen Orthographie*. This work, now in its twenty-fourth edition, is the current standard reference work on German orthography (Dudenredaktion 2006).

Efforts to standardize pronunciation led to the publication of Theodor Siebs's *Deutsche Bühnenausprache* in 1898, which was modeled on northern German pronunciation (one exception being that <sp> and <st> were pronounced [ʃp] and [ʃt]).[46] Although the first edition was intended to codify the language of the stage, later editions were less narrow in scope (Siebs 1969).

Since the ENHG period, the German language has seen further development of analytic structures (although on a less grand scale than previously). Objects that were in the genitive case in Luther's time have been given up in favor of prepositional objects (or have been replaced by accusative objects).

(50) a. *hoffe ich liechtes* (Luther, cited in Stedje 2001:156)
         hope I light-genitive
     b. modern German: *auf etwas hoffen* 'to hope for something'

(51) a. *brauch der Zeit* (Luther, cited in Stedje 2001:156)
         need the-genitive time
     b. modern German: *etwas* (accusative) *brauchen* 'to need something'

An analytic subjunctive (*würde helfen* 'would help') has developed alongside the (older) synthetic subjunctive (*hülfe* 'would help'). This can be viewed as a response to the uncertainty that arose (*hälfe* or *hülfe*?) because of the leveling of the distinction between the singular and plural in the stem of the preterite, on which this subjunctive form is based (Stedje 2001:157).

By roughly 1900, the NHG standard can be viewed as having been established. After the founding of the German Empire in 1871, a certain amount of uniformity was achieved through the codification of orthography and pronunciation. Changes have continued to take place since then, of course. "Duden" is now an institution: what was once a spelling dictionary has evolved into a twelve-volume reference work that treats topics such as pronunciation, grammar, style, and usage – in addition to spelling. And spelling remains as controversial an issue as ever. Reforms were proposed (but not carried out) in 1944 and again in 1996. The 1996 reforms, which were met with much opposition and are still hotly debated, became official – with modifications – on August 1, 2006. Although we can now speak of a German standard language, there is still much variation throughout the German-speaking region, in the colloquial language (in pronunciation, "grammar," and vocabulary), in the versions of German that can be identified by national boundaries, and in the dialects, the very local versions of German that are not bound by the rules of the standard. The topic of regional variation is taken up in the following chapter.

Exercises

1. Apply Grimm's Law to the following PIE roots to discover Modern English derivatives.

	PIE	Modern English
(a)	*pent- 'to tread, go'	_____ind
(b)	*dheub- 'deep, hollow'	_____ee_____
(c)	*ters- 'dry'	_____irst
(d)	*kerd- 'heart'	_____ear_____
(e)	*ghos-ti- 'stranger, guest, host'	_____ues_____
(f)	*del- 'to recount, count'	_____ell
(g)	*bher- 'to carry'	_____ear
(h)	*gerbh- 'to scratch'	_____arve
(i)	*demə- 'to constrain, force'	_____ame
(j)	*kel- 'to be prominent'	_____ill

2. Use what you know about the High German Consonant Shift (and the changes that affected *d and *þ) to determine the German cognates of the following words in English.
   (a) **plant**; (b) **tongue**; (c) **kiss**; (d) to **sleep**; (e) to **break**; (f) **vat**; (g) **tame**; (h) **dapper**; (i) **th**orn; (j) **tug**

3. The following words were borrowed from Latin. Use your knowledge of the High German Consonant Shift to determine if they were borrowed before or after this shift.
   (a) *Altar* (Lat. *altāre*); (b) *kauf-* (Lat. *caup-*); (c) *Patient* (Lat. *patiēns*); (d) *Pfeil* (Lat. *pīlum*); (e) *Pfirsich* (Lat. *persica*); (f) *Pilger* (Lat. *pelegrīnus*); (g) *Rettich* (Lat. *radix*); (h) *Senf* (Lat. *sināpis*); (i) *Teppich* (Lat. *tapētum*); (j) *Zoll* (Lat. *tolonīum*)

4. Find evidence for weakening of unstressed syllables, Secondary Umlaut, Palatalization, and Final Fortition in the following MHG text (from *Das Nibelungenlied*; de Boor 1988:3).

> Ez wuohs in Búrgónden   ein vil édel magedîn,
> daz in allen landen   niht schœners mohte sîn,
> Kriemhilt geheizen: si wart ein scœne wîp.
> dar umbe muosen degene   vil verlíesén den lîp.

> There grew a royal child in Burgundy –
> In all the world none lovelier than she.
> Her name was Kriemhild. Great her beauty when,
> In womanhood, she cost the lives of many men.

(Ryder 1962:43)

(*wuohs* = NHG *wuchs*; *sîn* = NHG *sein*; *wart* = NHG *ward* 'wurde'; *wîp* = NHG *Weib* 'Frau'; *verlíesén* = NHG *verlieren*; *lîp* = NHG *Leib* 'Leben')

5. Identify the following texts as OHG, MHG, or ENHG. Provide evidence that supports your conclusions.[47]

   (a) *Der kunig zu Babylonien, hatte sein reych auch mit rauben vnnd gewalt genummenn*
       der König zu Babylonien hatte sein Reich auch mit Rauben und Gewalt genommen

   (b) *Thô quad zi imo thaz uuîb: 'hêrro, gib mir thaz uuazzar, thaz mih ni thurste noh ni queme hera scephen'.*
       da sprach zu ihm das Weib Herr gib mir das Wasser dass mich nie durste noch nie komme hierher schöpfen

   (c) *Swer mit sünden sî geladen, der sol sîn herze in riuwe baden.*
       wer mit Sünden sei geladen der soll sein Herz in Reue baden

   (d) *Uuurdun sum erkorane, Sume sâr verlorane.*
       wurden einige ausgewählt einige sofort verloren

   (e)
       mit sîme stabe, den er truoc,
       dâ mite er ûf daz houbet sluoc
       den knaben edele unde clâr,
       daz im diu scheitel und daz hâr
       von rôtem bluote wurden naz.

       mit seinem Stab den er trug da mit er auf das Haupt schlug den Knaben edel und schön dass ihm die Scheitel[48] und das Haar von rotem Blut wurden nass

NOTES

1 The <th> in *thu* was pronounced like the <th> in Eng. *thing*.

2 A word of caution is in order here. Because this text is a translation from Latin, the word order it exhibits does not necessarily reflect accurately the rules of Old High German syntax. See section 5.2.3 for further discussion.

3 Various terms for the reconstructed parent language of the Germanic languages can be found in the literature: "Proto-Germanic" (*Urgemanisch*), "Common Germanic" (*Gemeingermansich*), etc. We use the simple term "Germanic" to refer to this reconstructed form.

4 We use Fortson's (2004) symbols for the reconstructed sounds of PIE; they are similar to IPA symbols.

5 This does not take into account the laryngeals, a class of sounds whose exact phonetic values are not known. The laryngeals are generally believed to have been fricatives articulated in the back of the mouth and throat. However, they have no certain consonantal reflexes outside the Anatolian branch of PIE (Fortson 2004: 56).

6 In historical linguistics, an asterisk is used to denote a reconstructed form – one that is not preserved in any written documents.

7 The dual is used to signal two entities.

8 The perfect, traditionally viewed as a fourth tense, is now held to be a stative that acquired a secondary use as a past tense (Fortson 2004:81).

9 See Fortson 2004:81–83 for further discussion of the various grammatical distinctions in the PIE categories for tense, voice, and mood.

10 This is the definition of topicalization that Fortson (2004:144) provides for the process in PIE.

11 A clitic is an unstressed word that cannot stand alone but must attach to a neighboring stressed word, with which it forms a unit. The *m* in *I'm* and the *s* in *she's*, for example, are clitics.

12 For further discussion of PIE, see, for example, Fortson 2004 and Watkins 1998.

13 In diachronic (historical) as well as synchronic linguistics (see chapter 2, section 2.3), the symbol "<" means '(comes) from' or '(is) derived from', and ">" means 'becomes' or 'changes to',

14 In an essay published in 1818, the Danish philologist Rasmus Rask first described the sound correspondences that form the basis of Grimm's Law. Jacob Grimm, who had independently discovered these correspondences and then read Rask's work, published his formulation (generally considered the definitive description) in 1822 in the second edition of his *Deutsche Grammatik*.

15 The voiced aspirated stops were voiced stops followed by a puff of breath or a brief period of breathy voice (murmur) (Fortson 2004:50). Breathy voice is produced with the arytenoids apart and the ligamental vocal cords vibrating (Ladefoged 1971:8).

16 The fifteen different PIE stops in Table 5.1 have been reduced to nine in Table 5.2. In Germanic, the palatal velars merge with the plain velars. To simplify the discussion, we have left out the PIE labiovelars. The *th* sound in a word like Eng. *think* ([θ]), is represented with the symbol *þ* (thorn), since this is commonly found in the handbooks.

17 The Sanskrit examples are from Fortson 2004:302.

18 See Iverson and Salmons 1995 for an account for this exception to Grimm's Law.

19 The PIE and Germanic forms in (7) are from Fortson 2004:303. The symbol h_2 in (7a) stands for one of the IE laryngeals.

20 English *choose* and its cognate in German, *küren* 'to choose', provide evidence for leveling of the *s/r* alternation: English has leveled the alternation in favor of *s* (with *s* in all forms of the paradigm) and German has leveled it in favor of *r*.

21 These examples are from Fortson 2004:304.

22 In Gothic, *ō* is spelled with *o*.

23 The vocative case marks words (nouns and pronouns) that are used to address someone. In the sentence *Beth, are you planning to go?* the noun *Beth* has a vocative role.

24 The instrumental case marks words (nouns and pronouns) used to express instrument or means. In Germanic, the instrumental was of limited use even in the oldest surviving texts (Fortson 2004:304).

25 The middle in PIE could also express the passive voice. Fortson (2004:83) argues that it is best to regard the middle as having been a mediopassive, capable of expressing either middle or passive meaning depending on context.

26 The terms "strong" and "weak" were coined by Jacob Grimm.

27 The origin of this dental suffix has long been a topic of discussion; it is generally believed to have developed from the same root as the English verb *do*.

28 The runic inscriptions, the oldest documents in Germanic, date back to roughly the middle of the first century AD. These inscriptions make use of the Germanic runic alphabet known as the futhark, named after its first six letters: *f u þ a r k*. For further information on the runes, see, for example, Krause and Jankuhn 1966, Robinson 1992, and Antonsen 1975, 2002.

29 In synthetic languages, words are composed of more than one morpheme. In purely analytic languages, each word contains a single morpheme. Grammatical categories like number and tense are not realized as affixes in such languages, but are expressed as separate words.

30 Cognates are words (in two or more different languages) that derive historically from the same word. They are similar in form, but not necessarily identical because of sound changes that may affect one language but not another. Cognates are also similar but not necessarily identical in meaning because of semantic changes that may affect a word in one language but not another.

31 See Stedje 2001:60 for examples of some additional environments in which *p *t *k remain unshifted.

32 Some consonants that appeared between *a* and *i* functioned initially as a barrier to Primary Umlaut, for example, *ht*: OHG *mahti* 'powers (*Mächte*)'. The barriers were eventually overcome in the Middle High German period. The later umlaut of short *a* is subsumed under Secondary Umlaut (see below in the text and section 5.3.2).

33 Consonants as well as vowels were affected by the Germanic accent shift. The changes were progressive, and those affecting consonants were earlier than those affecting vowels. For further details of these *Auslautsgesetze* 'laws of finals', see, for example, Bach 1970:60–61 and Boutkan 1995.

34 There is only one example of a dual form, *unkēr* (first person genitive dual), in a work by Otfrid (Braune 2004:241).

35 The preterite is also used to express the pre-past; that is, it has the sense of a past perfect (Schrodt 2004:128).

36 Extraposition is the movement of an element from its normal position to a position at the end of a sentence. In the subordinate clause *weil mein Freund viel besser war als ich* 'because my friend was a lot better than I', the comparative phrase *als ich* 'than I' has been extraposed.

37 The beginning of the MHG period is also considered to be 1100 or 1150 (rather than 1050) because of the absence of literary works in the vernacular during the century following the OHG period. The end of the MHG period is also debated, some scholars (following Jacob Grimm) placing it at 1500.

38 In normalized MHG orthography, long vowels are indicated with a circumflex (e.g., *â*, *ê*, etc.). The long umlauted vowels are *æ*, *œ*, and *iu* [y:]. The affricate [ts] is represented with *z* (*zuo* 'to'), *tz* when in intervocalic position (*setzen* 'to set'). The *s*-sound that developed from *t* is represented with the symbol ʒ (*waʒʒer* 'water') to distinguish it from the affricate as well as the *s*-sound inherited from Germanic (*hûs* 'house').

39 The alliterative German phrase that describes this process, *die mitteldeutsche Monophthongierung*, is a good mnemonic for remembering the dialect area that was affected.

40 The period in the forms in (41) signals a syllable boundary.

41 Gothic script (*Frakturschrift*), in use since the fifteenth century, makes use of two kinds of *s* symbols: a long *s*, which appears in medial position, and a round *s*, which appears word-finally.

42 The second person singular preterite stem differed from the first and third person stems; it contained the root vowel of the plural stem – with umlaut: *ich nam* 'I took'; *du næme* 'you took'; *wir nâmen* 'we took'.

43 The "present subjunctive" of MHG corresponds to the present Subjunctive I of Modern Standard German; the "preterite subjunctive" of MHG corresponds to the present Subjunctive II of Modern Standard German.

44 This description of ENHG word order is based on Ebert *et al.* 1993.

45 The largest Swiss chanceries and presses had switched to *das Gemeine Deutsch* at the beginning of the NHG period.

46 Northern German pronunciation was held to be purer than that of German spoken elsewhere, since it was based on the written language. In northern Germany, Low German had long been the variety used in speech, although High German was used for writing. When speakers in the cities began to use High German as the spoken medium, they modeled their pronunciation on the written word (Stedje 2001:155).

47 These texts are from Bachmann 1970, Ebert *et al.* 1993, and Braune *et al.* 1994. They have been modified slightly to remove some of the effects of normalized orthography.

48 The noun *Scheitel* is now masculine.

6   Regional variation

6.1   The standard–colloquial–dialect continuum

At the one end of the German standard–colloquial–dialect continuum is the standard language. The standard language is the supraregional variety codified in works such as the *Duden* grammar (Dudenredaktion 2005) and pronouncing dictionary (Mangold 2005). At the other end of the continuum are the dialects, the local or regional varieties. Between these two extremes is the colloquial language (*Umgangssprache*), which exhibits regional variation in pronunciation, grammar, and lexicon, but not to the degree found in the dialects.[1]

Various terms are used in German to refer to the standard language; some common terms are *Hochsprache*, *Schriftsprache*, and *Standardsprache*. The non-technical term *Hochdeutsch* is also used to refer to the standard language. Virtually all native speakers interpret this term as synonymous with *Hochsprache* and are unaware of its technical sense. In its technical sense, *Hochdeutsch* means 'High German' and refers to those dialects that participated in the High German Consonant Shift (see the discussion in chapter 5, section 5.3.2).[2]

The standard language is the variety that is typically described in grammar books and dictionaries, the variety that is used in school (in Germany) and taught to foreigners. Barbour and Stevenson label this variety "formal Standard German," since it is the variety that represents the speech and writing of educated people in formal situations; it is comparable not to standard English, but to formal standard English (1990:135).[3]

What is considered the norm in Standard German can differ significantly from common practice. For example, although colloquially and regionally, the preposition *wegen* 'because of' is common with the dative case (*wegen dem Wetter* 'because of the weather'), this is considered incorrect in the standard language (Dudenredaktion 2001:928), where the genitive is required (*wegen des Wetters*). Language textbooks are beginning to address such differences between the standard and everyday usage. Lovik *et al.* (2007:423), for example, note that while the genitive case is common with prepositions like *wegen* in written texts, it is increasingly being replaced by the dative case in spoken German.

The status of the standard language differs from region to region. In German-speaking Switzerland, no member of the native population speaks Standard German as a native language, although most speakers do acquire a certain level of proficiency in it. In southern Germany and Austria, native speakers of Standard German are a smaller proportion of the population than native speakers in northern Germany (Barbour and Stevenson 1990:136).[4]

Although Standard German can be characterized as a supraregional variety, with a uniform grammar and spelling, it does exhibit regional variation. For example, there are some meanings for which there is no supraregional lexeme. A well-known example is southern German *Samstag* 'Saturday' and northern German *Sonnabend* 'Saturday'.[5] The words for 'butcher' are also regionally bound (Clyne 1995:89): *Fleischer* (east central and some west central), *Metzger* (southern and central), and *Schlachter* (northern). Although several different consonantal *r*-sounds are accepted as standard pronunciation, their distribution can be described in regional terms: Uvular *r* predominates in northern, central, and south-western parts of the German-speaking area, alveolar *r* in south-eastern parts (C. Hall 2003:65). In general, however, the standard is a fairly uniform variety of German and regionalism is minimal.

The colloquial language can itself be divided up into different varieties, although scholars are not in agreement as to how many varieties should be recognized. Schönfeld (1977:170) distinguishes three varieties of German between the standard and the Low German dialect in the north of the former East Germany. Veith (1983) also recognizes three varieties of the colloquial in a study of the urban speech of Frankfurt, but his levels do not correspond exactly to those of Schönfeld. Barbour and Stevenson (1990:140) differentiate between two different types of colloquial German, colloquial Standard German and colloquial non-standard German, in part because German speakers recognize this division in their own speech. In our discussion of regional variation within the colloquial language (in section 6.1.3), we will make at most a distinction between these two levels of the colloquial.

It is important to keep in mind that although we can identify the major varieties of German on the continuum from the standard to dialect, there are often no clear or sharp dividing lines separating them. The nature of the divisions also differs from region to region. In the Low German area, for example, where dialects are very far from Standard German, the division between dialect and colloquial German is much sharper than in the Central German area, where dialects are closer to the standard, having made the greatest contribution historically to the development of the standard (Stevenson and Barbour 1990:141–142).

6.2   Variation in the colloquial

Variation in colloquial German can be described in regional terms. We will limit our discussion here to variation in the colloquial language spoken in Germany.[6] The regions that are important to this discussion are northern, central, and southern Germany. We will consider variation in pronunciation, in grammar, and in vocabulary.

6.2.1   Variation in pronunciation

In northern Germany, the suffix *-ung* is pronounced [ʊŋkʰ], not [ʊŋ], as in the standard language: *Reibung* 'friction' [ʁaɪp̆ʊŋkʰ] (rather than [ʁaɪp̆ʊŋ]). In addition, word-initial <sp> and <st> are pronounced with [s] rather than [ʃ]: *Spiel* 'game' [spiːl] (rather than [ʃpiːl]); *Stein* 'stone' [staɪ̯n] (rather than [ʃtaɪ̯n]). In northern and central Germany, /k/ (<g>) in coda position is pronounced as a fricative ([x] or [ç], depending on the quality of the preceding vowel), not as a stop, as in Standard German: *Tag* 'day' [tʰaːx] (instead of [tʰaːkʰ]), *Teig* 'dough' [tʰaɪ̯ç] (instead of [tʰaɪ̯kʰ]).[7] In southern Germany, the /k/ in the suffix *-ig* is pronounced as a stop, not as a fricative, which is standard: *wichtig* 'important' [vɪçtʰɪkʰ] (rather than [vɪçtʰɪç]). Word-initial [ç] is realized in southern Germany as [kʰ]: *Chemie* 'chemistry' [kʰemiː] (rather than [çemiː]). In southern and especially south-western Germany, there is a tendency to pronounce medial and final <sp> and <st> with [ʃ] instead of [s], which is standard: *Wespen* 'wasps' [vɛʃpm̩], *Wurst* 'sausage' [vʊɐ̯ʃtʰ]. One of the salient regional pronunciations involving vowels is the substitution in northern and central Germany of [eː] for [ɛː], the pronunciation of long <ä>: *Käse* [kʰeːzə] (for standard [kʰɛːzə]). For further discussion of non-standard pronunciations in colloquial German, see, for example, Barbour and Stevenson 1990:151–155, Durrell 1992:13, and C. Hall 2003.

6.2.2   Variation in grammar

There is less regional variation in grammar (morphology, syntax) than in pronunciation or vocabulary, but there are a number of well-known deviations from the standard that are typical of the north or the south.

The use of *am* + nominalized infinitive + *sein* is the typical northern German way of expressing progressive meaning overtly: *Mein Vater ist am Schreiben* for Standard German *Mein Vater schreibt gerade* 'My father is writing' (Durrell 1992:16). According to *Duden* (Dudenredaktion 2001:63), similar progressive constructions with *beim* or *im* in place of *am* are considered standard; the use of *am* is a regional colloquialism (found particularly in the Rhineland and in Westphalia).

Table 6.1 *Personal pronouns in northern colloquial non-standard German*

	'I'	'you (singular)'	'he'	'she'	'it'
Nominative	*ich/ick(e)*	*du*	*er*	*sie*	*es/et*
Oblique	*mi(r)*	*di(r)*	*ihm*	*ihr*	*es*

The splitting of "*da*-compounds" is another characteristic of northern German syntax. In Standard German, words formed using *da* followed by a preposition (*davon* 'from it/them'; *dafür* 'for that/it') cannot be split into their component parts and separated by other sentence constituents. *Dafür kann ich nichts* 'I can't help it.' In northern German, splitting is the norm in the colloquial language: *Da kann ich nichts für.*

In the north, in the variety of the colloquial language that Barbour and Stevenson label "colloquial non-standard German," the accusative–dative distinction is absent, a feature shared by northern German dialects. Table 6.1 displays the forms of the personal pronoun in the singular (from Barbour and Stevenson 1990:162), which illustrate this feature. The oblique case is the non-nominative case, the case used when either the accusative or the dative would be used in the standard language. The absence of an accusative–dative distinction in the colloquial non-standard German of the north is no doubt the cause of the confusion of accusative and dative found in the colloquial standard of this region. For example, one might hear *Er hat* **mir** (dative) *gesehen* 'He has seen me' in the north instead of the standard *Er hat mich* (accusative) *gesehen* (Durrell 1992:16).

The use of the preposition *nach* 'to' instead of *zu* 'to' is a characteristic of colloquial German in the north. One hears *nach dem Bahnhof* 'to the train station' instead of the standard *zum Bahnhof*.

One sees a certain amount of regional variation in the choice of auxiliary verb. In the colloquial language in northern Germany we find the auxiliary *sein* rather than *haben* used with the verbs *beginnen* and *anfangen*, both meaning 'to begin': *Ich bin begonnen/angefangen* 'I have begun' (Durrell 1992:16). In the south, we find the auxiliary *sein* instead of *haben* used with *liegen* 'to lie', *sitzen* 'to sit', and *stehen* 'to stand': *Ich bin gelegen/gesessen/gestanden* 'I have lain/sat/stood.'

The plural formation of nouns also exhibits regional variation. In the north, the use of the plural ending *-s* has increased (Durrell 1992:16): *die Doktors* 'the doctors' (for standard *die Doktoren*). It often replaces the zero-plural found in Standard German: *die Wagens* 'the cars' (for standard *die Wagen*). Some non-standard plurals found in the south are the following (Durrell 1992:17):

(1)   South   Standard
   a.   *die Wägen* 'the cars'   *die Wagen*
   b.   *die Stücker* 'the pieces'   *die Stücke*
   c.   *die Stiefeln* 'the boots'   *die Stiefel*

Another non-standard feature of nouns in the south is gender. A number of nouns exhibit genders that differ from those in Standard German (Durrell 1992:17).

(2)   South   Standard
   a.   *der Butter* 'the butter'   *die Butter*
   b.   *der Radio* 'the radio'   *das Radio*
   c.   *der Gewalt* 'the violence' *die Gewalt*
   d.   *die Bach* 'the brook'   *der Bach*
   e.   *der Kartoffel* 'the potato' *die Kartoffel*

The use of past tense forms shows regional variation in the colloquial language. Speakers in the south typically do not use the past; they use the present perfect instead. Because of the lack of past forms, southern speakers do not have a past perfect; they use the double present perfect to express a past event that precedes another past event (see section 4.3.4): *Ich habe es vergessen gehabt* 'I had forgotten it' (instead of Standard German *Ich hatte es vergessen*). Some speakers in the south have past tense forms in their speech, but only those of the verbs *haben* 'to have' and *sein* 'to be'. These speakers use the present perfect for all verbs other than *haben* and *sein*. Because they have past forms for *haben* and *sein*, they also have the past perfect, as in the standard language.[8]

6.2.3   Variation in vocabulary

As Durrell (1992:20) points out, it is sometimes difficult to separate regionalism from style level in the lexicon. Many regional words are limited to the colloquial language, whereas others are used in all speech styles. The examples in Tables 6.2 and 6.3 are some of the more well-known regional variants with their counterparts in the standard language. None of the examples is restricted to the colloquial language, although some are more common in the colloquial language than in more formal speech.

6.3   German in Switzerland

6.3.1   Diglossia

German-speaking Switzerland has been used in the linguistic literature as a classic example of diglossia, a situation in which a community uses two distinct

Table 6.2 *Vocabulary in northern German*
(modified from Durrell 1992:20)

North	Standard
das Abendbrot 'supper'	*das Abendessen*
denn 'then'	*dann*
flöten 'to whistle'	*pfeifen*
die Gören 'children'	*die Kinder*
der Kasten 'drawer'	*die Schublade*
kloppen 'to hit'	*schlagen*
kucken 'to look'	*sehen*
der Pott 'pot'	*der Topf*
der Schlips 'necktie'	*die Krawatte*
die Wurzel 'carrot'	*die Mohrrübe*

Table 6.3 *Vocabulary in southern German*
(modified from Durrell 1992:21–22)

South	Standard
arg 'very'	*sehr*
geschwind 'fast'	*schnell*
die gelbe Rübe 'carrot'	*die Mohrrübe*
der Kamin 'chimney'	*der Schornstein*
das Mädel 'girl'	*das Mädchen*
die Orange 'orange'	*die Apfelsine*
der Rahm 'cream'	*die Sahne*
reden 'to speak'	*sprechen*
schauen 'to look'	*sehen*
sieden 'to boil'	*kochen*

forms of the same language, one, the prestige form, learned in school and used in one set of contexts (or domains), the other acquired as a native language and used in another set of contexts (Ferguson 1959). In Switzerland, the two distinct forms are Swiss Standard German (SSG), similar to the standard language of Germany, and *Schweizerdeutsch*, a cover term for all German dialects spoken in Switzerland. There is no colloquial language (*Umgangssprache*), as there is in Germany, to mediate between SSG and the local Swiss dialects.

Although it is common to treat German-speaking Switzerland as a classic case of diglossia, the term does not currently apply in the strict sense, since SSG, in contrast to dialect, does not have the status of a prestige variety. Barbour and Stevenson (1990:213) argue that both varieties have positive prestige, but for different reasons and to different extents.[9]

It has generally been argued that SSG is used in writing and formal speech, and dialect in informal speech. Although these may have been the traditional domains of the two varieties, this division does not reflect current practice. Dialect is being used increasingly in informal speech in formal domains (on radio and television, in church services, in the military, in secondary and post-secondary education, etc.) and even in formal speech (Clyne 1995:43, Werlen 2004). According to Barbour and Stevenson (1992:213), for the vast majority of German Swiss, SSG is a variety of German used exclusively for writing. The relationship between the two varieties of German used in Switzerland is thus treated by many linguists as a special kind of diglossia, diglossia based on medium (*mediale Diglossie*), where (in general) the standard language is used for writing, and dialect for speaking (e.g., Sieber and Sitta 1986:20, Ramseier 1988.17). Rash (1998.50) suggests that the term "functional diglossia" may be preferable, since it describes a situation in which each variety is allocated certain functions. Werlen (2004:22) also points out the shortcomings of a simple model of medial diglossia, noting, for example, that Swiss German dialects are written as well as spoken: dialect is used in obituaries, for postcards, and especially in electronic communication (e-mail, text-messaging).[10]

The relationship between SSG and the Swiss dialects is less clear-cut than a textbook definition of diglossia might suggest – whether defined in terms of domain, medium, or function. Barbour and Stevenson argue that it is probably more appropriate to speak of tendencies rather than absolute rules, with one variety more likely to be used in a given situation than another variety. Ramseier (1988:545) argues that SSG and dialect cannot be neatly separated; their domains can be viewed as overlapping. This situation, where two varieties may be appropriate in a given situation, can lead to a greater degree of code-switching, that is, switching from one language variety to another within a single conversation (Barbour and Stevenson 1990:214).

6.3.2   Swiss Standard German

Although SSG is similar to the Standard German used in Germany, there are differences between the two – in pronunciation, orthography, morphology, and vocabulary. Some of the more well-known differences are described in the following sections.[11] To avoid any confusion in terminology, we will refer to the Standard German spoken in Germany as German Standard German (GSG).

6.3.2.1 Pronunciation   Boesch (1957) provided guidelines for the pronunciation of SSG that sought a middle ground between a pronunciation heavily influenced by dialect and one adhering strictly to the GSG norm. Some of these suggestions were included in the nineteenth edition (1969) of the pronouncing dictionary by Siebs (Russ 1994:85). The *Duden* pronouncing dictionary (Mangold 2005) aims to provide a supraregional standard and thus does not address the pronunciation of SSG.

Vowels in SSG differ from those in GSG mainly in length. In some words we find long vowels where GSG has short vowels; in other words we find the opposite (Meyer 1989:26–27).

(3)　　German Standard German　　Swiss Standard German
   a.　　*br*[a]*chte* 'brought'　　*br*[aː]*chte*
   b.　　*H*[ɔ]*chzeit* 'wedding'　　*H*[oː]*chzeit*
   c.　　*Ged*[ɛ]*chtnis* 'memory'　　*Ged*[ɛː]*chtnis*
   d.　　*d*[yː]*ster* 'gloomy'　　*d*[ʏ]*ster*
   e.　　*Kr*[eː]*bs* 'cancer'　　*Kr*[ɛ]*bs*
   f.　　*N*[iː]*sche* 'niche'　　*N*[ɪ]*sche*

One of the salient differences in the pronunciation of consonants in SSG involves the pronunciation of <ch>. The velar fricative [x] tends to be used for word-initial <ch>, where GSG requires [ç] or [kʰ]. The velar fricative is also often substituted for GSG [ç] in words like *ich* 'I' and *sicher* 'sure' (Clyne 1995:48).

(4)　　German Standard German　　Swiss Standard German
   a.　　[ç]*emie* 'Chemistry'　　[x]*emie*
   b.　　[ç]*ina* 'China'　　[x]*ina*
   c.　　[kʰ]*ronik* 'chronicle'　　[x]*ronik*
   d.　　[kʰ]*or* 'chorus'　　[x]*or*
   e.　　*i*[ç] 'I'　　*i*[x]
   f.　　*si*[ç]*er* 'sure'　　*si*[x]*er*

The <g> in the -*ig* suffix is pronounced as [k] when GSG requires [ç] (Ammon *et al.* 1995:257).

(5)　　German Standard German　　Swiss Standard German
   a.　　*ewi*[ç] 'eternal'　　*ewi*[k]
   b.　　*erledi*[ç]*t* 'dealt with'　　*erledi*[k]*t*

Another important feature of SSG is the absence of *r*-Vocalization. SSG has a consonantal pronunciation of <r> where GSG has a vocalized *r*: *bitte*[r] 'bitter' (GSG *bitt*[ɐ]).

SSG differs from GSG in various ways prosodically. One difference involves word stress. In words borrowed from French, SSG exhibits stress on the initial syllable, whereas GSG has non-initial stress.

(6)　　German Standard German　　Swiss Standard German
   a.　　*Büˈffet* 'sideboard'　　ˈ*Büffet*
   b.　　*Büˈro* 'office'　　ˈ*Büro*
   c.　　*Fiˈlet* 'fillet'　　ˈ*Filet*

There is a general consensus that German-speaking Swiss can be recognized by their intonation (Ammon 1995:257). According to Panizollo (1982:41–42), the stressed syllables preceding the nucleus in SSG are low in pitch and the unstressed syllables following them take on a slightly rising cadence. In GSG, the pitch of prenuclear speech is in the medium range and the cadences are relatively level. Ammon points out that it is not clear to what extent SSG intonation differs from the intonation of Swiss dialects or possibly of the entire Alemannic dialect region (1995:258).

6.3.2.2 Orthography An important systemic difference between SSG and GSG orthography – one that is acknowledged in the *Duden* spelling dictionary – is the substitution in SSG of <ss> for <ß> (Dudenredaktion 2006:95). The use of <ß> is not taught in school and it is rarely found in Swiss German texts (Rash 1998:154).[12]

Words of foreign origin tend to retain their original orthography more often in SSG than in GSG (Meyer 1989:33; Rash 1998:155).

(7)   German Standard German   Swiss Standard German
    a.   *Debüt* 'debut'   *Début*
    b.   *Mokassin* 'moccasin'   *Mocassin*
    c.   *schick* 'elegant'   *chic*
    d.   *Soße* 'sauce'   *Sauce*
    e.   *Resümee* 'summary'   *Résumé*

Sometimes differences in spelling between SSG and GSG indicate differences in pronunciation (Ammon 1995:254).

(8)   German Standard German   Swiss Standard German
    a.   *Müsli* 'muesli'   *Müesli*
    b.   *Züricher* 'native of Zürich'   *Zürcher*

6.3.2.3 Morphology   A comparison of SSG and GSG reveals differences in derivational morphology. For example, affixes like *-ung*, *-nis*, and *-keit* are common in both SSG and GSG, but the following words, which contain them, are unknown in GSG (Rash 1998:157):

(9)   Swiss Standard German
    a.   *-ung*   *Gastung* 'guests' (collective)
    b.   *-nis*   *Betreffnis* 'installment' (cf. *Teilbetrag*)
    c.   *-keit*   *Sehnlichkeit* 'yearning' (cf. *Sehnsucht*)
    d.   *-schaft*   *Dorfschaft* 'people in a village'
    e.   *-ler*   *Bähnler* 'railroad worker' (cf. *Bahnarbeiter*)

Other affixes (from dialect) are found only in SSG (Rash 1998:159).

(10)   Swiss Standard German
   a.   *-et*   *der Heuet* 'hay harvest' (cf. *Heuernte*)
   b.   *-ete*   *das Tanzete* 'dancing' (cf. *das Tanzen*)

Diminutives formed with the suffix *-li* are particularly common in SSG and do not necessarily designate entities that are small: *Rüebli* 'carrot(s)', *Peterli* 'parsley', *Pullöverli* 'pullover' (Rash 1998:157–158).

The verbal suffix *-ieren* is often used in SSG when GSG would simply have *-en*.

(11)   German Standard German   Swiss Standard German
   a.   *campen* 'to camp'   *campieren*
   b.   *grillen* 'to grill'   *grillieren*
   c.   *handikapen* 'to handicap'   *handicapieren*
   d.   *parken* 'to park'   *parkieren*

In the formation of compounds we find differences between SSG and GSG in the use of inflectional affixes and linking elements. Compounds in SSG sometimes have inflectional affixes or linking elements between the two members of a compound where their GSG counterparts do not.

(12)   German Standard German   Swiss Standard German
   a.   *Uhrmacher* 'watch maker'   *Uhrenmacher*
   b.   *Landgemeinde* 'rural community'   *Landsgemeinde*

Sometimes GSG compounds have these inflectional affixes and linking elements and their SSG counterparts do not.

(13)   German Standard German   Swiss Standard German
   a.   *Tageblatt* 'daily paper'   *Tagblatt*
   b.   *Sonntagsausgabe* 'Sunday edition' *Sonntagausgabe*

6.3.2.4 Vocabulary   While SSG has many lexical items in common with German spoken in southern Germany and Austria (e.g., *Orange* 'orange'), it also has words that are unique to SSG. Table 6.4 lists some of the more common lexical items peculiar to SSG along with their GSG counterparts. In some cases, a SSG word will exist in GSG, but with a different meaning. For example, SSG *Kleid* means 'suit', whereas in GSG it means 'dress'; SSG *schlimm* means 'clever', whereas in GSG it means 'bad'.

Gender assignment in nouns is another area in which SSG differs from GSG.

Table 6.4 *Vocabulary in Swiss Standard German*
(modified from Durrell 1992:23–24)

Swiss Standard German	German Standard German
die Base 'aunt'	*die Tante*
der Camion 'truck'	*der Lastwagen*
der Coiffeur 'haircutter'	*der Friseur*
der Führer 'car driver'	*der Autofahrer*
glätten 'to iron'	*bügeln*
der Hausmeister 'homeowner'	*der Hausbesitzer*
die Maturität (school-leaving exam)	*das Abitur*
merci 'thank you'	*danke*
Rösti 'fried potatoes'	*Bratkartoffeln*
schlimm 'clever'	*schlau*
das Velo 'bicycle'	*das Fahrrad*
der Vortritt 'right-of-way'	*der Vorfahrt*

(14)   German Standard German   Swiss Standard German
   a. *die Couch* 'couch'   *der Couch*
   b. *die Semmel* 'roll'   *der Semmel*
   c. *das Drittel* 'third'   *der Drittel*

In the case of the word for 'radio', gender assignment in SSG is identical to gender assignment in colloquial German in southern Germany (*der Radio*), in contrast to gender assignment in GSG (*das Radio*).

6.4   German in Austria

6.4.1   Overview

In Austria, as in central and southern Germany, we find a standard–colloquial–dialect continuum. Wiesinger (1990:443) makes a four-way distinction when describing the speech varieties in Austria (particularly in the east and south): primary dialect, regional dialect, colloquial speech, and the standard, which we label Austrian Standard German (ASG). ASG, described below, differs in pronunciation, grammar, and vocabulary from GSG. With the exception of the dialects of Vorarlberg in the west, which (like Swiss German) are Alemannic dialects, Austrian dialects belong to the Bavaro-Austrian dialect area. Colloquial speech reflects a leveling between dialect and the standard. For example, in the Weinviertel of Lower Austria about 20 to 70 kilometers from Vienna, *heim* [hoɐm] 'home' is used in primary dialect in the phrase meaning 'to go home'. In ASG, 'home' is rendered as *nach Haus* [nɑːx hɑoz]. The colloquial form, *zu Haus* [dz aoz] 'home', acts as a mediating intermediate form (Wiesinger 1990:444–445).[13] Most speakers have competence in more than one variety of speech in the continuum from standard to dialect and will use these varieties differently depending on the situation and conversational partner.

Roughly three-quarters of the population in Austria can be regarded as dialect speakers, with the use of dialect being stronger in rural areas and small towns than in cities. However, dialect is becoming restricted more and more to conversations with close friends and family, and colloquial speech and the standard are used with greater frequency as the social distance between conversational partners and the formality of the conversational situation increases. In general, colloquial language is favored as the form of everyday speech in the middle and upper classes, especially in towns.[14]

6.4.2   Austrian Standard German

The main Austrian work that codifies ASG is the *Österreichisches Wörterbuch* (Back *et al.* 2006), now in its fortieth edition, with over 80,000 entries. The current version, which follows the most recent spelling reforms, aims to describe Austrian German, in particular the features in vocabulary, pronunciation, grammar, and phraseology that are peculiar to the language. It includes many technical terms as well as common vocabulary. In addition to pronunciation, grammatical information (gender, genitive and plural endings, etc.), and definitions, lexical entries include information regarding style (e.g., *ugs.* = *umgangssprachlich* 'colloquial'), origin, and regional distribution. In this respect it describes more than just the standard language. It includes the official spelling rules of 2006 and provides pertinent information and overviews on language and grammar as well as spelling, and thus codifies more than just spelling, vocabulary, and pronunciation.

Some examples of the special features of ASG pronunciation, grammar, and vocabulary are provided in the following sections.

6.4.2.1 Pronunciation   One Austrian feature in the pronunciation of vowels is the use of [ɔ] (instead of [a]) as the realization of /a/ (C. Hall 2003:87).[15]

(15)   German Standard German   Austrian Standard German
    a. [a]*st* 'branch'   [ɔ]*st*
    b. *B*[a]*cke* 'cheek'   *B*[ɔ]*cke*

Another systemic difference in the pronunciation of vowels involves the diphthong /aɪ/. In GSG this is realized as [aɪ]; in ASG, the vocalic member of the diphthong has a less "open" pronunciation. According to Hall (2003:104), for example, a typical realization of this diphthong in Austria is [ɛe̞]. A word like *kein* 'no', for example, would be pronounced *k*[ɛɛ̯]*n* in ASG rather than *k*[aɪ̯]*n*, as in GSG.

A feature of the pronunciation of vowels in ASG that is lexically governed involves schwa ([ə]). In words borrowed from French, word-final schwa is deleted. For example, GSG [ə] in the following words is not pronounced in ASG: *Chanc*[ə] 'chance', *Cliqu*[ə] 'clique', *Nuanc*[ə] 'nuance'.

As in SSG, there are differences between ASG and GSG in vowel length in a number of words. Some of the words that exhibit such differences are also found in SSG; others are not. The following examples exhibit pronunciations that are unique to ASG (Back *et al.* 2006).

(16)   German Standard German   Austrian Standard German
    a. *Ch*[ɒ]*f* 'boss'   *Ch*[ɐ̯]*f*
    b. *H*[uː]*sten* 'cough'   *H*[ʊ]*sten*
    c. *Beh*[øː]*rde* 'authorities'   *Beh*[œ]*rde*
    d. *Gran*[iː]*t* 'granite'   *Gran*[ɪ]*t*

Although ASG has both [ç] and [x] in its phonetic inventory, it differs from GSG in the distribution of these sounds. In particular, ASG has [x] following /r/ instead of [ç], as in GSG (Clyne 1995:37).

(17)   German Standard German   Austrian Standard German
    a. *dur*[ç] 'through'   *dur*[x]
    b. *Kir*[ç]*e* 'church'   *Kir*[x]*e*

AGS has initial [k] in words of foreign origin where GSG has [ç], a feature it shares with colloquial German spoken in southern Germany (Back *et al.* 2006:869).

(18)   German Standard German   Austrian Standard German
    a. [ç]*ina* 'China'   [k]*ina*
    b. [ç]*emie* 'chemistry'   [k]*emie*

Word accent in ASG differs from that in GSG in a number of words, examples of which are the following (Back *et al.* 2006:809):

(19)   German Standard German   Austrian Standard German
    a. *Vati'kan* 'Vatican'   *'Vatikan*
    b. *'Tabak* 'tobacco'   *Ta'bak*
    c. *Mathema'tik* 'mathematics'   *Mathe'matik*

6.4.2.2 Grammar   In word formation we find various differences between ASG and GSG. For example, a derivational suffix that is particularly productive in ASG but not found in GSG is *-(e)rl* (Clyne 1995:39).[16]

(20) a. *Hintertürl* 'back door'
     b. *Schnackerl* 'hiccups'
     c. *Wimmerl* 'pimple'[17]

In the formation of compounds, we find differences between ASG and GSG (and SSG) in the use of inflectional affixes and linking elements.

(21)   German Standard German   Austrian Standard German
     a. *Toilettenpapier* 'toilet paper'   *Toilettepapier*
     b. *Fabrikbesitzer* 'factory owner'   *Fabriksbesitzer*
     c. *Aufnahmeprüfung* 'entrance exam'   *Aufnahmsprüfung*

There are various differences between ASG and GSG in the conjugation of particular verbs. Like SSG and colloquial southern German, ASG uses the auxiliary *sein* 'to be' in the present perfect with the verbs *liegen* 'to lie', *sitzen* 'to sit', and *stehen* 'to stand'. A feature unique to ASG is the absence of distinct past participle forms for the modal verbs *dürfen* 'to be allowed to', *können* 'to be able to', and *mögen* 'to like'. Instead of using past participles in the perfect, as in GSG, we find the infinitive in ASG. For example, we find ASG *hat dürfen* 'has been allowed to' instead of GSG *hat gedurft* (Clyne 1995:40).

A feature that is unique to the syntax of ASG is the placement of the auxiliary in subordinate clauses with two infinitives. In GSG the order is auxiliary verb + main verb + modal verb. In ASG, the order is main verb + auxiliary verb + modal verb.

(22)   . . . *obwohl sie andauernd etwas **sagen hatte wollen*** . . . (attested; cited in Stubkjær 1993:48)
          although she constantly something to-say had to-want
          ' . . . although she constantly had wanted to say something . . . '
          GSG: . . . *hatte sagen wollen*

6.4.2.3 Vocabulary   There are many lexical items that are unique to ASG. Table 6.5 lists some of the common words that are distinctively Austrian. Some nouns in ASG have genders that differ from those in GSG. For example, we find ASG *der Gehalt* 'salary', in contrast to GSG *das Gehalt*. There are a number of examples where an ASG word has a choice of gender, but GSG has only one (Clyne 1995:40).

(23)   German Standard German   Austrian Standard German
     a. *die Brezel* 'pretzel'   *die/das Brezel*
     b. *der Kunde* 'client'   *der/die Kunde*
     c. *der Monat* 'month'   *der/das Monat*

Table 6.5 *Vocabulary in Austrian Standard German*

Austrian Standard German	German Standard German
die Abwasch 'sink'	*das Spülbecken*
Feber 'February'	*Februar*
Flugpost 'airmail'	*Luftpost*
Jänner 'January'	*Januar*
die Jause 'snack'	*die Zwischenmahlzeit*
das Nachtmahl 'supper'	*das Abendessen*
der Polster 'cushion'	*das Kissen*
die Putzerei 'dry cleaners'	*die chemische Reinigung*
raunzen 'to moan, whine'	*jammern*
die Schale 'cup'	*die Tasse*
der Sessel 'chair'	*der Stuhl*
das Spital 'hospital'	*das Krankenhaus*

Some nouns in ASG have plural forms that differ from those in GSG. For example, *Kragen* 'collar' and *Wagen* 'car' have an umlaut in the plural in ASG (*Krägen*, *Wägen*), whereas they have "zero" plurals in GSG (*Kragen*, *Wagen*).

6.5   German in the East and West

Germany was a divided nation for 45 years, beginning with its division into four occupation zones in 1945 and then into two separate states in 1949, the German Democratic Republic (GDR) and the Federal Republic of Germany (FRG), and ending with reunification in 1990. Although each state produced independent grammars and spelling and pronunciation dictionaries during the period of division, significant differences between the two varieties of German were to be found not in morphology, syntax, orthography, or pronunciation, but in the lexicon.[18] The very different political ideologies and economic and social realities of the two states were reflected at the level of vocabulary, in the inventory of lexical items, and in the meanings and use of these items.

In the GDR, new words were created (with borrowed and/or native material) to express new entities and concepts (Russ 1994:107–111).

(24) a. *das Aktiv* 'work team' (*Elternaktiv, Ernteaktiv, Gewerkschaftsaktiv, Lernaktiv, Parteiaktiv*)

   b. *die Aspirantur* 'research assistantship'

   c. das *Kombinat* 'large state concern' (*Fischkombinat, Textilkombinat*)

   d. *das Kollektiv* 'work or production group for the achievement of common goals' (*Autorenkollektiv, Architektenkollektiv, Jugendkollektiv, Schriftstellerkollektiv, Schulkollektiv*)

Existing words were given new meanings (Russ 1994:107–108).

(25) a. *Brigade* (new meaning: 'work team or group')
     b. *differenzieren* (new meaning: 'assess the delivery of agricultural
         products')

Words acquired connotations in the GDR that differed from their connotations
in the FRG. Words like *Kommunist* 'communist', *Revolution* 'revolution', and
Klassenkampf 'class struggle' had positive connotations in the GDR, but negative connotations in the FRG, whereas the opposite was true of words like
christlich 'Christian', *idealistisch* 'idealistic', and *Dissident* 'dissident' (Russ
1994:108). The influence of English also differed in the two countries. Many
words borrowed from English made their way into the language in the FRG,
whereas only a handful could be found in the GDR, for example, *das Meeting*
'political meeting', *die Rallye* 'car or motorcycle rally', and *der Broiler* 'roast
chicken' (Clyne 1995:72).

   In the GDR there was also a "public register," used by the party and its func-
tionaries, the government, schools, military, and media (Hellmann 1978:27–30;
Fraas and Steyer 1992:175).[19] This public means of communication was not
limited to party and government officials; each citizen had some competence
(passive/active) in this register (Hellmann 1978:27). It was characterized by
its use of abstract lexical items, nominalizations, compound adjectives, clus-
tering of noun phrases, especially in the genitive, and repetition, and "by its
verbosity and semantic barrenness" (Clyne 1995:69). In the following example,
note in particular the use of the genitive (*der Qualität und* [*der*] *Wirksamkeit
der . . . Betreung* 'of the quality and effectiveness . . . of the care'; *des Betriebs-
gesundheitswesens* 'of the workplace health-care system') and the compound
adjective (*arbeitsmedizinischen* 'industrial medical').

(26)   *Die Verordnung orientiert auf die weitere Erhöhung der Qualität
         und Wirksamkeit der ambulanten medizinischen sowie
         arbeitsmedizinischen Betreuung in den Einrichtungen des
         Betriebsgesundheitswesens.*
         'The regulation gives directions concerning the further increase in
         quality and effectiveness of out-patients' medical and industrial
         medical care in institutions of health in the workplace.' (attested;
         Clyne 1995:69)

The private register, in contrast, was not so strikingly different from its West
German counterpart (Fraas and Steyer 1992:176). For example, the Berlin wall
was called the *antifaschistischer Schutzwall* 'anti-Fascist rampart of protection'
in the public register, but was simply the *Mauer* 'wall' in the private register
(Schlosser 1999:163–164).

During the period of division, there was a long-standing debate about the status of German in the two states: Were there two different national varieties of German, on a par with the national varieties in Austria and Switzerland – the *Viervariantenthese* 'four varieties thesis' (Lerchner 1974) – or one? Although this debate is now moot,[20] one can still ask to what extent the linguistic differences that existed prior to the *Wende* and subsequent reunification remain today.[21]

One of the most important changes in the language of the East was the disappearance of the old public register (Fraas and Steyer 1992:176), the reclaiming of an unmanipulated public language (Schlosser 1999:184). A "semipublic" register, which had been used in intellectual circles, in the churches, and in opposition groups, spread into the public domain (Fraas and Steyer 1992:175–177). The new public discourse conformed quickly to the model of the West (Fraas and Steyer 1992:176).

Differences in the lexicon, however, did not disappear – at least not entirely. Some words that were unique to the GDR lexicon persist as regional terms, and are labeled as such in the most recent *Duden* spelling dictionary (Dudenredaktion 2006): *der Broiler* 'roast chicken', *die Datsche* 'country cottage', *die Plaste* 'plastic', *die Zielstellung* 'objective'. Although there are other terms whose referents no longer exist, these terms continue to be used in discussions of the past and they can still be found in reference works. The *Duden* spelling dictionary definitions of terms like *erweiterte Oberschule* 'upper secondary school' and *Elternaktiv* 'parent representatives of a school class', for example, include the phrase *in der DDR* 'in the GDR', an indication of their "historical" status.

The official attitude towards foreign words has changed since the fall of the Wall. A once negative (official) view of English words in the GDR has given way to an increase in their use. Schönfeld and Schlobinski (1995:125–126), for example, note a considerable rise in the number of foreign words used in East Berlin, and cite the following examples from English: *Timing, out, Crash-Kurs, Count-down, Discounter*.

Following forty years of separation, however, with different manners of speaking, different expressions, the special use of particular words, special linguistic habits, attitudes, and behavior, and very different experiences (Müller 1994:119), linguistic unity has not been a simple process. Good (1993) speaks of a *Kultur des Mißverständnisses* 'culture of misunderstanding' in a united Germany. In a brief article on the difficulties in communication between Germans from the East and West, Fraas (1993:260) writes of the constant sense of speaking at cross-purposes (*aneinander vorbeireden*) – in spite of a shared native language – that characterizes an internal division in a politically united Germany. In his assessment of the linguistic differences that still exist nine years after the end of the GDR, Schlosser (1999:245) writes that *innere*

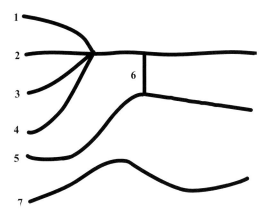

Key:
1. *ik/ich* isogloss (Ürdingen Line)
2. *maken/machen* isogloss (Benrath Line)
3. *Dorp/Dorf* isogloss (Eifel Barrier)
4. *dat/das* isogloss (Hunsrück Barrier)
5. *appel/apfel* isogloss (Germersheim Line)
6. *pund/fund* isogloss
7. *Kind/Chind* isogloss (Sundgau-Bodensee Barrier)

Figure 6.1 Isoglosses of the High German Consonant Shift (modified from Wells 1985:428)

Einheit 'internal unity' has by no means been achieved, and that only through constant efforts towards mutual understanding can it be attained.[22]

6.6   The German dialects

6.6.1   Introduction

The modern German dialects are typically classified into three dialect areas, Upper German, Central German, and Low German. Upper and Central German together comprise the High German area. As mentioned in chapter 5, the extent to which the High German Consonant Shift affected a dialect determines its classification as Upper, Central, or Low German. The shift began in the south and made its way northward. The furthest north was the shift of final *k to *ch*. The *ik/ich* isogloss delineates the extent of this shift (see Figure 6.1).[23] North of this isogloss, Germanic *k in word-final position remains unshifted, as in *ik* 'I'; south of this isogloss final *k shifted to *ch* [x], as in *ich*. The *ik/ich* isogloss is also known as the Ürdingen Line (*Ürdinger Linie*), since Ürdingen is the town where the isogloss crosses the Rhine. The shift of medial *k did not spread as far north; it is represented by the *maken/machen* isogloss, known as the Benrath Line (*Benrather Linie*), since it crosses the Rhine at Benrath (a district of Düsseldorf). The major isoglosses of the High German Consonant Shift that play a role in delineating the modern German dialects are sketched in Figure 6.1. The Low German dialects lie to the north of the *maken/machen* isogloss; the Upper German dialects lie to the south of the *appel/apfel* isogloss; and the Central German dialects lie between the two. The remaining isoglosses play a role in determining the dialect boundaries within these three main dialect areas (see below for further discussion).

Two other sound changes, in addition to the High German Consonant Shift, are used to classify the modern German dialects: the (Early) New High German (NHG) Diphthongization (which, roughly speaking, did not affect the Low German dialects or the Alemannic area of the Upper German dialects) and the (Early) New High German (NHG) Monophthongization (which affected essentially only the Central German dialects).

The discussion in the following sections presents further details of the geographic spread of these sound changes (the High German Consonant Shift, NHG Diphthongization, and NHG Monophthongization) and the role they play in the delineation of the three major dialect areas and the dialects within these areas. Additional salient features of the dialects are also identified. Only the main divisions and subdivisions in each of the three dialect areas will be identified and discussed briefly.[24]

In the discussion of German in Switzerland and Austria (in sections 6.3 and 6.4), the role of dialect in comparison to the standard language and colloquial speech was addressed. What can be said about dialect use in Germany? The situation in central and southern Germany is similar to the situation in Austria in that there is a standard–colloquial–dialect continuum. The following examples (from Große 1955, cited in König 2004:135) illustrate some of the many possible gradations from dialect to standard in the Meißen (Upper Saxon) dialect area in central Germany.

(27)   *s ward bāe uanfang mid rāin*
         s ward bāle ānfang mit rān
         s wärd balde ānfang mit rächn
         s werd balde anfang dse rächn
         s wird bald anfang dsu rēchnen
         (*es wird bald anfangen zu regnen* 'it will soon begin to rain')

In northern Germany, there is no continuum of colloquial speech between the standard and dialect. Colloquial speech is more a stylistically relaxed form of the standard, and there is a gap between dialect on the one hand and the standard on the other (König 2004:135).[25] Dialects in the north are further removed from the standard than in central and southern Germany because of the absence of the effects of the High German Consonant Shift in the north.

In both Germany and Austria, there has been a decline in local dialects in favor of regional ones because of factors such as urbanization, commuter mobility, and improved communication and educational opportunities. In southern Germany, dialects are used far more than in the north, where they are more stigmatized (Clyne 1995:118). South Germans have a high degree of local identity, so dialect is more likely to serve as a marker of identity in southern Germany than in the north (Clyne 1995:97–98). Dialects have acquired new functions in recent years. For example, dialect is now being used for radio call-in shows; radio weather reports; radio, TV, and street advertisements; columns in local and regional newspapers; and slogans and pamphlets of action groups (Clyne 1995.112, Stevenson 1997:63). Dialect has also become the language of protest, and a resurgence of dialect use in Germany and Austria is closely connected with the "green" (conservation) movement (Clyne 1995:112–113). Dialect revival (localization) can also be viewed as part of the resistance to globalization (manifested linguistically, for example, in the spread of English as the leading international language); see Fishman 1998. This revival of dialect can be seen in spite of a continuing movement away from dialect in many parts of Germany, motivated in part by the role of the standard language in education (Clyne 1995:118–119).

6.6.2   Upper German dialects

The Upper German dialects lie to the south of the *appel/apfel* isogloss, that is, south of the Germersheim Line.[26] The German dialects south of this line underwent the full extent of the High German Consonant Shift, traditionally illustrated with the words *ich* 'I', *machen* 'to make', *Dorf* 'village', *das* 'the', *Apfel* 'apple', and *Pfund* 'pound'.

The Upper German dialect area is typically divided into three further areas, Alemannic, Upper Franconian, and Bavaro-Austrian.[27] Each of these areas is further subdivided: Alemannic into Swabian and Low, High, and Highest Alemannic; Upper Franconian into South and East Franconian; and Bavaro-Austrian into North, Central, and South Bavaro-Austrian.

The Alemannic dialects are spoken in the German-speaking area of Switzerland, in the Austrian Vorarlberg, in Alsace (France), and in the German state of Baden-Württemberg.

With the exception of Swabian (see below), the Alemannic dialects retain the MHG monophthongs *î, û,* and *iu* [u:] ([u:]*f Schw*[i:]*zerd*[y:]*tsch* 'auf Schweizerdeutsch'). That is, they were not affected by the NHG Diphthongization. They were also not affected by the NHG Monophthongization. Like all Upper German dialects (with the exception of most Upper Franconian dialects), the

Alemannic dialects retain the MHG diphthongs *ie*, *uo*, and *üe* as diphthongs, with /iɐ̯/ in *lieb* 'dear', either /iɐ̯/ or /yɐ̯/ in *müde* 'tired', and /uɐ̯/ in *gut* 'good' (Barbour and Stevenson 1990:88).

Swabian is the one Alemannic dialect that diphthongized the MHG monophthongs *î*, *û*, and *iu*. MHG *î* and *iu* are both realized as /əi/ in Swabian: *steif* [ʃdəif] 'stiff'; *heulen* [həilə] 'to cry'; MHG *û* is realized as /əu/: *Raupe* [rəup] 'caterpillar' (Russ 1990c:346). Another feature of Swabian phonology is the loss of *n* before *s*, with nasalization of a preceding vowel (Niebaum and Macha 1999:197): *Gans* [gãs] 'goose' (Stevenson 1997:71).

The Alemannic dialects in the narrow sense (the Swiss German dialects), with their retention of the MHG monophthongs and diphthongs, provide us with a living example of features of an earlier stage of the language that are no longer found (in this combination) in other varieties of German. The German dialects in Wallis (Highest Alemannic dialects), which have retained the long vowels of OHG endings in essentially unreduced form, are particularly fascinating. For example, the plural forms of *Tag* 'day' in Wallis German are *Taga* (nominative, accusative), *Tago* (genitive), and *Tagu(n)* (dative) (Schirmunski 1962:163). Other examples are *schi sägunt* (*sie sagen*) 'they say' and *trichu* (*trinken*) 'to drink' (Baur 1983:148).

The *Kind*/*Chind* isogloss (see Figure 6.1) serves to distinguish Low Alemannic (*Kind*) from High (and Highest) Alemannic (*Chind*).

All the Alemannic dialects (as well as the Upper Franconian dialects) form diminutives with an *l*-suffix that ends in a vowel (Niebaum and Macha 1999:197). In High Alemannic, for example, we find -*li* or -*eli*: *Hündli*, *Hündeli* 'doggy' (Russ 1990b:380). In Swabian, the diminutive suffix is -*le* (Niebaum and Macha 1999:197).

The following sentences from Züritüütsch, spoken in the Canton of Zürich, illustrate some features of (High) Alemannic (from Russ 1990b: 380–381):

(28)   Züritüütsch

En chüele Wind strycht über s Land und bewegt daa und deet es Gresli. D Luft isch na chalt, und wänn e Bluem wott uufgaa, so verschrickt si ab der Chüeli und planget uf der Wëërmi vo der Sune.

Ein kühler Wind streicht über das Land und bewegt da und dort ein Gräslein. Die Luft ist noch kalt, und wenn eine Blume sich aufmachen will, so erschrickt sie von der Kühle und sehnt sich nach der Wärme von der Sonne.

'A chilly wind brushes over the countryside and moves blades of grass here and there. The air is still cold and when a flower wants to open itself up it recoils from the chill and longs for the warmth of the sun.'

Notice the *ch* for initial *k in words like *Chüeli* (*Kühle*) 'chill' and *chalt* (*kalt*) 'cold', a feature of High Alemannic. Another feature of High Alemannic is the diminutive suffix -*li* in *Gresli* (*Gräslein*) 'blade of grass'. A feature that belongs to Alemannic proper is the "old" diphthongs in *chüel-* (*kühl-* < MHG *küel-*) 'cool' and *Bluem* (*Blume* < MHG *bluome*) 'flower'. The "old" monophthong *û* in *uufgaa* (*aufgehen* < MHG *ûfgân*) 'to open' is a feature of Upper German in general.

The Upper Franconian dialects are spoken in southern central Germany north of the Swabian dialect area and west of the North Bavaro-Austrian dialect area. In these dialects (as in Swabian and the Bavaro-Austrian dialects), the MHG monophthongs *î*, *û*, and *iu* have been diphthongized. For example, in East Franconian we find [zaɪ] *sein* 'his' < MHG *sîn* and [zɑʊv] *saufen* 'to drink' < MHG *sûfen* (Rowley 1990:414). In addition, most of the Upper Franconian dialects differ from all the other Upper German dialects through their monophthongization of the MHG diphthongs *ie*, *uo*, and *üe*. In East Franconian we find, for example, [biə] *Bier* 'beer' < MHG *bier* and [gənux] *genug* 'enough' < MHG *genuoc* (Rowley 1990:414). The Upper Franconian dialects are thus very similar to the Central German dialects with respect to NHG Diphthongization and Monophthongization (the Central German dialects underwent both sound changes). However, given their full participation in the High German Consonant Shift, the Upper Franconian dialects are classified as Upper rather than Central German.

Like the Alemannic dialects, Upper Franconian forms diminutives with an *l*-suffix that ends in a vowel. In Upper Franconian, the diminutive suffix is -*la* (Niebaum and Macha 1999:197). The first and third person plural present indicative verb endings are -*e(n)* in Upper Franconian, in contrast to Swabian, in which they are -*et* (Niebaum and Macha 1999:197).

The Bavaro-Austrian dialects are spoken primarily in southern Germany and Austria. North Bavaro-Austrian is spoken in the Upper Palatinate and Upper Franconia; Central Bavaro-Austrian is spoken in Upper and Lower Bavaria and Upper and Lower Austria; South Bavaro-Austrian is spoken in the Austrian states of Styria (*Steiermark*), Carinthia (*Kärnten*), and Tyrol.

One of the features that distinguishes the Bavaro-Austrian dialects from the other Upper German dialects is the use of old dual forms, *es* and *eŋk*, in place of the second person plural forms of the personal pronouns, *ihr* and *euch* (Schirmunski 1962:29). A second feature is the form of the diminutive suffix. In the Bavaro-Austrian dialects, this suffix is -*el* (-*l*, -*erl*) (Niebaum and Macha 1999:197). For example, the North Bavaro-Austrian diminutive of [ghɔts] (*Katze*) 'cat' is [ghatsl] or [ghatsərl] (Rowley 1990:434).

The various Bavaro-Austrian dialects can be distinguished from each other by at least one feature. In North Bavaro-Austrian, MHD *uo* has become *ou*: MHG *bruoder* 'brother' > *Brouder* (*Bruder*). In the other Bavaro-Austrian dialects it has become *ua*: *Bruader* (Niebaum and Macha 1999:198). In Central

Bavaro-Austrian, *l* before a consonant is vocalized: *Salz* 'salt' > *Soiz*; *Feld* 'field' > *Föit* (Niebaum and Macha 1999:198). In South Bavaro-Austrian, Germanic **k* has been shifted to [kx] initially, when geminated, and sometimes following a consonant: *kxluəg* (*klug*) 'clever', *trukxə* (*trocken*) 'dry', *deŋkxə* (*denken*) 'to think' (Schirmunski 1962:30).

The following sentences, from southern Central Bavaro-Austrian, contain some words with features that are typical of this dialect area (Wiesinger 1990:500–502).[28]

(29)   Southern Central Bavaro-Austrian
  a. [dɐ vɔ̃ödɐ hɔ̃üdn rɛχt gɛɐn khɔ̃üp den ɔɪdn kχraɪdzbraːvm mɔ̃ː]
     Der Vater hat ihn recht gern gehabt, den alten kreuzbraven Mann.
     'Father liked him a lot, the very brave man.'
  b. [dɔː iz aʊz gwɛɪn mãĩ vɔ̃ödɐ hɔ̃üd niks glap vɔ̃ gaɪstɐ]
     . . . da ist es aus gewesen, mein Vater hat nichts geglaubt von Geistern.
     '. . . then it was finished, my father did not believe anything about ghosts.'
  c. [i muɐs ɛŋkχ ʒɔ̃ː vɐdzëːn]
     Ich muss es euch schon erzählen.
     'I must tell you.'
  d. [liɐwɐ vriːz ɪn zëïm]
     Lieber fresse ich ihn selber.
     'I'd rather eat it myself.'
  e. [un hɔ̃ː voijɐ gmɔχt]
     und habe Feuer gemacht
     'and made a fire'

In (29a), the [ɪ] in [ɔɪdn] (*alten*) 'old' is an example of vocalized *l*, a feature of Central Bavaro-Austrian. The affricate [kχ] in [kχraɪdzbraːvm] (*kreuzbraven*) 'very brave' in (29a) and [ɛŋkχ] (*euch*) 'you' in (29c) is a feature of South Bavaro-Austrian, but it is not surprising to find it in neighboring southern Central Bavaro-Austrian. We find evidence of the NHG Diphthongization in [aʊz] (*aus* < MHG *ûs*) 'out' and [mãĩ] (*mein* < MHG *mîn*) 'my' in (29b), typical of the Upper German area (with the exception of the Alemannic dialects proper). The word [liɐwɐ] (*lieber*) 'rather' in (29d), with the old diphthong [iɐ], demonstrates the absence of the NHG Monophthongization, typical of all Upper German dialects (with the exception of Upper Franconian). The old dual form [ɛŋkχ] for the second person plural pronoun *euch* 'you' in (29c) is a feature that is typically Bavaro-Austrian. Various words in (29), in addition to those with the affricate [kχ], provide evidence of the High German Consonant Shift, which is characteristic of the entire Upper German area: [aʊz] (*aus*;

cf. Eng. *out*); [vɐdzë:n] (*erzählen*; cf. Eng. *tell*); [gmɔχt] (*gemacht*; cf. Eng. *make*).

6.6.3   Central German dialects

The Central German dialects lie to the north of the *appel/apfel* isogloss (the Germersheim Line) and to the south of the *ik/ich* and *maken/machen* isoglosses (the Ürdingen and Benrath lines, respectively). The Benrath line is typically cited as the boundary that separates the Central German dialects from their Low German neighbors to the north. It crosses the Rhine at Benrath and runs to the east in the area of Magdeburg and Berlin. The Germersheim Line begins in the west, south of Saarbrücken, crossing the Rhine at Germersheim, and then goes north-east, to the east of Frankfurt, and then east, south of Erfurt, to the Czech border.

The isoglosses of the High German Consonant Shift that lie between the the Benrath Line and Germersheim Line (see Figure 6.1) play an important role in distinguishing the major Central German dialects from each other. The *pund/fund* isogloss (running roughly north–south to the east of Kassel) separates the West Central German dialects (*pund*) from the East Central German dialects (*fund*). In the west, the *Dorp/Dorf* isogloss (Eifel Barrier) separates Ripuarian (*Dorp*) from Mosel Franconian (*Dorf*), and the *dat/das* isogloss (Hunsrück Barrier) separates Mosel Franconian (*dat*) from Rhenish Franconian (*das*). The isoglosses in the west, from the Benrath Line to the Germersheim Line, are known as the Rhenish fan (*Rheinischer Fächer*) because of the fan-like shape they form as they spread out from east to west (see Figure 6.1). The two main East Central German dialects are Thuringian and Upper Saxon.

NHG Monophthongization is a feature that applies to all the Central German dialects. In South Hessian (a Rhenish Franconian dialect), for example, we find monophthongs for the MHG diphthongs *ie*, *uo*, and *üe*: *liib* (*lieb*) 'dear', *Bluud* (*Blut*) 'blood', *griise* (*grüßen*) 'to greet' (Durrell and Davies 1990:226). The Central German dialects typically have also undergone NHG Diphthongization. For example, in South Hessian we find diphthongs for the MHG monophthongs *î*, *û*, and *iu* [y:]: *draiwe* (*treiben*) 'to drive', *Braud* (*Braut*) 'bride', and *haid* (*heute*) 'today' (Durrell and Davies 1990:226). Only Riuparian and some Rhenish Franconian dialects do not show diphthongization.

A morphological feature that is characteristic of all Central German dialects is the use of the diminutive suffix -*chen*. A morphological feature that serves to distinguish Upper Saxon from its neighbor to the west, Thuringian, is the retention of final -*n* in the infinitive: Upper Saxon [sa:gən] (*sagen* 'to say'), [le:sən] (*lesen* 'to read'); Thuringian [sa:gə], [le:sə] (Bergmann 1990:293).

The phrases and sentences in (30) are from Westpfälzisch, a dialect of Rhenish Franconian. In this area we expect to find shifted *p*, *t*, and *k*, with the exception of unshifted *-pp- and *p-, as well as NHG Monophthongization and Diphthongization.

(30)   Westfälisch[29]

    a. [fɔr siwə pʰɛnɪç] (Karch 1980:16)
        für sieben Pfennig
        'for seven pennies'

    b. [leːdigliç hameːr unɐ uns di ebl̩ fədɛːld gəhad] (Karch 1980:86)
        Lediglich haben wir unter uns die Äpfel verteilt gehabt.
        'We had simply divided up the apples among us.'

    c. [sundɒˑgs medɒːgs kɒmɐ dɛs jɔ mɒxə] (Karch 1980:12)
        Sonntags mittags kann man das ja machen.
        'Sunday afternoons one can do that.'

    d. [jɔː n̩ dɒn hɔd mɐ saːi haːusɒːwətʰ] (Karch 1980:12)
        Ja, und dann hat man seine Hausarbeit.
        'Yes, and then one has one's housework.'

    e. [dan kumə diˑ buːwə] (Karch 1980:20)
        Dann kommen die Buben.
        'Then the boys come.'

    f. [mir wɔlnə diːfbrunə bɔːrə] (Karch 1980:26)
        Wir wollen einen Tiefbrunnen bohren.
        'We want to drill a deep well.'

In (30a) we see unshifted *p- in [pʰɛnɪç] (*Pfennig*) 'penny', and in (30b) we find unshifted *-pp- in [ebl̩] (*Äpfel*) 'apples'. Examples of shifted *k and *p can be found in [mɒxə] (*machen*) 'to make' in (30c) and in [diːf] (*tief*) 'deep' in (30f). The phrase [saːi haːusɒːwətʰ] (*seine Hausarbeit*) 'one's housework' in (30d) provides evidence of NHG Diphthongization (MHG *sîn* > *sein* and MHG *hûs* > *Haus*). The words [buːwə] (*Buben*) 'boys' (< MHG *buoben*) in (30e) and [diːf] (*tief*) 'deep' (< MHG *tief*) in (30f) provide evidence of NHG Monophthongization.

6.6.4   Low German dialects

The Low German dialects are spoken north of the Benrath Line in an area that extends from the Dutch–German border in the west, the Dano-German border in the north, and the German–Polish border in the east. The Low German area is traditionally divided into West and East Low German. West Low German is subdivided into North Saxon in the north and Westphalian and Eastphalian in the south; East Low German is subdivided into Mecklenburgish-West Pomeranian in the north and Brandenburgish in the south (Goltz and Walker 1990:31).

The Low German dialects are characterized by the general absence of the effects of the High German Consonant Shift. In contrast to the Upper German dialects, where we find the words *ich*, *machen*, *Dorf*, *das*, *Apfel*, and *Pfund* (see section 6.6.2), in the Low German dialects we find *ik*, *maken*, *Dorp*, *dat*, *Appel*, and *Pund*. An exception is the area between the Benrath Line and the Ürdingen Line, where Germanic **k* in word-final position has been shifted to [ç] in a small number of monosyllabic words such as *ich* 'I'. The dialects in this area are nevertheless characterized as Low German (Barbour and Stevenson 1990:80).

The Low German dialects (with the exception of some Westphalian dialects) have not diphthongized the Middle Low German (MLG) monophthongs *ī*, *ū*, and *ǖ* (comparable to the MHG monophthongs *î*, *û*, and *iu*). Compare, for example, the following North Central Westphalian words, which all exhibit monophthongal reflexes of these MLG monophthongs, with their NHG cognates, which contain diphthongs (Durrell 1990:71).

(31)	Westphalian	MLG	NHG cognates
a.	/iː/ *Tiid*	*ī*	*Zeit* 'time'
b.	/uː/ *Huus*	*ū*	*Haus* 'house'
c.	/yː/ *Hüüser*	*ǖ*	*Häuser* 'houses'

There is no process of monophthongization in the Low German dialects that is comparable to the NHG Monophthongization, since MLG had monophthongs (e.g., *ē* and *ō*) that corresponded to the MHG diphthongs (*ie* and *uo*).

The Low German dialects also have an initial [s] before a consonant, where Central and Upper German dialects have [ʃ]: [s]*ten* (*Stein*) 'stone', [s]*nīden* (*schneiden*) 'to cut' (Schirmunski 1962:31).

All the Low German dialects have a single plural ending (one for all persons) in the present tense: *-et* in the West Low German dialects, *-(e)n* in the East Low German (Niebaum and Macha 1999:195). All Low German dialects also have a single non-nominative case for the personal pronouns. In the Eastphalian dialects this corresponds to the accusative form in Standard German: *mik* (*mich*) 'me'; *dik* (*dich*) 'you'. In all other Low German dialects it corresponds to the dative form in Standard German: *mi* (*mir*) 'me'; *di* (*dir*) 'you' (Niebaum and Macha 1999:196).

The following sentences are from an East Low German dialect of Mecklenburgish-West Pomeranian (Schönfeld 1990:99, 131).[30]

(32) a. [vat mɔːkt diːn jʊŋ]
        Was macht dein Junge?
        'How is your son?'

  b. [ɪk hɛv hyːæt haɛ hɛt zɪk dat baen brɔːǧn]
        Ich habe gehört, er hat sich das Bein gebrochen.
        'I have heard that he has broken his leg.'

Notice the unshifted *t in [vat] in (32a) and [dat] in (32b) and the unshifted *k in [mɔːkt] in (32a) and [ɪk] and [zɪk] in (32b). Notice also the MLG monophthong ī in [diːn] in (32a). The form of the third person singular masculine pronoun in the nominative, *hae* in (32b), is another feature of Low German dialects, one that it has in common with English (*he*), in contrast to the High German dialects (*er*).

Exercises

1. Identify which of the following words exhibit GSG pronunciation. Provide the GSG pronunciation for those that do not.
   (a) *Chemiker* [ˈkʰeːmikʰɐ]
   (b) (*eine*) *Blumage* [p̌laˈmaːʃ]
   (c) (*sie*) *dachte* [ˈt̪aːxtʰə]
   (d) *genehmigt* [kəˈneːmɪçtʰ]
   (e) *Leber* [ˈleːp̌ər]
   (f) *wuchs* [ˈvʊks]
   (g) *Monate* [ˈmoːnatʰə]
   (h) *Tier* [ˈtʰiːɐ̯]
2. Consult works like Meyer 1989 and Back *et al.* 2006 to determine how the following words differ from their GSG counterparts (e.g., in pronunciation, gender, meaning, spelling, inflection, etc.).
   (a) SSG *einladen*
   (b) SSG *die Strasse*
   (c) SSG *der Park*
   (d) SSG *der Couch*
   (e) SSG *die Badanstalt*
   (f) ASG *die Brosche*
   (g) ASG *liegen*
   (h) ASG *das Cola*
   (i) ASG *der Zugsverkehr*
   (j) ASG *dreifärbig*
3. The following words are found in SSG, ASG, northern German, or southern German. What are their GSG equivalents?
   (a) *röntgenisieren*
   (b) *klönen*
   (c) *der Advokat*
   (d) *das Billett*
   (e) *die Gasse*
   (f) *die Stulle*
   (g) *garagieren*

(h) *das Nachtessen*

(i) *plätten*

(j) *die Kassa*

4. Keeping in mind what you know about the spread of the High German Consonant Shift, NHG Diphthongization, and NHG Monophthongization, identify the following texts as Upper, Central, or Low German.[31] Provide evidence in support of your conclusions.

(a) [haɪ lɛˑdə zɪk dɑt ʀɑt ʔuːt fɑn œˑnə – ʔʊn faˑʁt lɔˑoš – mɪt‿dɛn ʀɒː . . . zɑ zɪn dɑ°‿tœɪm]

er lieh sich das Rad aus von dem – und fährt los – mit dem Rad . . . so sind die Zeiten

(b) [nõː guɐd . . . hiat neːm ɐn haɪzl ɔːwɐ ɪz d ˈlɒndʒdrɔs vɐˈbaɪ ˈgɒŋə . . . nɔːxn ˈbraɪttõñts ʑ̩ʑkɪ z̩ waɪ deɪz zake aʊv dɛ ʑdɪ ʊs liɐŋ]

nun gut . . . hart neben dem Häuslein aber ist die Landstraße vorbeige-gangen . . . nach dem Brauttanz sieht das Weib das Säckel auf der Straße liegen

(c) [ʔʊn mɔjẽs‿ʃʀaɪt‿dan dɪ ˈmama – maxt‿dɑ̊t‿də ʀɒˑʊs kʊmt – ʔɛt geˑt‿tsɛˑ‿ɪt]

und morgens schreit dann die Mama – macht dass ihr raus kommt – es wird Zeit

(d) [əz ɪʒ næxtɪ nɔ laŋ lɪəxt ksɪ ɪ də tsʊmftʃtʊbən‿ʊnd ɪ də wiːrtshyzər . . . dər ʃtatʃribər pfiːft tswyʃʃə zinə tsændə dyrə]

es ist gestern-Abend noch lange Licht gewesen in den Zunftstuben und in den Wirtshäusern . . . der Stadtschreiber pfeift zwischen seinen Zähnen durch

NOTES

1 The transcriptions in this chapter for varieties of German other than the standard language spoken in Germany are taken from their original sources and thus do not follow the conventions established in chapter 1. Lenis stops are typically transcribed using the symbols *b*, *d*, and *g*; the fortis stops are transcribed using *p*, *t*, and *k*; aspiration of fortis stops is often not indicated.

2 The stereotype that "High German (the *Hochsprache*) comes from the north (e.g., Hanover)" reflects the fact that the first codified *pronunciation* of the standard (Siebs 1898) was based on the pronunciation of the north. See chapter 5, section 5.6, for further details.

3 See chapter 5 for a discussion of the process by which Standard German developed and was established.

4 The Standard German spoken in Switzerland, Swiss Standard German, and the standard spoken in Austria, Austrian Standard German, differ from the Standard German spoken in Germany, German Standard German. See sections 6.3.2 and 6.4.2

for discussion of the ways in which these national varieties of Standard German differ from German Standard German.

5 *Samstag* is making headway in the west and north, no doubt in part because of the use of *Samstag* by the railway and postal service (to better distinguish 'Saturday' from *Sonntag* 'Sunday'); *Sonnabend* is still common in the east, however (Dudenredaktion 2001: 735).

6 The linguistic situation in Switzerland and Austria will be treated in sections 6.3 and 6.4.

7 For further discussion, see chapter 1, section 1.2.4.7.

8 See Barbour and Stevenson 1990:168 for discussion of other examples of regional variation in the use of past tense forms.

9 See Barbour and Stevenson 1990:213 for further discussion.

10 See Werlen (2004:21–24) for further discussion of the factors that play a role in the choice of SSG versus dialect.

11 For further discussion of the linguistic characteristics of SSG, see, for example, Panizzolo 1982, Meyer 1989, Ammon *et al.* 1995:251–282, Clyne 1995:47–49, and Rash 1998:154–166.

12 See Rash (1998:154–155) for a discussion of the reasons given for the absence of <ß> in SSG orthography.

13 The phonetic transcriptions here are from Wiesinger 1990:444–445.

14 This summary of the linguistic situation in Austria is from Wiesinger 1990: 447.

15 This is also a feature of speech in Bavaria (C. Hall 2003:87).

16 Derivational suffixes are those suffixes that are used to create new lexemes (words).

17 *Wimmerl* 'pimple' is also used in colloquial speech in Bavaria.

18 Two separate volumes of the *Duden Rechtschreibung* appeared during this time, one published in West Germany (Mannheim), the other in East Germany (Leipzig). See Russ 1994:102–107 for a discussion of these two works and others that codified the two national varieties of German, as well as a discussion of the minor differences (in spelling, pronunciation, and grammar) between the two varieties.

19 I follow Clyne (1995:69) and use the term "public register" for what is referred to as "öffentliche Sprache" ('public speech') or "öffentlicher Sprachgebrauch" ('public usage') in works such as Hellmann 1978 and Fraas and Steyer 1992.

20 By the 1980s there was already a general consensus that although there were two different communication communities (*Kommunikationsgemeinschaften*), there was still a single speech community (Schlosser 1999:234).

21 The word *Wende* is the term that is now used for the transitional period between the peaceful revolution in the GDR in the fall of 1989 and the incorporation of the GDR into the FRG (reunification) on October 3, 1990.

22 For a comprehensive treatment of the sociolinguistic issues that have played a role during the periods of national disunity and unity in Germany since 1945, see Stevenson 2002.

23 An isogloss is a line drawn on a dialect map that indicates where one variant of a linguistic form is used (on one side of the line) and where another variant is used (on the other side of the line).

24 Further dialects can be identified within the main subdivisions, but will not be addressed here.

25 See König (2004:134) for a map that illustrates graphically the continuum in central and southern Germany and the absence of a continuum in the north.

26 Strictly speaking, the Upper German dialects lie to the south of the Speyer Line, the *pund/pfund* isogloss, which diverges (southward) from the *appel/apfel* isogloss briefly in the area around the Rhine (Frings 1956:125). The Germersheim Line, however, is typically cited as the northern border of the Upper German dialects.

27 We follow here the Upper German divisions in Stevenson 1997:70. Instead of the term "Bavarian" we use "Bavaro-Austrian" to reflect the fact that these dialects are spoken in Bavaria and Austria.

28 The phonetic transcriptions of southern Central Bavaro-Austrian have been simplified somewhat. The symbol [χ] stands for a voiceless uvular fricative. The "velopalatals" [ï ï ë ë] and "palato-velars" [ü ö ö ɔ̃] are slightly centralized mid-tongue vowels with "something of a [y] and [ø] quality" (Wiesinger 1990:510).

29 These phonetic transcriptions of Westpfälzisch have been simplified somewhat. The vowel [ɒ] found in these examples is characterized by Karch (1980:2) as a rounded low back vowel. Vowels that are half long are indicated by using the half-length mark, ˑ.

30 The diacritic ° indicates that a segment is voiceless.

31 These (slightly altered) texts are from Keller 1961, Bethge and Bonnin 1969, and Russ 1990a. The linking symbol, ‿, indicates the absence of a break.

7   Sociolinguistic issues

7.1   Introduction

The subfield of linguistics known as sociolinguistics deals with the relationship between language and society.[1] Sociolinguistic research seeks to achieve a better understanding of the nature of language by investigating the way in which language functions in social contexts.[2]

A concept that is important in sociolinguistic investigation is the notion of variety. A variety is any form of language used by a particular group of speakers that can be identified in social, regional, or situational terms. Language varieties that can be defined according to the social groups to which their speakers belong are known as social dialects or sociolects. Sociolects can be identified in terms of the social class of their speakers, their ethnicity, religion, occupation, education, and so on. Those varieties of language that are associated with a particular geographical area and that can thus be defined in regional terms are dialects (in the narrow sense of the term). The varieties of language known as registers are the special forms that are used when dealing with a specific subject matter or when engaged in a particular activity.[3] Law and medicine, for example, are well-known technical registers. Styles are those varieties of a language that differ according to their level of formality. Styles can range from very formal to very informal.

In this chapter we will look at some issues in German sociolinguistics, a number of which involve different varieties of German. (Regionally defined varieties – dialects – were discussed in chapter 6.) Section 7.2 deals with the topic of style and the kinds of linguistic variation that can be found in German that are based on differences in levels of formality. Section 7.3 discusses the forms of address in German and the rules that underlie the system of address, which are determined by the social relationships between speakers and addressees. Some issues in language and gender are treated in section 7.4. The issues discussed here address recent efforts to change the ways in which gender is encoded in German. Section 7.5 deals with the characteristics of *Jugendsprache* 'youth speech', which is probably best treated as a kind of jargon, a register characterized by obscure vocabulary, among other things. Section 7.6 deals with the language of foreign workers, and section 7.7 treats language contact, in particular the borrowing that has played and continues to play a role in German as a result of language contact.

7.2   Style

7.2.1   Introduction

The situation in which language is used plays an important role in determining one's speech style, that is, the level of formality of one's speech. In a casual conversation with friends, an informal speech style would be appropriate. If one were to give a speech in a highly formal situation, very formal speech would be required. Although style is best viewed as a continuum from very informal to very formal, it is useful to identify several levels for the purpose of comparison: colloquial (informal), neutral, and formal.

The medium of discourse can have an effect on style. For example, written language tends to be more formal than spoken language. There are of course exceptions. A personal letter would not as a rule contain highly formal language; it could be quite informal, depending on the relationship between the writer and the addressee. A speech delivered in a formal setting would typically employ formal language. However, if a speech were not spontaneous, but read from a text written prior to delivery, it would simply be an example of written language delivered orally. News broadcasts are another example of written language that is spoken aloud.

The level of formality is manifested in all aspects of language. It affects pronunciation, word choice, grammatical structures used, and so on. For example, in a setting where informal language would be appropriate, it would be odd for a speaker to use vocabulary that is marked as formal. If someone were having a casual conversation with friends and mentioned that someone had died, it would be odd to express this using the verb *ableben* 'to pass away' – marked as *gehoben* 'elevated' in the *Duden Rechtschreibung* dictionary (Dudenredaktion 2006:155) – rather than the neutral *sterben* 'to die'. One could even imagine a situation where *abkratzen* 'to kick the bucket' (labled *derb* 'crude' in Dudenredaktion 2006:155) would be more appropriate than *ableben*. In the following sections we will look at some additional examples of the ways in which differences in style (levels of formality) can have an effect on language.

7.2.2   Stylistic variation

7.2.2.1 Pronunciation   The discussion of the phonetics and phonology of German in chapter 1 focused on the pronunciation of individual sounds and the pronunciation of these sounds in words in isolation. In actual speech, however, words are not pronounced in isolation, but in utterances, and in utterances one typically does not find the careful pronunciation of words said in isolation – the pronunciation found in dictionaries like the *Duden Aussprachewörterbuch* (Mangold 2005). Both tempo and style have an effect on pronunciation, and the faster the tempo and more informal the style, the greater the frequency in the assimilation, reduction, and deletion of sounds. Even in slow, formal speech, however, which is characterized by clear, careful enunciation, one can find examples of reduction. In the following discussion we will focus on the informal end of the style continuum and look at examples of assimilation, reduction, and deletion that can be found in colloquial speech. Keep in mind that we are dealing with formality and informality in the standard language. Similar, but different, processes will be found in other varieties of German.

Assimilation takes place when two segments become more alike in one or more features. Recall, for example, the examples of assimilation discussed in chapter 1 (voicing assimilation, Velar Fricative Assimilation, Nasal Assimilation). The following are some examples of assimilation that can be found in colloquial speech (Kohler 1995:207–210; C. Hall 2003:141–144).[4]

(1)   Assimilation
   a.   [tkʰ]→ [kkʰ]   *hat kein* 'has no' [ˈhak kʰaɪn]
   b.   [sʃ]→ [ʃʃ]   *schönes Spiel* 'nice game' [ʃøːnəʃ ˈʃpiːl]
   c.   [nm]→ [mm]   *kann man* 'can one' [kʰam man]
   d.   [mp̆]→ [mm]   *zum Beispiel* 'for example' [tsʊmˈmaɪʃpiːl]
   e.   [f]→ [v]   *hoff' ich* 'hope I' [hɔvɪç]

The examples in (1a) through (1c) involve assimilation of place of articulation (of stops, fricatives, and nasals). (1d) is an example of assimilation of manner of articulation (a stop becomes a nasal). (1e) involves voicing assimilation: a voiceless fricative becomes voiced between two voiced segments (vowels).

When vowels are in unstressed positions, they are subject to a number of reduction processes. Vowel Shortening, discussed in chapter 1 (section 1.2.4.1), applies in all pronunciation styles of German, including formal speech.

(2)   Vowel Shortening
   a.   *den* 'the' /teːn/→ [ten]
   b.   *nun* 'now' /nuːn/→ [nun]

Further reduction processes affect vowels in colloquial speech. Centralization reduces tense vowels to their lax counterparts.

(3)   Centralization
   a.   *den* 'the' [ten]→ [tɛn]
   b.   *nun* 'now' [nun]→ [nʊn]

Reduction to /ə/ further weakens (and centralizes) vowels.

(4)   Reduction to /ə/
    a.   *den* 'the' [tɛn]→ [tən]
    b.   *nun* 'now' [nʊn]→ [nən]

Schwa Deletion is the final stage in the reduction of vowels.

(5)   Schwa Deletion
    a.   *den* 'the' [tən]→ [tn̩]
    b.   *ein* 'a' (/aɪn/→ [aɪn]→) [ən]→ [n]

In colloquial speech, Schwa Deletion is much less restricted than in "standard" pronunciation (the pronunciation represented in the rule presented in chapter 1). For example, in standard pronunciation, schwa must be preceded by a stop or fricative in order to be deleted before /n/. In colloquial speech, schwa can be deleted without any preceding consonant, as the pronunciation of *ein* in the following sentence demonstrates.

(6)   *Wollen Sie ein Foto?* 'Do you want a photo?'
        ['vɔln zi ən 'foːtʰo]→ ['vɔln zɪ n̩ 'foːtʰo] (C. Hall 2003:151)

Schwa is also typically deleted in verb endings.

(7) a.   *ich mache* 'I make'→ *ich mach*
    b.   *ich habe* 'I have'→ *ich hab*
    c.   *konnte ich* 'could I'→ *konnt ich*

Consonants as well as vowels are deleted in colloquial speech. This often affects geminate consonants (Kohler 1995:210–211; C. Hall 2003:147).

(8)   Geminate reduction
    a.   *kommen* 'to come'   ['kʰɔmm̩]→ ['kʰɔm]
    b.   *mitteilen* 'to communicate'   ['mɪttʰaɪln̩]→ ['mɪtʰaɪln̩]

It also affects /tʰ/ when it occurs in the middle of a consonant cluster (Kohler 1995:208–209; C. Hall 2003:146).

(9)   Deletion of /tʰ/
    a.   /stʰl/→ [sl]   *festlich* 'festive' [fɛslɪç]
    b.   /ltʰs/→ [ls]   *hältst* '(you) hold' [hɛlstʰ]

A number of word classes in German are made up of words that are typically unstressed in connected speech (e.g., pronouns, determiners, adverbs, prepositions, auxiliary verbs, conjunctions). When unstressed, these words are susceptible to various types of "reduction," and in their reduced forms are known as "weak forms" (*schwache Formen*).[5] For example, the various reduced forms of the determiners *den* 'the' and *ein* 'a' discussed above, as well as those of the adverb *nun* 'now', are all weak forms. Additional examples of reduced forms from other word classes are the following (see Kohler 1995:211–220 and C. Hall 2003:148–157 for additional examples and further discussion):

(10) a. *ihm* 'him'   /iːm/ [im], [ɪm], [əm], [m]
    b. *ist* 'is'   /ɪstʰ/ [ɪs], [s]
    c. *vor* 'before'   /foːr/ [foɐ̯], [fɔɐ̯], [fɐ]
    d. *und* 'and'   /ʊntʰ/ [ʊn], [ən]

The following example compares the careful pronunciation of a sentence (one that would be produced by applying the rules in chapter 1) with one that would be characteristic of informal speech (Mangold 2005:67):

(11)   *Was haben sie denn der Frau gesagt?* 'What have they said to the woman?'
    a. careful speech: [vas ˈhaːp̩m̩ zi tɛn teɐ̯ fʁaʊ̯ k̬əˈzaːktʰ]
    b. informal speech: [vas ˈhan zə n tɐ fʁaʊ̯ k̬əˈzaːtʰ]

The careful pronunciation of this sentence contains instances of assimilation, reduction, and deletion. Unstressed long vowels are shortened (*sie* /ziː/ → [zi]); schwa is deleted in *haben* and then /n/ is assimilated to the preceding /p/ (/haːpən/ → [haːp̩m̩]). The informal pronunciation of this sentence, however, exhibits many more examples of reduction and deletion. A long stressed vowel is shortened in *haben*; a short tense vowel is reduced to schwa in *sie*. Vowels are deleted in *denn* and *der*, and consonants are deleted in *haben*, *denn*, and *gesagt*.

    7.2.2.2 Vocabulary   Many lexical items in German are unmarked with respect to the stylistic level to which they belong. They are neutral and would not be inappropriate in an informal or a formal setting. Words such as *Straße* 'street', *lesen* 'to read', and *Liter* 'liter', for example, do not have any special stylistic status and could be used in essentially any situation regardless of the level of formality. Other items are marked and thus appropriate only for situations where informal or formal speech is expected. The word *blöd*, for example, is a colloquial way of saying *dumm* 'dumb' and would be viewed as an odd choice of lexical item in a formal speech situation. Just as odd would be the use of the elevated form *Gatte* to speak of one's husband in an informal setting.

    Table 7.1 provides some examples of words that are essentially synonymous but that differ in their level of formality. Words that are colloquial are typically marked as such in dictionaries, but only highly formal lexical items tend to be identified as formal vocabulary. For example, all but one of the words (phrases) that are characterized as colloquial in Table 7.1 are marked "ugs."

Table 7.1 *Stylistic variation in vocabulary (modified from Durrell 1992:25–28)*

Colloquial	Neutral	Formal
protzen	*angeben* 'to show off'	*sich rühmen*
langen	*ausreichen* 'to be sufficient'	*genügen*
	die Backe 'cheek'	*die Wange*
der Sprit	*das Benzin* 'gas', 'petrol'	*der Treibstoff*
hereinlegen	*betrügen* 'to deceive'	
blöd	*dumm* 'dumb'	*töricht*
futtern	*essen* 'to eat'	*speisen, tafeln*
die Polente	*die Polizei* 'police'	
mies	*schlecht* 'bad'	*übel*
fix	*schnell* 'fast'	*flink*
klauen	*stehlen* 'to steal'	*entwenden*
den Mund halten	*still sein* 'to be quiet'	*schweigen*
der Quatsch	*der Unsinn* 'nonsense'	*der Nonsens*
abhauen	*weggehen* 'to leave'	*sich entfernen*

(*umgangssprachlich* 'colloquial') in the most recent *Duden* spelling dictionary (Dudenredaktion 2006), whereas only *tafeln* 'to dine' is marked as being formal ("geh." = *gehoben* 'elevated'). Notice that not all entries in the neutral column in Table 7.1 have corresponding forms in both the colloquial and formal columns. In cases like these, the neutral form can be used to fill the gap. Some colloquial language is considered crude or vulgar and is identified accordingly in dictionaries (*derb* 'crude'; *vulgär* 'vulgar'). For example, a synonym of the colloquial *hereinlegen* 'to take somebody for a ride' is *bescheißen* 'to cheat', which is labeled "derb" in Dudenredaktion 2006:246 (cf. *scheißen* 'to shit'). For further examples of stylistic variation in the lexicon, see Durrell 1992:25–28.[6]

7.2.2.3 Grammar The stylistic variation found in German grammar is probably best exemplified by a comparison of colloquial German with formal Standard German, the variety of German that is codified in, for example, the *Duden* grammar (Dudenredaktion 2005), since the grammatical structures found in neutral style are often similar to those found at the formal level (Durrell 1992:18). An excellent data source is the *Duden* dictionary entitled *Richtiges und gutes Deutsch* (Dudenredaktion 2001), which deals with questions about usage (*Zweifelsfälle*) and thus provides information on what is current in colloquial German and what is acceptable in the (formal) standard. Durrell 1992:18–19, which provides a list of grammatical structures that are typical of colloquial German and the corresponding structures that are acceptable in formal written German, is also an excellent source of information.

The first two frequently asked questions under the heading *Genitivattribut* 'genitive attribute' in the *Duden* usage dictionary involve the acceptability of phrases like the following (Dudenredaktion 2001:350):

(12) a. *meinem Bruder sein Zimmer*
         my-dat. brother his room 'my brother's room'
     b. *das Haus von meinen Eltern*
         the house of my-dat. parents 'my parents' house'

Both phrases (which make use of the dative case or a dative preposition) are common in colloquial German,[7] but are to be avoided in the standard language (Dudenredaktion 2001:353). The corresponding phrases found in the standard language exhibit the genitive case.[8]

(13) a. *das Zimmer meines Bruders*
         the room my-gen. brother-gen. 'my brother's room'
     b. *das Haus meiner Eltern*
         the house my-gen. parents 'my parents' house'

As mentioned in chapter 6 (section 6.1), the use of the dative case with prepositions like *wegen* 'because of' is the norm in colloquial speech, but considered incorrect in the standard language, where the genitive is required.

According to the *Duden* usage dictionary, it is generally considered impolite or colloquial to use demonstrative pronouns instead of personal pronouns to refer to people unless demonstrative meaning is intended (Dudenredaktion 2001:223).

(14)   *Ich weiß es von meinem Vater. Der* (standard: *Er*) *hat es im Betrieb gehört.*
         'I know about it from my father. He heard it at work.'

The use of the definite article with personal names is common in colloquial German and is also found in administrative language (Dudenredaktion 2001:658).

(15) a. colloquial: *Die Inge hat mich verlassen.* 'Inge left me.'
     b. administrative: *die Frau Schmidt* 'Mrs. Schmidt'

In the (formal) standard, an article is not used with a personal name unless an adjective precedes it (Dudenredaktion 2001:657).

(16) a. *Hans ist ein braver Junge.* 'Hans is a good boy.'
     b. *der kleine Karl* 'little Karl'

The use of a preposition + *was* 'what' instead of a prepositional adverb beginning with *wo-* is another feature that distinguishes colloquial speech from the standard language.

(17)   *Mit was* (standard: *Womit*) *soll das Brett befestigt werden?*
        (Dudenredaktion 2001:697)
        'With what should the board be attached?'

The colloquial German use of *tun* + infinitive is characterized as an "unnecessary extension of the predicate" in the *Duden* usage dictionary; it is considered incorrect in the standard language (Dudenredaktion 2001:835).[9]

(18)   *Sie tut gerade schreiben.* (standard: *Sie schreibt gerade.*)
        she does just-now write 'She's writing.'

Only when the infinitive is preposed for purposes of emphasis is this construction considered acceptable in the written standard (Dudenredaktion 2005: 434).

(19)   *Verstehen tut er wie gewöhnlich nichts.*
        understand does he as usual nothing 'As usual he understands nothing.'

When the verb *brauchen* functions as an auxiliary (with modal meaning similar to *müssen* 'to have to'), it is typically used without *zu* in the spoken language (Dudenredaktion 2001:184). This usage is thus common in spoken neutral German as well as in colloquial German.

(20) a.   spoken: *Du brauchst nicht kommen.* 'You don't need to come.'
     b.   written: *Du brauchst nicht zu kommen.*

In the written language (at the neutral and formal style levels), *brauchen* is typically used with *zu*.

Several issues involving word order differentiate colloquial German from the formal standard. In colloquial (and spoken neutral) German, the conjunction *weil* 'because' is often used with main clause (verb-second) word order (Dudenredaktion 2001:930).

(21) a.   colloquial: *Sie kann nicht kommen, weil sie hat keine Zeit.*
     b.   formal: . . . *weil sie keine Zeit hat.*

Although verb-second word order with *weil* is considered incorrect in the standard language, its use in the spoken language is becoming increasingly common – an indication that *weil* is undergoing a change in status from a subordinating (verb-final) to a coordinating (verb-second) conjunction (Dudenredaktion 2001:930).

In the colloquial language, one often finds main clauses used instead of relative clauses (Durrell 1992:19).[10]

(22) a. colloquial: *Es gibt Leute, die reden im Schlaf.*
         it gives people they speak in sleep 'There are people who talk in
         their sleep.'
     b. formal: *Es gibt Leute, die im Schlaf reden.*

Although these clauses are used to further modify an entity and correspond to
relative clauses in formal German, they are not necessarily relative clauses with
aberrant (verb-second rather than verb-final) word order. Küper (1991:134),
for example, argues that main clause (verb-second) word order is required in
these clauses because they begin with a demonstrative pronoun, not with a
relative pronoun.[11] This would then be another example of the increased use of
demonstrative pronouns in the colloquial language in comparison to the formal
(see the discussion above regarding the use of demonstrative pronouns in place
of personal pronouns).

   Demonstrative as well as personal pronouns that would otherwise occur
sentence-initially (in the Vorfeld) are often omitted in the spoken language
(Dudenredaktion 2005:894).

(23) a. *Peter? Hat mich wirklich überrascht.* (*Der hat mich . . .*)
         'Peter? (He) really surprised me.'
     b. *Wo ist Anna? – Arbeitet heute zu Hause.* (*Sie arbeitet heute . . .*)
         'Where is Anna? – (She's) working at home today.'

These pronouns can be recovered (determined) from the context, and are
expendable when speaking, when shortcuts tend to be taken.

   For further examples of stylistic variation in German grammar, see Durrell
1992:18–19.

7.3   Address

7.3.1   A brief history

The German language did not always make a *du/Sie* distinction in its forms of
address. The "original" pronoun used to address a single person was *du*. We
find evidence of this in the *Hildebrandslied*, when Hildebrand and Hadubrand
address each other as strangers, not knowing that they are father and son.

(24)   *eddo hwelihhes cnuosles du sis* (Braune *et al.* 1994:84)
        and which lineage you are

The first evidence of a special pronoun of politeness (which has its roots in
Latin practices) is Otfrid's use of *ir* (a second person plural form) in the ninth
century to address the Bishop of Salomo of Konstanz (Bach 1970:194; Besch

1998:92–93). But even in the twelfth century the use of *ir* is still not a regular occurrence. The German *Rolandslied*, by Pfaffe Konrad, which is based on a French original, only uses *du*, although the French source exhibits the polite form *vos* (Bach 1970:194). With the spread of chivalric culture, however, which was greatly influenced by the French tradition, came an increase in the use of *ir* (= modern German *ihr*) as a pronoun of politeness, modeled on the French use of *vos* (= modern French *vous*). By the sixteenth century, *Ihr* was regularly used among the nobility and upper middle class.[12] The pronoun *du* was exchanged by members of the lowest social classes; the members of these classes were also addressed with *du* by those of higher rank (Metcalf 1938:11).

During the sixteenth century, *Ihr* usage spread to the lower social classes and *Ihr* was even used occasionally to address servants and beggars. This increase in the use of *Ihr* caused it to lose its value as a pronoun of politeness, which led to the development of new pronouns of politeness (Metcalf 1938:11). By the middle of the seventeenth century, the forms *Er* and *Sie*-singular (< *sie* 'she') had acquired this function. *Er* and *Sie*-singular were the pronominal developments of *Herr* and *Frau*, the nominal forms of address that had encroached on the territory of *Ihr* among the lower nobility and the upper middle class (Metcalf 1938:64).[13] The following example of this use of *Herr* as a form of address is from a play by Jacob Ayrer, written at the end of the sixteenth century (cited in Metcalf 1938:60):

(25)   *Mich dunkt, der Herr beschweret sey Mit einer grosen Melancholey.*
         'Me thinks, the lord is [= you are] burdened with a great
         melancholy.'

The *Sie*-plural form of address, which came into use at the end of the seventeenth century, has its origin in pronominal extensions of abstract nominal forms of address like *Eure Majestät* 'Your Majesty' and *Eure Gnade* 'Your Grace'. The pronominal forms, like the abstractions themselves, were used increasingly with plural verbs and were therefore identified with the plural third person pronouns (Metcalf 1938:109–110).

By the beginning of the eighteenth century, there were five different types of address for an individual: *du*, *Ihr*, *Er/Sie*-singular, *Sie*-plural, and abstractions (e.g., *Majestät* 'Majesty', *Durchlaucht* 'Highness', *Gnaden* 'Grace', *Exzellenz* 'Excellency').[14] This proliferation of forms, however, eventually led to simplification, yielding the two forms we find today, *du* and *Sie*-plural.

7.3.2   The address system

The traditional "modern" use of *du* and *Sie* is one that can be characterized by the contrast of the notions intimate (*du*) versus polite/respectful (*Sie*) (Besch

1998:14). Many of the conventions that governed this use of *du* and *Sie* until the late 1960s are still valid today. Those conventions that can be considered traditional (pre-1968) are the following (Clyne 1995:130–131; Besch 1998:14–15): Family members, relatives, children under fifteen, friends, animals, and God are all addressed with *du*. Members of groups that have a strong bond (e.g., members of clubs, sports groups, fraternities, some political parties, etc.) address each other with *du*. Asymmetry can be found in the child–adult relationship, in that children are addressed with *du*, but older children are urged to address adult strangers with *Sie*. Clyne (1995:130) characterizes *Sie* as the unmarked pronoun of address and *du* as being marked as the pronoun of solidarity (Brown and Gilman 1960).[15] The use of *du* can also be viewed as signaling disrespect, however, as evidenced by the fines that have been imposed on citizens for addressing the police with *du*.[16] In 1987, for example, a fine of 300 DM for addressing a police officer with *du* was increased to 2,500 DM for using *du* with an added insult, *Du blöde Sau* 'You stupid son-of-a-bitch' (Besch 1998:56–58). As a sign of friendship, people can decide to address each other with *du*, a decision that is sometimes celebrated with a ritual drink (*Brüderschaft trinken*) and is subject to certain conventions. For example, it is the older person who is expected to make the offer of *du*.[17]

Changes to this traditional system can be linked to the changes that came about following the German student movement in the late 1960s. Before this period, students addressed each other and their instructors with *Sie*; *du* was used only for special friends. Bayer (1979) characterizes this system of address as one based on an unmarked pronoun for formality (*Sie*) versus a marked one for intimacy (*du*). In the late 1960s, as a protest against conventional social relationships, students began to use *du* for communication with each other. According to Bayer (1979), this new system of address is based on an unmarked pronoun for solidarity (*du*) versus a marked one for social distance (*Sie*). When both address systems were employed in a speech situation, misunderstandings were often the result. This led to a certain amount of uncertainty when addressing others, uncertainty that still exists today. Zimmer (1986:53) characterizes the "*du/Sie*-conflict" (do I say *du* or *Sie*?), which repeatedly raises the question of one's own social identity and group membership, as a common daily occurrence.

One of the changes in the use of *du* and *Sie* that is evident today is the more widespread use of *du* among members of the younger generation (Clyne 1995:131). The use of *du* among university students has become the norm, although much of its status as a signal of ideology and solidarity has been lost; it is simply an extension of the *du* of school children, used as the automatic form of address among young people up to roughly age thirty (Besch 1998:25). A longitudinal study based on opinion polls showed more Germans in 1993

(34%) than in 1974 (25%) who were willing to use *du* with people they had not known for a long time, a tendency that was strongest among people in the 16–29 age group (59%) (Clyne 1995:131). Ideological beliefs play a greater role in promoting the use of *du* than they did previously. Not just membership in a political party or club, but similarly radical or progressive political or social views will trigger an automatic *du* relationship (Clyne 1995:134). Although *du* is used more widely than it was prior to the late 1960s, *Sie* has by no means been displaced. Stevenson (1997:139) suggests that the trend could in fact be moving in the opposite direction.

Traditionally, *du* is used with a person's first name; *Sie* is used with *Herr/Frau* and a person's last name, title, or title and last name. There is also the less common combination of *Sie* plus first name, used, for example, in TV and radio interviews with athletes and entertainers, where the use of first names may be based on the Anglo-American practice (Clyne 1995:135).

There are national and regional differences in the practices that character-ize the current system of address. In southern Germany and Austria, *du* is used more than in northern Germany; it is also used more in rural areas than in urban ones (Clyne 1995:136). A 1993 survey showed that East Germans are more reluctant to enter into a quick *du* relationship than West Germans (Clyne 1995:137). In Austria, one finds *du* in combination with titles, which are used frequently: *Du, lieber Herr Hofrat!* 'You, Mr. Counsellor!' (Muhr 1993:31).

7.4   Language and gender

7.4.1   Equal treatment

One of the issues in the study of language and gender involves the ways in which women use language in comparison to men. Numerous studies have described women's speech as being different from that of men (e.g., Baron 1986, Arliss 1991). Another issue, the focus of this discussion, involves the way in which women are represented in language, in particular the forms used to address them and the terminology used to describe them.

In the late 1970s, inspired by the work on language and gender by linguists such as Mary Ritchie Key (1975) and Robin Lakoff (1975), feminist linguists in Germany began to call for the equal treatment of women and men in language (e.g., Guentherodt *et al.* 1980, Hellinger 1980, Pusch 1980). One type of unequal treatment they sought to replace was the subordinate, second-class, and "silent" treatment of women in examples like the following (Guentherodt *et al.* 1980:16, 19–20).

(26) a. *Herr Meier mit Frau* 'Mr. Meier and wife'
         non-sexist alternatives: *Frau Meier und Herr Meier* 'Mrs. Meier and
         Mr. Meier'; *das Ehepaar Meier* 'the Meier couple'
     b. *Fräulein Sell* 'Miss Sell' (cf. *Herr Sell* 'Mr. Sell')
         non-sexist alternative: *Frau Sell* 'Ms. Sell'[18]
     c. *Bundespräsident Scheel und Ehefrau Mildred* 'Federal President
         Scheel and wife Mildred'
         non-sexist alternative: *Bundespräsident Scheel und Dr. Scheel*
     d. *An die Familie Peter Dörsch* 'to the Peter Dörsch family'
         non-sexist alternative: *An Frau Eva Dörsch und Herrn Peter Dörsch*
         'to Mrs. Eva Dörsch and Mr. Peter Dörsch'

Another sexist practice was the use of the male (man) as the standard or
norm for people in general (Guentherodt *et al.* 1980:16–17).

(27) a. *Sehr geehrte Herren* 'Dear sirs'
         non-sexist alternative: *Sehr geehrte Damen und Herren*
     b. *der Glaube unserer Väter* 'the belief of our fathers'
         non-sexist alternative: *der Glaube unserer Vorfahren* 'the belief of
         our ancestors'
     c. *Weiblicher Kaufmann gesucht* 'female businessman wanted'
         non-sexist alternative: *Kauffrau gesucht* 'businesswoman wanted'
     d. *der Kontoinhaber* 'the account holder'
         non-sexist alternative: *die Kontoinhaber/innen* 'account holders'

Although expressions like *der Kontoinhaber* 'the account holder' and *der
Bewerber* 'the applicant' are considered generic forms that can refer to females
as well as males, the problem is that these forms are identical to the masculine forms. In addition, all words that must agree in gender with these
generic forms (because of the requirements of the grammar of German) are
masculine.

(28) *Jeder Passagier möge seinen Platz identifizieren.* (Trömel-Plötz
      1978:51)
      'Each passenger should identify his seat.'

As Pusch (1984:7) points out, the following statement, which is in her passport, is inaccurate (although grammatical) because it characterizes her as a
Deutscher, a male German:

(29) *Der Inhaber dieses Passes ist Deutscher.*
      the bearer of-this passport is German-masc.

7.4.2   Achieving linguistic equality

A number of general strategies have been proposed to deal with the issue of linguistic equality in German, with varying degrees of success. Linguistic equality is certainly more difficult to achieve in German than in English. For example, words that end in *-man* and *-ess* in English can be replaced by neutral terms: one can replace *policeman* with *police officer*, *fireman* with *firefighter*, *waiter* and *waitress* with *server*, and *steward* and *stewardess* with *flight attendant*. In German, however, because nouns have grammatical gender, and because those that refer to individuals are typically either masculine or feminine, it is much more difficult to find a neutral term. The use of a plural form (a common strategy in English) typically does not solve the problem. The plural *Studenten* 'students', for example, is based on the masculine *der Student*; *Studentinnen* 'students' is based on the feminine *die Studentin*.

A section in the *Duden* usage dictionary (Dudenredaktion 2001:392–398) addresses the equal treatment of women and men in the German language. According to *Duden*, the basic principles to be followed are visibility (when women are included they should be mentioned) and symmetry (when women and men are mentioned, they should be treated linguistically in an equal manner). Generic masculine forms – masculine forms (nouns, pronouns) that are used to refer to women as well as men – are thus out. Some of the current strategies employed in the effort to avoid sexist language and discussed in *Duden* are "splitting" (see below), various types of abbreviations, and alternative forms. These strategies are still quite controversial and they are by no means accepted universally, as a brief comparison of several online newspapers in section 7.4.4 reveals.

7.4.2.1 Splitting   "Splitting" is the explicit use of a feminine and a masculine form (instead of a single form). Some examples of full (non-abbreviated) double forms (*Paarformeln*) are the following (Dudenredaktion 2001:393).

(30) a.   *Kolleginnen und Kollegen*
           colleagues-fem. and colleagues-masc.
     b.   *Assistentin oder Assistent*
           assistant-fem. or assistant-masc.
     c.   *eine oder einer*
           one-fem. or one-masc.

According to *Duden*, this doubling is the most polite and most explicit variant of linguistic equality and should be used above all in addressing others personally. Women should be addressed exactly like men when using titles, first names, last names, job designations, and so on (Dudenredaktion 2001:393).

(31) a.   not acceptable: *Frau Meier hat mit Oberstudiendirektor*
            Dr. Lehmann gesprochen. 'Mrs. Meier spoke with Principal
            Dr. Lehmann.'
       b.   acceptable: *Studienrätin Dr. Meier hat mit Oberstudiendirektor*
            Dr. Lehmann gesprochen. 'Teacher Dr. Meier spoke with Principal
            Dr. Lehmann.'

Virtually all titles and job designations have feminine as well as masculine
forms, and feminine forms have become well established (Dudenredaktion
2001:827).

(32) a.   *Ministerpräsidentin N. N. sprach vor dem Kongress.*
            prime-minister-fem. N. N. spoke to the congress
       b.   *Berlinerin wurde erste Prorektorin in Speyer.*
            Berliner-fem. became first deputy-vice-chancellor-fem. in Speyer

The feminine titles *Doktorin* 'doctor' and *Professorin* 'professor' are typically
not used to address women, however. In the spoken language, women are
commonly addressed as *Frau Doktor* and *Frau Professor* (Dudenredaktion
2001:828).

   7.4.2.2 Abbreviations   In written texts, for reasons of economy, doubled forms can be abbreviated in various ways. In keeping with the use of
the term *Paarformeln* for unabbreviated doubled forms, abbreviated forms are
commonly referred to as *Sparformeln.*[19]
   A slash can be used as long as the doubled forms differ only by an ending
and a grammatically correct word is left if the slash is removed.

(33) a.   *Assistent und Assistentin > Assistent/-in* 'assistant'
       b.   *Mitarbeiter und Mitarbeiterinnen > Mitarbeiter/-innen* 'coworkers'
       c.   *jede und jeder > jede/-r* 'each'

Pairs like *Arzt und Ärztin* 'doctor' cannot be abbreviated with a slash because
these words differ by more than just an ending.
   Doubled forms can be abbreviated with the use of parentheses, which can
occur at the end of a word or in the middle of a word.

(34) a.   *Schüler(in)* 'pupil'
       b.   *Student(inn)en* 'students'
       c.   *eine(r)* 'one'
       d.   *jede(r)* 'each'

The use of parentheses with a feminine ending is not recommended, however,
because it gives the impression that the feminine form is subordinate and less
important (Dudenredaktion 2001:394).

The use of a capital -*I*- in the middle of a word as an abbreviation for doubled forms has been attested since the beginning of the 1980s.

(35) a. *KollegInnen* 'colleagues' (= *Kollegen und Kolleginnen*)
     b. *MitarbeiterInnen* 'coworkers'

According to *Duden*, this type of abbreviation is common, but it is just as commonly rejected, and in some agencies and institutions it is explicitly forbidden (Dudenredaktion 2001:394). The use of capital letters in the middle of a word can also be found in the names of products, companies, and services (*MiniDisc*, *DaimlerChrysler*, *TeleBanking*), but it is not something that is sanctioned by the official spelling rules (Dudenredaktion 2006:58).

   7.4.2.3 Alternative forms   Because abbreviations are not well suited for use in the spoken language, and full forms can be cumbersome, alternatives to splitting are useful. One common alternative is the conversion of participles to plural nouns.[20]

(36) a. *Studierende* 'those studying (students)'
     b. *Lehrende* 'those teaching (teachers)'
     c. *Gewählte* 'those elected'

A word designating an object rather than a word designating a person can be used.

(37)   *Leitung* 'leadership' (instead of *Leiter oder Leiterin* 'leader')

Adjectives can be used in place of doubled nouns.

(38)   *ärztlicher Rat* 'medical advice' (instead of *Rat der Ärztin/des Arztes* 'advice of the doctor')

Relative clauses can also be used in place of doubled forms.

(39) a. *Wer einen Mord begeht, wird bestraft.* 'Whoever commits murder will be punished.' (Instead of *Morderinnen und Mörder werden bestraft.* 'Murderers will be punished.')
     b. *Personen, die einen Antrag stellen* 'people who make an application' (instead of *Antragsteller und Antragstellerinnen* 'applicants')

Although potentially just as lengthy as doubled forms, relative clauses can be a stylistic improvement over splitting.

7.4.3   Legal language

The status of non-sexist language in legal spheres varies from one German-speaking country to another. In some cases, legal language reflects current usage norms as codified in *Duden* (Dudenredaktion 2001:392–398), in others it has not kept up. A comparison of the situation in Germany with that in Switzerland exemplifies the range of approaches to non-sexist language in legal texts.[21]

A 1991 report by a task force on legal language (*Arbeitsgruppe Rechtssprache*) set up by the German Federal Government distinguished between two types of legal language (*Rechtssprache*): official language (*Amtssprache*), used, for example, for administrative communication, judicial decisions, and forms; and legislative language (*Vorschriftensprache*), used to formulate laws and decrees (Hellinger 1995:306). The task force supported the principle of visibility of the female in official language and thus revision of forms, educational programs, examination regulations, and so on to include feminine occupational titles and terms of address, but also the use of alternatives to linguistic visibility such as nouns that refer to objects rather than people (*das Ministerium* 'department' instead of *der Minister* 'secretary'). The report argued, however, that the use of splitting in a headline did not preclude the use of the generic masculine in the following text (Hellinger 1995:306). Legislative language, on the other hand, was exempt from changes in its use of the generic masculine. Justification for this position included the claim that the use of sex-specific feminine and masculine nouns referring to humans in revised or new texts would cause inconsistencies with the traditional use of the generic masculine. In addition, it would be too costly in terms of time, money, and effort to revise the entire legal code, and the revisions would yield legal texts with "rather ugly formulations" (Hellinger 1995:306–307).

A 1991 report prepared by a Swiss task force set up by the Swiss Federal Government, in contrast to the German Federal Government report, supported visibility and symmetry in the two types of legal language it identified in Swiss Standard German, administrative language (*Verwaltungssprache*) and legislative language (*Gesetzessprache*). The co-existence of generic masculines in existing legislation and sex-specific masculines in new legislation was not viewed as a threat to legal consistency; the aesthetics of inclusive language was also not an issue. Acceptable means of achieving linguistic equality included abbreviations for double forms such as those using a slash (*Antragsteller/innen* 'applicants') and those with capital -*I*- (*AntragstellerInnen*), although not in legislative language (Hellinger 1995:307–308).

7.4.4   The print media

A brief comparison of several online newspapers provides an example of the range of current approaches in the German print media to the issue of non-sexist language. The text in these examples comes from the information the newspapers provide on readership, employees, contributors, and so on.

At one end of the range of approaches is the use of capital -*I*- in *die tageszeitung.*

(40)   *die tageszeitung: 250* **MitarbeiterInnen**, *7.000* **GenossInnen** *und*
        202.000 **LeserInnen** *(davon 84%, die exklusiv die taz lesen)*
        verpflichten sich taztäglich der Pressevielfalt. (www.taz.de [July 24,
        2007])
        '250 employees, 7,000 cooperative members, and 202,000 readers
        (84% of whom read the taz exclusively) commit taz-daily to media
        diversity.'

The use of *Paarformeln*, which can be found in newspapers like the *Frankfurter Rundschau* and *Die Zeit*, follows the principle of visibility and avoids the stigma attached to the use of abbreviations like capital -*I*-.

(41) a. *Frankfurter Rundschau: Jedes Jahr bewerben sich viele*
         Kandidatinnen und Kandidaten *auf einen Praktikumsplatz in der*
         FR-Redaktion. (www.fr-online.de [July 24, 2007])
         'Each year many candidates (-fem. and candidates-masc.) apply for
         an internship in the FR editorial department.'
     b. *Das sind 51 000* **Leserinnen** *und* **Leser** *(+3 Prozent) mehr als noch*
         vor einem Jahr. (www.zeit.de [August 3, 2007])
         'That's 51,000 more readers (-fem. and readers-masc.) (+3 percent)
         than a year ago.'

At the other end of the range of approaches is the use of the generic masculine plural – found, for example, in the *Frankfurter Allgemeine Zeitung* – which does not follow the principle of visibility.

(42)   *Frankfurter Allgemeine Zeitung: Die F.A.Z. hat täglich 910.000*
        Leser. (www.faz.net [July 24, 2007])
        'The F.A.Z. has 910,000 readers daily.'

In between these two "extremes" we find a mixture of forms in newspapers like the *Süddeutsche Zeitung* and the Swiss *Neue Zürcher Zeitung*.

(43) a. *Süddeutsche Zeitung: Für die Süddeutsche Zeitung arbeiten*
         etliche der besten **Journalisten** *Deutschlands . . . Damit ist die*
         Süddeutsche Zeitung für ihre Kern-Zielgruppe – **Höhergebildete**,
         Einkommensstarke, **Fach- und Führungskräfte** *– schon lange zum*
         Lieblingsmedium geworden. (www.sueddeutsche.de [July 24, 2007])
         'Quite a few of the best journalists work for the *Süddeutsche
         Zeitung* . . . With that, the *Süddeutsche Zeitung* has long since
         become the favorite medium for its core target audience: the highly
         educated, those in high-income brackets, specialists, executives.'

b. *Neue Zürcher Zeitung*: *Dabei müssen die* **Verfasserinnen und Verfasser** *von Meinungsbeiträgen den echten Vor- und Nachnamen nennen.* **Nutzern**, *welche die Richtlinien für Leser-Kommentare nicht befolgen, kann die Registrierung entzogen werden.*
(www.nzz.ch [July 24, 2007])
'In doing so, authors (-fem. and authors-masc.) of opinion pieces must provide their real first and last names. Users who do not follow the guidelines for reader commentaries can have their registration revoked.'

The example from the *Süddeutsche Zeitung* makes use of a generic masculine plural (*Journalisten*) as well as alternative forms, which include neutral plural forms derived from participles (*Hohergebildete*) and adjectives (*Einkommensstarke*) and plurals that do not refer explicitly to people (*Fach- und Führungskräfte*). The example from the *Neue Zürcher Zeitung* makes use of splitting (*Verfasserinnen und Verfasser*) as well as a generic masculine plural (*Nutzern*). While the interspersion of generic masculine plurals may be driven by stylistic considerations, linguists like Hellinger and Schräpel (1983:53–54) have argued that the criterion of visibility must have a higher priority than the criteria of stylistic elegance and economy.

7.5   Jugendsprache

7.5.1   Speakers and usage

The term *Jugendsprache* 'youth speech' is commonly used to refer to the variety of German spoken by young people, teenagers in particular. Barbour and Stevenson characterize *Jugendsprache* as a kind of jargon, which they define as a variety of a language spoken by a subculture group that is usually characterized by an inventive and frequently changing vocabulary (1990:6, 276). The purpose of jargon is to signal membership in a closed social group. The use of frequently changing vocabulary therefore makes it difficult for those who do not belong to the group to acquire the speech variety. Young people view their speech as more direct, spontaneous, and "cool" than adult speech, which they characterize as dry and serious (Schlobinski 1995:333). *Jugendsprache* thus has a distancing as well as an identity-building function; it also serves as a means of protest (Ehmann 2005:12) – an effect of the use of words that are considered vulgar or taboo in the standard language. Not all young Germans use *Jugendsprache*, however, and not every user of *Jugendsprache* uses it invariably: context plays an important role in determining use. Furthermore, *Jugendsprache* is not a homogeneous language variety; it differs from group to group and situation to situation (Schlobinski 1995:334). However, general features of *Jugendsprache* can be identified. These are discussed in the following section.

7.5.2   Linguistic features

7.5.2.1 Lexical features   The main features that distinguish *Jugend-sprache* from other varieties of German are lexical in nature. A number of glossaries and dictionaries have been published that deal with the lexicon of *Jugendsprache* (e.g., Müller-Thurau 1983; Ehmann 2001, 2005),[22] which is in a constant state of flux, as many words go out of style as quickly as they gain popularity. Popular means of enriching the vocabulary are through semantic change, borrowing, derivation and compounding, reduction, and other word-formation processes. While many of these processes are also common in the standard language, others are not, for example, "lexical mutation" (see the discussion below). These processes yield lexical items that are unique to the lexicon of *Jugendsprache*, although some will find their way into the colloquial language of other groups, as has, for example, the word *geil* 'terrific' < *geil* 'horny' (Schlobinski 1995:335).

A popular means of creating new words is by changing the meaning of an existing word. Some types of semantic change that can be found are broadening, narrowing, shift, amelioration, and pejoration.[23]

(44) a.   broadening: *hämmern* 'to hammer' > 'to hammer; to work hard'
     b.   narrowing: *tricky* 'wily; difficult' > 'wily'
     c.   shift: *Brett* 'board' > 'very good pop or hip-hop song'
     d.   amelioration: *porno* 'very' < *porno-* (e.g., *pornografisch* 'pornographic')
     e.   pejoration: *Massage* 'massage' > 'blow' (e.g., *Kopfmassage* 'blow to the head')

Many words are borrowed from English, often with a slight change in meaning. These words are easily "eingedeutscht" (integrated); they are inflected like German words and often serve as the base for derivation and other word-formation processes.

(45) a.   *Supporter* 'parents, grandparents, aunt; financially strong sponsor'
     b.   *muddeln* 'to muddle along'
     c.   *relaxt* 'calm, relaxed'

New words are created through derivation. For example, a number of verbs in Ehmann 2005:148–150 are formed with the prefix *ver-*:

(46) a.   *verchecken* 'to forget; to sell' (*checken* 'to check; to understand [colloquial]')
     b.   *verdackeln* 'to miss; to forget' (*der Dackel* 'dachshund')
     c.   *vereiern* 'to pull someone's leg'; 'to take someone for a ride'

The formation of superlatives is particularly productive. Androutsopoulos (1998:105) notes in particular the use of the prefixes *hyper-*, *mega-*, *ober-*, *super-*, *über-*, and *ultra-* in his (fanzine) corpus. Examples from Ehmann 2005 of words that contain these prefixes are the following:

(47) a.   *hypertonisch* 'fantastic'
     b.   *Mega-Deal* 'big (awesome) thing'
     c.   *superlustig* 'particularly funny; totally inept'
     d.   *ultra-geil* 'super terrific'

The suffixes *-i* and *-o* are particularly productive in *Jugendsprache*.

(48) a.   *der Behindi* (pronounced "Biheindi"; c.f. English *behind*) 'a backward person'
     b.   *der Dösi* 'sleepyhead, daydreamer'
     c.   *laschi* 'wimpy, boring'
     d.   *peino* 'embarrassing'
     e.   *der Trivialo* 'unimaginative person'
     f.   *der Karriero* 'career oriented person'

Conversion, another derivational process, also plays a role in creating new lexical items.

(49) a.   *müllen* 'to blather' (c.f. *Müll* 'garbage')
     b.   *zoffen* 'to quarrel' (c.f. *Zoff* 'trouble')

In addition to derivation, we also find examples of compounding in *Jugendsprache*. These compounds are often very creative, with the meaning of the parts not necessarily adding up to the meaning of the whole.

(50) a.   *Nagelstudio* 'brothel' ('nail studio')
     b.   *Milchtüte* 'twirp' ('milk carton')
     c.   *Rhythmuspräsident* 'drummer' ('rhythm president')
     d.   *Sehdeckel* 'eyes' ('sight lids')

The compound *Milchtüte*, for example, is a person, not a 'bag' (*Tüte*), and *Sehdeckel* are eyes, not eyelids.

Another word-formation process that enriches the *Jugendsprache* vocabulary is clipping, a type of reduction.

(51) a.   *Stino* (< *Stinknormalo*) 'super normal person'
     b.   *Compi* (< *Computer-Experte*) 'computer expert'
     c.   *Spezi* (< *Spezialist*) 'specialist'

As in the standard language, words that are the products of reduction can be used in other word-formation processes. The verb *alken* 'to booze it up', for example, can be viewed as derived (through conversion) from *Alk* 'alcohol', itself the product of clipping (< *Alkohol* 'alcohol'). Clippings are also used in the formation of compounds. The compound *Compi-Spezi* 'computer specialist' is in fact made up of two clippings.

Some words in the *Jugendsprache* lexicon do not fall into traditional word formation categories. A process that Ehmann terms "lexical mutation" is probably best described as the replacement of letters or morphemes of an existing word to create a new word – one that often has a different meaning.

(52) a. *labundig* 'lively, fun-loving' (cf. *lebendig* 'lively')
     b. *zotteln* 'to walk leisurely' (c.f. *zockeln* 'to plod')
     c. *mittenmang* 'right in the middle' (cf. *mittendrin* 'right in the middle')
     d. *vordergestern* 'totally out of fashion' (cf. *vorgestern* 'day before yesterday')

Vowels have been replaced in *labundig* and consonants in *zotteln*. In *vordergestern*, the morpheme *vor* 'before' has been replaced by the morpheme *vorder* 'front'. In *mittenmang*, *drin* 'inside' has been replaced by *mang*, which Ehmann (2005:95) views as being derived from *Menge* 'crowd, heap'. Other examples of word formation in *Jugendsprache* that are difficult to characterize are lexical items like *doppeldidoch* and *hoppeldihopp*.

(53) a. *doppeldidoch* '(emphatically) to the contrary!' (cf. *doch* 'to the contrary!')
     b. *hoppeldihopp* 'quickly' (cf. *hopp* 'quick')

The word *doppeldidoch* can be viewed as a product of compounding, but the "linking" material, -*di*-, adds a complicating twist to the process. One can see evidence of reduplication in *hoppeldihopp*, but there is more going on than simple reduplication. There is also clearly a connection between these two words (both contain the sequence -*eldi*-). The process of "lexical mutation," as well as the "creative wordplay" evidenced in lexical items like *doppeldidoch* and *hoppeldihopp*, are particularly striking examples of the inventiveness that characterizes the vocabulary of *Jugendsprache*.

Another characteristic feature of the *Jugendsprache* lexicon is the use of lexical items that are considered vulgar in the standard language. This is a feature that is common to the speech of young people in general; Cheshire (1982:155), for example, views swearing as an important symbol of "vernacular identity" for boys and girls. Androutsopoulos (1998:415) argues that the "vulgar" portion of the German *Jugendsprache* lexicon centers around five "word nests," groups of lexical items (words, phrases) that have as their basis a single morpheme.

(54) a. *arsch* 'ass'   *lahmarschig, verarschen*
     b. *fuck/fick* 'fuck'   *abgefuckt, ficken*
     c. *kack* 'crap'   *Kacker, abkacken*
     d. *kotz* 'puke'   *großkotzig, abkotzen*
     e. *scheiß/schiss* 'shit'   *Scheißer, Scheißdreck, beschissen*

Although these words are not found exclusively in *Jugendsprache*, their roots are used to create new lexical items that are (at least initially) unique to the speech of young people. Among the relatively new creations that can be found in Ehmann 2005 are the following:

(55) a.   *abkacken* 'to be bored' (Standard German: 'to fail completely')
    b.   *anfucken* 'to insult'
    c.   *Arsch-Raller* 'ass'
    d.   *Schneckenschiss* 'weakling; coward; rubbish'

Notice that these words can have meanings that are not considered vulgar. However, although their meaning may be innocent, their form still supplies them with a certain amount of "shock" value.

    7.5.2.2 Sentence level and discourse features   At the sentence level, one feature that characterizes *Jugendsprache* is the use of intensifiers such as *absolut*, *echt*, *total*, and *voll*.

(56)   *das ist **echt** gefragt, lange Haare und Assi sein* (attested; Androutsopoulos 1998:343)
    'that's really hot, long hair and being antisocial'

Intensifiers can be doubled, increasing the intensifying effect.

(57) a.   *Da waren wir **echt voll** begeistert.* (attested; Androutsopoulos 1998:351)
    'We were really massively excited.'
    b.   *Die Leute sind **echt total** nett.* (attested; Androutsopoulos 1998:351)
    'The people are really totally nice.'

One position in which intensifiers are used that is not typical of the standard language is before NP complements of copulative verbs like *sein* 'to be' (Androutsopoulos 1998:352).

(58) a.   *es ist **absolut** die Wucht, die ich hab* (attested; Androutsopoulos 1998:356)
    'it is absolutely the force that I have'
    b.   *Das ist **total** der Beschiss, das Ding* (attested; Androutsopoulos 1998:357)
    'That is totally the rip-off, that thing'

    Words like *echt* and *total* occur in the standard language as well as in *Jugendsprache* (although they are used differently in *Jugendsprache*). The word *ey*, on the other hand, can be considered a marker of *Jugendsprache*, since adults use words like *wa* and *ne* instead (Schlobinski 1995:333). *Ey* is used in expressive speech acts as an intensifier.[24]

(59)   *echt geil ey!* (Schlobinski 1995:333)
      'Really terrific!'

It also serves as an evaluation marker.

(60)   *scheiße, ey!* (Schlobinski 1995:333)
      'Shit!'

Ey is also used in communicative speech acts.[25] It can serve as an attention getter.

(61)   *ey, wann kommst'n?* (Schlobinski 1995:333)
      'Hey, when are you coming?'

It functions as an address signal.

(62)   *ey, Alter, was sagst du dazu?* (attested; Androutsopoulos 1998:479)
      'Hey, dude, what do you say?'

It also functions as a structuring signal, marking the structure of the discourse. It is used, for example, to signal the end of a discourse contribution (Schlobinski *et al.* 1993:137).

(63)   *ich haue ihr in den Bauch (.) sie merkt nichts ey* (Schlobinski *et al.* 1993:139)[26]
      'I hit her in the stomach; she doesn't notice anything.'

A class of words that also have discourse functions are "root words." These are formed by removing the infinitive suffix from a verb (Schlobinski 1995:322).

(64) a.   *ächz* 'moan, groan'
     b.   *seufz* 'sigh'
     c.   *stöhn* 'groan'
     d.   *würg* 'choke'

According to Schlobinski (1995:322), the purpose of these words is to express specific actions and to comment on them. For example, *würg* expresses dislike and revulsion (Schlobinski 1995:322), as the following (attested) example (from Androutsopoulos 1998:487) demonstrates:

(65)   Speaker A: *Ich habe mir mit so einem Teil . . . meinen rechten Zeigefinger abgesäbelt. Hier, schau mal, fehlt immer noch ein Stück.*
      'I sawed off a piece of my right index finger. Here, take a look, a piece is still missing.'
      Speaker B: *Würg.* 'Choke.'

In the following example, the speaker uses these root words to describe and comment on the act committed by making the preceding utterance.

(66)   [*In der Region gibt es*] *ein einziges Fanzine* [. . .], *dessen Macher ich
        übringens bin (protz prahl!!!)* (Androutsopoulos 1998:186)
        'In the region there's only one fanzine . . . by the way, I'm its
        producer (show off, brag!!!)'

According to Schlobinski (1995:323), root words were an invention of writers
who were faced with the task of translating English sound words into German.
These root words (as well as onomatopoeic words) became an essential component of comic-book language and eventually found their way into colloquial
speech via the language of young people (Dolle-Weinkauf 1990:70).

The use of intensifiers and other words with discourse functions (*ey*, root
words) are just some of the sentence level and discourse features that char
acterize *Jugendsprache*. For example, Androutsopoulos (1998:481–486) notes
the use of insults in *Jugendsprache* as well as the formulaic language that
characterizes forms of address, leave-taking, expressions of surprise, and so
on (508–522). For further discussion of these and other characteristics of
Jugendsprache, see, for example, Henne 1986, Schlobinski *et al.* 1993, and
Androutsopoulos 1998.

7.6   The German of foreign workers

7.6.1   *Speakers*

Foreigners in Germany can be divided into several categories, including, but not
limited to, *Arbeitsmigranten* (foreign workers), *Aussiedler* (former residents of
eastern European countries of German descent), and *Asylanten* (asylum seek-
ers). This discussion is concerned with *Arbeitsmigranten*, in particular those
who were initially recruited to work in German industry during the labor shortage in the 1950s. These workers were originally referred to as *Gastarbeiter*
'guest workers' because their stay was viewed as temporary. However, many
have remained in Germany for decades, many of their children have been born
there, and relatively few show an interest in leaving (Barbour and Stevenson 1990:194). Thus, terms such as *Migrant, Immigrant, Arbeitsmigrant*, and
ausländischer Arbeiter are used increasingly in the German literature in place
of the term *Gastarbeiter* (Clyne 1995:194). In addition to being inaccurate, the
term *Gastarbeiter* is considered offensive by a number of those to whom it
has been applied (Fennell 1997:2). Following Fennell 1997, the term "foreign
worker" is used here to refer to this group of foreigners.

The largest numbers of foreign workers in Germany come mainly from
Turkey, Italy, the former Yugoslavia, and Greece. They have tended to lead a
marginal existence because of their status as temporary members of the work

force and the government's position that Germany is *kein Einwanderungsland* (not an immigration country). Although the social conditions for foreign workers have improved since the 1950s (notoriously bad living conditions have gotten better), problems of integration, education, social equality, and racial tension remain (Fennell 1997:50).[27] Fennell argues that many of the social problems that foreign workers face would be alleviated if they had better proficiency in German. The linguistic skills of foreigners in Germany have been the focus of a number of studies since the late 1960s.[28] Some early studies sought to understand the "untutored" knowledge of foreign workers with the goal of improving language teaching programs for adults. Most studies, however, have focused on the linguistic features of Foreign Worker German (FWG) and the insights it can shed on the acquisition of a second language in general (Barbour and Stevenson 1990:195).

7.6.2   *Linguistic features*

The German of foreign workers varies from very rudimentary to more native-like. Regardless of the native language of a speaker, each level of proficiency exhibits common structural characteristics.[29] The speech of those with only a very basic competence in German can be characterized as highly simplified in comparison to Standard German, the target language. For example, articles, prepositions, pronouns, and verbs are deleted (Clyne 1968:131).

(67) a.   *Das Rinus.* (*Das ist der Rhein.* 'That is the Rhine.')
   b.   *Patiente essen.* (*Ich habe Patienten* [*das*] *Essen gebracht.* 'I brought patients food.')
   c.   *Krankenkasse viel Geld.* (*Von der Krankenkasse bekommt man viel Geld.* 'From the health insurance company you get a lot of money.')

One verb form, typically the infinitive, tends to be generalized (Clyne 1968:132–133).

(68) a.   *Ja, ich nicht viel **sprechen** deutsch.* (*spreche*)
         'Yeah, I don't speak German a lot.'
   b.   *Ich heute **bringen** Kartoffel mit Reis.* (*brachte*)
         'I brought potatoes with rice today.'
   c.   *Ich habe gut **sprechen**.* (*gesprochen*)
         'I have spoken well.'

There is a tendency to delete bound morphemes (Clyne 1968:135).

(69) a.   *Ein gut Kostum.* (*ein gutes Kostüm* 'a good suit')
   b.   *Viel schenke.* (*viele Geschenke* 'many gifts')

The generalized use of *nix* (*niks*) for *nicht, nichts, nie,* and *kein* is typical of FWG (Clyne 1995:195).

(70) a.   *niks mehr zurück* (Clyne 1968:135)
          (*nicht mehr zurück* 'not back again')
      b.   *niks gut Wetter* (Clyne 1968:135)
          (*nicht/kein gutes Wetter* 'not/no good weather')

The generalized use of the pronoun *du* is also common (Clyne 1968:135).

(71) a.   *Bitte du sprechen.* (said to the speaker's boss)
          please you speak
      b.   *kennt dir schenke* (said to the speaker's employer)
          could to-you give

The order subject–verb–object is favored (Bodemann and Ostow 1975:
139).[30]

(72)   *Und die Frau garnik verstehen Deutsch*
          and the woman nothing-at-all understand German 'And the woman
          doesn't understand any German.'

The auxiliary and main verb are kept maximally close together, although negation can occur between them, since negation occurs immediately before the main verb (Bodemann and Ostow 1975:139).

(73)   *Aber er wollte niks mache neue Fabrik.* (Bodemann and Ostow
          1975:138)
          but he wanted not make new factory 'But he didn't want to build a
          new factory.'

The non-verbal portion of phrasal verbs tends not to be separated from the verbal portion (Bodemann and Ostow 1975:139).

(74)   *Jetzt diese ältere Leute rausmachen.* (Bodemann and Ostow
          1975:137)
          (cf. *Jetzt macht er diese älteren Leute 'raus.* 'Now he's putting these
          older people out.')

Although the speech of some foreign workers shows evidence of fossilization (non-native features have become permanent), the speech of others can be characterized as being at an intermediate stage on the way to acquisition of the target language. A number of studies have sought to identify sequences of acquisition and stages on the continuum of development of FWG. The Heidelberg Research Project on "Pidgin-German,"[31] which studied the German of adult Italian and Spanish workers, found, for example, that the use of simple verb forms is learned first, and copula and modal verbs are acquired before the auxiliary (Klein and Dittmar 1979:131). Clahsen *et al.* (1983), who studied the acquisition of word order and negation by adult speakers from Italy, Spain, and Portugal, identified seven stages of development, where acquisition of one stage implies acquisition of the preceding stage. For example, if speakers are able to place adverbial phrases between the finite verb and the direct object (stage 6), they are also able to produce verb-second order in main clauses (stage 5).

(75)   Stage 5
        französich kann ich auch noch heute (Clahsen *et al.* 1983:141)
        French can I also still today 'I can still speak French today.'

(76)   Stage 6
        ich habe nur eine kleine weintraube (Clahsen *et al.* 1983:153)
        I have only a small bunch-of-grapes 'I only had a small vineyard.'[32]

In addition to investigating the different stages of acquisition, a number of studies of FWG have also studied the factors that correlate with successful progression towards linguistic competency in German. The Heidelberger Forschungsprojekt "Pidgin-Deutsch" (1975:129–131), for example, identified several social factors that play a role. The most important factor is the amount of contact with Germans during leisure time. The second most important factor is the age of the learner upon arrival in Germany. Other factors include the amount of contact with Germans at work, the type of employment, and the length of stay in Germany.

Although second- and third-generation foreigners do not have as much difficulty learning German as their parents, they still face problems because of bilingual education that is less than ideal (Clyne 1995:195). Fennell (1997:83) predicts, however, that the linguistic abilities of the children of foreign workers in Germany will develop like those of the offspring of foreigners in other immigration countries such as Australia and the United States, where second-generation speakers tend to be diglossic (speaking their parents' native language at home and English at school/work) and third-generation speakers are often monolingual in English. Fennell views the progression of third-generation immigrants in Germany to higher educational levels as an indication that they too are developing native fluency in German.

7.7   Language contact

7.7.1   A brief history

Although language contact can bring about changes in all areas of grammar (phonology, morphology, syntax, etc.), the vocabulary of a language is typically the most susceptible to change. Speakers of German may lament the current wave of borrowings from English, but history shows us that this is by no means a new phenomenon. The vocabulary of modern German displays evidence of centuries of contact with other languages.

Some of the earliest borrowings still found in German today are of Celtic origin. A number of words are assumed to stem from a period of contact with Celtic civilization during the Iron Age (Wells 1985:54) – Germanic and Celtic share the term *$\bar{\imath}$sarno- for 'iron' (Polomé 1972:64) – but it is often difficult to determine whether common vocabulary items reflect common stock or borrowing from one language into another. Polomé (1972:64) speculates that *Fichte* 'spruce' (OHG *fiuhta*) might reflect one of the oldest borrowings from Celtic into Germanic. Words that are generally held to be borrowings from Celtic because of their phonological features are *Amt* 'office' and *Reich* 'empire'.

Contact with Roman civilization during Germanic times left behind a significant number of loanwords from Latin that have survived into modern German. The following examples are from this first "Latin wave" (Waterman 1991:35–36; Stedje 2001:55).

(77)	German	Latin
a.	*Fenster* 'window'	*fenestra*
b.	*Kampf* 'battle'	*campus*
c.	*Kessel* 'kettle'	*catīnus*
d.	*Mauer* 'wall'	*mūrus*
e.	*Pfeffer* 'pepper'	*piper*
f.	*Plaume* 'plum'	*prūnum*
g.	*Pfund* 'pound'	*pondō*
h.	*Straße* 'street'	(*via*) *strāta*
i.	*Tisch* 'table'	*discus*
j.	*Ziegel* 'brick'	*tēgula*

The age of these borrowings can be seen in the evidence they provide of having undergone the High German Consonant Shift (they were borrowed into Germanic before the High German Consonant Shift). We can see the shift of $p > pf$ in *Kampf*, for example, and the shift of $t > z$ ([ts]) in *Ziegel*.

Words of Greek origin found their way into German, often via Latin, although the dissemination of some words is not a clear-cut matter (Wells 1985:56): *Kirche* 'church' (< Lat. *kyrica* < Gk. *kuri(a)kon* '(house) of the Lord'), *Almosen* 'alms', *Bischof* 'bishop', *Engel* 'angel', *Teufel* 'devil'.

The second wave of Latin words found their way into German vocabulary through the *Klosterkultur* in German monasteries during the Old High German period. Not just words involving religious matters, but also words from scribal culture, gardening, crafts, and so on were borrowed from Latin into German (Waterman 1991:71–72; Stedje 2001:69–70).

(78) German Latin
   a. *Altar* 'altar' *altāre*
   b. *Kloster* 'cloister' *claustrum*
   c. *predigen* 'to preach' *praedicāre*
   d. *Tinte* 'ink' *tincta*
   e. *schreiben* 'to write' *scrībere*
   f. *Tafel* 'tablet' *tabula*
   g. *Petersilie* 'parsley' *petrosilium*
   h. *Zweibel* 'onion' *cēpulla*
   i. *Pinsel* 'paintbrush' *pēnicillus*
   j. *Seide* 'silk' *sēta*

These words, unlike those borrowed earlier, did not undergo the High German Consonant Shift. The *p* in *Petersilie* and the *t* in *Tafel*, for example, remained unshifted. Many loan translations from Latin found their way into German during this period (Waterman 1991:72):[33] *Gotteshaus* 'house of God' < Lat. *domus Deī*; *Gewissen* 'conscience' < Lat. *conscientia*; *Wohltat* 'good deed' < Lat. *beneficium*.[34]

During the Middle High German period, the influence of French on German was particularly great. See chapter 5 (section 5.4.1) for a brief discussion of the words and affixes that were borrowed into German during this time. Some words from the Netherlands found their way into German as well: *Wappen* 'coat of arms' (cf. the related High German word *Waffen* 'weapon', with *f* < *p*), *Tölpel* 'fool'.

The Early New High German period saw borrowing from Latin (the third Latin wave), Greek (often via Latin), and Italian. Latin had a particularly strong influence on German during this period, through the Church, and to a greater degree through the intellectual movement of Humanism. According to Waterman (1991:120–121), the bulk of Latin loanwords that can still be found in German entered the language at this time, some examples of which (in the areas of theology, law, medicine, etc.) are the following: *Absolution* 'absolution', *Amnestie* 'amnesty', *Arterie* 'artery', *Doktor* 'doctor', *Hypothek* 'mortgage', *Kathedrale* 'cathedral', *Medizin* 'medicine', *Sekte* 'sect', *Student* 'student', *Text* 'text'.

Those words of Greek origin that found their way into German during this period include the following (Stedje 2001:132): *Akademie* 'academy', *Archiv* 'archive', *Chirurgie* 'surgery', *Epidemie* 'epidemic', *Grammatik* 'grammar', *Gymnasium* 'high school', *Mathematik* 'mathematics', *Orthographie* 'orthography', *Polizei* 'police', *Problem* 'problem'. Italian loans entered the language in the areas of music and finance (Stedje 2001:26): *Bass* 'bass', *Allegro* 'allegro', *Violine* 'violin', *Fagott* 'bassoon'; *Konto* 'account', *Kredit* 'credit', *Bilanz* 'balance'.

During the earlier portion of the New High German period, the influence of French on the German lexicon was once again particularly strong (see the discussion in chapter 5, section 5.6). Later on, during the eighteenth century, English loans found their way into the language, in particular through the influence of literary movements and politics and government. Some of the words and expressions that stem from this period are the following (Waterman 1991:177; Stedje 2001:151): *Blankvers* 'blank verse', *Humor* 'humor', *Opposition* 'opposition', *Parlament* 'parliament', *ein Gesetz einbringen* 'to introduce a bill', *zur Ordnung rufen* 'to call to order'. During the nineteenth century, the influence of English increased in a number of fields, including commerce, fashion, foods, and sports (Waterman 1991:177–178; Stedje 2001:151): *Beefsteak* 'steak', *Bonds, Match, Partner, Pullover, Rekord, Roastbeef, Scheck, Smoking* 'dinner jacket', *Sport, Streik, Trainer* 'coach'.

The influence of English increased during the twentieth century, with the impact of American English being particularly great following the Second World War. The following list of borrowings gives an idea of some of the areas of vocabulary that have been affected by this period of borrowing:

(79)   *Babysitter, die Band* (B[ɛ]nd), *Bestseller, Business, Comics, Computer, Handout, Jeans, killen, Layout, Look, Make-up, Manager, News, Quiz, Service, Spray, Team, Teenager, Trend*

It is not uncommon that a borrowed word will have a meaning in German that is somewhat different from its meaning in English. For example, a *Drink* is an alcoholic drink, a *Job* typically means temporary employment, and a *Meeting* is a political, scientific, or sports gathering.

The material borrowed from English includes more than just loanwords. There are also loan translations, loan "renditions," and semantic loans. A loan translation involves translating each part of a foreign word or expression into the native language, as the following loan translations from English demonstrate.

(80) a.   *Flutlicht* < *floodlight*
     b.   *Einkaufszentrum* < *shopping center*
     c.   *herumhängen* < *to hang around*

A loan rendition translates only a part of the foreign word into the native language.

(81) a.   *Luftbrücke* (literally 'air bridge') < *airlift*
     b.   *Übertreibung* (literally 'over driving') < *overstatement*
     c.   *Titelgeschichte* (literally 'title story') < *cover story*

Semantic loans expand the meaning of a word already in the language on the basis of a similar word in another language. For example, the verb *kontrollieren* originally meant 'to supervise, inspect', but on the basis of the English verb *to control*, it acquired the additional meaning 'to control'. Other examples of semantic loans from English are *feuern*, which acquired the meaning 'to fire' as in 'to let go', and *realisieren*, which acquired the meaning 'to realize' in the sense of 'to understand'.

There are a variety of social, political, and scientific reasons for the large number of borrowings from English that have found their way into German since the Second World War. Steffens (2003:5), touching briefly on the causes of the relatively large number of Anglo-Americanisms in German, mentions the following:[35] the economic assistance of the United States in the form of the Marshall Plan; the Federal Republic's policy of alliances, which was oriented towards the West; the dominance of the United States in the domains of science and technology; the dominance of English in international communication; the status of English as the first foreign language worldwide; the role model function of the American lifestyle. Steffens (2003:5) also mentions the importation of technical innovations together with the terms designating them as one of the reasons for the large number of Anglo-American loans in German. Other factors that Steffens notes include linguistic economy (Anglo-Americanisms are typically short and succinct); the close relationship between English and German; the higher stylistic and communicative value often ascribed to Anglo-Americanisms; and the desire to impress – to signal that one is educated, modern, and cosmopolitan or a member of a particular group.

7.7.2   Recent English influence

The *Überfremdung* 'foreign infiltration' of the German language – the rampant use of Anglo-Americanisms – is a topic that is currently of concern to linguists and non-linguists alike. For example, a national survey carried out by the Institut für Deutsche Sprache in 1999 determined that roughly one quarter of the population is concerned about changes in the language, the most important change being the increase in Anglo-Americanisms (Zifonun 2002:2).

In an article in *Die Zeit* titled "Sonst stirbt die deutsche Sprache" 'Otherwise the German language will die', Zimmer (1995:42) cites the following examples that demonstrate the degree to which English has had an impact on German.

(82) a.   *Miles & More führt ein flexibleres Upgrade-Verfahren ein: mit dem neuen Standby oneway Upgrade-Voucher kann direkt beim Check-in das Ticket aufgewertet werden.* (Lufthansa)
   b.   *In der Pipeline ist das Upgrade eines Kalibrationskits für Proofscreenmonitore und als Highlight ein Digitizer für CAD-Applikationen.* (a computer magazine)

One of Zimmer's concerns is that Germans do not take the trouble to replace English words by those that have been adapted to the German linguistic system;

he finds fault in particular with the lack of phonological and morphological assimilation of borrowed items. Pittner (2001:234), in response to Zimmer 1995, argues that speakers do a better job of integrating foreign words into German than Zimmer claims, citing the use of foreign stems in productive word-formation processes: for example, in the derivation of words like *computern* 'to use a computer', *auspowern* 'to completely use up one's power', and *Newcomerin* 'newcomer'.

In a report on a study of neologisms that entered German in the 1990s, Steffens (2003:5) notes that relatively many belong to relatively few domains.

(83) a. Computer/Internet: *doppelklicken, E-Mail, Homepage*
     b. Media: *Bezahlfernsehen, Latenightshow, Multiplexkino*
     c. Society: *Babyklappe, Minijob, Ostalgie*
     d. Sports: *Carvingski, Gelbsperre, inlineskaten*
     e. Economy: *Globalisierungsfalle, outsourcen, Scheinselbständigkeit*

Neologisms can also be found in the following areas:

(84) a. Banking and finance: *Eurogeld, Gewinnwarnung, Onlinebanking*
     b. Leisure and entertainment: *Hüpfburg, Infotainment, raven*
     c. Telecommunication: *Call-by-Call, Festnetz, Handy*

In an attempt to relativize the impression that neologisms are only borrowings from English, Steffens points out that more than half are the products of word-formation processes in German.

Zifonun (2002:8), like Steffens (2003:8), sees no danger of *Überfremdung* of the German language, given the tendency of speakers to integrate English loans into German. Although she argues that some developments deserve attention (e.g., the increased integration of uninflected words), she does not see the grammatical system of German as being in danger. She argues for the use of German terms whenever possible when services and information for the general public are involved. However, she does not view the assimilation (*Eindeutschung*) of Anglo-Americanisms in a negative light, calling it a *Glücksfall* 'godsend': According to Zifonun, a concise Anglo-Americanism is preferable to a bad translation. She concludes that today, just as in earlier times, German can be enriched by words from foreign languages.[36]

Exercises

1. Identify as many instances as possible of assimilation, reduction, and deletion in the following examples of colloquial speech.
   (a) *Der Kaffee ist teuer.* 'The coffee is expensive.' [tɐ kʰafe ɪs tʰɔɪɐ]
   (b) *Sie geht baden.* 'She's going swimming.' [zi ɡep paːtn̩]
   (c) *Wir sind nicht fertig.* 'We're not ready.' [vɐ zɪn nɪç feɐ̯tʰɪç]

(d) *Auf Wiedersehen.* 'Good-by.' [f viːʈɐzen]

(e) *Wir haben es geschafft.* 'We did it.' [vɐ hams kəʃaftʰ]

2. Consider the following sets of synonyms and determine the stylistic level of each member in the set (colloquial, neutral, formal).

   (a) *der Mann, der Alte, der Gatte*

   (b) *die Hochschulreife, das Abitur, das Abi*

   (c) *die Birne, der Kopf, das Haupt*

   (d) *verstehen, kapieren*

   (e) *das Zuchthaus, der Knast, das Gefängnis*

   (f) *etwas ausplaudern, etwas preisgeben, sich verplappern*

   (g) *verrückt, plemplem*

   (h) *entschlafen, hopsgehen, sterben*

3. List possible gender-inclusive alternatives to the following expressions:

   (a) *der Schüler* 'pupil'

   (b) *der Mitarbeiter* 'colleague'

   (c) *der Lehrer* 'teacher'

   (d) *der Polizist* 'police officer'

   (e) *der Rechtsanwalt* 'attorney'

   (f) *der Student* 'student'

   (g) *der Autor* 'author'

   (h) *der Koch* 'chef'

4. Identify the means by which the following words were added to the vocabulary of German *Jugendsprache* (derivation, conversion, compounding, etc.):

   (a) *supergeil*

   (b) *arschcool*

   (c) *Klampfer* 'guitarist' (*klampfen* 'to play guitar')

   (d) *Stip* 'scholarship' (*Stipendium* 'scholarship')

   (e) *Schlagi* 'drummer' (*Schlagzeuger* 'drummer')

   (f) *türlich* 'naturally' (*natürlich* 'naturally')

   (g) *Fun*

   (h) *Arschtyp*

   (i) *Straightheit*

   (j) *Brilli* 'someone who wears glasses'

5. What do the following words mean as they are used in German?

   (a) *der Bodybag*

   (b) *die Peperoni*

   (c) *das Ticket*

   (d) *der Dress*

   (e) *die City*

   (f) *der Slip*

   (g) *der Pony*

   (h) *der Flipper*

NOTES

1 For general introductions to sociolinguistics, see, for example, Dittmar 1973, 1997 (both in German), Hudson 1996, Trudgill 2000, and Wardhaugh 2002. For more comprehensive overviews, see Coulmas 1998 and Ammon *et al.* 2005.

2 A seminal figure in the study of language as it is spoken in its social context is William Labov, who has focused in particular on the issues of linguistic variation and change. See, for example, Labov 1994, 2001, and 2006.

3 The definition of the term "register" varies considerably in the literature. For example, it is often used to refer to "varieties according to use," in contrast to dialects (in the broad sense of the term), which are defined as "varieties according to user" (Hudson 1996:45). This notion of register is fairly complex, and involves several dimensions, including "field" (subject matter and activity), "mode" (means of communication), and "tenor" (variation in formality; relationship between participants) (Halliday 1978:33). We take a simpler (narrower) approach here (following, e.g., Wardhaugh 2002:50–51) and define registers as those varieties that differ according to subject matter and activity. We also separate the notion of style (tenor) from register.

4 The transcriptions here and elsewhere in this chapter conform to the conventions adopted in chapter 1.

5 The concept of "weak form" was originally used for English by Jones (1956:126–137).

6 Durrell (1992) uses the term "register" to refer to the stylistic level of language that is influenced by subject matter, medium, and situation, and identifies three main register types, which he labels R1, R2, and R3 (1992:3–8). These registers correspond roughly to the categories of style identified here (colloquial, neutral, and formal): R1 is everyday colloquial speech, R2 is a neutral register, and R3 is the register of modern written German.

7 Phrases like *meinem Bruder sein Zimmer* are more common in casual colloquial speech (*in salopper Umgangssprache*) (Dudenredaktion 2001:353).

8 The dative preposition *von* instead of the genitive is acceptable (and in fact required) in the standard language when case would not otherwise be expressed overtly, for example, in phrases like *der Preis von sechs Häusern* 'the price of six houses' (with the genitive instead of *von*, there would be no case marking on the noun *Häuser*). See Dudenredaktion 2001:353 for additional situations in which *von* in place of the genitive is acceptable in the standard language.

9 See Langer 2001 for discussion of the stigmatization of the *tun* + infinitive construction.

10 Relative clauses are of course also found in the colloquial language. In particular, they are found instead of the "extended" adjective phrases that are typical of formal written German (see section 3.4 for examples and further discussion).

11 Demonstrative pronouns are essentially identical in form to relative pronouns; compare Table 2.8 and Table 2.9.

12 Pronouns of "politeness" are capitalized here to distinguish them from their non-polite counterparts. For example, *Ihr* is the pronoun that means 'you (singular, polite)', whereas *ihr* simply means 'you (plural)'.

13 Abstract nominal constructions such as *Eure Majestät* 'Your Majesty' and *Eure Gnade* 'Your Grace' were used to address those at the highest levels of society (Metcalf 1938:64).

14 See Metcalf 1938 (which covers developments in the sixteenth through eighteenth centuries) for detailed discussion of the situations in which the various forms of address were used. Augst 1977:23–44 also provides a historical overview that includes usage conventions.

15 See Brown and Gilman (1960) for an analysis of the traditional "modern" use of *du* and *Sie* that is based on the notions of power and solidarity.

16 A speaker signals disrespect by not using *Sie*, the pronoun of respect.

17 See Besch 1998:16 for a discussion of the reasons for switching to *du* and further discussion of the conventions that govern this switch.

18 The use of *Fräulein* 'Miss' to address an unmarried woman has been replaced by *Frau* in official and administrative language (*Amts- und Verwaltungssprache*) as well as in colloquial speech (Klann-Delius: 2005:188). This use of *Frau* is similar to the use of *Ms.* in English, in that it is correct regardless of a woman's marital status.

19 The examples of abbreviations in this section are from Dudenredaktion 2001: 394.

20 The examples here of alternatives to splitting are from Dudenredaktion 2001: 398).

21 The situation in Austria with respect to legal language is similar to the situation in Germany (Clyne 1995:147).

22 See Neuland 1999:41–42 for additional dictionaries that deal with *Jugendsprache.*

23 The examples in this section are from Ehmann 2005.

24 According to Schlobinski *et al.* (1993:136), expressive speech acts are those with which speakers express subjective experiences, opinions, and judgments.

25 Communicative speech acts are those with which speakers organize their speech, structure topics and contributions, regulate conversation sequences, and so on (Schlobinski *et al.* 1993:136).

26 A single period between parentheses, (.), indicates a short pause.

27 See Fennell 1997 for a discussion of the living conditions, education, employment opportunities, and other aspects of the social conditions of foreign workers.

28 *Gastarbeiterlinguistik* has in fact become a recognized subfield of linguistics in Germany.

29 Many studies have sought to explain the commonalities in FWG and the deviations from Standard German. See Barbour and Stevenson 1990 for an overview of various theories that have been proposed. See also Fennell 1997 for a discussion of the issue of classifying FWG (pidgin, creole, etc.).

30 This as well as other examples from Bodemann and Ostow 1975 are reproduced here in standard orthography. Although non-standard pronunciation in the original examples is generally not indicated, non-standard inflection is.

31 Although various studies, including the Heidelberg Research Project on "Pidgin-German," refer to FWG as *Pidgindeutsch* 'pidgin-German', it cannot be considered a pidgin in the strict sense of the term. A pidgin is a highly simplified language that develops as a mixture of two of more languages in a language contact situation where speakers do not know each other's languages.

32 The speaker used the word *Weintraube* 'bunch of grapes', but meant instead to say *Weinberg* 'vineyard'.

33 A loan translation is a word or expression that has been formed by translating a corresponding word or expression in another language.

34 The prefix *ge-* was often used to translate Latin *con* 'with', as in *Gewissen* (< Lat. *conscientia*).

35 I use the term "Anglo-Americanisms" for words and expressions borrowed from American and/or British English.

36 For a book-length treatment of Anglicisms in German, see Onysko 2007.

Glossary

ablaut A vowel alternation used to signal grammatical distinctions; found in irregular verbs in German and English (e.g., *sing, sang, sung*; *singen* 'to sing', *sang* 'sang', *gesungen* 'sung').

acoustic phonetics The subfield of phonetics that deals with the physical properties of speech sounds.

acronym A word formed from the initial letters of the words in a name or a phrase (e.g., *NATO* < *North Atlantic Treaty Organization*).

adjective A category of word that describes a property that can be attributed to entities named by nouns (e.g., *schön* 'beautiful', *klein* 'small', *nett* 'nice').

adjunct An optional constituent (e.g., *vor dem Konzert* 'before the concert' in *Ich habe sie vor dem Konzert getroffen* 'I met her before the concert').

adjunction A syntactic operation that adjoins (attaches) one phrase, YP, to another phrase, XP, by creating a position to which YP can move. A copy of XP (a new XP node) is made above it that immediately dominates the two adjoined phrases, the old XP and the moved YP.

adposition A cover term for prepositions, postpositions, and circumpositions.

adverb A category of word that is often used to describe the action of a verb (e.g., *schnell* 'quickly'); adverbs can also modify adjectives and other adverbs (e.g., *sehr* 'very') and sentences (e.g., *leider* 'unfortunately').

affix An obligatorily bound morph that does not realize a lexeme (e.g., *un-* and *-s* in *unmasks*; *zer-* and *-t* in *zerstört* 'destroys').

affricate A stop followed by a fricative with essentially the same point of articulation (e.g., [pf] in *Pfund* 'pound', [ts] in *Zunge* 'tongue').

agent The thematic role of the entity that initiates or carries out an action and is capable of volition (e.g., the role of *Julia* in *Julia küsste ihr Kind* 'Julia kissed her child').

allomorph One of the realizations of a morpheme (e.g., /ə/, /ən/, and /s/ are some of the allomorphs of the nominal plural morpheme in German, e.g., in *Jahre* 'years', *Ohren* 'ears', and *Autos* 'cars').

allophone One of the phonetic realizations of a phoneme (e.g., [x] and [ç] are allophones of the German phoneme /x/, as in *Na*[x]*t* 'night' and *ni*[ç]*t* 'not').

alveolar ridge The ridge immediately behind the upper teeth.

ambisyllabicity The presence of a single segment in two neighboring syllables.

analogy A process in language change that alters the form of an existing word or morpheme because of its similarity to other words or morphemes. The process typically introduces greater regularity into the language (e.g., the use of a "regular" past form for *backen* 'to bake', *backte* 'baked', instead of the original "irregular" form *buk* 'baked').

analytic A type of language in which words are typically composed of a single morpheme.

anaphor A type of noun phrase that does not have independent reference; it receives its reference from the noun phrase to which it refers, its antecedent (e.g., *sich* 'himself' in *Der Bürgermeister verteidigte sich* 'The mayor defended himself' is an anaphor whose antecedent is *der Bürgermeister* 'the mayor').

antecedent A linguistic unit to which another (typically later) unit in the discourse refers (e.g., in *die Frau, mit der er verheiratet ist* 'the woman to whom he is married', *die Frau* 'the woman' is the antecedent of the relative pronoun *der* 'whom').

antepenultimate syllable The third-to-last syllable (e.g., *mo* in *Har.mo.ni.ka* 'harmonica').

approximant A speech sound produced when one articulator is close to another, but not close enough to produce audible friction (e.g., *w* in English *win*).

argument The arguments of a verb are the subject and the verbal complements (e.g., *zerstören* 'to destroy' has two arguments, a subject and an object).

articulatory phonetics The subfield of phonetics concerned with how human speech sounds are produced by the vocal organs.

arytenoid cartilages Two cartilages at the back of the larynx to which the vocal cords are attached.

aspect A category of the verb that expresses the internal temporal contour of an event or situation in various ways (e.g., as completed, ongoing, habitual, etc.).

aspiration The period of voicelessness accompanied by a burst of air following the release of a stop (e.g., the *p* in English *pin* [pʰɪn] and German *Pass* [pʰas] 'passport' is articulated with aspiration).

assimilation The change of a feature or features of one sound to match those of a neighboring sound (e.g., the change of [n] to [m] in *i*[m]*put* 'input').

attributive adjective An adjective that modifies a following noun (e.g., *rote* 'red' in *rote Rosen* 'red roses').

auditory phonetics The subfield of phonetics that investigates the way that speech sounds are perceived by listeners.

auxiliary verb A verb that accompanies the main (lexical) verb (e.g., *hat* 'has' in *hat gekauft* 'has bought'; *muss* 'must' in *muss kaufen* 'must buy').

back A feature that involves the placement of the body of the tongue and characterizes consonants as well as vowels; [+back] sounds are articulated behind the palatal region in the oral cavity.

base An item to which an affix is attached (e.g., *activate* serves as the base for the prefix *de-* in *deactivate*; *Lösung* serves as the base for the suffix *-en* in *Lösungen* 'solutions').

blend A new lexeme formed from parts of two or more existing lexemes (e.g., *brunch*, from *breakfast* and *lunch*; *jein* 'yes and no', from *ja* 'yes' and *nein* 'no').

breathy voice A state of the vocal cords in which the arytenoids are slightly apart and the ligamental cords are vibrating while allowing a high rate of airflow through the glottis.

case A morphosyntactic category that provides information about the grammatical role (subject, direct object, etc.) of an element in a sentence. The cases found in

German are nominative, accusative, dative, and genitive (e.g., *ich* 'I', *mich*, *mir*, *meiner*).

circumfix A discontinuous affix that surrounds the base to which it is attached (e.g., *ge . . . t* in *gekauft* 'bought').

circumposition A category of word that functions like a preposition but surrounds (rather than precedes) its NP complement (e.g., *von . . . an* in *von diesem Tag an* 'from this day on').

clause An expression that contains (minimally) a subject and a predicate (e.g., *Das Kind schläft* 'The child is sleeping'; *ob das Kind schläft* 'if the child is sleeping').

clipping A word-formation process that shortens an existing word by deleting part of it (e.g., *deli* from *delicatessen*; *Uni* from *Universität* 'university').

clitic An unstressed word that cannot stand alone but must be attached to a neighboring stressed word, with which it forms a unit (e.g., *s* in *she's*).

closed syllable A syllable that ends with a consonant (e.g., both syllables in *leng.then*; both syllables in *süp.lich* 'sweetish').

coda The segments that follow the nucleus of a syllable (e.g., [ls] in monosyllabic *Hals* [hals] 'neck').

code-switching The process whereby a speaker switches from one language variety to another within a single conversation.

cognates Words in two or more languages that have descended from the same word in their ancestor language (e.g., German *Zunge* 'tongue' and English *tongue*).

complement A phrase that combines with a word to create a larger phrase with that word as its head; the choice of complement is determined by properties of the head (e.g., in the VP *die Tür öffnen* 'open the door', the NP *die Tür* 'the door' is the complement of the V *öffnen* 'open').

complementary opposites Two words that have the type of oppositeness of meaning where the negative of one implies the positive of the other (e.g., *single* and *married*; *wahr* 'true' and *falsch* 'false').

complementary distribution When two sounds never occur in the same phonetic environment (e.g., German [i:], which only occurs in stressed syllables, and [i], which occurs in unstressed syllables).

complementizer A functional category that includes words like English *that*, *whether*, and *if*, and German *dass* 'that', *weil* 'because', and *ob* 'if'; a complementizer takes a sentence (IP) as a complement to form a complementizer phrase (CP).

complex word A word (lexeme) composed of more than one morpheme (e.g., *unlivable*, *hopefully*; *Zerstörung* 'destruction', *Erlaubnis* 'permission').

compound A lexeme formed by adjoining two or more lexemes (e.g., *girlfriend*, *football*; *Nachtmensch* 'night person', *Kaffeemühle* 'coffee grinder').

conditional sentence A sentence that consists of a main clause and a conditional clause, one which expresses a condition (e.g., *Wir spielen heute draußen, wenn es nicht regnet* 'We'll play outside today if it doesn't rain.').

consonant A speech sound produced by impeding the flow of air in some way (e.g., [p], [s], [m]).

consonantal A feature involving the presence or absence of obstruction in the vocal tract; a sound is [+consonantal] if it is produced with major obstruction in the vocal tract.

constituent One of the components out of which a phrase is built up (e.g., *das* and *Buch* are the constituents of the NP *das Buch* 'the book').

contextual inflection The inflection required by the syntactic context in which a word form occurs (e.g., the first person singular ending on the verb, *-e*, required by the presence of the subject *ich* 'I' in *Ich komme* 'I'm coming').

continuant A feature that characterizes sounds made with free or nearly free airflow through the center of the oral cavity. Vowels and fricatives are [+continuant]; stops, nasals, and laterals are [−continuant].

converses Two words that are relational opposites; they express a relationship between two entities by expressing the position (direction, role, etc.) of one with respect to the other from two alternative points of view (e.g., *vor* 'before' and *nach* 'after'; one can say either *A kommt vor B* 'A comes before B' or *B kommt nach A* 'B comes after A').

conversion The creation of a new lexeme by changing the part of speech of an existing lexeme without the use of affixation (e.g., the verb *dirty* from the adjective *dirty*; *salzen* 'to salt' from *Salz* 'salt').

copula A "linking verb" whose main function is to link the subject of a sentence with the predicate (e.g., *be, become, remain*; *sein* 'to be', *werden* 'to become', *bleiben* 'to remain').

copulative compound A type of compound in which each member of the compound is equal; one member does not modify another (e.g., *Alsace-Lorraine*; *schwarzweiß* 'black and white').

coronal A feature that characterizes sounds produced with the blade of the tongue raised from its neutral position (e.g., [ʃ] is [+coronal]; [ç] is [−coronal]).

creaky voice A state of the vocal cords in which the arytenoids hold one end of the vocal cords tightly together so that they can vibrate only at the other end.

degree A grammatical category in the inflection of adjectives; used to express comparison. The degrees found in German are positive, comparative, and superlative (e.g., *alt* 'old', *älter* 'older', *ältest* 'oldest').

derivation A word-formation process that creates a new lexeme, typically by adding an affix to a base (e.g., *rethink* from *think*; *dornig* 'thorny' from *Dorn* 'thorn').

determiner A functional category that serves as the specifier of a noun phrase (e.g., *the, a, this*; *der* 'the', *ein* 'a', *dieser* 'this').

diacritic A small mark added to a phonetic symbol to change its value in some way (e.g., the wedge, ˎ, placed under a symbol to indicate that the sound is voiced, [t̬]).

dialect A variety of a language that is associated with a particular geographical area or social group.

diglossia A situation in which a community uses two distinct forms of the same language: a prestige form learned in school and used in one set of contexts, and a vernacular form acquired as a native language and used in another set of contexts. This term is also applied to contexts in which two different languages function in the same way.

diphthong A vowel in which there is a change in quality within a single syllable (e.g., the vowels in *dry, cow, toy*; the vowels in *klein* 'small', *laut* 'loud', and *deutsch* 'German').

diphthongization A process in which a monophthong becomes a diphthong (e.g., MHG [uː] became ENHG [au̯]).

direct object The NP complement of a transitive verb (e.g., *den Ball* in *Er schlug den Ball hart* 'He hit the ball hard'); the more directly affected NP complement of a ditransitive verb (e.g., *ein Buch* in *Sie schenkte ihm ein Buch* 'She gave him a book').

distinctive feature A feature that is capable of distinguishing one phoneme from another (e.g., the feature [back], which distinguishes the phoneme /uː/ from /yː/ in German).

ditransitive A verb that takes two NP objects, a direct object and an indirect object, is ditransitive (e.g., *geben* 'to give': *Ich gab meinem Sohn eine Gitarre* 'I gave my son a guitar').

dominance A relationship between nodes in a tree diagram. X dominates Y if it is higher in the tree than Y and connected to Y by a continuous set of lines that branch downward. X immediately dominates Y if no other nodes intervene.

dual The value for the morphosyntactic category of number that indicates two (e.g., the Gothic pronoun *wit* 'we two' is a dual form).

epenthesis A process that inserts a sound in the middle of a word (e.g., the insertion of [p] in the pronunciation of *warmth* as *warm|p|th*).

epistemic modality The type of modality that expresses a speaker's degree of confidence in the truth of a proposition.

evidentiality A semantic category that involves the expression of different attitudes towards the source of the information in the proposition.

event time The time at which an event (situation) takes place.

experiencer The thematic role of the entity that feels or perceives something (e.g., the role of *das Kind* 'child' in *Das Kind sieht den Ball* 'The child sees the ball').

extraposition The movement of an element from its normal position to a position at the end of a sentence.

feature A characteristic of some aspect of language. Phonetic features characterize the properties of sounds (e.g., [voice], [aspirated], [sonorant]). Grammatical features identify grammatically relevant characteristics of words and phrases (e.g., [feminine], [plural], [past]).

finite A finite verb in German is a verb form inflected for person, number, tense, and mood (e.g., *läuft* 'runs'); a finite clause is a clause that contains such a verb.

foot A stressed syllable and any following unstressed syllables that intervene before the next stressed syllable (e.g., ˈschö.ne.re ˈHaa.re 'more beautiful hair' is made up of two feet, *schönere* and *Haare*).

fossilization When non-native features become permanent in the speech of a language learner.

free variation The substitution of one sound for another without a change in meaning (e.g., ha[ʁ]t , ha[ɐ̯]t 'hard').

fricative A type of consonant produced by placing two articulators close together to create a narrow passage through which air is forced, producing a turbulent airflow (e.g., [f], [z], [ç]).

front A feature of vowels that involves the position (from front to back in the mouth) of the highest point of the tongue; [+front] vowels are produced with the highest point of the tongue at the front of the mouth (e.g., [iː], [ɛ], [œ]).

functional category A category of word that conveys grammatical information rather than semantic content (e.g., determiners, conjunctions).

gender A morphosyntactic category that divides nouns into classes; the relevant genders in German are masculine, feminine, and neuter.

generative-transformational syntax A version of generative grammar that recognizes a "transformational component" that mediates between the underlying structure of sentences and their surface structure.

glottis The space between the vocal cords.

goal The thematic role of the entity towards which a motion takes place (e.g., the role of *Italien* 'Italy' in *Wir sind nach Italien gereist* 'We traveled to Italy').

gradable antonyms Two words that occur at the opposite ends of a scale that includes intermediate terms; the negative of one term does not necessarily imply the positive of the other (e.g., *big* and *little*; *heiß* 'hot' and *kalt* 'cold').

grammatical function The function of a noun phrase in a sentence (e.g., subject, direct object, indirect object).

grammatical word A word defined by its position in a paradigm (e.g., 'dative plural of HAUS', which is realized by the word form *Häusern* 'houses').

head The element around which a phrase is built; the obligatory element in a phrase (e.g., N in NP, V in VP).

high A feature of both consonants and vowels; [+high] sounds are produced by raising the body of the tongue above its neutral position.

homorganic Having the same place of articulation.

hyponym A semantically more specific word whose meaning is included in the meaning of a more general word (e.g., *Eiche* 'oak tree' is a hyponym of *Baum* 'tree').

immediate constituent One of the parts into which a linguistic unit is immediately divisible (e.g., NP, VP, and Infl are the immediate constituents of IP).

imperative The mood used to express commands and requests.

indicative The mood used to express statements of fact and questions.

indirect object The less directly affected NP complement of a ditransitive verb, typically in the dative case in German (e.g., *ihm* in *Sie schenkte ihm ein Buch* 'She gave him a book').

indirect speech Reported speech (in contrast to a direct quote); used to report what someone said, asked, or commanded (e.g., *She said that she was sick*, in contrast to *She said, "I'm sick"*).

infinitive The non-finite form of a verb typically used as the citation form. In German, the infinitive is formed with the basic stem and the suffix *-(e)n* (e.g., *lieben* 'to love', *sammeln* 'to collect').

inflection The creation of different word forms of a lexeme, typically through the addition of affixes (e.g., the creation of the verb form *lacht* 'laughs' by adding the suffix *-t* to the stem *lach* 'laugh').

inherent inflection The inflection that is required because of the information that a speaker chooses to convey (e.g., the plural suffix *-er* on *Kinder* 'children'; the superlative suffix *-st* on the adjective *kleinst* 'smallest').

instrument The thematic role of the entity with which an action is performed (e.g., the role of *einem scharfen Messer* 'a sharp knife' in *Sie beschneidet die Stiele mit einem scharfen Messer* 'She cuts the stems with a sharp knife').

intonation The changes in pitch over the course of an utterance.

intonational phrase Each intonation pattern that contains a nucleus.

intransitive verb A verb that does not take a direct object (e.g., *fallen* 'to fall', *schlafen* 'to sleep').

isogloss A line drawn on a dialect map to separate the area in which one linguistic form is used from the area in which a variant form is used.

Item and Arrangement A model of morphology that views words as the "arrangement" (concatenation) of morphemes, each realized by a particular morph.

Item and Process A model of morphology that views words as the output of dynamic processes such as affixation, vowel change, etc.

jargon A register characterized by obscure vocabulary; used to signal membership in a closed social group.

larynx The part of the windpipe (trachea) that contains the vocal cords; commonly called the voice box.

lateral A sound produced by allowing air to escape on either side of the tongue (e.g., the *l* sound in *Lippe* 'lip').

lax vowel In German, a vowel that is produced closer to the mid-central position of the vowel area than its tense counterpart (e.g., the vowels in *ich* 'I', *dünn* 'thin', *muss* 'must', *denn* 'because', *Köln* 'Cologne', *oft* 'often').

length The duration of a sound relative to the duration of other sounds (e.g., the *a* sound in *Staat* 'state' is [+long]; the *a* sound in *Stadt* 'city' is [−long]).

lexeme An abstract unit of vocabulary that is realized by one or more word forms (e.g., *Haus*, *Hause*, *Hauses*, *Häuser*, and *Häusern* are all word forms of the lexeme HAUS 'house').

lexical category A category of word that has semantic content; includes the categories noun, verb, adjective, preposition, adverb.

lingua franca A language used for communication purposes between groups of speakers with different native languages.

linking element The *-(e)s-* that occurs between two elements in a compound in German (e.g., *Wohnungsmangel* 'housing shortage', *Kindesalter* 'childhood').

liquid A cover term for laterals and various types of *r* sounds.

loan rendition A word formed by translating only part of the elements of a foreign word literally into the native language (e.g., *Luftbrücke*, literally 'air bridge', from *airlift*).

loan translation A word formed by translating each of the elements of a foreign word or expression into the native language (e.g., *Flutlicht*, from *floodlight*).

loanword A word borrowed from a foreign language that has been integrated in the new language (e.g., *Streik* 'strike', from *strike*).

location The thematic role that specifies the place where something is located or takes place (e.g., the role of *dem Haus* 'the house' in *Die Kinder spielten vor dem Haus* 'The children played in front of the house').

low A feature of both consonants and vowels; [+low] sounds are produced by lowering the body of the tongue below its neutral position.

manner of articulation The way in which the airstream is impeded (by the lips, tongue, velum, etc.) in the production of a speech sound.

matrix clause The superordinate clause in which another clause is embedded (e.g., *Die Frau ist meine Schwester* 'The woman is my sister' is the matrix clause in the sentence *Die Frau, die dort steht, ist meine Schwester* 'The woman who is standing there is my sister').

matrix verb The main verb of the matrix clause (e.g., *glauben* 'to think' in *Ich glaube, sie hat Recht* 'I think she's right').

meronym A word that designates an entity that is a part of another entity (e.g., *Zehe* 'toe' is a meronym of *Fuß* 'foot').

mid A term used in the characterization of tongue height in the classification of vowels. A mid vowel is made with the tongue neither raised nor lowered; in a three-way contrast, mid vowels can be characterized as [−high] and [−low].

minimal pair Two words that differ in meaning and that are identical in form except for one sound that occurs in the same place in each word (e.g., *leiden* 'to suffer' and *neiden* 'to envy').

Mittelfeld The portion of a German sentence that occurs between the finite and non-finite verb forms in a main clause.

modal verb An auxiliary verb that expresses modality (e.g., *können* 'can', *müssen* 'must', *sollen* 'should').

modality A semantic category that involves the expression of different attitudes towards or degrees of commitment to a proposition.

monophthong A vowel (a pure vowel) in which there is no change in quality within a single syllable (e.g., the vowels in *bit*, *bet*, and *bat*; those in *Kind* 'child', *Mann* 'man', and *gut* 'good').

monophthongization A process by which a diphthong becomes a monophthong (e.g., MHG *guot* 'good' became ENHG *gut*).

mood Modality distinctions that are marked by verbal inflection. The three moods that are relevant in German are indicative, subjunctive, and imperative.

morph The realization of a morpheme; the constituent elements of a word form (e.g., the word form *Wohnung* 'dwelling' is made up of two morphs, /voːn/ and /ʊŋ/).

morpheme The smallest unit of language that bears meaning; realized by morphs (e.g., the morpheme {wohn} 'dwell' is realized by the morph /voːn/).

morphology The study of the structure of words.

morphosyntactic category A category that is referred to by rules in both morphology and syntax; a category that plays a role in the paradigm of a lexeme (e.g., case, number, person, tense).

Nachfeld The portion of a German sentence that follows the non-finite verb forms in a main clause.

nasal A feature used to describe sounds produced by lowering the velum (e.g., [m] is [+nasal]; [f] is [−nasal]).

nasal sound A speech sound produced by lowering the velum so that the airstream is allowed to pass through the nasal passages.

natural class A class of sounds that have a feature (or features) in common (e.g., front rounded vowels, voiceless fricatives).

node Any point connected by a line in a tree diagram.

noun A category of word that is used to name entities (e.g., *Erde* 'earth', *Stolz* 'pride', *Kind* 'child').

nucleus (intonation) The most prominent stressed syllable in a stretch of speech; associated with a change in pitch (e.g., the syllable *ein-* in *Das musst du doch einsehen!* 'But you have to recognize that!').

nucleus (syllable) The core of a syllable, usually a vowel (e.g., the monophthong in *dass* 'that', the diphthong in *mein* 'my').

number A morphosyntactic category that expresses contrasts that involve countable quantities. The number contrasts in German are singular and plural.

obstruent The class of consonants that includes stops, fricatives, and affricates.

onset The segment or segments in a syllable that precede the nucleus (e.g., the first two segments, [ʃm], in monosyllabic *schmal* 'narrow').

open syllable A syllable that ends in a vowel (e.g., both syllables in *be.tray*; both syllables in *Ki.no* 'cinema').

oral sound A speech sound produced by raising the velum against the back of the throat so that the airstream passes only through the mouth.

palate The hard palate is the front part of the roof of the mouth; the soft palate (velum) is the soft area at the back of the roof of the mouth.

participle The non-finite forms of a verb other than the infinitive. German has two participles, the present participle (e.g., *tanzend* 'dancing') and the past participle (e.g., *getanzt* 'danced').

patient The thematic role of the entity that undergoes an action and often undergoes a change of state (e.g., the role of *seinen Sohn* 'his son' in *Der Vater umarmte seinen Sohn* 'The father hugged his son').

penultimate syllable The second-to-last syllable (e.g., *tro* in *Zi.tro.ne* 'lemon').

percept The thematic role of the entity that is felt or perceived (e.g., the role of *den Ball* in *Das Kind sieht den Ball* 'The child sees the ball').

periphrasis The use of a multi-word expression in place of a single word (e.g., the use of *würde kommen* instead of *käme* to express 'would come').

person A morphosyntactic category that identifies the participants in a situation. A typical distinction is among first person (the speaker or a group including the speaker), second person (the person or persons addressed), and third person (anyone else).

phone A speech sound.

phoneme The minimal unit in the sound system of a language, capable of making contrasts in meaning; an abstract unit with phonetic variants (e.g., /l/, /r/, /z/, which contrast in the words *Lippe* 'lip', *Rippe* 'rib', *Sippe* 'clan').

phonemic transcription A representation of speech sounds using only phonemes as symbols (e.g., /zɪxər/, representing the pronunciation of *sicher* 'safe').

phonetic transcription A representation of speech sounds that provides phonetic detail as well as phonemic distinctions (e.g., [zɪçɐ], representing the pronunciation of *sicher* 'safe').

phonetics The study of the sounds of human speech; three branches of this field of study are articulatory phonetics, acoustic phonetics, and auditory phonetics.

phonology The study of the sound systems of languages.

phonotactics The permissible sequences of segments (sounds, phonemes) in a given language.

phrase An expression larger than a word that acts as a syntactic unit, with at least two levels of representation, the word level and the phrase level (e.g., *der Apfel* 'the apple', *nach Hause gehen* 'go home').

phrase structure rule A rule that indicates how a phrase is formed out of its constituent parts (e.g., PP → P NP).

pidgin A highly simplified language that develops as a mixture of two of more languages in a language contact situation where speakers do not know each other's languages.

pitch The auditory property of a sound that allows listeners to place it on a scale ranging from low to high.

place of articulation The place in the vocal tract where the airstream is impeded in the production of a consonant.

plural The value for the grammatical category of number that indicates more than one entity.

portmanteau morph A morph that realizes more than one morpheme (e.g., /tʰ/ in *liebt* 'loves', which realizes the morphemes {third person}, {singular}, {present}, {indicative}).

postposition A category of word that functions like a preposition but follows (rather than precedes) its NP complement (e.g., *entlang* 'along', as in *die Straße entlang* 'along the street').

pragmatics The study of those aspects of meaning determined by the context in which language is used (e.g., time and place of an utterance; attitudes, beliefs, and assumptions of speakers and hearers).

predicative An element used as a predicate is said to be predicative (e.g., the adjective *klein* 'little' in *Die Kinder sind klein* 'The children are little'; the noun *Ärztin* 'doctor' in *Meine Frau ist Ärztin* 'My wife is a doctor').

prefix An affix that is attached to the beginning of its base (e.g., *un-* in *unklar* 'unclear').

preposition A category of word typically used to designate location in time or space (*vor* 'before', *hinter* 'behind'); it precedes the NP with which it forms a prepositional phrase (e.g., *vor dem Konzert* 'before the concert').

pronoun A category of word that can be used to substitute for a noun phrase (e.g., *es* 'it', *sie* 'she').

prosodic phonology Aspects of phonology such as pitch, loudness, and tempo, which are not properties of individual sounds.

proto-language A reconstructed language for which there are no preserved records; presumed to be the ancestor of one or more known languages.

realization The physical expression of an abstract linguistic unit (e.g., the morph /frau̯/ is a realization of the morpheme {frau} 'woman').

reduction (morphology) A noun that is a shortened (reduced) version of a complex noun or a phrase (e.g., *Demo*, from *Demonstration* 'demonstration').

reduction (phonology) A cover term for phonological processes that "reduce" sounds (e.g., the shortening of long vowels; centralization, which reduces tense vowels to their lax counterparts).

reduplication A process of affixation that makes use of an affix created by repeating part (or all) of the base to which it is attached (e.g., *Pinkepinke* 'dough', from *Pinke* 'money').

reference time The time from which an event is viewed.

reflexive pronoun A pronoun used to refer back to the subject of a sentence or clause (e.g., *sich* in *Er verteidigte sich* 'He defended himself').

register A variety of language used when dealing with a specific subject matter or when engaged in a particular activity (e.g., the technical register of legal language).

relative clause A clause embedded in an NP that modifies the head noun (e.g., *den sie fährt* 'that she drives' in *der Wagen, den sie fährt* 'the car that she drives').

root The portion of a word form that is left when all affixes have been removed (e.g., *stör* in *Zerstörung* 'destruction').

root modality A type of modality that contrasts with epistemic modality; expresses notions like obligation, permission, and ability.

round A feature that characterizes sounds made by protruding the lips (e.g., [ʊ] in *muss* 'must' is [+round], [ɪ] in *ich* 'I' is [−round])

rounded Sounds that are produced with the lips protruding (e.g., [ʊ], [ɔ]).

schwa The name for the vowel [ə], a mid central lax unrounded vowel, which never occurs in a stressed syllable in German (e.g., the final vowel in *bitte* 'please').

scrambling The movement of a constituent in a clause from its normal position to further forward in the clause (e.g., in *Dann holte mich mein Vater ab* 'Then my father picked me up', the direct object, *mich* 'me', has been scrambled from its normal position following the subject to a position preceding it).

semantic loan A type of borrowing in which an existing word acquires a new, secondary meaning on the basis of another meaning that its translation has in the lending language (e.g., the extension of the meaning of *feuern* 'to fire, shoot' to include the meaning 'to let go [from a job]' on the basis of this meaning of English *fire*).

semantics The study of meaning in language.

simplex word A word that has no affixes and is not part of a compound (e.g., *Frau* 'woman', *Wagen* 'car').

singular The value for the grammatical category of number that indicates one entity.

sociolect A language variety that can be defined according to the social group to which its speakers belong.

sociolinguistics The study of the relationship between language and society; the investigation of the way in which language functions in social contexts.

sonorant A feature that characterizes sounds produced when air flows smoothly through the vocal tract. Vowels, nasals, and liquids are [+sonorant].

source The thematic role of the entity from which a motion takes place (e.g., the role of *dem Auto* 'the car' in *Die Frau steigt aus dem Auto* 'The woman gets out of the car').

specifier A word that makes the meaning of its head more precise and marks a phrase boundary (e.g., the determiner *diese* 'these' in *diese Bücher* 'these books').

speech time The time of an utterance.

spirant Another term for "fricative."

spread glottis A feature that characterizes sounds with an active glottal opening gesture. Stops that are [+spread glottis] are often aspirated.

standard language The prestige, supraregional variety of a language used by the government and mass media, taught in schools and to foreigners.

stem The portion of a word form that serves as a base for inflectional affixes (e.g., *missversteh* in *missversteht* 'misunderstands').

stop A type of consonant (also known as "plosive") produced by a complete closure in the vocal tract (e.g., [p], [t], [k]).

stress The degree of force used in the production of a syllable; syllables that are stressed are perceived as more prominent than other syllables. Factors that can play a role in determining prominence include length, loudness, and pitch.

stress-timed A term used to describe the pronunciation of a language in which stressed syllables recur at regular intervals of time (e.g., English and German).

style A variety of a language that differs from another in its level of formality.

subcategorization The assignment of a lexical item to a subclass (subcategory) of the syntactic category to which it belongs, typically with respect to the types of phrases with which it can occur (e.g., the verb *verteidigen* 'to defend' is subcategorized for an NP complement).

subjunctive The mood used to mark a clause as expressing something other than a statement of what is certain.

subordinate compound A compound in which one element modifies the other (e.g., *Kaffeemühle* 'coffee grinder', where *Kaffee* 'coffee' describes the kind of grinder).

suffix An affix that is attached to the end of its base (e.g., *-lich* in *monatlich* 'monthly').

suppletion A situation in which two forms in the paradigm of a lexeme show no phonological similarity (e.g., *good* and *better*; *gut* 'good' and *besser* 'better').

surface structure The structure at the level of the spoken language rather than at a deeper or more abstract (underlying) level.

syllable A unit of speech built around a peak of sonority (the nucleus), typically a vowel. The additional parts of a syllable are the onset and coda.

syllable-timed A term used to describe the pronunciation of a language in which each syllable takes up approximately the same amount of time (e.g., French).

syncretism Identity between two forms in the paradigm of a lexeme (e.g., *studiert* 'studies', a third person singular form of STUDIEREN 'to study', and *studiert* 'studied', the past participle).

synonyms Two words that have the same meaning in some or all contexts (e.g., *couch* and *sofa*; *Nomen* 'noun' and *Substantiv* 'noun').

syntax The study of the structure of sentences.

synthetic A type of language in which words are typically composed of more than one morpheme.

tag question A question formed by attaching a tag, and interrogative fragment, to the end of a statement (e.g., in German, the tag question *Sie kommt, nicht wahr?* 'She's coming, isn't she?' is formed with the tag *nicht wahr*).

telic A term used to refer to events that have a clear endpoint (e.g., *ein Haus bauen* 'to build a house', *durchs Ziel gehen* 'to cross the finishing line').

tense (feature) A feature used to distinguish between (1) tense and lax vowels; (2) finite and non-finite verbs and clauses.

tense (verb) A morphosyntactic category of the verb that is used to express the time at which the action denoted by the verb takes place.

tense vowel In German, a vowel that is produced further from the mid-central position of the vowel area than its lax counterpart (e.g., the vowels in *nie* 'never', *früh* 'early', *Schuh* 'shoe', *Schnee* 'snow', *Öl* 'oil', *Sohn* 'son').

thematic role The semantic role played by an entity involved in a situation or event (e.g., agent, patient, goal, location).

theme The thematic role of the entity that is moved by an action or whose location is described (e.g., the role of *das Gemälde* 'the painting' in *Das Gemälde hängt jetzt in meinem Zimmer* 'The picture is hanging in my room now').

topicalization The movement of a constituent to the front of a sentence so that it can function as a topic, the person or thing about which something is said (e.g., the movement of the direct object, *day passes*, to sentence-initial position in *Day passes you can buy online*).

topological model An approach to German sentence structure that divides a sentence up into fields (the Vor-, Mittel-, and Nachfeld).

trace An empty element (marked by the symbol *t*) that is left behind in syntactic structure in each position out of which a constituent moves.

transitive verb A verb that takes a direct object (e.g., *schlagen* 'to hit', *verteidigen* 'to defend').

tree diagram A diagram that represents the internal hierarchical structure of a phrase or sentence.

trill A sound produced by holding an articulator loosely close to another articulator, so that the airstream sets it in vibration.

umlaut The partial assimilation of a vowel to a vowel in a following syllable (e.g., the fronting of OHG *a* in *lang* 'long' to *e* in *lengiro* 'longer' because of the influence of the following front vowel *i*). A vowel alternation used to signal grammatical distinctions that is the result of assimilation to a following vowel is also known as umlaut (e.g., the vowel alternation used to signal the plural in nouns, as in *Fuß* 'foot' and *Füße* 'feet').

underlying structure The structure generated by phrase structure rules; a more abstract level than surface structure.

utterance A stretch of speech.

uvula The small piece of soft tissue that hangs down from the rear portion of the velum.

valency The number and type of arguments that occur with a verb (e.g., the verb *schlafen* 'to sleep' requires a subject and thus has a valency of 1; the verb *schlagen* 'to hit' requires a subject and direct object and thus has a valency of 2).

velum The soft area at the back of the roof of the mouth; also called the soft palate.

verb A category of word that is used to describe actions and states; in German it is inflected for person, number, tense, etc. (e.g., *laufen* 'to run', *sein* 'to be').

vocal cords The two pairs of folds of muscle and ligament attached to the inner sides of the thyroid cartilage at the front of the larynx and to the two arytenoid cartilages at the back of the larynx.

vocal tract The air passages above the larynx.

voice (feature) A feature that distinguishes between voiced and voiceless sounds.

voice (grammatical) A grammatical category that allows a speaker to alter the pairing of thematic roles with grammatical functions; the main distinction is between active and passive voice. In the active sentence *Sie reparierte den Wagen* 'She repaired the car', the PATIENT, *Wagen*, is a direct object; in the passive sentence, *Der Wagen wurde repariert* 'The car was repaired', the PATIENT is a subject.

voiced A glottal state in which the vocal cords are brought close together, but not completely closed, so that the air passing through them causes them to vibrate (e.g., [a], [v], and [l] are voiced).

voiceless A glottal state in which the vocal cords are spread apart and the airstream passes freely through the space between them (e.g., [p], [f], and [ç] are voiceless).

Vorfeld The portion of a German sentence that precedes the finite verb in a main clause.

vowel A speech sound produced without a closure of the mouth or a narrowing of the speech organs to a degree that would produce audible friction when the airstream passes through the mouth (e.g., [ɪ], [a], [ʊ]).

wh-phrase A phrase containing a wh-word, a word that (in English) begins with *wh* (*who*, *what*, *which*, *where*, *when*), or a word with a similar syntax (*how*); German wh-words typically begin with *w* rather than *wh* (*wer* 'who', *was* 'what', *welch* 'which', *wo* 'where', *wann* 'when', *wie* 'how').

Word and Paradigm A model of morphology that takes the lexeme and its paradigm of word forms as its starting point; the different word forms are derived by processes or operations that apply to the lexeme.

word form The smallest stretch of speech that can occur in isolation; the form (orthographic or phonological) in which a lexeme occurs (e.g., *Mutter*, *Mütter*, and *Müttern* are the word forms that realize the lexeme MUTTER 'mother').

References

Abney, Steven Paul. 1987. The English noun phrase in its sentential aspect. Cambridge, MA: MIT dissertation.

Allan, Keith. 1986. *Linguistic meaning.* 2 vols. London: Routledge & Kegan Paul.

Ammon, Ulrich. 1995. *Die deutsche Sprache in Deutschland, Österreich und der Schweiz: Das Problem der nationalen Varietäten.* Berlin: de Gruyter.

Ammon, Ulrich, Norbert Dittmar, Klaus J. Mattheier, and Peter Trudgill (eds.). 2005. *Sociolinguistics: An international handbook of the science of language and society.* 2nd edn. 3 vols. Berlin and New York: Mouton de Gruyter.

Anderson, Stephen R. 1992. *A-morphous morphology.* Cambridge University Press.

Androutsopoulos, Jannis K. 1998. *Deutsche Jugendsprache: Untersuchungen zu ihren Strukturen und Funktionen.* Frankfurt am Main: Lang.

Antonsen, Elmer H. 1975. *A concise grammar of the older runic inscriptions.* Tübingen: Niemeyer.

2002. *Runes and Germanic linguistics.* Berlin and New York: Mouton de Gruyter.

Arliss, Laurie P. 1991. *Gender communication.* Englewood Cliffs, NJ: Prentice Hall.

Augst, Gerhard. 1977. *Sprachnorm und Sprachwandel: Vier Projekte zu diachroner Sprachbetrachtung.* Wiesbaden: Athenaion.

Bach, Adolf. 1970. *Geschichte der deutschen Sprache.* 9th edn. Heidelberg: Quelle & Meyer.

Bachmann, Albert. 1970. *Mittelhochdeutsches Lesebuch mit Grammatik und Wörterbuch.* 19th edn. Zurich: Beer.

Back, Otto, *et al.* 2006. *Österreichisches Wörterbuch.* 40th edn. Vienna: öbvhpt.

Barbour, Stephen, and Patrick Stevenson. 1990. *Variation in German: A critical approach to German sociolinguistics.* Cambridge University Press.

Baron, Dennis E. 1986. *Grammar and gender.* New Haven: Yale University Press.

Barthel, Ulrich. 1994. Die Logik der Adjektivdeklination: eine Unterrichtseinheit. *Zielsprache Deutsch* 25.34–42.

Bartke, Susanne. 1998. *Experimentelle Studien zur Flexion und Wortbildung: Pluralmorphologie und lexikalische Komposition im unauffälligen Spracherwerb und im Dysgrammatismus.* Tübingen: Niemeyer.

Bauer, Laurie. 2003. *Introducing linguistic morphology.* Washington, DC: Georgetown University Press.

Baur, Arthur. 1983. *Was ist eigentlich Schweizerdeutsch?* Winterthur: Gemsberg-Verlag.

Bayer, Klaus. 1979. Die Anredepronomina *Du* und *Sie:* Thesen zu einem semantischen Konflikt im Hochschulbereich. *Deutsche Sprache* 3.212–219.

Bech, Gunnar. 1963. Zur Morphologie der deutschen Substantive. *Lingua* 12.177–189.

Becker, Thomas. 1998. *Das Vokalsystem der deutschen Standardsprache.* Frankfurt am Main: Lang.

Beckman, Jill, Michael Jessen, and Catherine Ringen. To appear. German fricatives: Coda devoicing or positional faithfulness? *Phonology.*

Benware, Wilbur A. 1986. *Phonetics and phonology of Modern German: An introduction.* Washington, DC: Georgetown University Press.

1987. Accent variation in German nominal compounds of the type (A(BC)). *Linguistische Berichte* 108.102–127.

Bergmann, Gunter. 1990. Upper Saxon. *The dialects of modern German: A linguistic survey,* ed. Charles V. J. Russ, 290–312. London: Routledge.

Besch, Werner. 1998. *Duzen, Siezen, Titulieren: Zur Anrede im Deutschen heute und gestern.* 2nd edn. Göttingen: Vandenhoeck & Ruprecht.

Bethge, Wolfang, and Gunther M. Bonnin. 1969. *Proben deutscher Mundarten.* Tübingen: Niemeyer.

Bierwisch, Manfred. 1967. Some semantic universals of German adjectivals. *Foundations of Language* 3.1–36.

1987. Semantik der Graduierung. *Grammatische und konzeptuelle Aspekte von Dimensionsadjektiven,* ed. Manfred Bierwisch and Ewald Lang, 91–286. Berlin: Akademie-Verlag.

Blevins, Juliette. 1995. The syllable in phonological theory. *The handbook of phonological theory,* ed. John A. Goldsmith, 206–244. Cambridge, MA: Blackwell.

Boase-Beier, Jean, and Ken Lodge. 2003. *The German language: A linguistic introduction.* Malden, MA: Blackwell.

Bodemann, Y. Michael, and Robin Ostow. 1975. Lingua Franca und Pseudo-Pidgin in der Bundesrepublik: Fremdarbeiter und Einheimische im Sprachzusammenhang. *Sprache ausländischer Arbeiter. Zeitschrift für Literaturwissenschaft und Linguistik,* Heft 18, ed. Wolfgang Klein, 122–146. Göttingen: Vandenhoeck & Ruprecht.

Boesch, Bruno. 1957. *Die Aussprache des Hochdeutschen in der Schweiz: Eine Wegleitung.* Zürich: Schweizer Spiegel.

Booij, Geert. 2002. *The morphology of Dutch.* Oxford University Press.

2005. *The grammar of words: An introduction to linguistic morphology.* Oxford University Press.

de Boor, Helmut (ed.). 1988. *Das Nibelungenlied.* 22nd edn., ed. and rev. Roswitha Wisniewski. Mannheim: Brockhaus.

Boost, Karl. 1955. *Neue Untersuchungen zum Wesen und zur Struktur des deutschen Satzes: Der Satz als Spannungsfeld.* Berlin: Akademie-Verlag.

Bornschein, Matthias, and Matthias Butt. 1987. Zum Status des s-Plurals im gegenwärtigen Deutsch. *Linguistik in Deutschland: Akten des 21. Linguistischen Kolloquiums,* Groningen 1986, ed. Werner Abraham and Ritva Århammar, 135–53. Tübingen: Max Niemeyer.

Boutkan, Dirk. 1995. *The Germanic "Auslautgesetze."* Amsterdam and Atlanta, GA: Rodopi.

Braun, Peter. 1982. Bestände und Veränderungen in der deutschen Wortbildung am Beispiel der *be-*Verben. *Muttersprache* 92.216–226.

Braune, Wilhelm. 2004. *Althochdeutsche Grammatik I. Laut und Formenlehre.* 15th edn., ed. Ingo Reiffenstein. Tübingen: Niemeyer.

Braune, Wilhelm, Karl Helm, and Ernst A. Ebbinghaus. 1994. *Althochdeutsches Lesebuch*. 17th edn. Tübingen: Niemeyer.

Breuer, Christoph, and Raalf Dorow. 1996. *Deutsche Tempora der Vorvergangenheit*. Trier: Wissenschaftlicher Verlag Trier.

Brown, Roger, and Albert Gilman. 1960. The pronouns of power and solidarity. *Style in language*, ed. Thomas A. Sebeok, 253–276. Cambridge, MA: MIT Press.

Brünner, Gisela, and Angelika Redder. 1983. *Studien zur Verwendung der Modalverben*. Tübingen: Narr.

Buscha, Joachim, Gertraud Heinrich, and Irene Zoch. 1993. *Modalverben*. 8th edn. Leipzig and New York: Langenscheidt Verlag Enzyklopädie.

Cahill, Lynne, and Gerald Gazdar. 1999. German noun inflection. *Journal of Linguistics* 35.1–42.

Carstairs, Andrew. 1986. Macroclasses and paradigm economy in German nouns. *Zeitschrift für Phonetik, Sprachwissenschaft und Kommunikationsforschung* 39.3–11.

Chambers, W. Walker, and John R. Wilkie. 1970. *A short history of the German language*. London: Methuen.

Cheshire, Jenny. 1982. Linguistic variation and social function. *Sociolinguistic variation in speech communities*, ed. Suzanne Romaine, 153–175. London: Arnold.

Choi, Hye-Won. 1999. *Optimizing structure in context: Scrambling and information structure*. Stanford, CA: CSLI Publications.

Clahsen, Harald, Jürgen M. Meisel, and Manfred Pienemann. 1983. *Deutsch als Zweitsprache: Der Spracherwerb ausländischer Arbeiter*. Tübingen: Narr.

Clahsen, Harald, Monika Rothweiler, Andreas Woest, and Gary F. Marcus. 1992. Regular and irregular inflection in the acquisition of German noun plurals. *Cognition* 45.225–255.

Claßen, Kathrin, Grzegorz Dogil, Michael Jessen, Krzysztof Marasek, and Wolfgang Wokurek. 1998. Stimmqualität und Wortbetonung im Deutschen. *Linguistische Berichte* 174.202–245.

Clements, George N., and Samuel Jay Keyser. 1983. *CV phonology: A generative theory of the syllable*. Cambridge, MA: MIT Press.

Clyne, Michael. 1968. Zum Pidgin-Deutsch der Gastarbeiter. *Zeitschrift für Mundartforschung* 35.130–139.

  1995. *The German language in a changing Europe*. Cambridge University Press.

Coates, Jennifer. 1983. *The semantics of the modal auxiliaries*. London and Canberra: Croom Helm.

Comrie, Bernard. 1976. *Aspect: An introduction to the study of verbal aspect and related problems*. Cambridge University Press.

  1979. Russian. *Languages and their status*, ed. Timothy Shopen, 91–151. Cambridge, MA: Winthrop Publishers.

  1985. *Tense*. Cambridge University Press.

Corbett, Greville G. 1991. *Gender*. Cambridge University Press.

Coulmas, Florian (ed.). 1998. *The handbook of sociolinguistics*. Oxford and Cambridge, MA: Blackwell.

Cruse, D. A. 1986. *Lexical semantics*. Cambridge University Press.

Cruttenden, Alan. 2001. *Gimson's pronunciation of English*. 6th edn. London: Arnold.

Curme, George O. 1960. *A grammar of the German language*. 2nd edn. New York: Ungar.

Dickens, David B. 1983. Teaching attributive adjective endings and adjectival nouns: An attempt at simplification. *Die Unterrichtspraxis* 16.103–106.

Dittmar, Norbert. 1973. *Soziolinguistik: Exemplarische und kritische Darstellung ihrer Theorie, Empirie und Anwendung*. Frankfurt am Main: Athenäum.

1997. *Grundlagen der Soziolinguistik: Ein Arbeitsbuch mit Aufgaben*. Tübingen: Niemeyer.

Dolle-Weinkauf, Bernd. 1990. *Comics: Geschichte einer populären Literaturform in Deutschland seit 1945*. Weinheim and Basel: Beltz.

Donalies, Elke. 2002. *Die Wortbildung des Deutschen: Ein Überblick*. Tübingen: Narr.

Dowty, David R. 1986. Thematic roles and semantics. *Berkeley Linguistics Society* 12.340–354.

Drach, Erich. 1940 [1963]. *Grundgedanken der deutschen Satzlehre*. Darmstadt: Wissenschaftliche Buchgesellschaft. [Reprint of the 3rd edn.]

Drosdowski, Günther (ed.). 1984. *Duden: Grammatik der deutschen Gegenwartssprache*. 4th edn. Mannheim: Bibliographisches Institut.

Dudenredaktion. 2001. *Duden: Richtiges und gutes Deutsch*. 5th edn. Mannheim: Dudenverlag.

2005. *Duden: Die Grammatik*. 7th edn. Mannheim: Dudenverlag.

2006. *Duden: Die deutsche Rechtschreibung*. 24th edn. Mannheim: Dudenverlag.

Durrell, Martin. 1988. Some problems of contrastive lexical semantics. *Understanding the lexicon: Meaning, sense and world knowledge in lexical semantics*, ed. Werner Hüllen and Rainer Schulze, 230–241. Tübingen: Niemeyer.

1990. Westphalian and Eastphalian. *The dialects of modern German: A linguistic survey*, ed. Charles V. J. Russ, 59–90. London: Routledge.

1992. *Using German: A guide to contemporary usage*. Cambridge University Press.

1999. Review of *Experimentelle Studien zur Flexion und Wortbildung*, by Susanne Bartke. *American Journal of Germanic Linguistics and Literatures* 11.238–243.

2002. *Hammer's German grammar and usage*. 4th edn. Chicago: McGraw-Hill.

Durrell, Martin, and Winifred V. Davies. 1990. Hessian. *The dialects of modern German: A linguistic survey*, ed. Charles V. J. Russ, 210–240. London: Routledge.

Dürrenmatt, Friedrich. 1952 [1967]. *Der Richter und sein Henker*. Einsiedeln: Benziger Verlag.

Ebert, Robert Peter, Oskar Reichmann, Hans-Joachim Solms, and Klaus-Peter Wegera. 1993. *Frühneuhochdeutsche Grammatik*. Tübingen: Niemeyer.

Ehmann, Hermann. 2001. *Voll konkret: Das neueste Lexikon der Jugendsprache*. Munich: Beck.

2005. *Endgeil: Das voll korrekte Lexikon der Jugendsprache*. Munich: Beck.

Eisenberg, Peter. 1998. *Grundriß der deutschen Grammatik*. Vol. 1, *Das Wort*. Stuttgart and Weimar: J. B. Metzler.

Erich, Veronika, and Heinz Vater. 1989. Das Perfekt im Dänischen und Deutschen. *Tempus – Aspekt – Modus: Die lexikalischen und grammatischen Formen in den germanischen Sprachen*, ed. Werner Abraham and Theo Janssen, 103–32. Tübingen: Niemeyer.

Eroms, Hans-Werner. 1980. *Be-Verb und Präpositionalphrase: Ein Beitrag zur Grammatik der deutschen Verbalpräfixe*. Heidelberg: Carl Winter.

1986. *Funktionale Satzperspektive.* Tübingen: Niemeyer.

Fagan, Sarah M. B. 1992. *The syntax and semantics of middle constructions: A study with special reference to German.* Cambridge University Press.

1996. The epistemic use of German and English modals. *Germanic linguistics: Syntactic and diachronic,* ed. Rosina L. Lippi-Green and Joseph C. Salmons, 15–34. Amsterdam and Philadelphia: John Benjamins.

2001. Epistemic modality and tense in German. *Journal of Germanic Linguistics* 13.197–230.

Fennell, Barbara A. 1997. *Language, literature, and the negotiation of identity: Foreign worker German in the Federal Republic of Germany.* Chapel Hill: University of North Carolina Press.

Ferguson, Charles A. 1959. Diglossia. *Word* 15.325–340.

Féry, Caroline. 1993. *German intonational patterns.* Tübingen: Niemeyer.

1997. Uni und Studis: die besten Wörter des Deutschen. *Linguistische Berichte* 172.401–489.

Firbas, Jan. 1964. On defining the theme in Functional Sentence Perspective. *Travaux linguistiques de Prague* 2.239–256.

Fishman, Joshua. 1998. The new linguistic order. *Foreign Policy* 113.26–40.

Fleischer, Wolfgang, and Irmhild Barz. 1995. *Wortbildung der deutschen Gegenwartssprache.* Tübingen: Niemeyer.

Fischer-Jørgensen, Eli. 1969. Untersuchungen zum sogenannten festen und losen Anschluss. *Kopenhagener Germanistische Studien 1: Peter Jørgensen zu seinem 70. Geburtstag am 12.9.1969 gewidmet,* ed. Karl Hyldgaard-Jensen and Steffen Steffensen, 138–164. Copenhagen: Akademisk Forlag.

Foley, William A., and Robert D. Van Valin, Jr. 1984. *Functional syntax and universal grammar.* Cambridge University Press.

Fortson, Benjamin W., IV. 2004. *Indo-European language and culture: An introduction.* Malden, MA: Blackwell.

Fox, Anthony. 1984. *German intonation: An outline.* Oxford: Clarendon Press.

2005. *The structure of German.* 2nd edn. Oxford University Press.

Fraas, Claudia. 1993. Verständigungsschwierigkeiten der Deutschen. *Muttersprache* 103.260–263.

Fraas, Claudia, and Kathrin Steyer. 1992. Sprache der Wende – Wende der Sprache? Beharrungsvermögen und Dynamik von Strukturen im öffentlichen Sprachgebrauch. *Deutsche Sprache* 20.172–184.

Frings, Theodor. 1956. *Sprache und Geschichte.* Vol. 1. Halle: Niemeyer.

Frisch, Max. 1957 [1966]. *Homo Faber: Ein Bericht.* Frankfurt am Main: Suhrkamp.

Fullerton, G. Lee. 1977. On teaching the subjective use of modal auxiliaries. *Die Unterrichtspraxis* 10.73–78.

Giegerich, Heinz J. 1985. *Metrical phonology and phonological structure: German and English.* Cambridge University Press.

1987. Zur Schwa-Epenthese im Standarddeutschen. *Linguistische Berichte* 112.449–469.

1989. *Syllable structure and lexical derivation in German.* Bloomington: Indiana University Linguistics Club.

Gívon, Talmy. 1990. *Syntax: A functional–typological introduction.* Amsterdam and Philadelphia: John Benjamins.

Goldberg, Adele, and Farrell Ackerman. 2001. The pragmatics of obligatory adjuncts. *Language* 798–814.

Goltz, Reinhard H., and Alastair G. H. Walker. 1990. North Saxon. *The dialects of modern German: A linguistic survey*, ed. Charles V. J. Russ, 31–58. London: Routledge.

Good, Colin. 1993. Über die "Kultur des Mißverständnisses" im vereinten Deutschland. *Muttersprache* 103.249–259.

Gordon, Raymond G., Jr. (ed.) 2005. *Ethnologue: Languages of the world*. 15th edn. Dallas: SIL International.

Grebe, Paul. 1973. *Duden: Grammatik der deutschen Gegenwartssprache*. 3rd edn. Mannheim: Bibliographisches Institut.

Greule, Albrecht. 1983. *Abi, Krimi, Sponti*: Substantive auf -*i* im heutigen Deutsch. *Muttersprache* 94.207–217.

1996. Reduktion als Wortbildungsprozess der deutschen Sprache. *Muttersprache* 106.193–203.

Große, Rudolf. 1955. *Die meißnische Sprachlandschaft: Dialektgeographische Untersuchungen zur obersächsischen Sprach- und Siedlungsgeschichte*. Halle: Niemeyer.

Gruber, Jeffrey. 1965. Studies in lexical relations. Cambridge, MA: MIT dissertation.

Grüter, Theres. 2003. Hypocoristics: The case of *u*-formation in Bernese Swiss German. *Journal of Germanic Linguistics* 15.27–63.

Guentherodt, Ingrid, Marlis Hellinger, Luise F. Pusch, and Senta Trömel-Plötz. 1980. Richtlinien zur Vermeidung sexistischen Sprachgebrauchs. *Linguistische Berichte* 69.15–21.

Günther, Hartmut. 1974. *Das System der Verben mit BE- in der deutschen Sprache der Gegenwart: Ein Beitrag zur Struktur des Lexikons der deutschen Grammatik*. Tübingen: Niemeyer.

1987. Wortbildung, Syntax, *be*-Verben und das Lexikon. *Beiträge zur Geschichte der deutschen Sprache und Literatur* 109.179–201.

Hale, Mark. 1987. Wackernagel's Law and the language of the Rigveda. *Studies in memory of Warren Cowgill (1929–1985)*, ed. Calvert Watkins, 38–50. Berlin: de Gruyter.

Hall, Christopher. 2003. *Modern German pronunciation: An introduction for speakers of English*. 2nd edn. Manchester University Press.

Hall, Tracy Alan. 1992. *Syllable structure and syllable-related processes in German*. Tübingen: Niemeyer.

2005. Paradigm uniformity effects in German phonology. *Journal of Germanic Linguistics* 17.225–264.

Halle, Morris, and Jean Roger Vergnaud. 1980. Three-dimensional phonology. *Journal of Linguistic Research* 1.83–105.

Halliday, M. A. K. 1978. *Language as social semiotic: The social interpretation of language and meaning*. Baltimore: University Park Press.

Harbert, Wayne. 1995. Binding theory, control, and *pro*. *Government and binding theory and the minimalist program: Principles and parameters in syntactic theory*, ed. Gert Webelhuth, 77–240. Oxford: Blackwell.

Haspelmath, Martin. 2000. Periphrasis. *Morphologie: Ein internationales Handbuch zur Flexion und Wortbildung*, ed. Geert Booij, Christian Lehmann, Joachim

Mugdan, Wolfgang Kesselheim, and Stavros Skopeteas, 654–664. Vol. 1. Berlin: de Gruyter.

Hawkins, John A. 1986. *A comparative typology of English and German: Unifying the contrasts*. London: Croom Helm.

Heidelberger Forschungsprojekt "Pidgin-Deutsch." 1975. *Sprache und Kommunikation ausländischer Arbeiter: Analysen, Berichte, Materialien*. Kronberg: Scriptor.

Heike, Georg. 1972. *Phonologie*. Stuttgart: J. B. Metzler.

Heine, Bernd. 1995. Agent-oriented vs. epistemic modality: Some observations on German modals. *Modality in grammar and discourse*, ed. Joan Bybee and Suzanne Fleischman, 17–53. Amsterdam and Philadelphia: John Benjamins.

Hellinger, Marlis. 1980. Zum Gebrauch weiblicher Berufsbezeichnungen im Deutschen – Variabilität als Ausdruck außersprachlicher Machtstrukturen. *Linguistische Berichte* 69.37–58.

1995. Language and gender. *The German language and the real world: Sociolinguistic, cultural, and pragmatic perspectives on contemporary German*, ed. Patrick Stevenson, 277–314. Oxford: Clarendon Press.

Hellinger, Marlis, and Beate Schräpel. 1983. Über die sprachliche Gleichbehandlung von Frauen und Männern. *Jahrbuch für Internationale Germanistik* 15. 40–69.

Hellmann, Manfred. 1978. Sprache zwischen Ost und West – Überlegungen zur Wortschatzdifferenzierung zwischen BRD und DDR und ihren Folgen. *Sprache und Kultur: Studien zur Diglossie, Gastarbeiterproblematik und kulturellen Integration*, ed. Wolfgang Kühlwein and Günter Radden, 15–54. Tübingen: Narr.

Henne, Helmut. 1986. *Jugend und ihre Sprache: Darstellung, Materialien, Kritik*. Berlin: de Gruyter.

Hoberg, Ursula. 1981. *Die Wortstellung in der geschriebenen deutschen Gegenwartssprache*. Munich: Hueber.

Höhle, Tilman. 1982. Explikation für "normale Betonung" und "normale Wortstellung." *Satzglieder im Deutschen: Vorschläge zur syntaktischen, semantischen und pragmatischen Fundierung*, ed. Abraham Werner, 75–165. Tübingen: Stauffenburg.

Hopper, Paul J., and Sandra A. Thompson. 1980. Transitivity in grammar and discourse. *Language* 56.251–299.

Hudson, R. A. 1996. *Sociolinguistics*. 2nd edn. Cambridge University Press.

Itô, Junko. 1986. Syllable theory in prosodic phonology. Amherst, MA: University of Massachusetts dissertation.

Itô, Junko, and Armin Mester. 1997. Sympathy theory and German truncations. *Selected phonology papers from the Hopkins Optimality Workshop/University of Maryland Mayfest 1997*, ed. Viola Miglio and Bruce Morén, 117–138. College Park, MD: University of Maryland.

Iverson, Gregory K., and Joseph C. Salmons. 1995. Aspiration and laryngeal representation in Germanic. *Phonology* 12.369–396.

Jackendoff, Ray. 1972. *Semantic interpretation in generative grammar*. Cambridge, MA: MIT Press.

1987. The status of thematic relations in linguistic theory. *Linguistic Inquiry* 18.369–411.

Janda, Richard D. 1991. Frequency, markedness, and morphological change: On predicting the spread of noun-plural *-s* in Modern High German and West Germanic.

Escol '90, ed. Yongkyoon No and Mark Libucha, 136–53. Ithaca, NY: Cornell Linguistics Circle Publications.

Jespersen, Otto. 1904. *Phonetische Grundfragen*. Leipzig: Teubner.

Jessen, Michael. 1988. Die dorsalen Reibelaute [ç] und [x] im Deutschen. *Linguistische Berichte* 117.371–396.

  1998. *Phonetics and phonology of tense and lax obstruents in German*. Amsterdam and Philadelphia: John Benjamins.

  1999. German. *Word prosodic systems in the languages of Europe*, ed. Harry van der Hulst, 515–545. Berlin: Mouton de Gruyter.

  2007. Rounded or unrounded offset in the German EU-diphthong. *Manuscript.*

Jessen, Michael, and Catherine Ringen. 2002. Laryngeal features in German. *Phonology* 19.189–218.

Johnson, Sally. 1998. *Exploring the German language*. London: Arnold.

Jones, Daniel. 1956. *An outline of English phonetics*, 8th edn. Cambridge: Heffer.

Karch, Dieter. 1980. *Proben westpfälzischer Ortsmundarten*. Lincoln: University of Nebraska.

Keller, R. E. 1961. *German dialects: Phonology and morphology, with selected texts*. Manchester University Press.

Key, Mary Ritchie. 1975. *Male/female language, with a comprehensive bibliography*. Metuchen, NJ: Scarecrow Press.

Kim, Gyung-Uk. 1983. *Valenz und Wortbildung: Dargestellt am Beispiel der verbalen Präfixbildung mit* be-, ent-, er-, miß-, ver-, zer-. Würzburg: Königshausen & Neumann.

Kinne, Michael. 2000. *Die Präfixe* post-, prä- *und neo-: Beiträge zur Lehn-Wortbildung*. Tübingen: Narr.

Kiparsky, Paul. 1966. Über den deutschen Akzent. *Übersuchungen über Akzent und Intonation im Deutschen*, 69–98. Berlin: Akademie-Verlag.

Kirkwood, Henry W. 1969. Aspects of word order and its communicative function in English and German. *Journal of Linguistics* 5.85–107.

Klann-Delius, Gisela. 2005. *Sprache und Geschlecht: Eine Einführung*. Stuttgart: J. B. Metzler.

Klein, Wolfgang, and Norbert Dittmar. 1979. *Developing grammars: The acquisition of German by foreign workers*. Heidelberg and New York: Springer.

Kloeke, W. U. S. van Lessen. 1982. *Deutsche Phonologie und Morphologie: Merkmale und Markiertheit*. Tübingen: Niemeyer.

Klosa, Annette. 1996. *Negierende Lehnpräfixe des Gegenwartsdeutschen*. Heidelberg: C. Winter.

Kobler-Trill, Dorothea. 1994. *Das Kurzwort im Deutschen: Eine Untersuchung zu Definition, Typologie und Entwicklung*. Tübingen: Niemeyer.

Kohler, Klaus J. 1979. Kommunikative Aspekte satzphonetischer Prozesse im Deutschen. *Phonologische Probleme des Deutschen*, ed. Heinz Vater, 13–39. Tübingen: Narr.

  1990. Segmental reduction in connected speech in German: Phonological facts and phonetic explanations. *Speech production and speech modeling*, ed. William J. Hardcastle and Alain Marchal, 69–92. Dordrecht: Kluwer.

  1994. Glottal stops and glottalization in German. *Phonetica* 51.38–51.

  1995. *Einführung in die Phonetik des Deutschen*. 2nd edn. Berlin: Erich Schmidt.

König, E., and G. Nickel 1970. Transformationelle Restriktionen in der Verbalsyntax des Englischen und Deutschen. *Probleme der kontrastiven Grammatik*, ed. Hugo Moser *et al.*, 70–81. Düsseldorf: Pädagogischer Verlag Schwann.

König, Werner. 2004. *dtv-Atlas Deutsche Sprache*. 14th edn. Munich: Deutscher Taschenbuch Verlag.

Köpcke, Klaus-Michael. 1982. *Untersuchungen zum Genussystem der deutschen Gegenwartssprache*. Tübingen: Niemeyer.

Köpke, Klaus-Michael, and David A. Zubin. 1984. Sechs Prinzipien für die Genuszuweisung im Deutschen: Ein Beitrag zur natürlichen Klassifikation. *Linguistische Berichte* 93.26–50.

Koster, Jan. 1975. Dutch as an SOV language. *Linguistic Analysis* 1.111–136.

Krause, Olaf. 2002. *Progressiv im Deutschen: Eine empirische Untersuchung im Kontrast mit Niederländisch und Englisch*. Tübingen: Niemeyer.

Krause, Wolfgang, and Herbert Jankuhn. 1966. *Die Runeninschriften im älteren Futhark*. Göttingen: Vandenhoeck and Ruprecht.

Krech, Eva-Maria, Eduard Kurka, Helmut Stelzig, Eberhard Stock, Ursula Stötzer, and Rudi Teske. 1982. *Großes Wörterbuch der deutschen Aussprache*. Leipzig: Bibliographisches Institut.

Küper, Christoph. 1991. Geht die Nebensatzstellung im Deutschen verloren? Zur pragmatischen Funktion der Wortstellung in Haupt- und Nebensätzen. *Deutsche Sprache* 19.133–158.

Labov, William. 1994. *Principles of linguistic change*. Vol. 1, *Internal factors*. Oxford: Blackwell.

2001. *Principles of linguistic change*. Vol. 2, *Social factors*. Oxford: Blackwell.

2006. *The social stratification of English in New York City*. 2nd edn. Cambridge University Press.

Ladefoged, Peter. 1971. *Preliminaries to linguistic phonetics*. Chicago: University of Chicago Press.

Laetz, Hans Gottlieb. 1969. Analysis of the syntactical and semantic usages of *müssen* in contemporary German. Stanford University dissertation.

Lakoff, Robin. 1975. *Language and woman's place*. New York: Harper & Row.

Langer, Nils. 2001. *Linguistic purism in action: How auxiliary* tun *was stigmatized in Early New High German*. Berlin: de Gruyter.

Lass, Roger, and John M. Anderson. 1975. *Old English phonology*. Cambridge University Press.

Leirbukt, Oddleif. 1988. Über Zeitreferenz und Modalitätsart ("subjektiv"/"objektiv") in deutschen Modalverbkonstruktionen. *Gedenkschrift für Ingerid Dal*, ed. John Ole Askedal, Cathrine Fabricius-Hansen, and Kurt Erich Schöndorf, 168–81. Tübingen: Niemeyer.

Leisi, Ernst. 1967. *Der Wortinhalt: Seine Struktur im Deutschen und Englischen*. Heidelberg: Quelle & Meyer.

Lenerz, Jürgen. 1977. *Zur Abfolge nominaler Satzglieder im Deutschen*. Tübingen: Narr.

Lerchner, Gotthard. 1974. Zur Spezifik der deutschen Sprache in der DDR und ihrer gesellschaftlichen Determination. *Deutsch als Fremdsprache* 11.259–265.

Litvinov, Viktor P., and Vladimir I. Radčenko. 1998. *Doppelte Perfektbildungen in der deutschen Literatursprache*. Tübingen: Stauffenburg.

Lötscher, Andreas. 1981. Abfolgeregeln für Ergänzungen im Mittelfeld. *Deutsche Sprache* 9.44–60.

Lovik, Thomas A., J. Douglas Guy, and Monika Chavez. 2007. *Vorsprung: A commu-nicative introduction to German language and culture.* 2nd edn. Boston and New York: Houghton Mifflin.

Lyons, John. 1995. *Linguistic semantics: An introduction.* Cambridge University Press.

Mangold, Max. 2005. *Duden: Aussprachewörterbuch.* 6th edn. Mannheim: Duden-verlag.

Marcus, Gary F., Ursula Brinkmann, Harald Clahsen, Richard Wiese, and Steven Pinker. 1995. German inflection: The exception that proves the rule. *Cognitive Psychology* 29.189–256.

Mathesius, Vilém. 1929 [1983]. Functional linguistics. *Praguiana: Some basic and less known aspects of the Prague Linguistic School,* ed. Josef Vachek, 121–142. Amsterdam and Philadelphia: John Benjamins.

Matthews, P. H. 1991. *Morphology.* Cambridge University Press.

Meineke, Eckhard, and Judith Schwerdt. 2001. *Einführung in das Althochdeutsche.* Paderborn: Schöningh.

Meinhold, Gottfried, and Eberhard Stock. 1982. *Phonologie der deutschen Gegen-wartssprache.* Leipzig: VEB Bibliographisches Institut.

Metcalf, George J. 1938. *Forms of address in German (1500–1800).* St. Louis, n. p.

Meyer, Kurt. 1989. *Wie sagt man in der Schweiz? Wörterbuch der schweizerischen Besonderheiten.* Mannheim: Dudenverlag.

Mihm, Arend. 2004. Zur Geschichte der Auslautverhärtung und ihrer Erforschung. *Sprachwissenschaft* 29.133–206.

Moulton, William G. 1956. Syllabic nuclei and final consonant clusters in German. *For Roman Jakobson: Essays on the occasion of his sixtieth birthday, 11 October 1956,* comp. by Morris Halle, Horace G. Lunt, Hugh McLean, and Cornelis H. van Schooneveld, 372–381. The Hague: Mouton.

1962. *The sounds of English and German.* Chicago: University of Chicago Press.

Muhr, Rudolf. 1993. Pragmatische Unterschiede in der deutschsprachigen Kommu-nikation: Österreich – Deutschland. *Internationale Arbeiten zum österreichischen Deutsch und seinen nachbarsprachlichen Bezügen,* ed. Rudolf Muhr, 26–38. Vienna: Hölder-Pichler-Tempsky.

Müller, Gereon. 1998. *Incomplete category fronting: A derivational approach to rem-nant movement in German.* Dordrecht and Boston: Kluwer.

Müller, Gerhard. 1994. Der "Besserwessi" und die "innere Mauer": Anmerkungen zum Sprachgebrauch im vereinigten Deutschland. *Muttersprache* 104.118–136.

Müller-Thurau, Claus Peter. 1983. *Lass uns mal 'ne Schnecke angraben: Sprache und Sprüche der Jugendszene.* Düsseldorf: Econ.

Muthmann, Gustav. 1996. *Phonologisches Wörterbuch der deutschen Sprache.* Tübingen: Niemeyer.

Neef, Martin. 1996. *Wortdesign: Eine deklarative Analyse der deutschen Verbflexion.* Tübingen: Stauffenburg.

Neuland, Eva. 1999. *Jugendsprache.* Heidelberg: Julius Groos.

Niebaum, Hermann, and Jürgen Macha. 1999. *Einführung in die Dialektologie des Deutschen.* Tübingen: Niemeyer.

Onysko, Alexander. 2007. *Anglicisms in German: Borrowing, lexical productivity, and written codeswitching.* Berlin and New York: de Gruyter.

Palmer, F. R. 1990. *Modality and the English modals*. 2nd edn. London and New York: Longman

Panizzolo, Paolo. 1982. *Die schweizerische Variante des Hochdeutschen*. Marburg: Elwert.

Paul, Hermann. 1998. *Mittelhochdeutsche Grammatik*. 24th edn., rev. Peter Wiehl and Siegfried Grosse. Tübingen: Niemeyer.

Pinker, Steven. 1999. *Words and rules: The ingredients of language*. New York: Basic Books.

Piroth, Hans Georg, and Peter M. Janker. 2004. Speaker-dependent differences in voicing and devoicing of German obstruents. *Journal of Phonetics* 32.81–109.

Pittner, Karin. 2001. Deutsch – eine sterbende Sprache? *Beiträge zu Sprache und Sprachen 3: Vorträge der 6. Münchner Linguistik-Tage*, ed. Karin Pittner and Robert J. Pittner, 229–237. Munich: lincom europa.

Pokorny, Julius. 1959–1969. *Indogermanisches etymologisches Wörterbuch*. 2 vols. Bern: Francke.

Polomé, Edgar C. 1972. Germanic and the other Indo-European languages. *Toward a grammar of Proto-Germanic*, ed. Frans van Coetsem and Herbert L. Kufner, 43–69. Tübingen: Niemeyer.

Pümpel-Mader, Maria, Elsbeth Gassner-Koch, Hans Wellmann, and Lorelies Ortner. 1992. *Deutsche Wortbildung: Typen und Tendenzen in der Gegenwartssprache. Eine Bestandsaufnahme des Instituts für Deutsche Sprache, Forschungsstelle Innsbruck. Fünfter Hauptteil: Adjektivkomposita und Partizipialbildungen*. Berlin: de Gruyter.

Pusch, Luise F. 1980. Das Deutsche als Männersprache – Diagnose und Therapievorschläge. *Linguistische Berichte* 69.59–74.

—— 1984. *Das Deutsche als Männersprache: Aufsätze und Glossen zur feministischen Linguistik*. Frankfurt am Main: Suhrkamp.

Ramat, Paolo. 1998. The Germanic languages. *The Indo-European languages*, ed. Anna Giacalone Ramat and Paolo Ramat, 380–414. London and New York: Routledge.

Ramers, Karl Heinz. 1992. Ambisilbische Konsonanten im Deutschen. *Silbenphonologie des Deutschen*, ed. Peter Eisenberg, Karl Heinz Ramers, and Heinz Vater, 246–83. Tübingen: Niemeyer.

Ramseier, Markus. 1988. *Mundart und Standardsprache im Radio der deutschen und rätoromanischen Schweiz: Sprachformgebrauch, Sprach- und Sprechstil im Vergleich*. Aarau, Frankfurt am Main, and Salzburg: Sauerländer.

Rappaport, Malka, and Beth Levin. 1988. What to do with θ-roles. *Thematic relations*, ed. Wendy Wilkins, 7–36. San Diego: Academic Press.

Rash, Felicity. 1998. *The German language in Switzerland: Multilinguialism, diglossia and variation*. Bern: Lang.

Reichenbach, Hans. 1947. *Elements of symbolic logic*. London and New York: Macmillan.

Robinson, Orrin W. 1992. *Old English and its closest relatives*. Stanford University Press.

—— 2001. *Whose German? The ach/ich alternation and related phenomena in "standard" and "colloquial."* Amsterdam and Philadelphia: John Benjamins.

Roelcke, Thorsten. 1997. *Sprachtypologie des Deutschen: Historische, regionale und funktionale Variation*. Berlin: de Gruyter.

Rohdenburg, Günther. 1974. *Sekundäre Subjektivierungen im Englischen und Deutschen: Vergleichende Untersuchungen zur Verb- und Adjektivsyntax.* Bielefeld: Cornelsen-Velhagen & Klasing.

Rowley, Anthony R. 1990. East Franconian. *The dialects of modern German: A linguistic survey*, ed. Charles V. J. Russ, 394–416. London: Routledge.

Rubach, Jerzy. 1990. Final devoicing and cyclic syllabification in German. *Linguistic Inquiry* 21.79–94.

Russ, Charles V. J. (ed.). 1990a. *The dialects of modern German: A linguistic survey.* London and Routledge.

1990b. High Alemannic. *The dialects of modern German: A linguistic survey*, ed. Charles V. J. Russ, 364–393. London: Routledge.

1990c. Swabian. *The dialects of modern German: A linguistic survey*, ed. Charles V. J. Russ, 337–363. London: Routledge.

1994. *The German language today. A linguistic introduction.* London and New York: Routledge.

Ryder, Frank G. (trans.). 1962. *The song of the Nibelungs: A verse translation from the Middle High German* Nibelungenlied. Detroit: Wayne State University Press.

Saeed, John I. 2003. *Semantics.* 2nd edn. Oxford: Blackwell.

Schipporeit, Luise, and F. W. Strothmann. 1970. Verbal tenses and time phrases in German. *Die Unterrichtspraxis* 3.29–46.

Schirmunski, V. M. 1962. *Deutsche Mundartkunde: Vergleichende Laut- und Formenlehre der deutschen Mundarten.* Berlin: Akademie-Verlag.

Schlobinski, Peter. 1995. *Jugendsprachen*: Speech styles of youth subcultures. *The German language and the real world: Sociolinguistic, cultural, and pragmatic perspectives on contemporary German*, ed. Patrick Stevenson, 315–337. Oxford: Clarendon Press.

Schlobinski, Peter, Gaby Kohl, and Irmgard Ludewigt. 1993. *Jugendsprache: Fiktion und Wirklichkeit.* Opladen: Westdeutscher Verlag.

Schlosser, Horst Dieter. 1999. *Die deutsche Sprache in der DDR zwischen Stalinismus und Demokratie: Historische, politische und kommunikative Bedingungen.* 2nd edn. Cologne: Verlag Wissenschaft und Politik.

Schmidt, Günter Dietrich. 1987. Das Affixoid. Zur Notwendigkeit und Brauchbarkeit eines beliebten Zwischenbegriffes der Wortbildung. *Deutsche Lehnwortbildung. Beiträge zur Erforschung der Wortbildung mit entlehnten WB-Einheiten im Deutschen*, ed. Gabriele Hoppe *et al.*, 53–101. Tübingen: Narr.

Schmidt, Wilhelm. 2000. *Geschichte der deutschen Sprache: Ein Lehrbuch für das germanistische Studium.* 8th edn. Stuttgart: S. Hirzel.

Schönfeld, Helmut. 1977. Zur Rolle der sprachlichen Existenzformen in der sprachlichen Kommunikation. *Normen in der sprachlichen Kommunikation*, ed. Wolfdietrich Hartung *et al.*, 163–208. Berlin: Akademie-Verlag.

1990. East Low German. *The dialects of modern German: A linguistic survey*, ed. Charles V. J. Russ, 91–135. London: Routledge.

Schönfeld, Helmut, and Peter Schlobinski. 1995. After the Wall: Social change and linguistic variation in Berlin. *The German language in the real world: Sociolinguistic, cultural, and pragmatic perspectives on contemporary German*, ed. Patrick Stevenson, 117–134. Oxford: Clarendon Press.

Schrodt, Richard. 2004. *Althochdeutsche Grammatik II. Syntax.* Tübingen: Niemeyer.

Seiler, Hansjakob. 1962. Laut und Sinn: Zur Struktur der deutschen Einsilber. *Lingua* 11.375–87.

Seymour, Richard. 1959. A note on teaching the German adjective. *Modern Language Journal* 43.276–278.

Shannon, Thomas F. 1987. On some recent claims of relational grammar. *Berkeley Linguistics Society* 13.247–262.

Sieber, Peter, and Horst Sitta. 1986. *Mundart und Standardsprache als Problem der Schule.* Aarau, Frankfurt am Main, and Salzburg: Sauerländer.

Siebs, Theodor. 1898. *Deutsche Bühnenaussprache: Ergebnisse der Beratungen zur ausgleichenden Regelung der deutschen Bühnenaussprache, die vom 14. bis 16. April 1898 im Apollosaale der Königlichen Schauspielhauses zu Berlin stattgefunden haben.* Berlin: Ahn.

 1969. *Deutsche Aussprache: Reine und gemäßigte Hochlautung mit Aussprachewörterbuch,* 19th edn., ed. Helmut de Boor, Hugo Moser, and Christian Winkler. Berlin: de Gruyter.

Sievers, Eduard. 1893. *Grundzüge der Phonetik zur Einführung in das Studium der Lautlehre der indogermanischen Sprachen.* Leipzig: Breitkopf.

Smith, Carlota S. 1997. *The parameter of aspect.* 2nd edn. Dordrecht and Boston: Kluwer.

Spiekerman, Helmut. 2000. *Silbenschnitt in deutschen Dialekten.* Tübingen: Niemeyer.

Stedje, Astrid. 2001. *Deutsche Sprache gestern und heute: Einführung in Sprachgeschichte und Sprachkunde.* Munich: Fink.

Steffens, Doris. 2003. Nicht nur Anglizismen...Neue Wörter und Wendungen in unserem Wortschatz. *Sprachreport* 4.2–9.

Steinmetz, Donald. 1986. Two principles and some rules for gender in German: Inanimate nouns. *Word* 37.189–217.

Stevenson, Patrick. 1997. *The German-speaking world: A practical introduction to sociolinguistic issues.* London and New York: Routledge.

 2002. *Language and German disunity: A sociolinguistic history of East and West in Germany, 1945–2000.* Oxford University Press.

Stötzer, Ursula. 1989. Zur Betonung dreiteiliger Substantivkomposita. *Deutsch als Fremdsprache* 26.263–265.

Strauss, Steven L. 1982. *Lexicalist phonology of English and German.* Dordrecht: Foris.

Stubkjær, Flemming T. 1993. Zur Reihenfolge der Verbformen des Schlußfeldes im österreichischen Deutsch. *Internationale Arbeiten zum österreichischen Deutsch und seinen nachbarsprachlichen Bezügen,* ed. Rudolf Muhr, 39–52. Vienna: Hölder-Pichler-Tempsky.

Tanaka, Hiroyuki. 1964. Die Konsonantenverbindungen im Deutschen. *Muttersprache* 74.169–177.

Titze, Ingo R. 2000. *Principles of voice production.* 2nd printing. Iowa City, IA: National Center for Voice and Speech.

Trier, Jost. 1965. Unsicherheiten im heutigen Deutsch. *Sprachnorm, Sprachpflege, Sprachkritik,* ed. Hugo Moser, 11–27. Düsseldorf: Schwann.

Trömel-Plötz, Senta. 1978. Linguistik und Frauensprache. *Linguistische Berichte* 57.49–68.

Trubetzkoy, Nikolaj S. 1939 [1977]. *Grundzüge der Phonologie.* Göttingen: Vandenhoeck & Ruprecht.

Trudgill, Peter. 2000. *Sociolinguistics: An introduction to language and society.* 4th edn. London: Penguin.

Twain, Mark. 1996. *A tramp abroad.* Oxford University Press.

Uszkoreit, Hans. 1987. *Word order and constituent structure in German.* Stanford, CA: Center for the Study of Language and Information.

van Dam, Jan. 1940. *Handbuch der deutschen Sprache.* Vol. 2, *Wortlehre.* Groningen: J. B. Wolters.

Vater, Heinz. 1975. *Werden* als Modalverb. *Aspekte der Modalität,* ed. Joseph P. Calber and Heinz Vater, 71–148. Tübingen: Narr.

1992. Zum Silben-Nukleus im Deutschen. *Silbenphonologie des Deutschen,* ed. Peter Eisenberg, Karl Heinz Ramers, and Heinz Vater, 100–133. Tübingen: Narr.

1994. *Einführung in die Zeit-Linguistik.* 3rd edn. Hürth-Efferen: Gabel.

Vaux, Bert. 1998. The laryngeal specifications of fricatives. *Linguistic Inquiry* 29.497–511.

Veith, Werner H. 1983. Die Sprachvariation in der Stadt: Am Beispiel von Frankfurt am Main. *Muttersprache* 93.82–90.

Vendler, Zeno. 1967. *Linguistics in philosophy.* Ithaca: Cornell University Press.

Vennemann, Theo. 1970. The German velar nasal: A case for abstract phonology. *Phonetica* 22.65–81.

Vikner, Sten. 1995. *Verb movement and expletive subjects in the Germanic languages.* Oxford University Press.

Wackernagel, Jacob. 1892. Über ein Gesetz der indogermanischen Wortstellung. *Indogermanische Forschungen* 1.333–436.

Wahrig, Gerhard. 2000. *Deutsches Wörterbuch.* 7th edn., ed. Renate Wahrig-Burfeind. Gütersloh: Bertelsmann Lexikon.

Wängler, Hans-Heinrich. 1960. *Grundriss einer Phonetik des Deutschen, mit einer allgemeinen Einführung in die Phonetik.* Marburg: N. G. Elwert.

Wardhaugh, Ronald. 2002. *An introduction to sociolinguistics.* 4th edn. Oxford: Blackwell.

Waterman, John T. 1991. *A history of the German language: With special reference to the cultural and social forces that shaped the standard literary language.* Rev. edn. Prospect Heights, IL: Waveland Press.

Watkins, Calvert. 1998. Proto-Indo-European: Comparison and reconstruction. *The Indo-European languages,* ed. Anna Giacalone Ramat and Paolo Ramat, 25–73. London: Routledge.

Webelhuth, Gert. 1992. *Principles and parameters of syntactic saturation.* Oxford University Press.

Weinrich, Harald. 1964. *Tempus: Besprochene und erzählte Welt.* Stuttgart: W. Kohlhammer.

1993. *Textgrammatik der deutschen Sprache.* Mannheim: Dudenverlag.

Welke, Klaus. 1965. *Untersuchungen zum System der Modalverben in der deutschen Sprache der Gegenwart.* Berlin: Akademie-Verlag.

Wells, C. J. 1985. *German: A linguistic history to 1945.* Oxford: Clarendon Press.

Werlen, Iwar. 2004. Zur Sprachsituation der Schweiz mit besonderer Berücksichtigung der Diglossie in der Deutschschweiz. *Bulletin Suisse de Linguistique Appliqué* 79.1–30.

Wiese, Richard. 1986. Schwa and the structure of words in German. *Linguistics* 24.695–724.

1988. *Silbische und lexikalische Phonologie: Studien zum Chinesischen und Deutschen*. Tübingen: Niemeyer.

1996. *The phonology of German*. Oxford University Press.

2001. Regular morphology vs. prosodic morphology? The case of truncations in German. *Journal of Germanic Linguistics* 13.131–177.

Wiesinger, Peter. 1990. The central and southern Bavarian dialects in Bavaria and Austria. *The dialects of modern German: A linguistic survey*, ed. Charles V. J. Russ, 438–519. London: Routledge.

Wipf, Joseph. 2004. Extended attribute constructions in German radio newscasts: Analysis and implications. *Die Unterrichtspraxis* 37.143–147.

Wöllstein-Leisten, Angelika, Axel Heilmann, Peter Stepan, and Sten Vikner. 1997. *Deutsche Satzstruktur: Grundlagen der syntaktischen Analyse*. Tübingen: Stauffenburg.

Wurzel, Wolfgang Ullrich. 1970. *Studien zur deutschen Lautstruktur*. Berlin: Akademie-Verlag.

1994. Gibt es im Deutschen noch eine einheitliche Substantivflexion? Oder: Auf welche Weise ist die deutsche Substantivflexion möglichst angemessen zu erfassen? *Funktionale Untersuchungen zur deutschen Nominal- und Verbalmorphologie*, ed. Klaus-Michael Köpcke, 29–44. Tübingen: Niemeyer.

Zifonun, Gisela. 2002. Überfremdung des Deutschen: Panikmache oder echte Gefahr? *Sprachreport* 3.2–9.

Zifonun, Gisela, Ludger Hoffmann, Bruno Strecker, *et al.* 1997. *Grammatik der deutschen Sprache*. 3 vols. Berlin: Walter de Gruyter.

Zimmer, Dieter E. 1986. *Redens Arten: Über Trends und Tollheiten im neudeutschen Sprachgebrauch*. Zürich: Haffmans Verlag.

1995. Sonst stirbt die deutsche Sprache. *Die Zeit* 26.42.

Zwart, C. Jan-Wouter. 1997. *Morphosyntax of verb movement: A minimalist approach to the syntax of Dutch*. Dordrecht and Boston: Kluwer.

Index

abbreviation 102, 258–260
ablaut 57, 75, 80, 88, 97, 107, 113n.72, 186
(*Der*) *Abrogans* 188
A.c.I. construction 143
acronym 102–104
address, forms of 252–255
  in FWG 270
  history of 252–253
adjective 90, 116, 119, 259
  attributive 71, 110n.33, 124
  and case 120–122
  comparative form 71, 150–151, 190
  inflection of 70–75
  predicative 71–72, 110n.33, 111n.35,
    124–125
  strong endings 72
  superlative form 71, 111n.35
  weak endings 72–73
  see also compound
adjective phrase 63, 124–125, 193–194
  extended 125, 278n.10
adjunct 128
adjunction 135–136, 141–142
adverb 92, 116, 124–126, 141–142, 146n.15,
  250–251; *see also* compound
adverb phrase 124–126, 176–177
affix 55–56, 99, 106, 212n.29
  derivational 90, 108n.3
  inflectional 56, 90, 98–99, 108n.3, 223,
    227
affixoid 99–100
affricate 18–19, 188–189, 212n.38, 236
AGENT thematic role 169–170, 172–173, 176
Alemannic dialects 189, 194, 201, 222, 224,
  232–235; *see also* Swabian, *Züritüütsch*
allomorph 55
allophone 15
alpha notation 32
alveolar ridge 5
ambisyllabicity 34
analytic form 111n.45, 187, 192, 197–199,
  208

analytic language 111n.45, 199
anaphor 142
Anglo Americanism 275–276
antonymy 150–152
apex 12
approximant 13, 48n.6
arytenoid cartilages 4–5, 50n.36, 211n.15
aspect 153–155
  habitual 122, 155
  imperfective 153–154
  perfective 153
  progressive 155, 161–163, 216
aspiration 11, 21, 23–24, 49n.16, 184–185,
  241n.1
Aspiration (rule) 23–24
assimilation 21, 26, 190, 248
  in colloquial German 246
  see also Nasal Assimilation, Velar Fricative
    Assimilation, voicing assimilation
Auslautverhärtung, *see* Final Fortition
Auslautsgesetze (laws of finals) 212n.33
Austrian Standard German (ASG) 224–228
  grammar 226–227
  legal language 279n.21
  pronunciation 225–226
  vocabulary 227–228
auxiliary verb 85, 113n.78, 116, 129, 197, 199,
  251, 270
  future 179n.14, 192
  inflection of 81, 82
  passive 172
  in perfect tenses 77, 160, 161, 178n.11,
    179n.16, 192, 217, 227
  in past subjunctive 83–84, 85
  position of 139, 227, 270

back feature 26–27, 30–31
base 56
Bavaro-Austrian dialects 224, 233, 235–237
BENEFICIARY thematic role 146n.11
Benrath line (*Benrather Linie*) 231, 232,
  237–239

310